Love Me,
Love Me Not

9

IO SAKISAKA

Contents

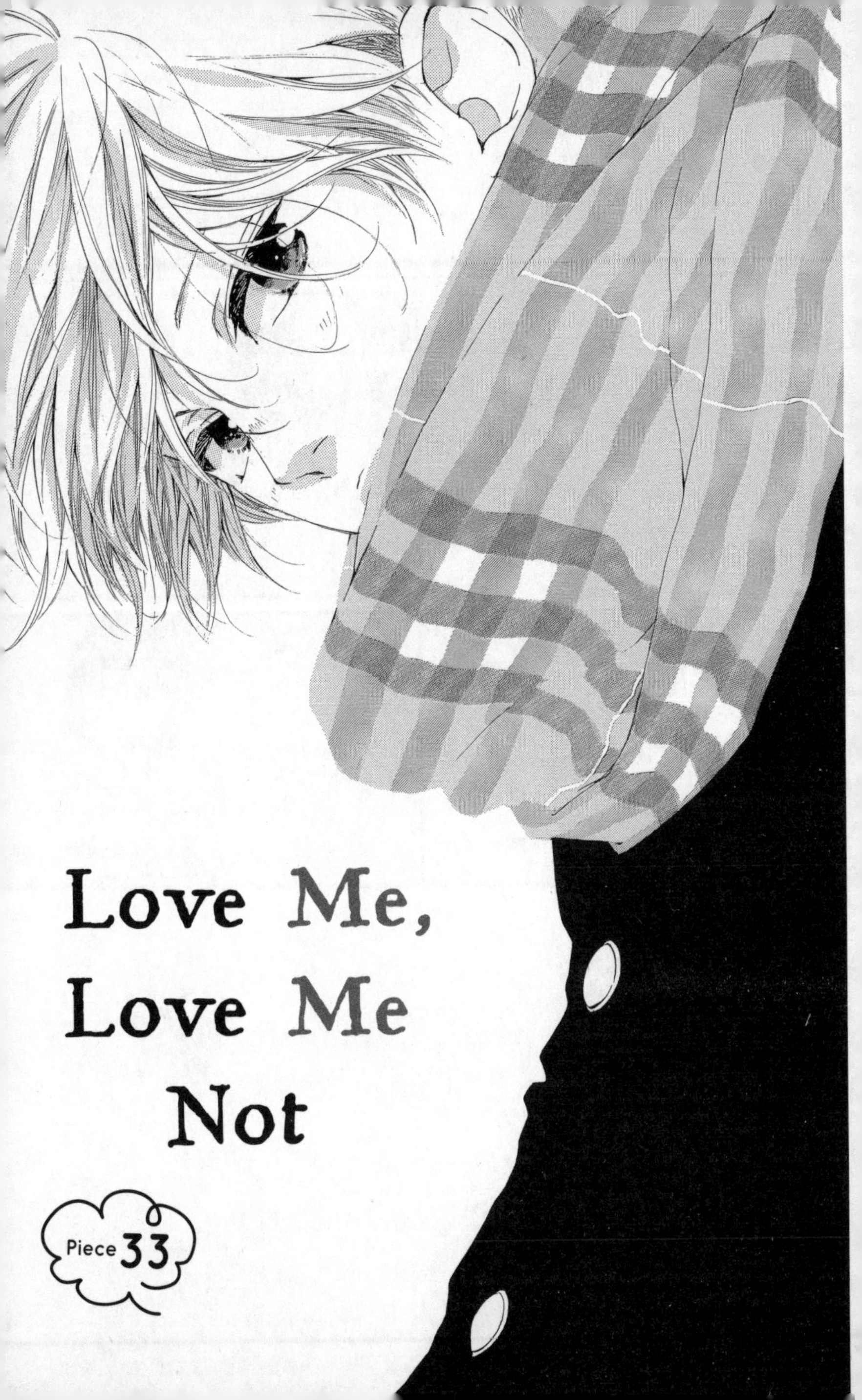
Love Me,
Love Me
Not
Piece 33

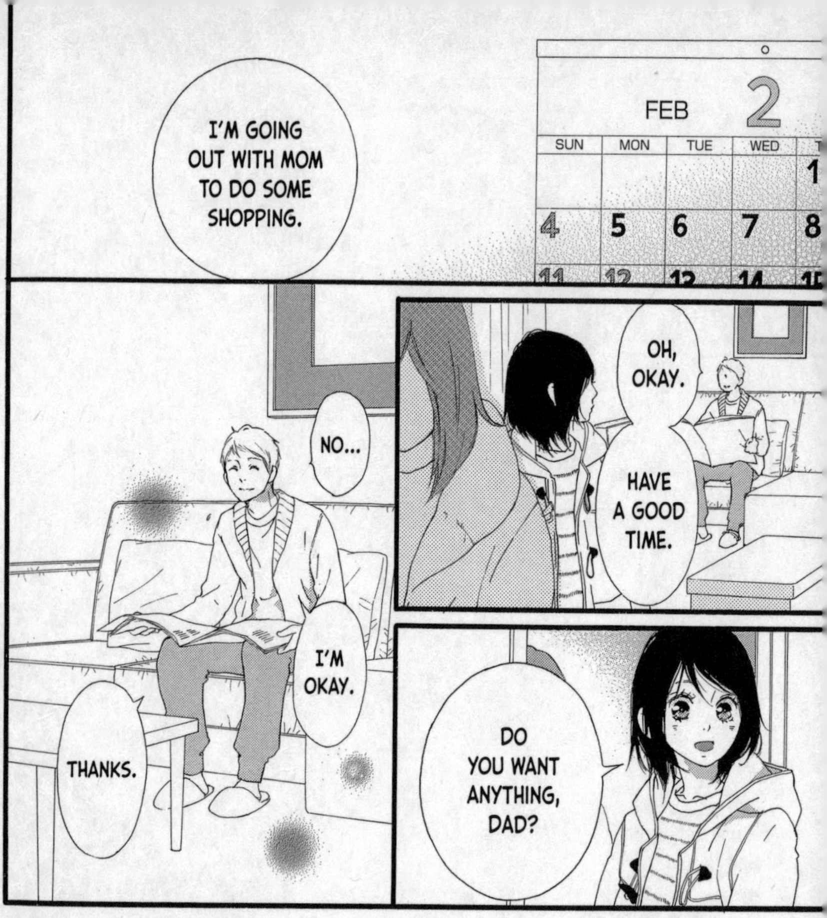
FEB 2
SUN MON TUE WED
I'M GOING OUT WITH MOM TO DO SOME SHOPPING.
OH, OKAY.
HAVE A GOOD TIME.
DO YOU WANT ANYTHING, DAD?
NO...
I'M OKAY.
THANKS.

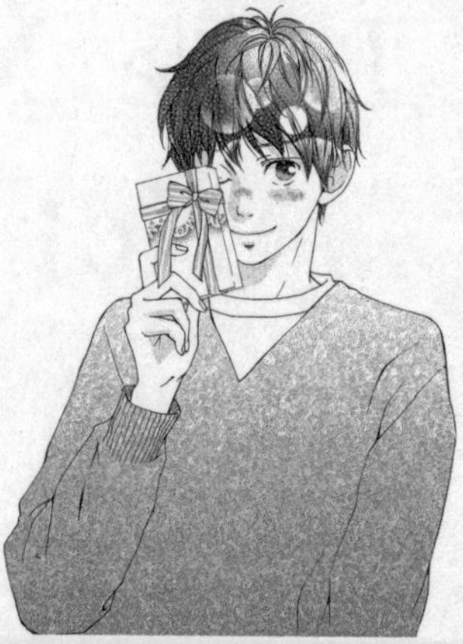

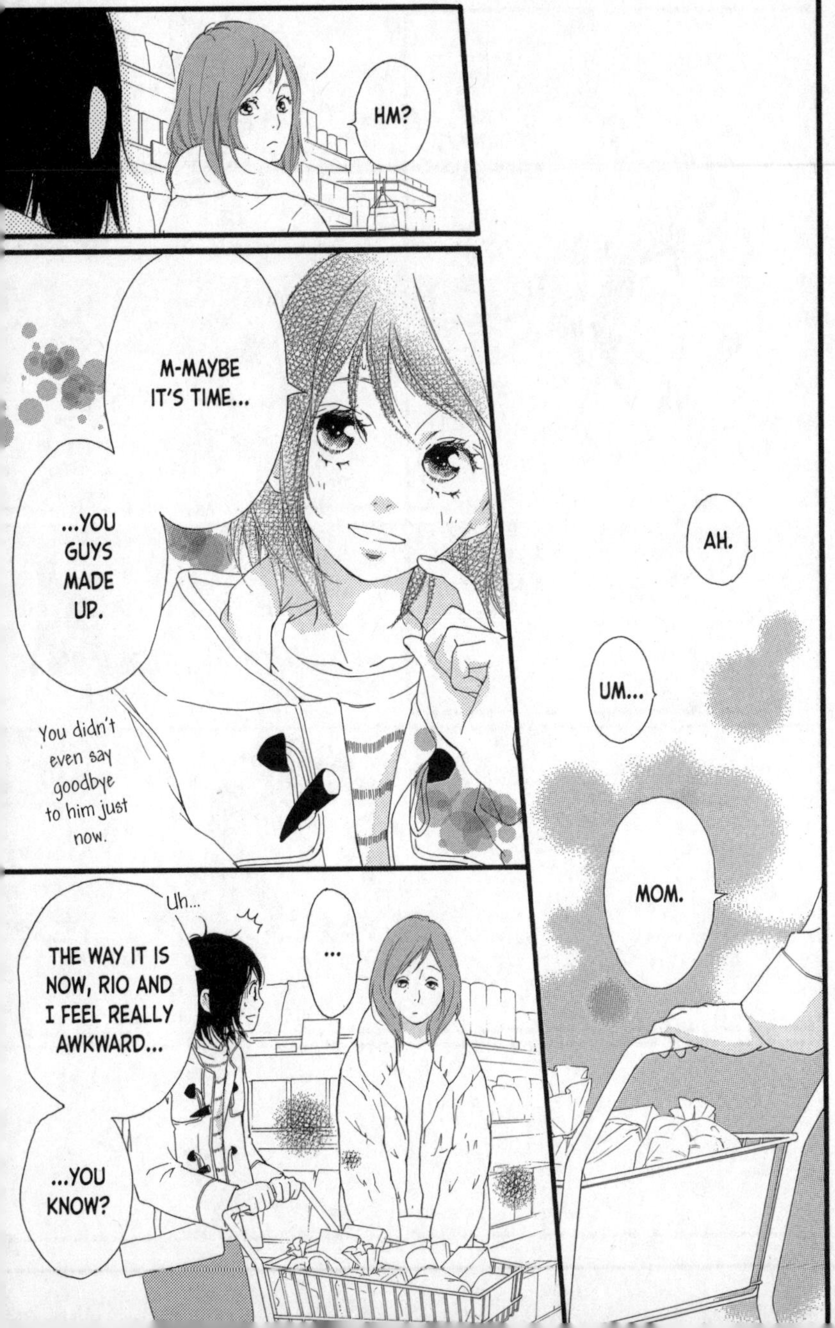
AH.
UM...
MOM.
HM?
M-MAYBE IT'S TIME...
...YOU GUYS MADE UP.
You didn't even say goodbye to him just now.
...
Uh...
THE WAY IT IS NOW, RIO AND I FEEL REALLY AWKWARD...
...YOU KNOW?

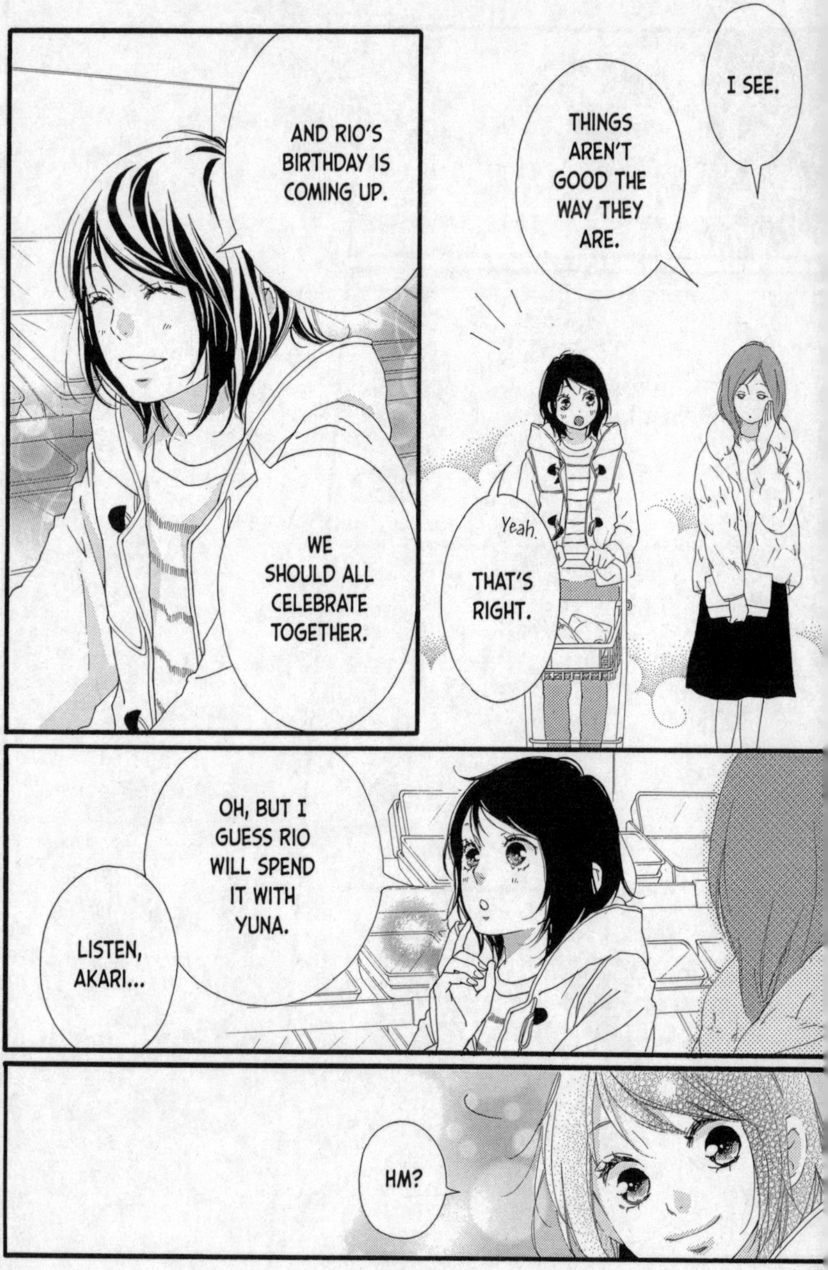
I SEE.
THINGS AREN'T GOOD THE WAY THEY ARE.
Yeah.
THAT'S RIGHT.
AND RIO'S BIRTHDAY IS COMING UP.
WE SHOULD ALL CELEBRATE TOGETHER.
OH, BUT I GUESS RIO WILL SPEND IT WITH YUNA.
LISTEN, AKARI...
HM?

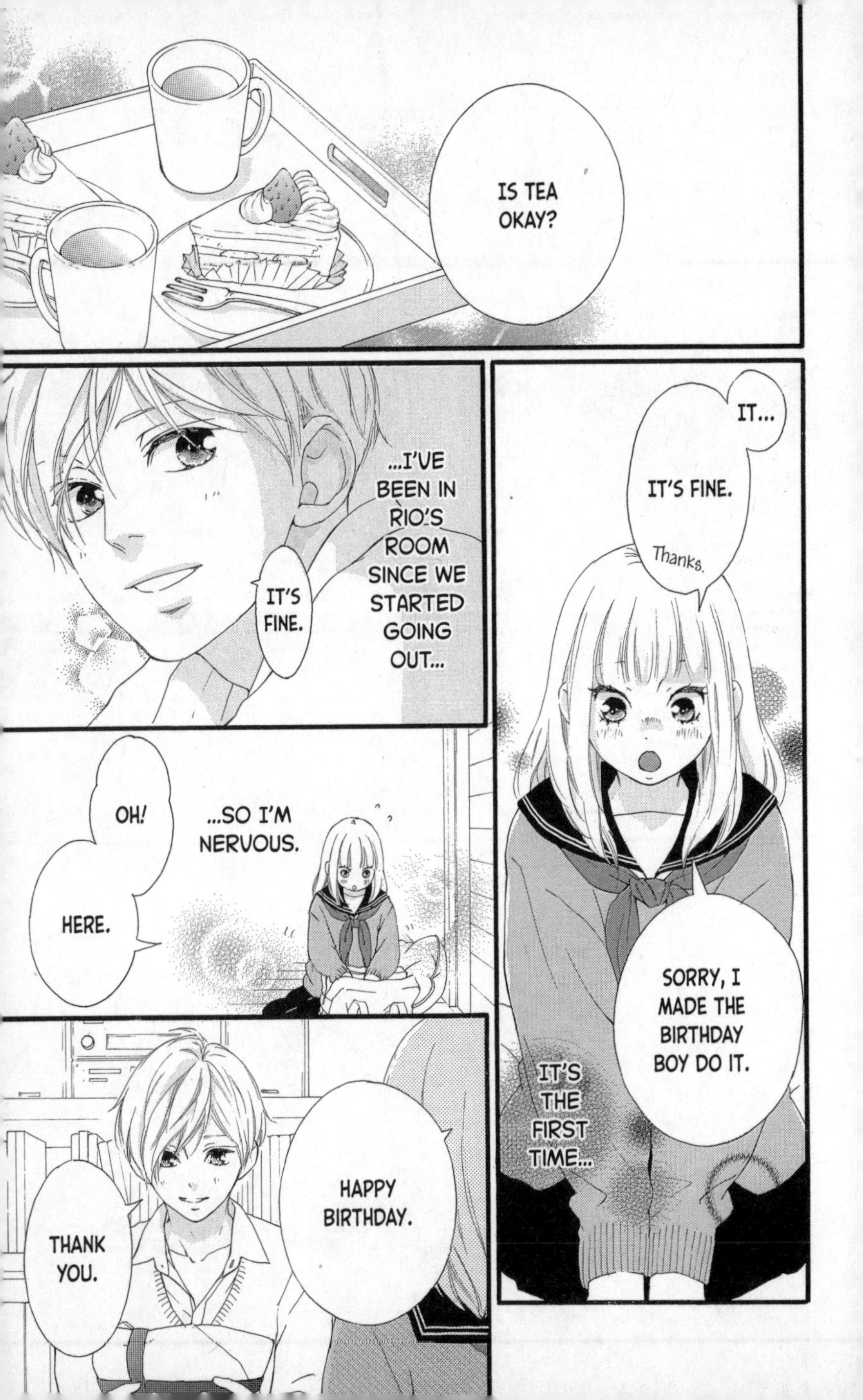
IS TEA OKAY?
IT... IT'S FINE.
Thanks.
SORRY, I MADE THE BIRTHDAY BOY DO IT.
IT'S THE FIRST TIME...
...I'VE BEEN IN RIO'S ROOM SINCE WE STARTED GOING OUT...
IT'S FINE.
...SO I'M NERVOUS.
OH! HERE.
HAPPY BIRTHDAY.
THANK YOU.

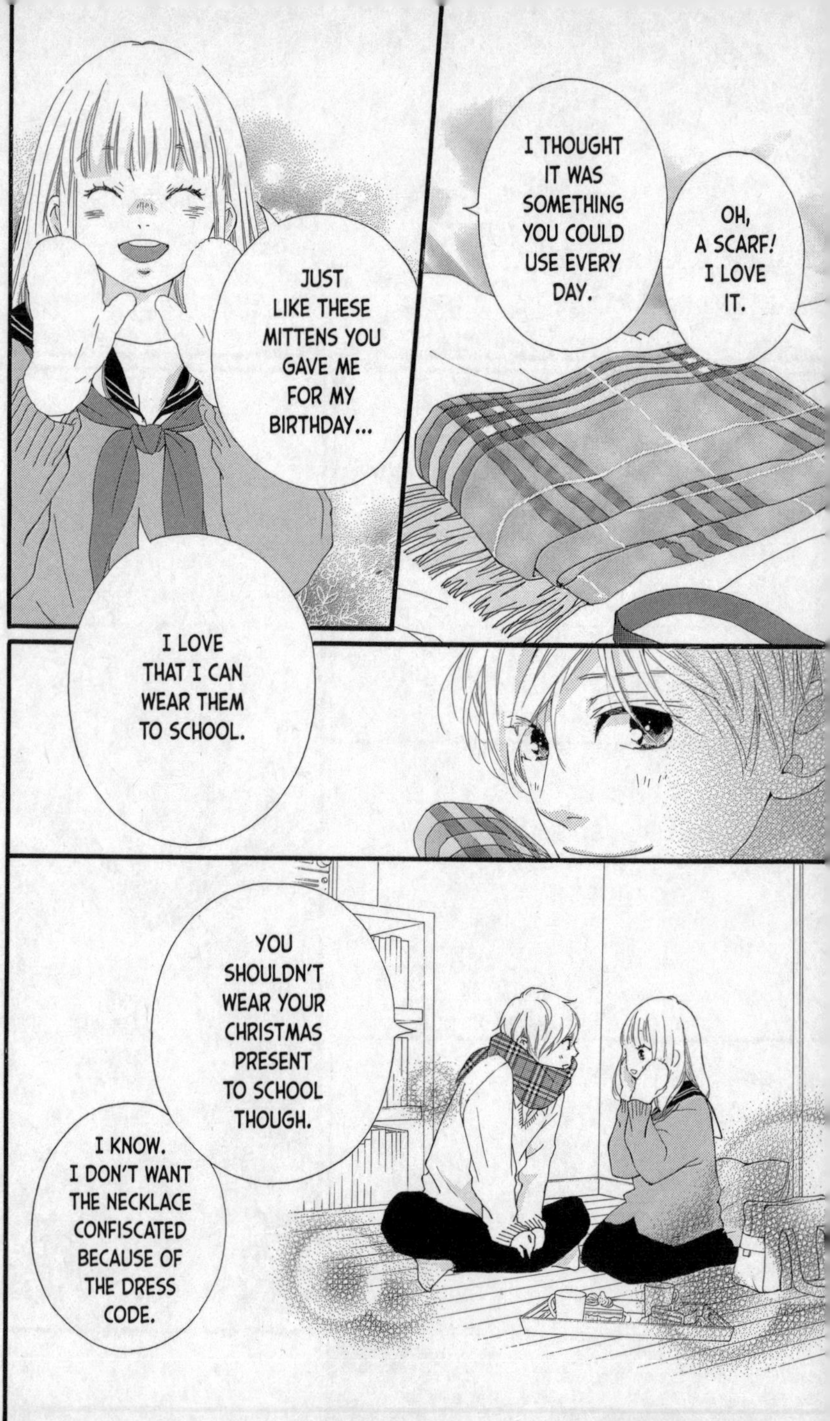
OH, A SCARF! I LOVE IT.
I THOUGHT IT WAS SOMETHING YOU COULD USE EVERY DAY.
JUST LIKE THESE MITTENS YOU GAVE ME FOR MY BIRTHDAY...
I LOVE THAT I CAN WEAR THEM TO SCHOOL.
YOU SHOULDN'T WEAR YOUR CHRISTMAS PRESENT TO SCHOOL THOUGH.
I KNOW. I DON'T WANT THE NECKLACE CONFISCATED BECAUSE OF THE DRESS CODE.

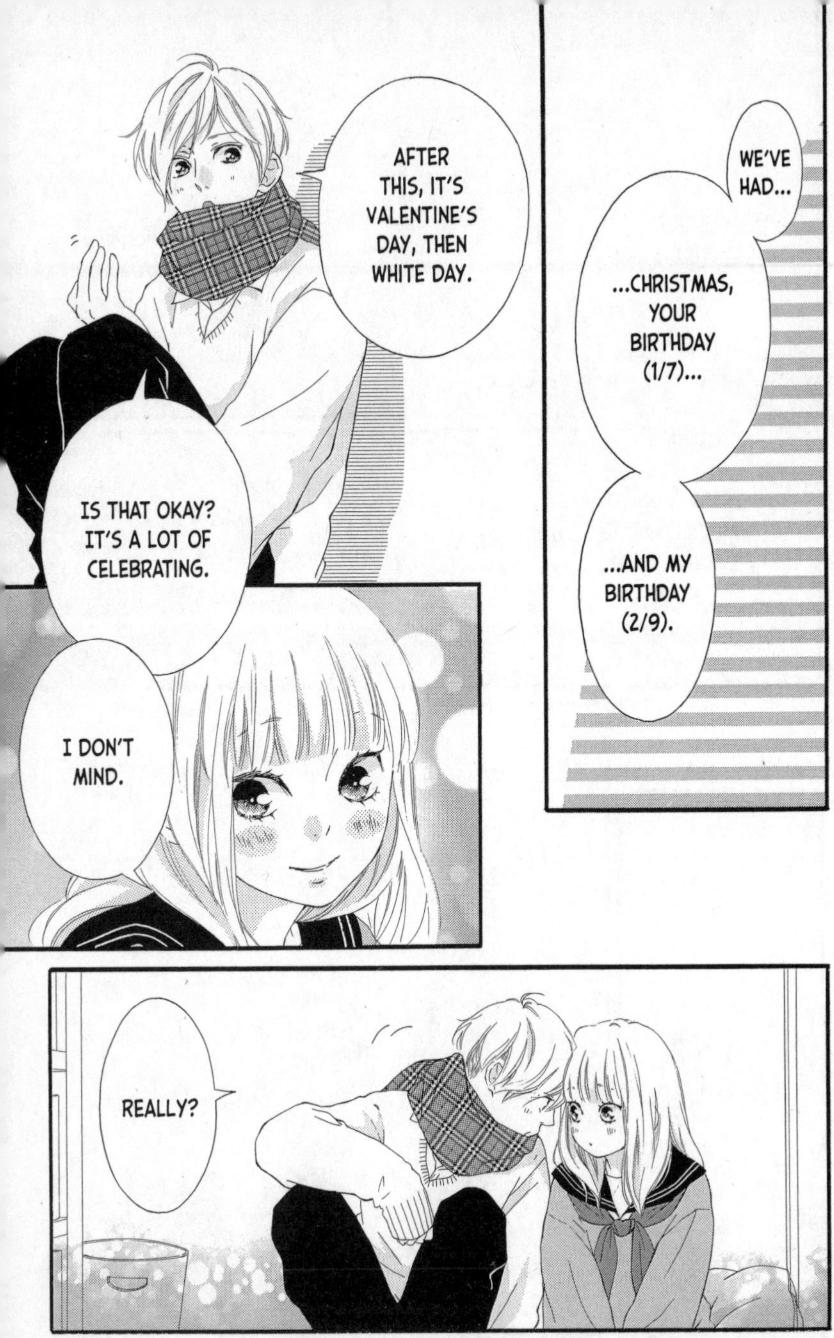
WE'VE HAD...
...CHRISTMAS, YOUR BIRTHDAY (1/7)...
...AND MY BIRTHDAY (2/9).
AFTER THIS, IT'S VALENTINE'S DAY, THEN WHITE DAY.
IS THAT OKAY? IT'S A LOT OF CELEBRATING.
I DON'T MIND.
REALLY?

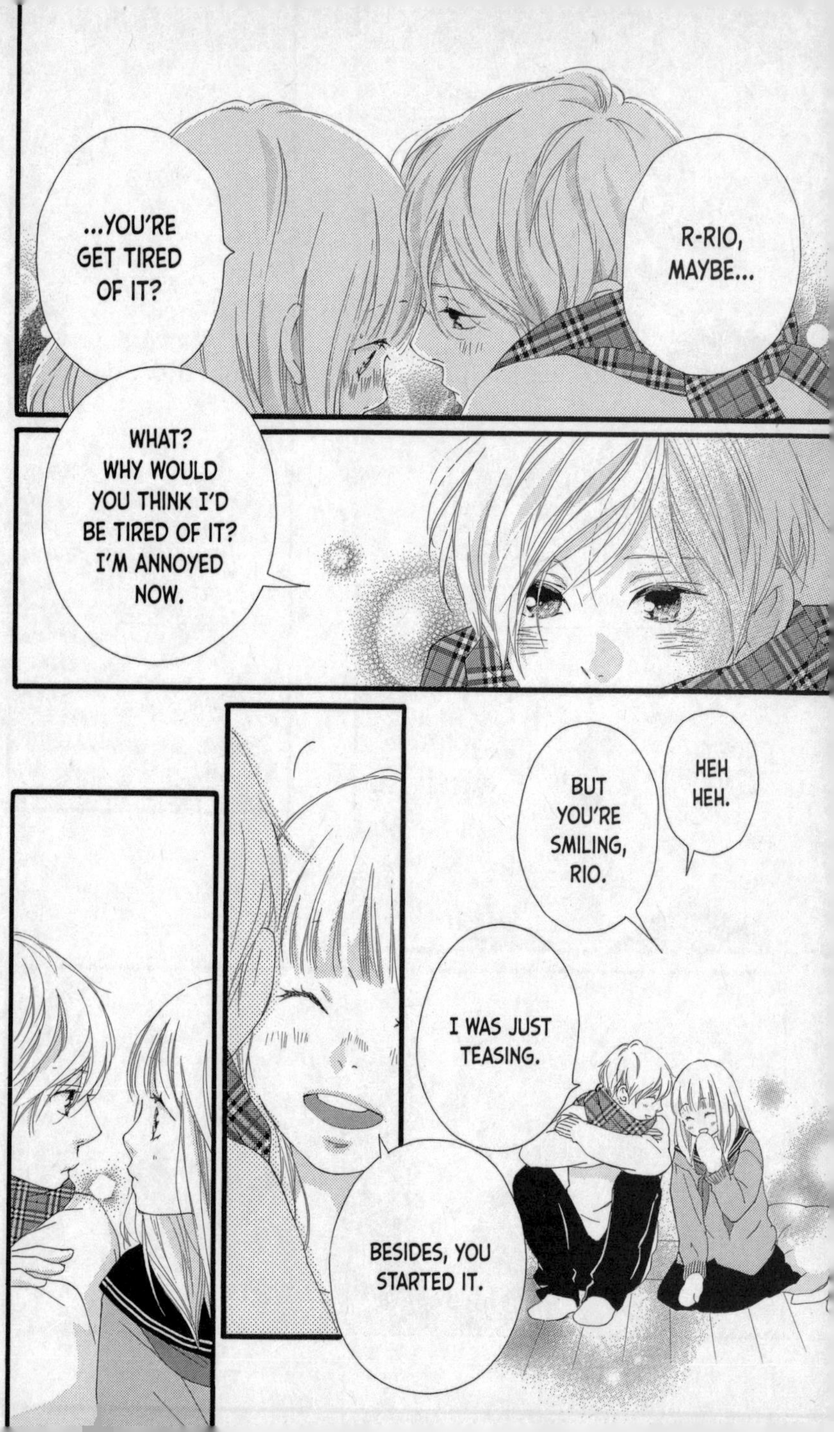
R-RIO, MAYBE...
...YOU'RE GET TIRED OF IT?
WHAT? WHY WOULD YOU THINK I'D BE TIRED OF IT? I'M ANNOYED NOW.
HEH HEH.
BUT YOU'RE SMILING, RIO.
I WAS JUST TEASING.
BESIDES, YOU STARTED IT.

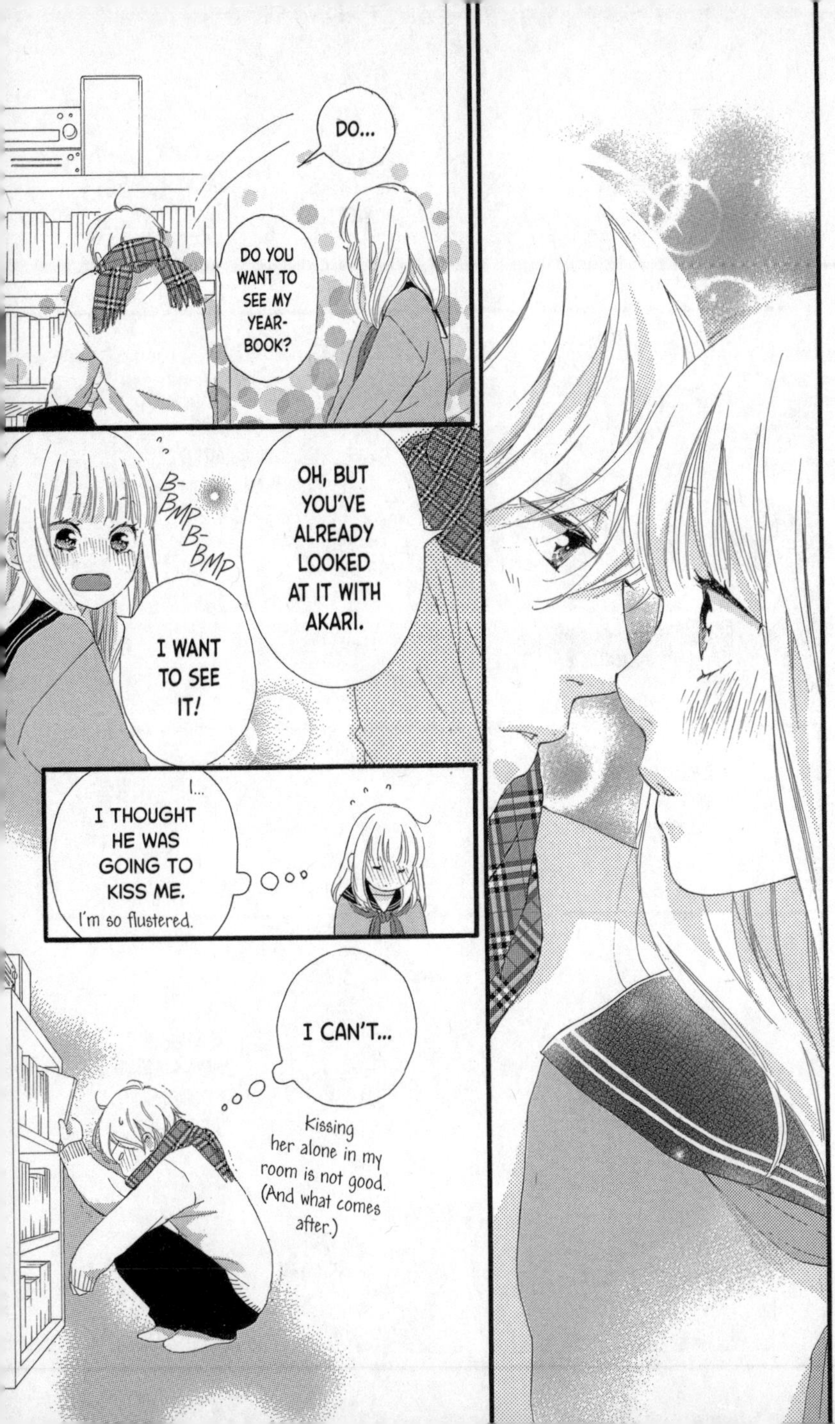
DO...
DO YOU WANT TO SEE MY YEAR-BOOK?
OH, BUT YOU'VE ALREADY LOOKED AT IT WITH AKARI.
B-BMP B-BMP
I WANT TO SEE IT!
I...
I THOUGHT HE WAS GOING TO KISS ME.
I'm so flustered.
I CAN'T...
Kissing her alone in my room is not good. (And what comes after.)

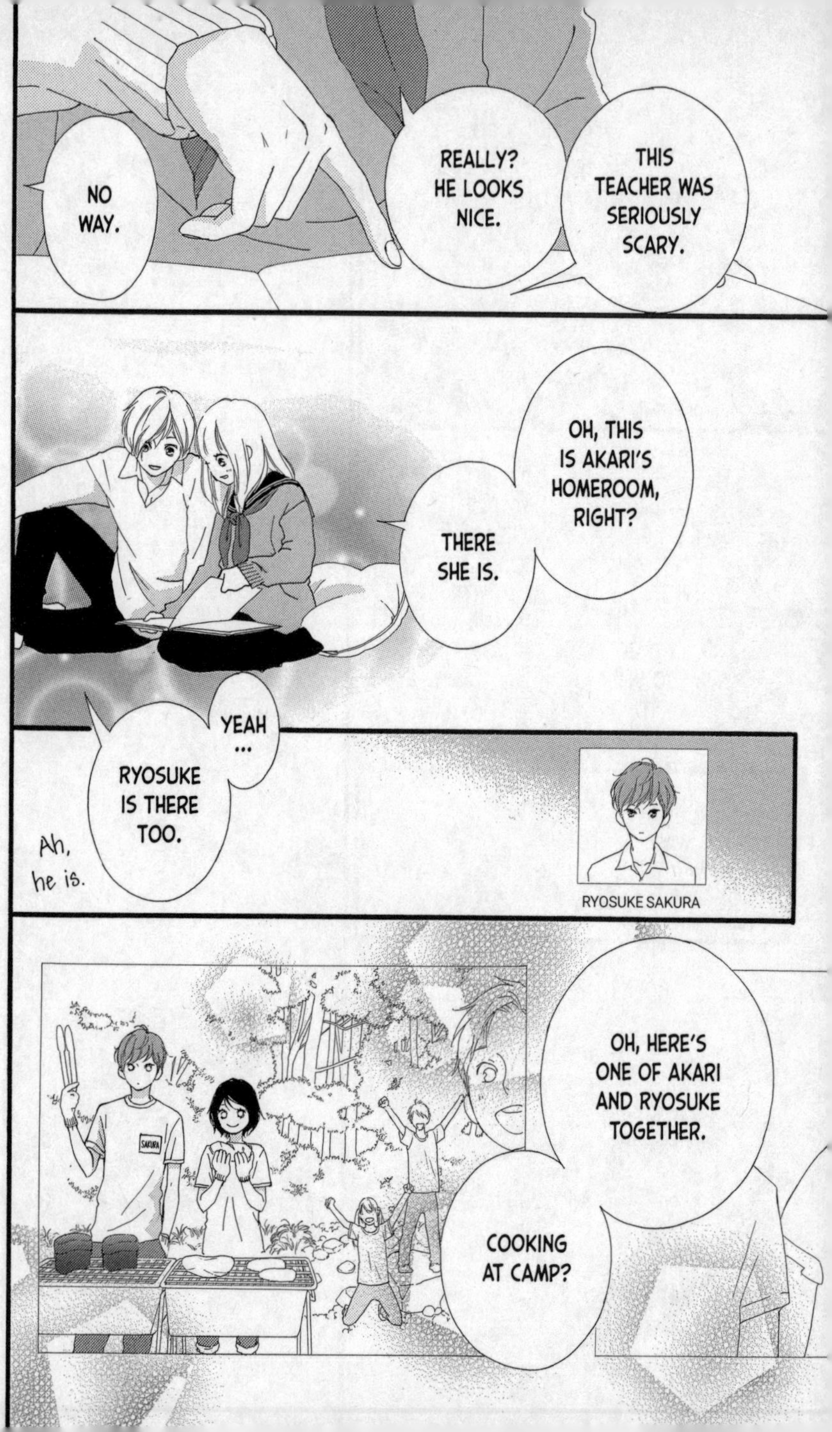
THIS TEACHER WAS SERIOUSLY SCARY.
REALLY? HE LOOKS NICE.
NO WAY.
OH, THIS IS AKARI'S HOMEROOM, RIGHT?
THERE SHE IS.
RYOSUKE SAKURA
YEAH...
RYOSUKE IS THERE TOO.
Ah, he is.
OH, HERE'S ONE OF AKARI AND RYOSUKE TOGETHER.
COOKING AT CAMP?
SAKURA

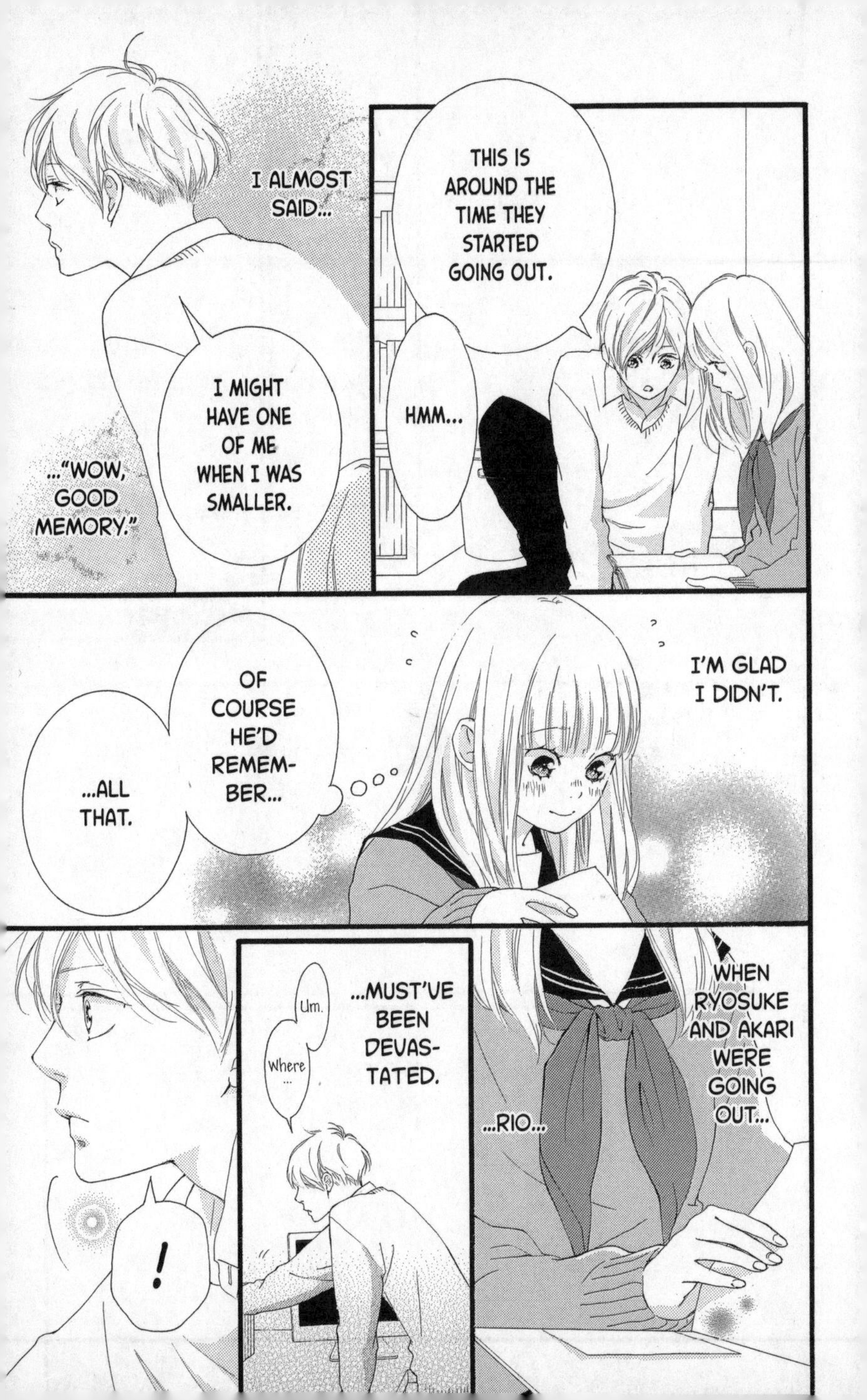
THIS IS AROUND THE TIME THEY STARTED GOING OUT.
HMM...
I ALMOST SAID...
I MIGHT HAVE ONE OF ME WHEN I WAS SMALLER.
..."WOW, GOOD MEMORY."
I'M GLAD I DIDN'T.
OF COURSE HE'D REMEMBER...
...ALL THAT.
WHEN RYOSUKE AND AKARI WERE GOING OUT...
...RIO...
...MUST'VE BEEN DEVASTATED.
Um.
Where...
!

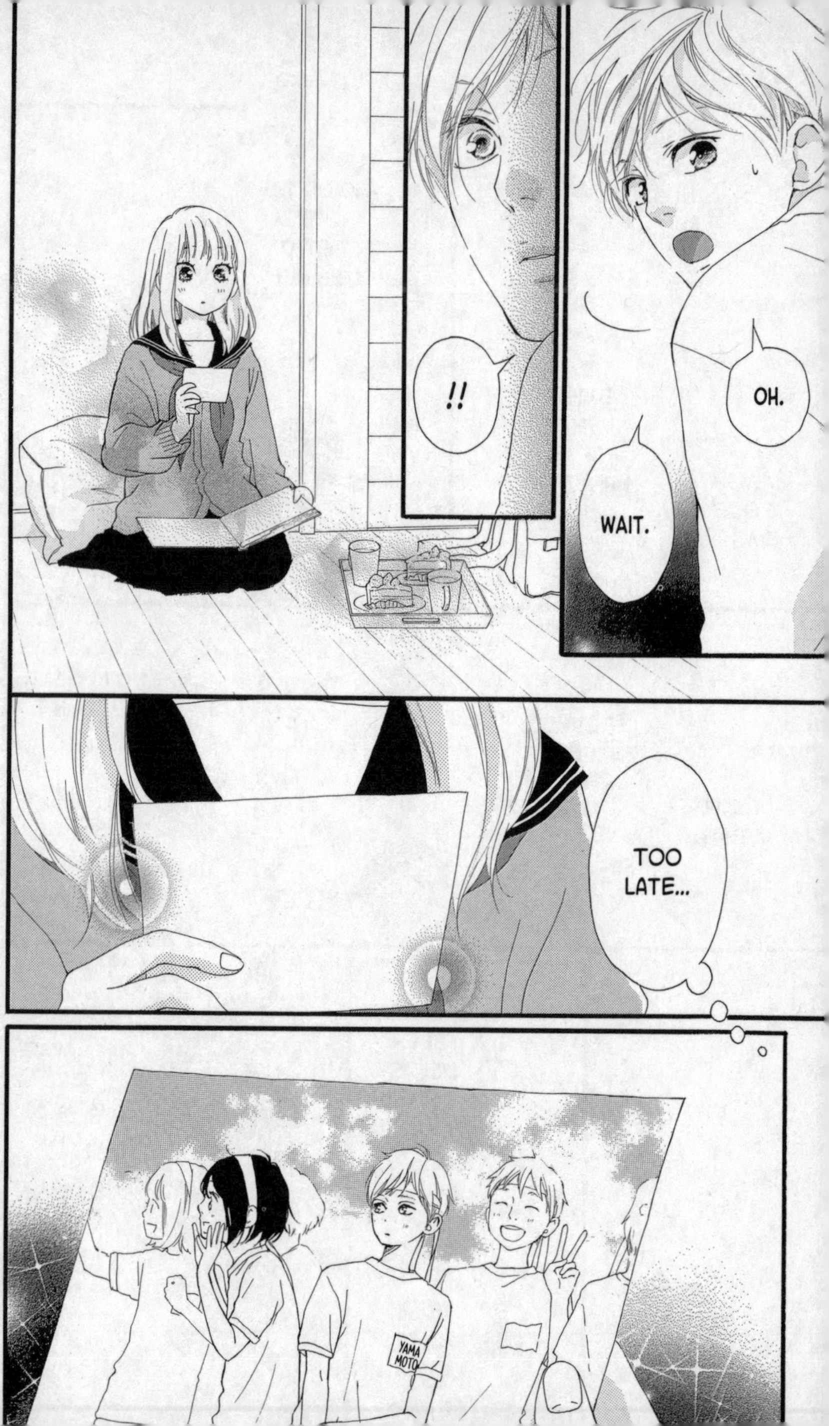
OH.
WAIT.
!!
TOO LATE...

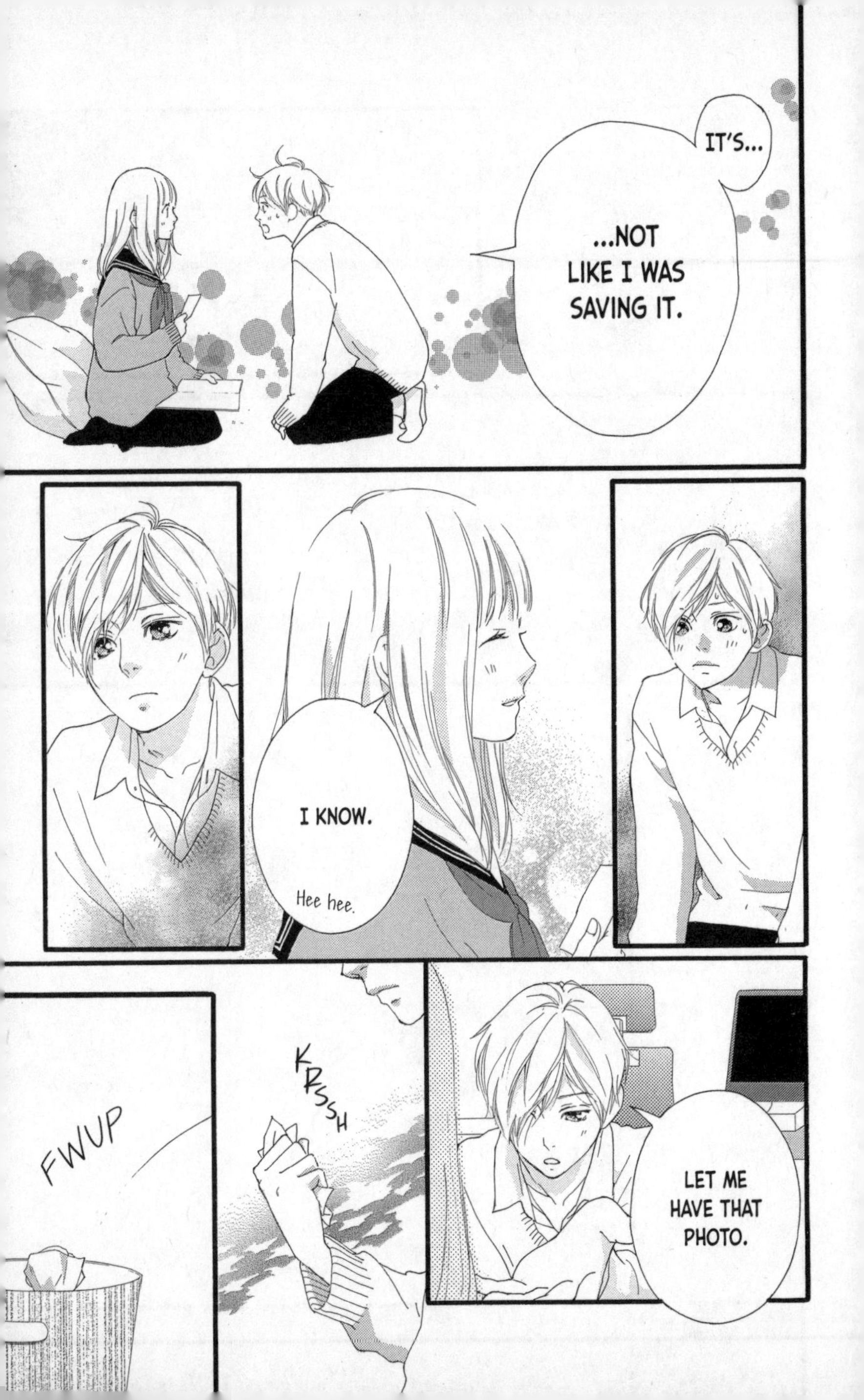
IT'S...
...NOT LIKE I WAS SAVING IT.
I KNOW.
Hee hee.
LET ME HAVE THAT PHOTO.
KRSSH
FWUP

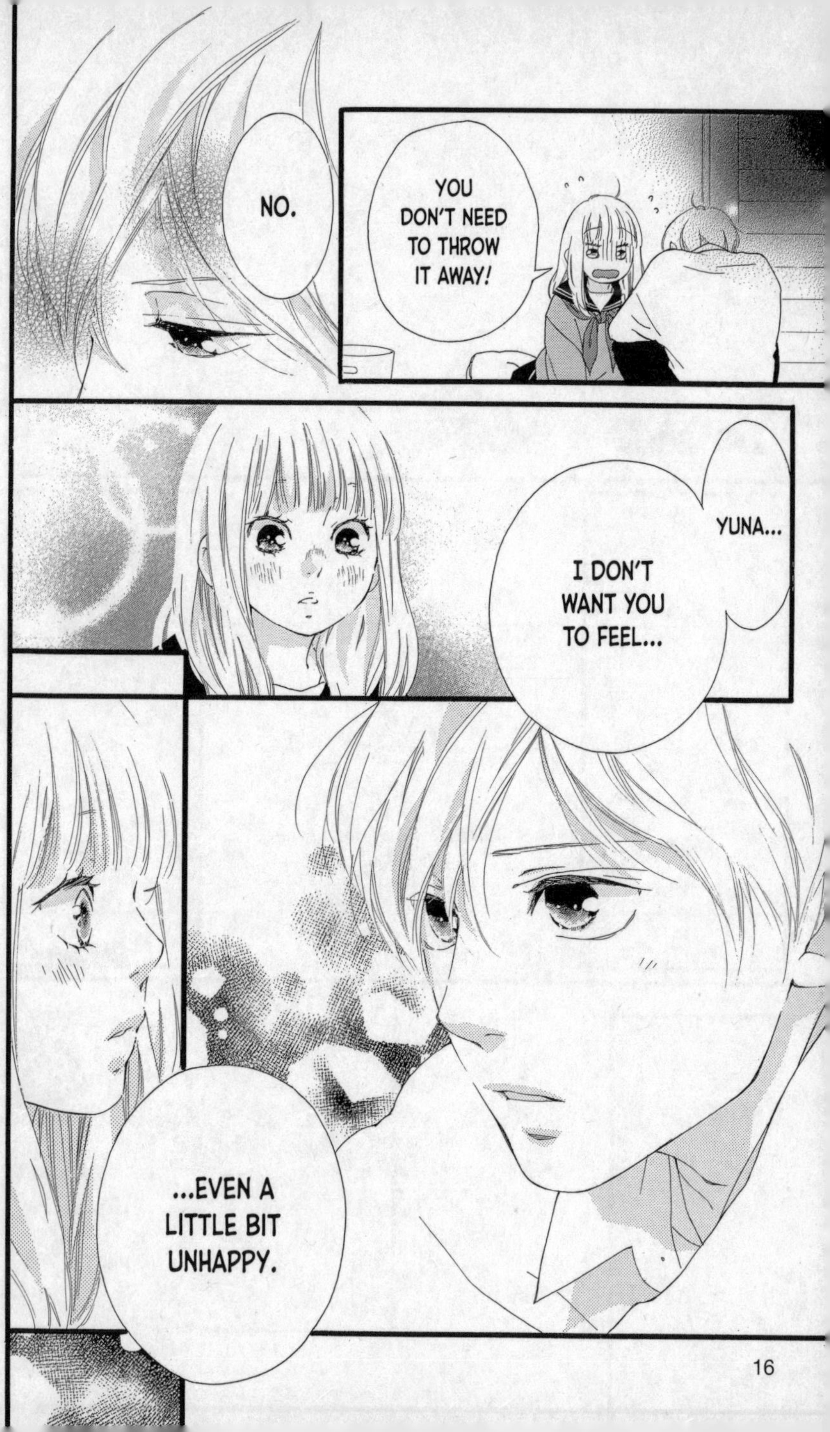
YOU DON'T NEED TO THROW IT AWAY!
NO.
YUNA...
I DON'T WANT YOU TO FEEL...
...EVEN A LITTLE BIT UNHAPPY.

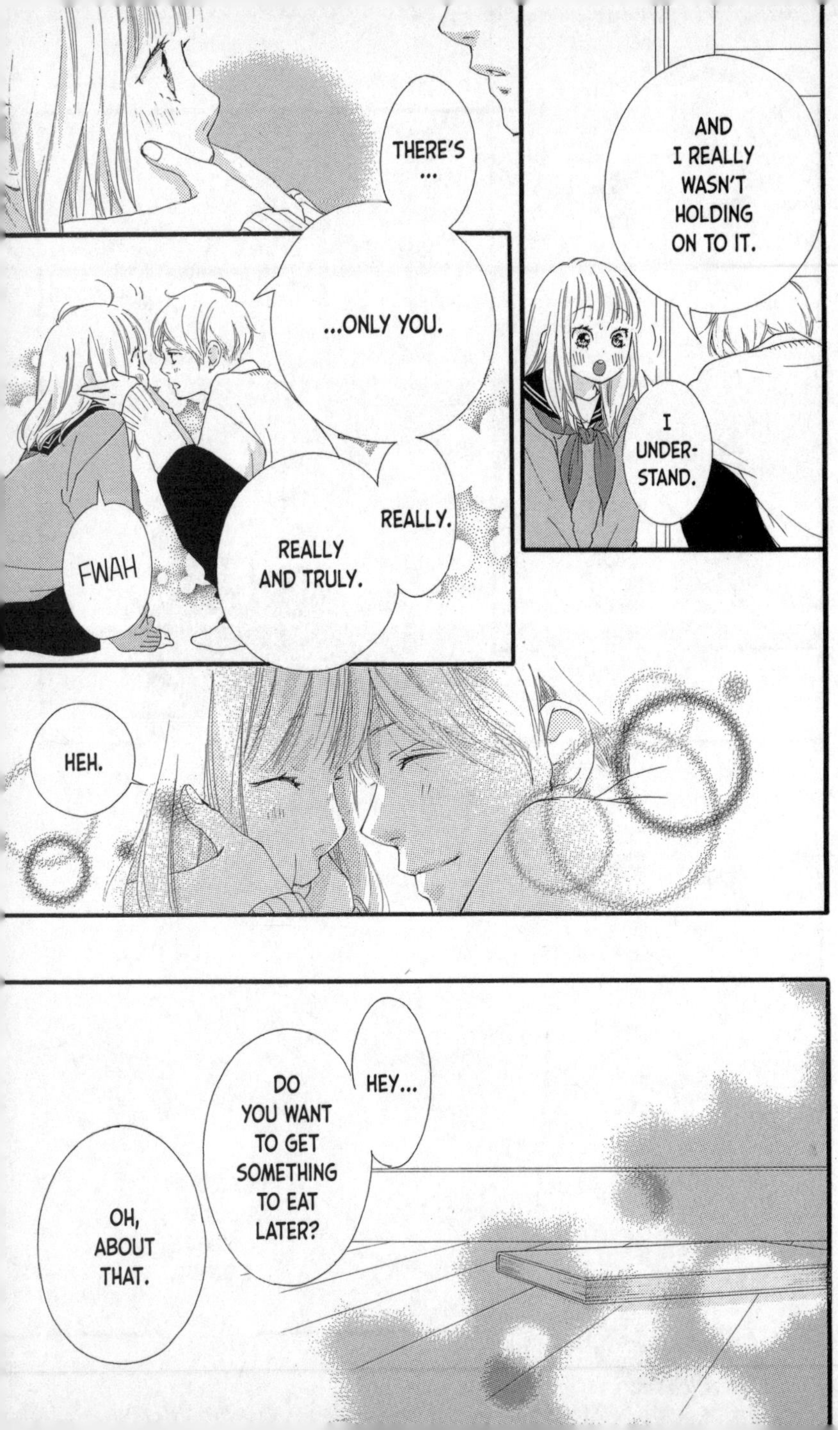
AND I REALLY WASN'T HOLDING ON TO IT.
I UNDER-STAND.
THERE'S ...
...ONLY YOU.
REALLY.
REALLY AND TRULY.
FWAH
HEH.
HEY...
DO YOU WANT TO GET SOMETHING TO EAT LATER?
OH, ABOUT THAT.

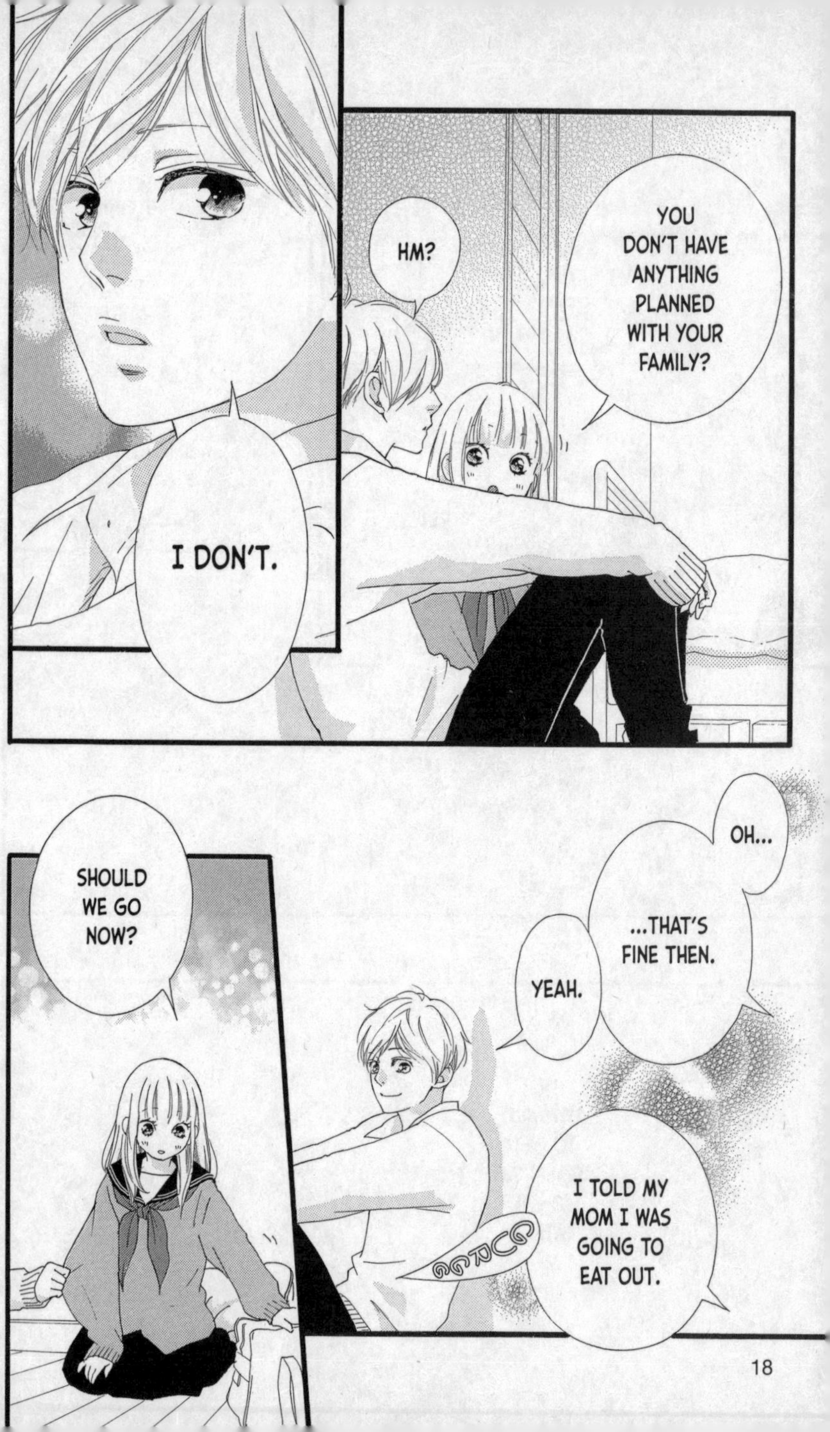
YOU DON'T HAVE ANYTHING PLANNED WITH YOUR FAMILY?
HM?
I DON'T.
OH...
...THAT'S FINE THEN.
YEAH.
I TOLD MY MOM I WAS GOING TO EAT OUT.
SHOULD WE GO NOW?

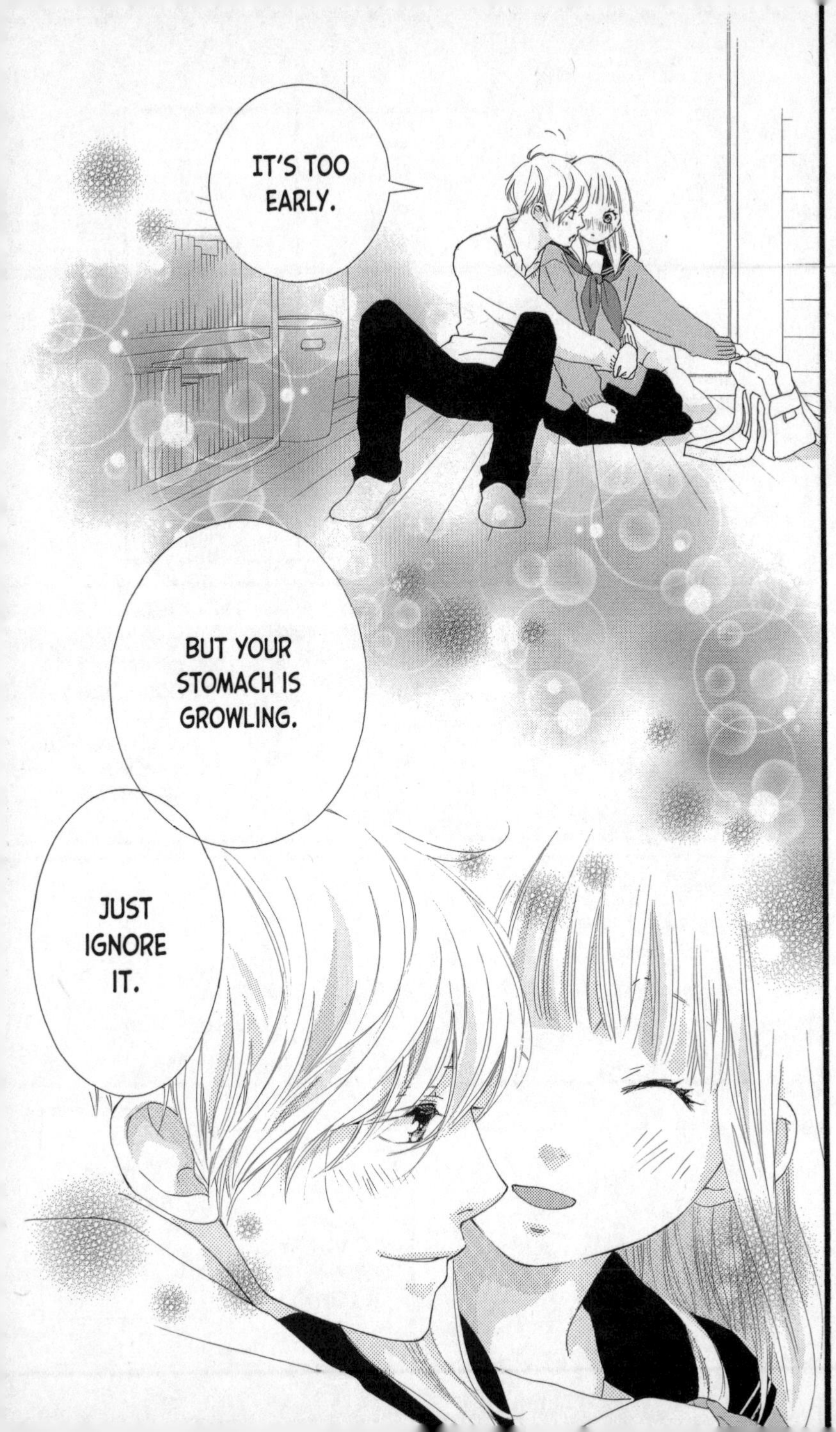
IT'S TOO EARLY.
BUT YOUR STOMACH IS GROWLING.
JUST IGNORE IT.

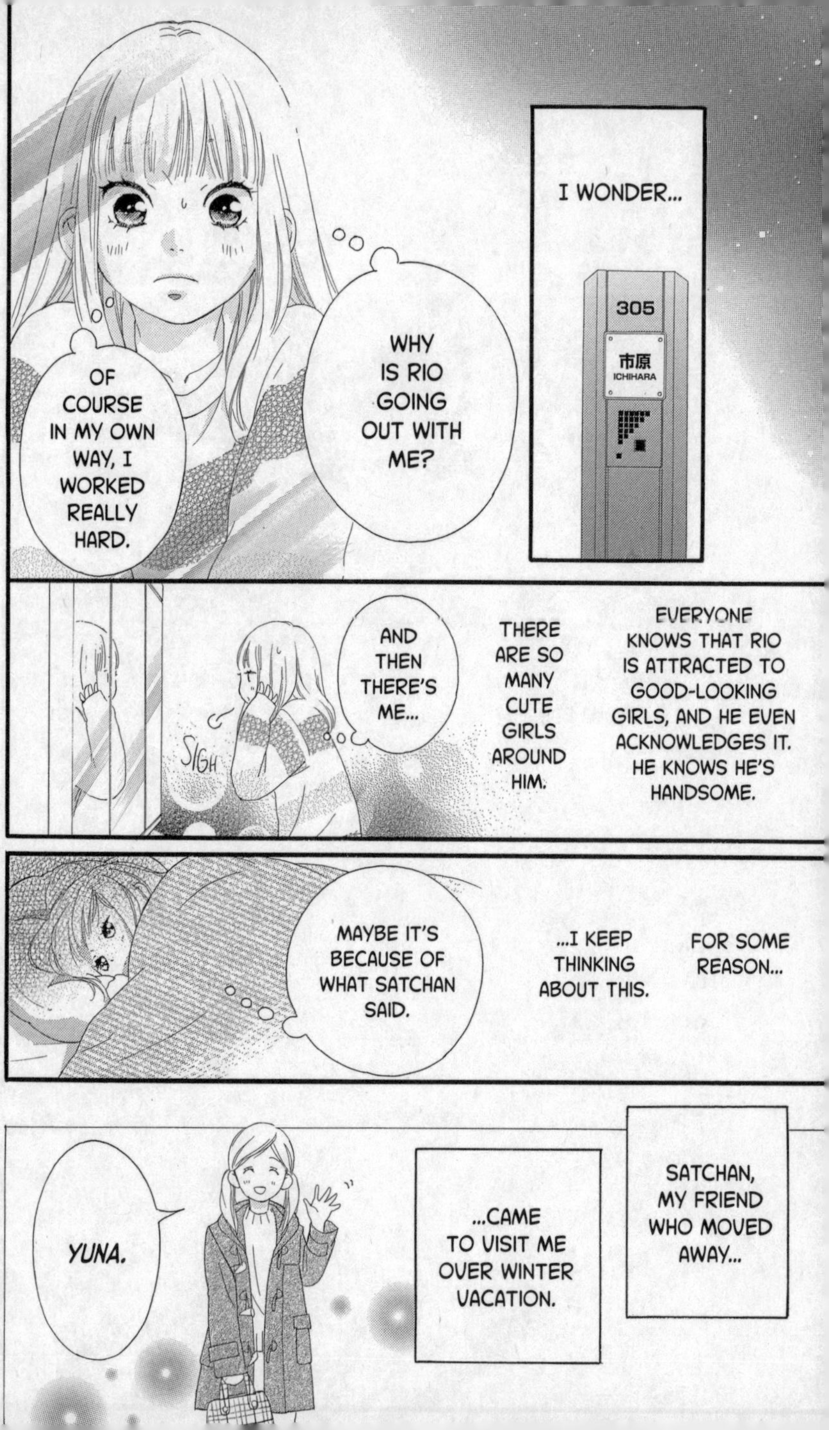
I WONDER...
305
市原
ICHIHARA
WHY IS RIO GOING OUT WITH ME?
OF COURSE IN MY OWN WAY, I WORKED REALLY HARD.
EVERYONE KNOWS THAT RIO IS ATTRACTED TO GOOD-LOOKING GIRLS, AND HE EVEN ACKNOWLEDGES IT. HE KNOWS HE'S HANDSOME.
THERE ARE SO MANY CUTE GIRLS AROUND HIM.
AND THEN THERE'S ME...
SIGH
FOR SOME REASON...
...I KEEP THINKING ABOUT THIS.
MAYBE IT'S BECAUSE OF WHAT SATCHAN SAID.
SATCHAN, MY FRIEND WHO MOVED AWAY...
...CAME TO VISIT ME OVER WINTER VACATION.
YUNA.

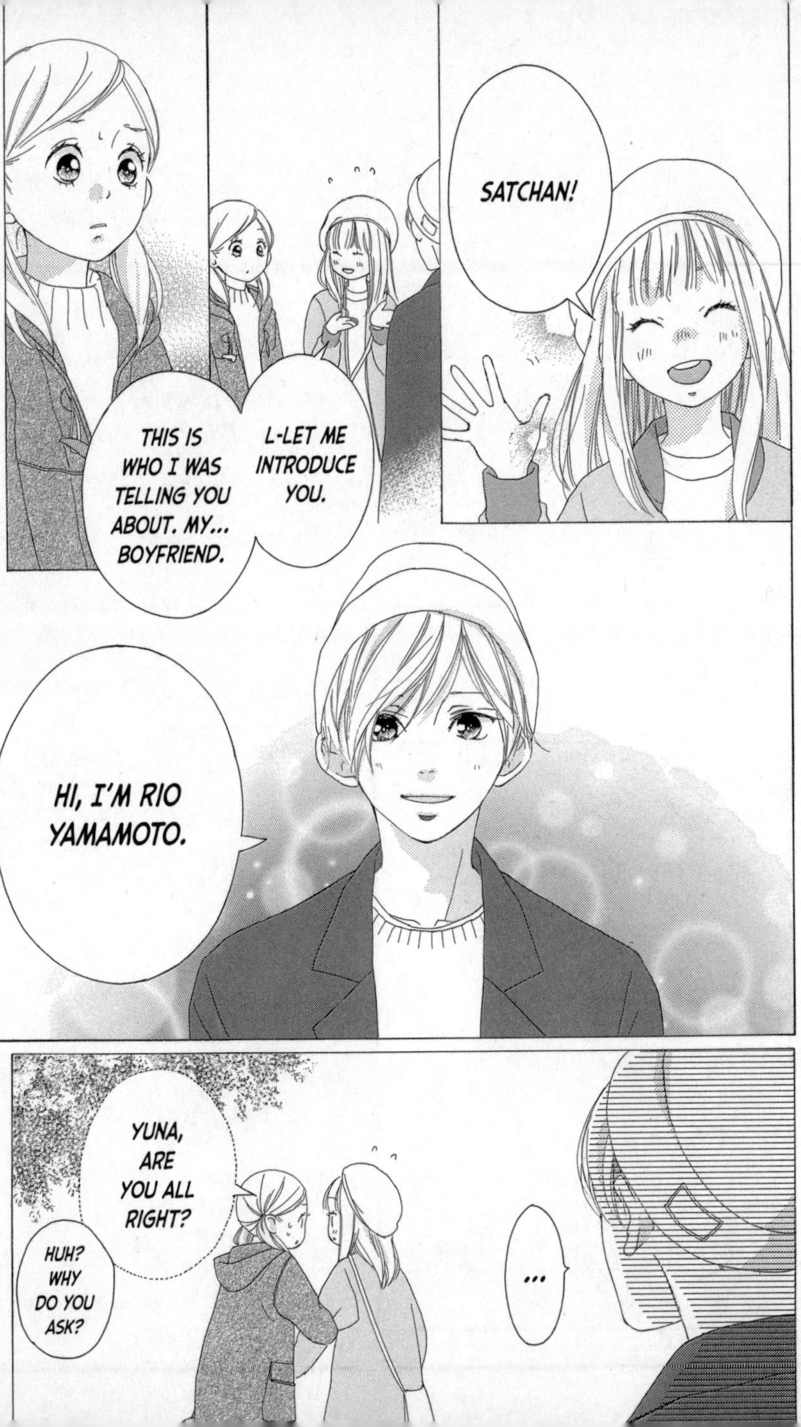
SATCHAN!
L-LET ME INTRODUCE YOU.
THIS IS WHO I WAS TELLING YOU ABOUT. MY... BOYFRIEND.
HI, I'M RIO YAMAMOTO.
...
YUNA, ARE YOU ALL RIGHT?
HUH? WHY DO YOU ASK?

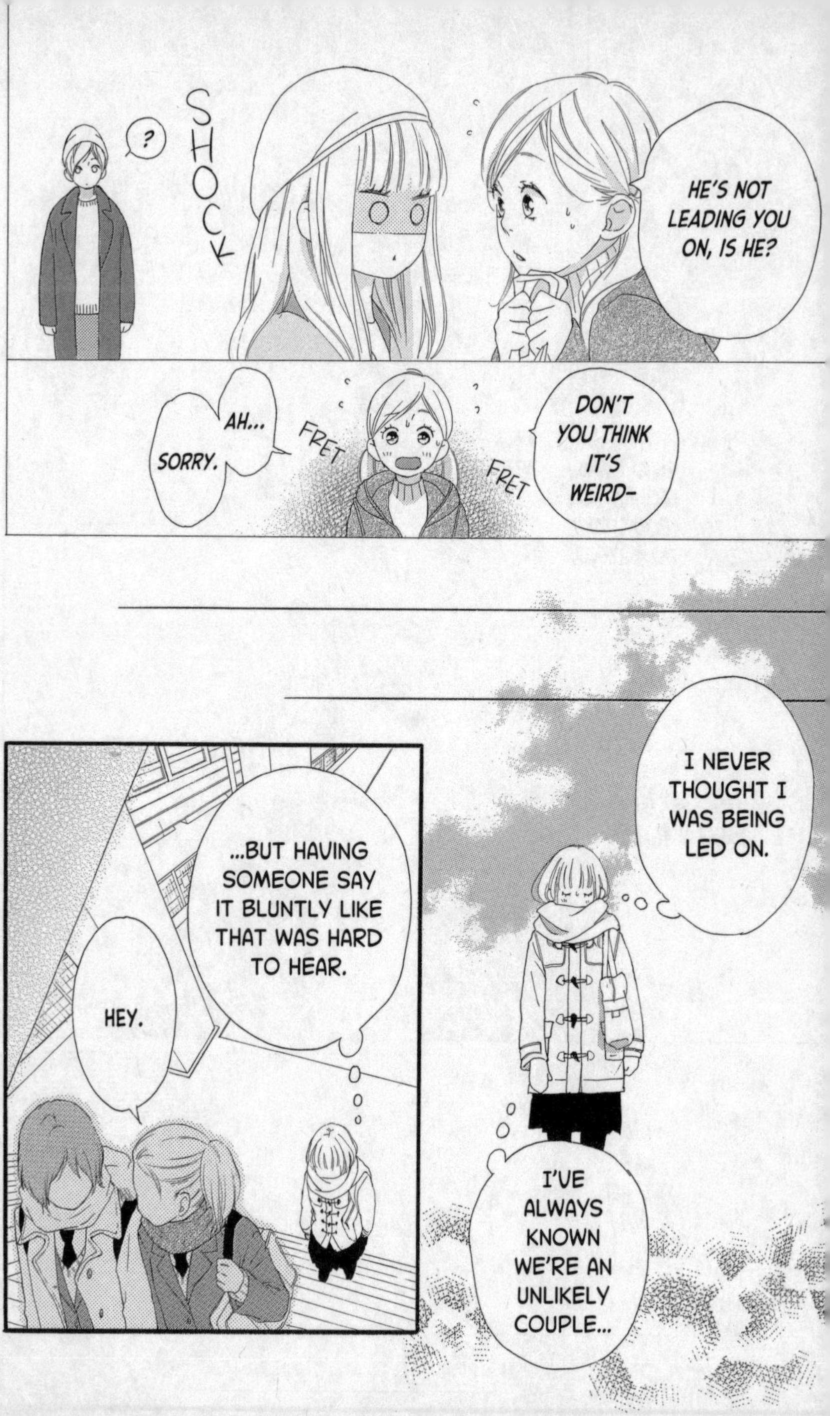
HE'S NOT LEADING YOU ON, IS HE?
SHOCK
?
DON'T YOU THINK IT'S WEIRD–
FRET
FRET
AH... SORRY.
I NEVER THOUGHT I WAS BEING LED ON.
I'VE ALWAYS KNOWN WE'RE AN UNLIKELY COUPLE...
...BUT HAVING SOMEONE SAY IT BLUNTLY LIKE THAT WAS HARD TO HEAR.
HEY.

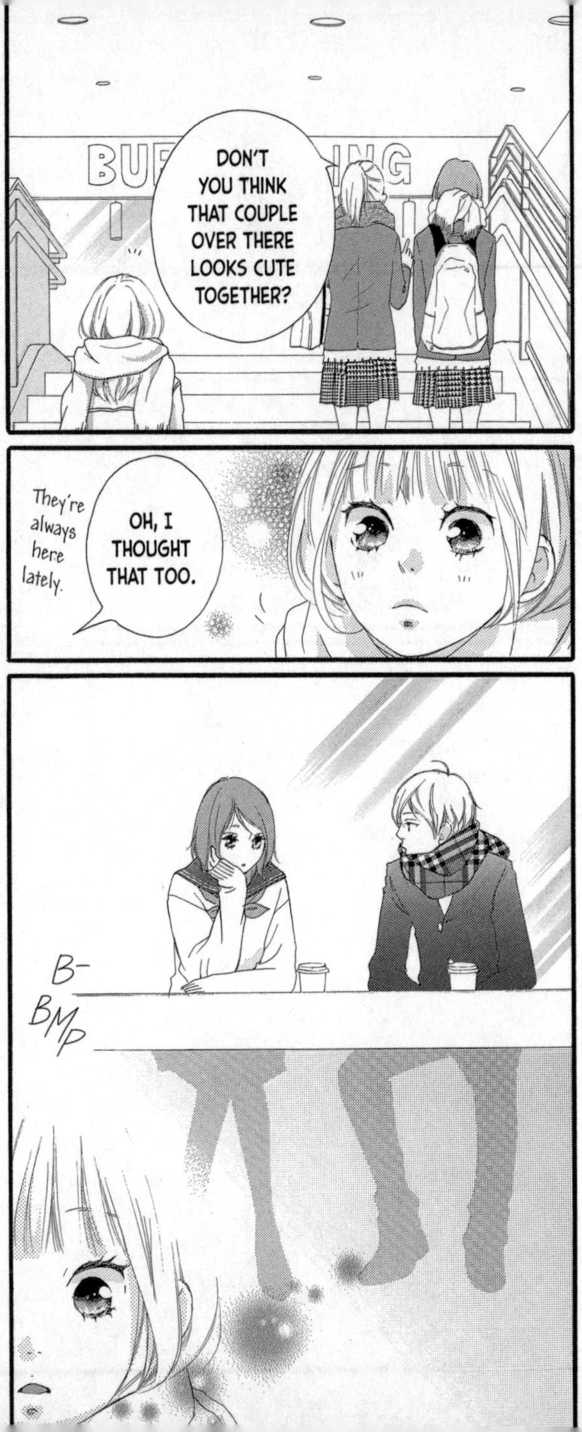
DON'T YOU THINK THAT COUPLE OVER THERE LOOKS CUTE TOGETHER?
OH, I THOUGHT THAT TOO.
They're always here lately.
B-BMP

The Bollywood movie *Baahubali* is really super fun. There was crazy laughing, floods of tears and everyone was super excited chatting afterwards about it. I loved it all. It's been a while since I watched a movie that raised my blood pressure like that, and I was very happy. On top of that, I got to go to an audience participation screening of *Baahubali*. It's the first time I've ever watched a movie with a penlight. And being able to play the tambourine during it? I'd never been to an audience participation screening, and I'd always thought it sounded fun, but it was even better than I had imagined. But never mind all that! The Baahubali character is so cool. Everyone I went with had their hearts stolen. You can't help but fall for him.

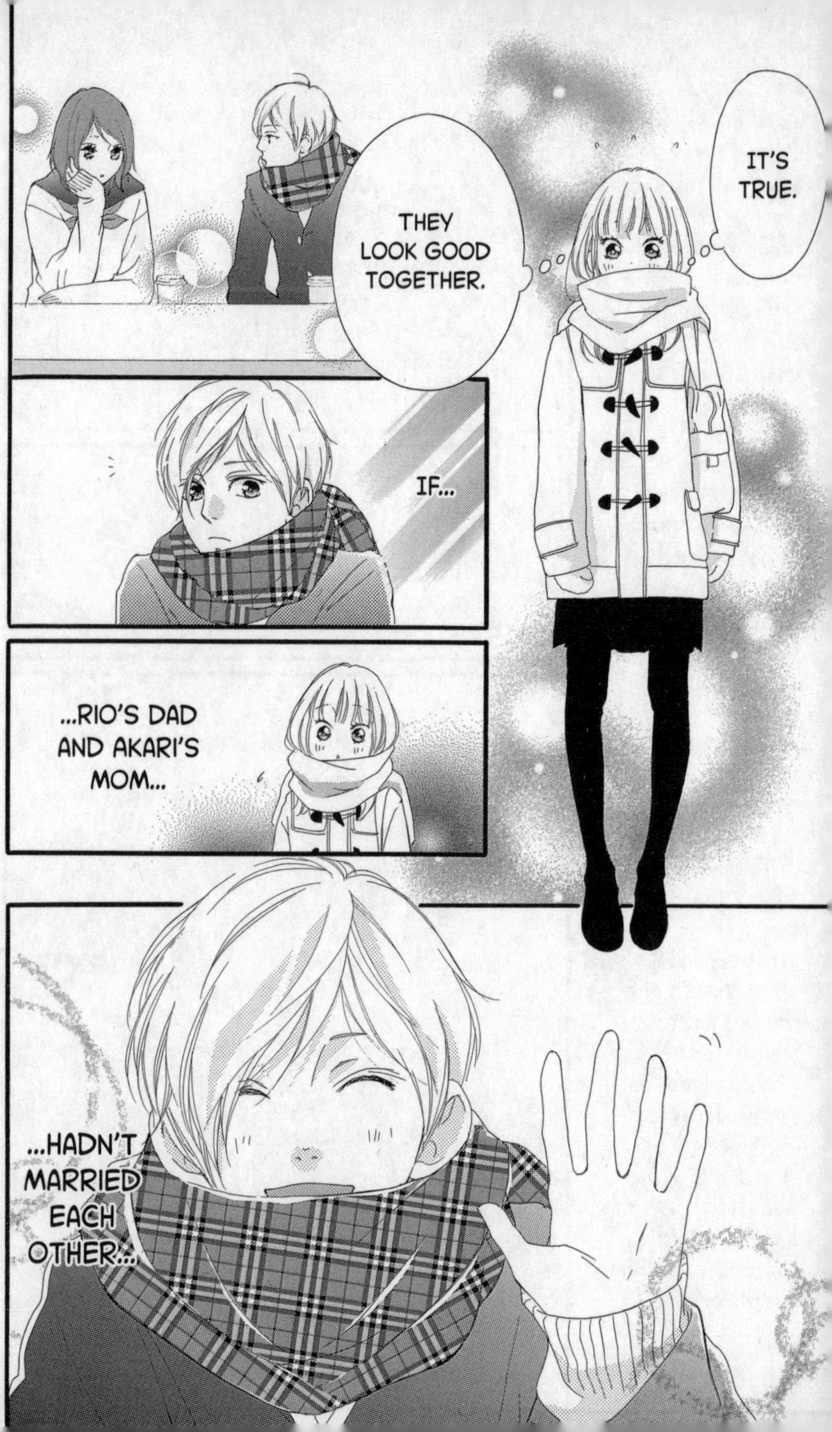
IT'S TRUE.
THEY LOOK GOOD TOGETHER.
IF...
...RIO'S DAD AND AKARI'S MOM...
...HADN'T MARRIED EACH OTHER...

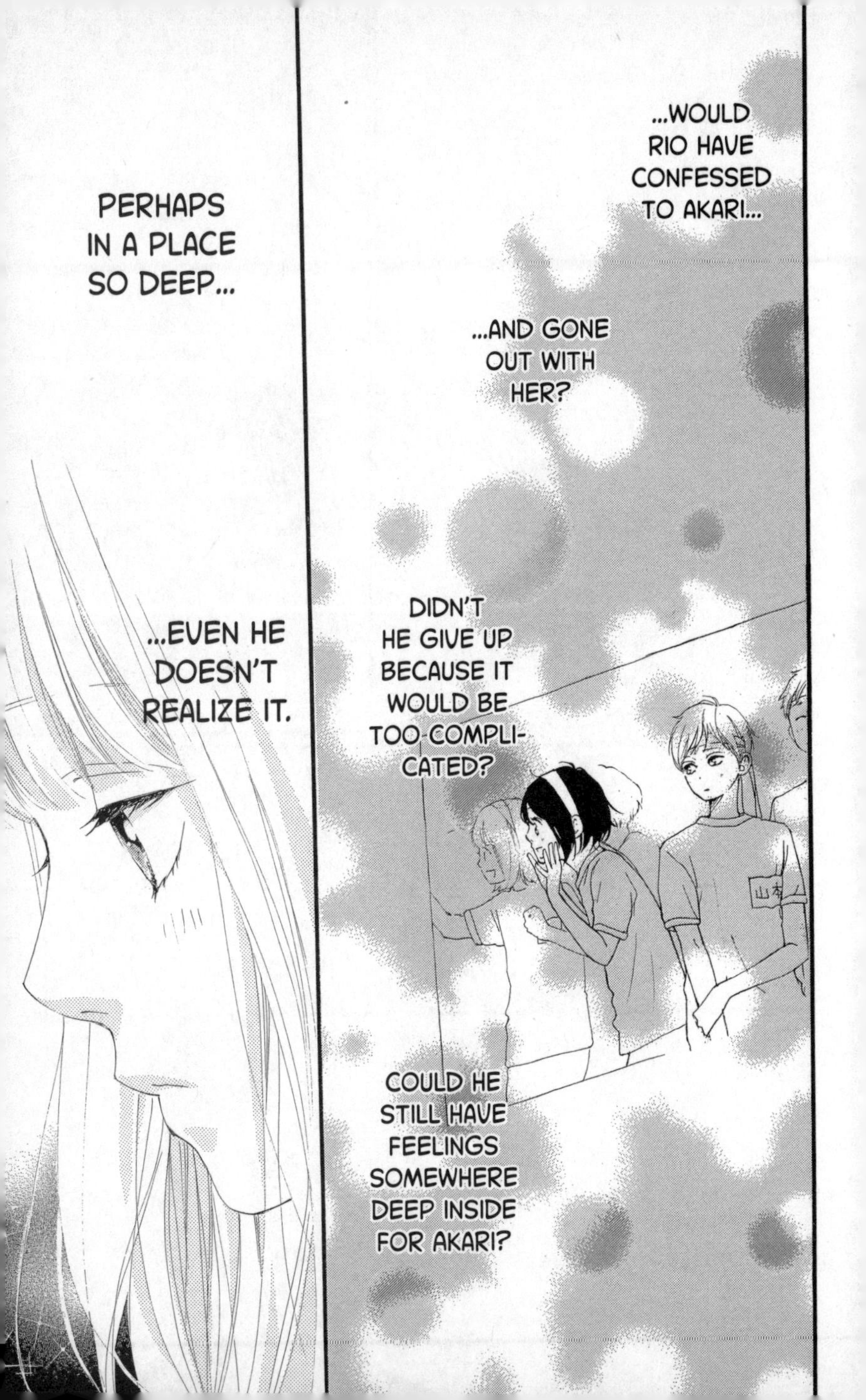
...WOULD RIO HAVE CONFESSED TO AKARI...
...AND GONE OUT WITH HER?
DIDN'T HE GIVE UP BECAUSE IT WOULD BE TOO COMPLI-CATED?
COULD HE STILL HAVE FEELINGS SOMEWHERE DEEP INSIDE FOR AKARI?
PERHAPS IN A PLACE SO DEEP...
...EVEN HE DOESN'T REALIZE IT.

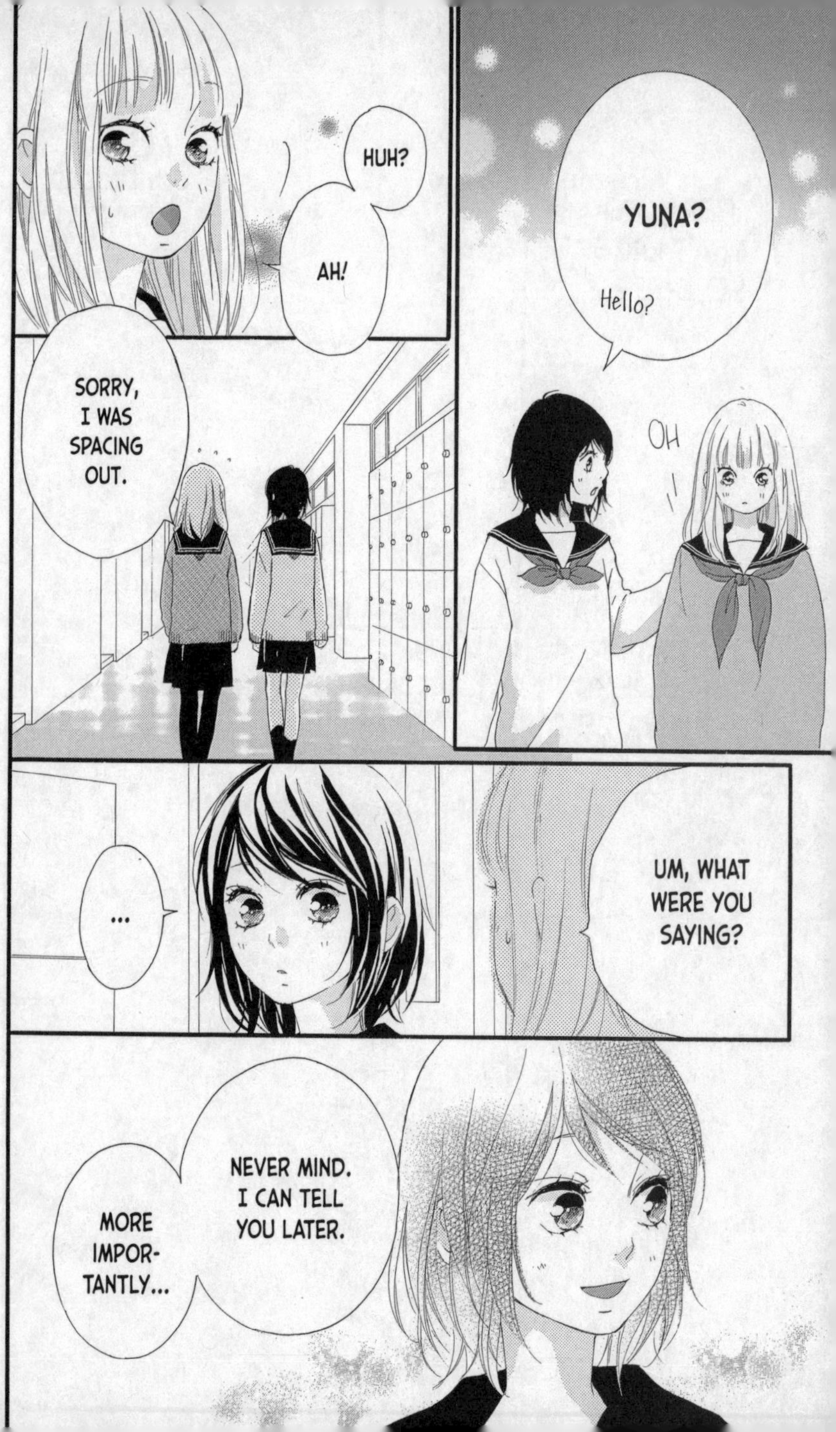
YUNA?
Hello?
OH
HUH?
AH!
SORRY, I WAS SPACING OUT.
UM, WHAT WERE YOU SAYING?
...
NEVER MIND. I CAN TELL YOU LATER.
MORE IMPOR-TANTLY...

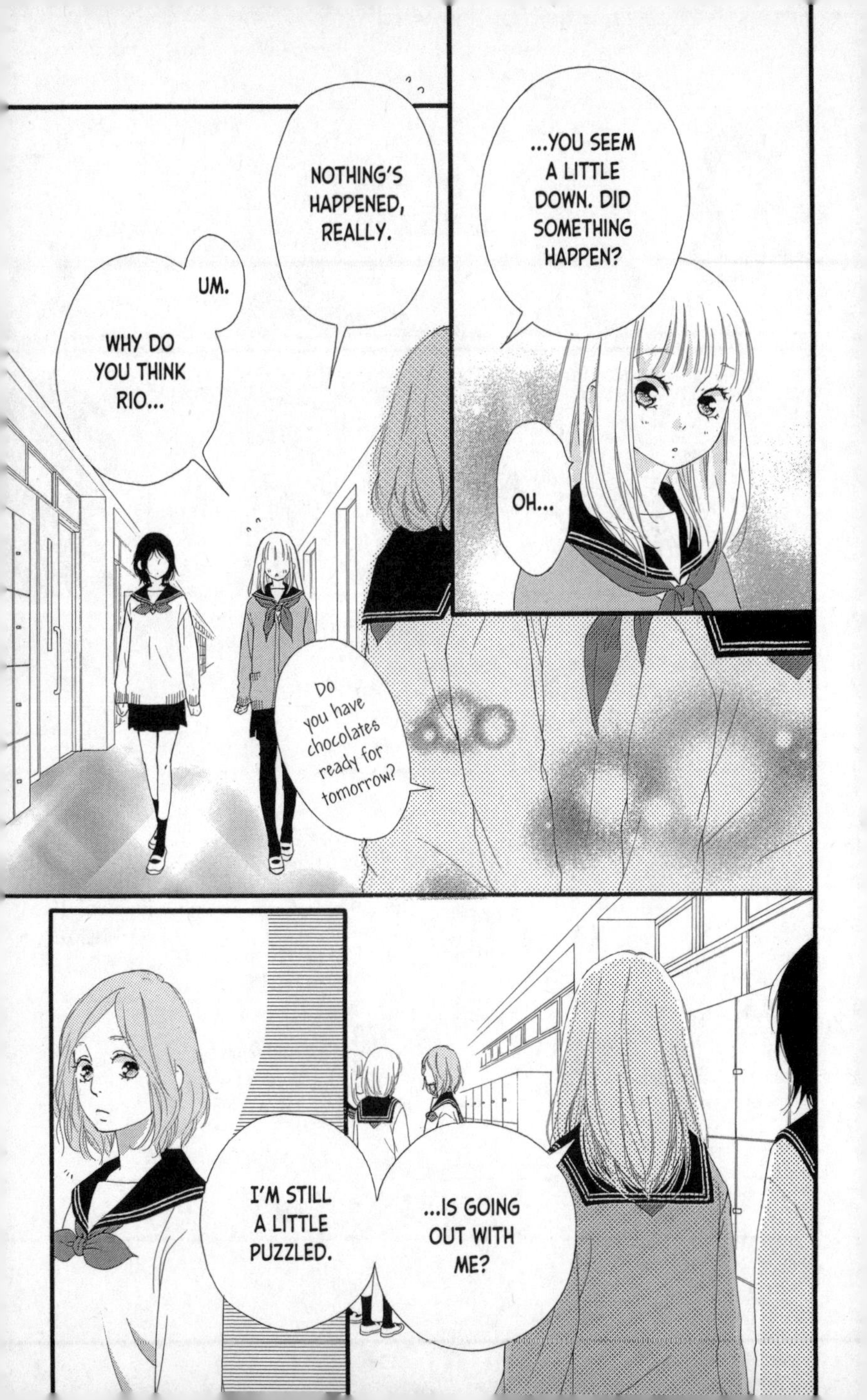
...YOU SEEM A LITTLE DOWN. DID SOMETHING HAPPEN?
OH...
Do you have chocolates ready for tomorrow?
NOTHING'S HAPPENED, REALLY.
UM.
WHY DO YOU THINK RIO...
...IS GOING OUT WITH ME?
I'M STILL A LITTLE PUZZLED.

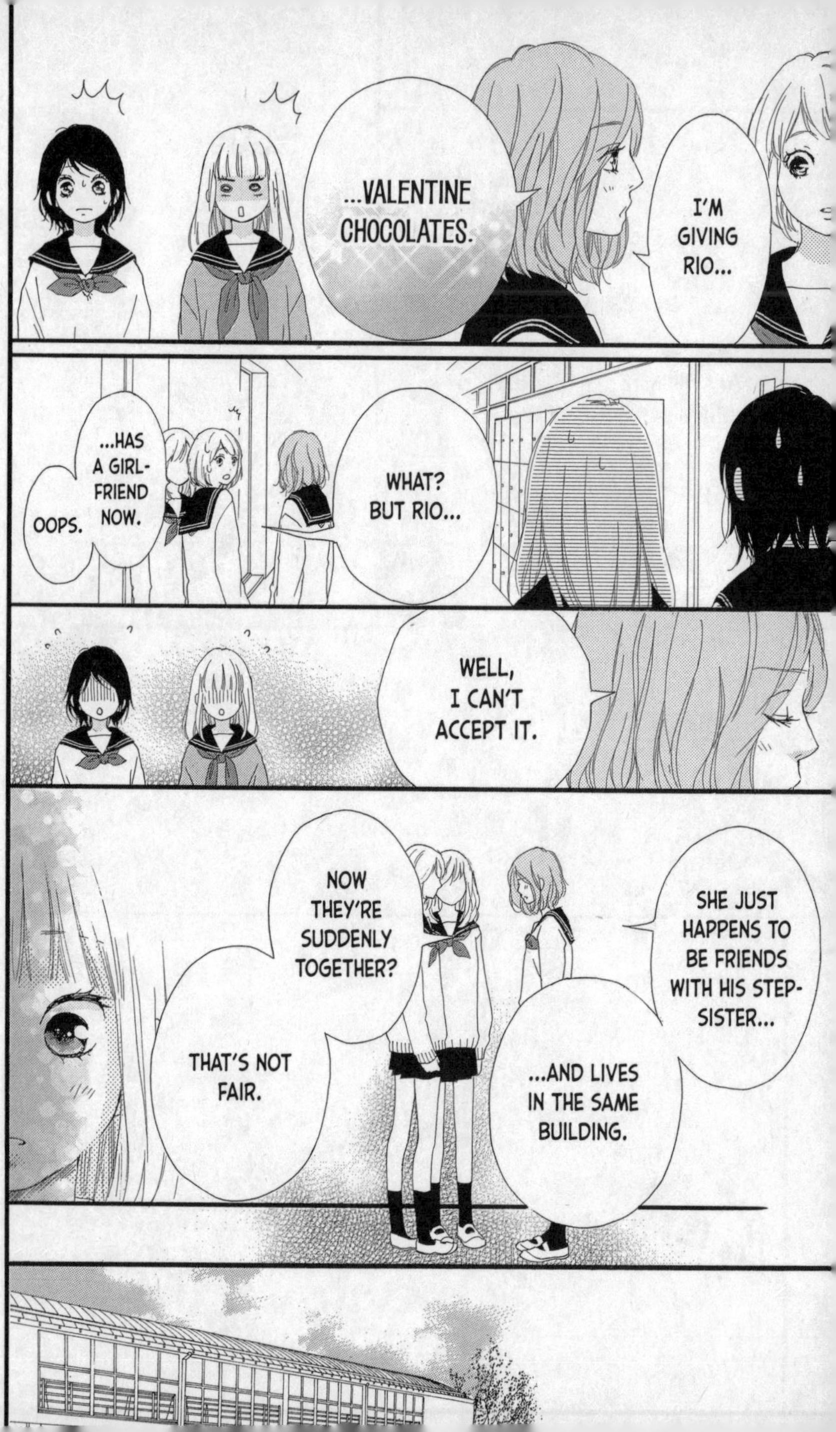

I'M GIVING RIO...
...VALENTINE CHOCOLATES.
WHAT? BUT RIO...
...HAS A GIRLFRIEND NOW.
OOPS.
WELL, I CAN'T ACCEPT IT.
SHE JUST HAPPENS TO BE FRIENDS WITH HIS STEPSISTER...
...AND LIVES IN THE SAME BUILDING.
NOW THEY'RE SUDDENLY TOGETHER?
THAT'S NOT FAIR.

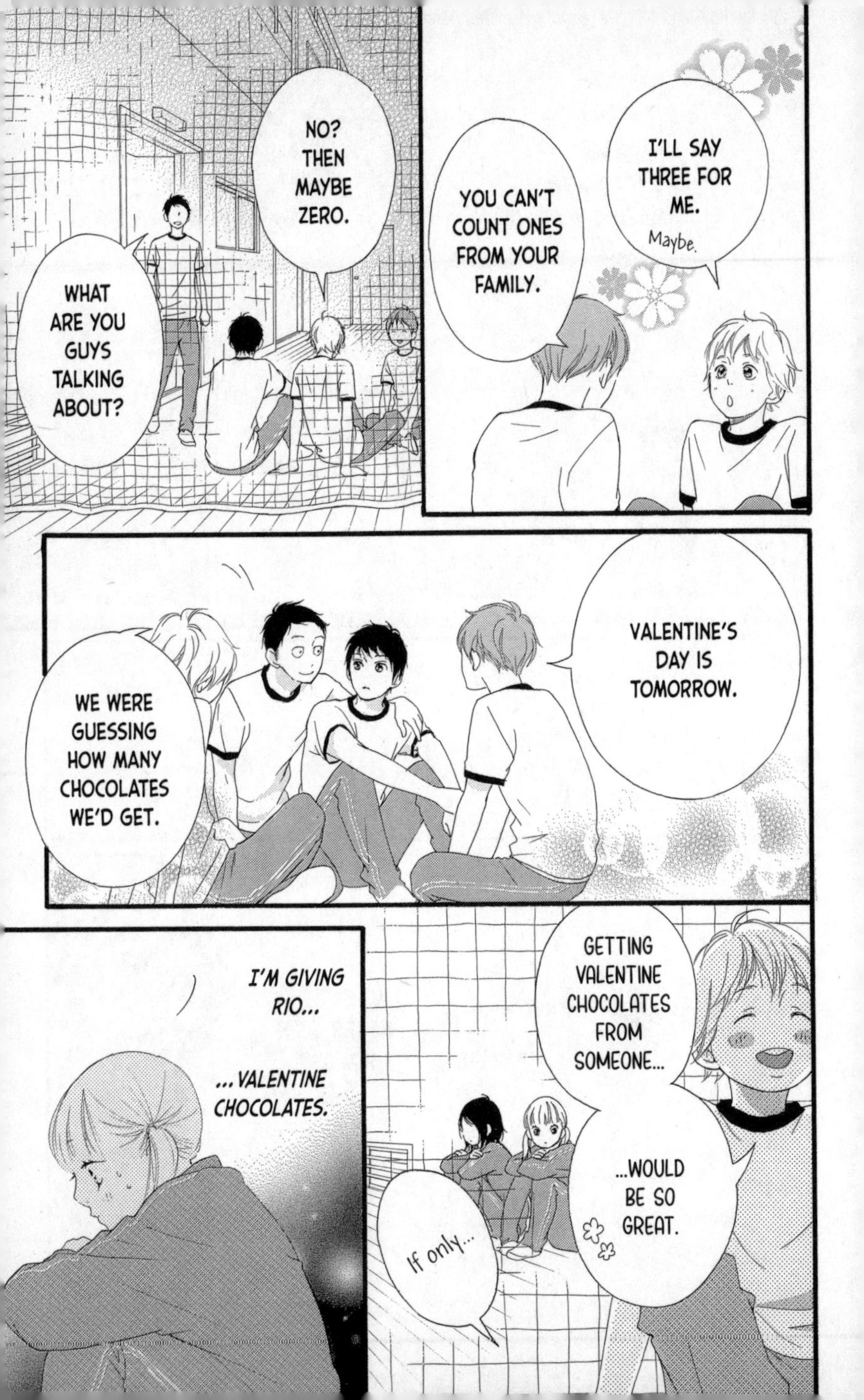
I'LL SAY THREE FOR ME.
Maybe.
YOU CAN'T COUNT ONES FROM YOUR FAMILY.
NO? THEN MAYBE ZERO.
WHAT ARE YOU GUYS TALKING ABOUT?
VALENTINE'S DAY IS TOMORROW.
WE WERE GUESSING HOW MANY CHOCOLATES WE'D GET.
GETTING VALENTINE CHOCOLATES FROM SOMEONE...
...WOULD BE SO GREAT.
If only...
I'M GIVING RIO...
...VALENTINE CHOCOLATES.

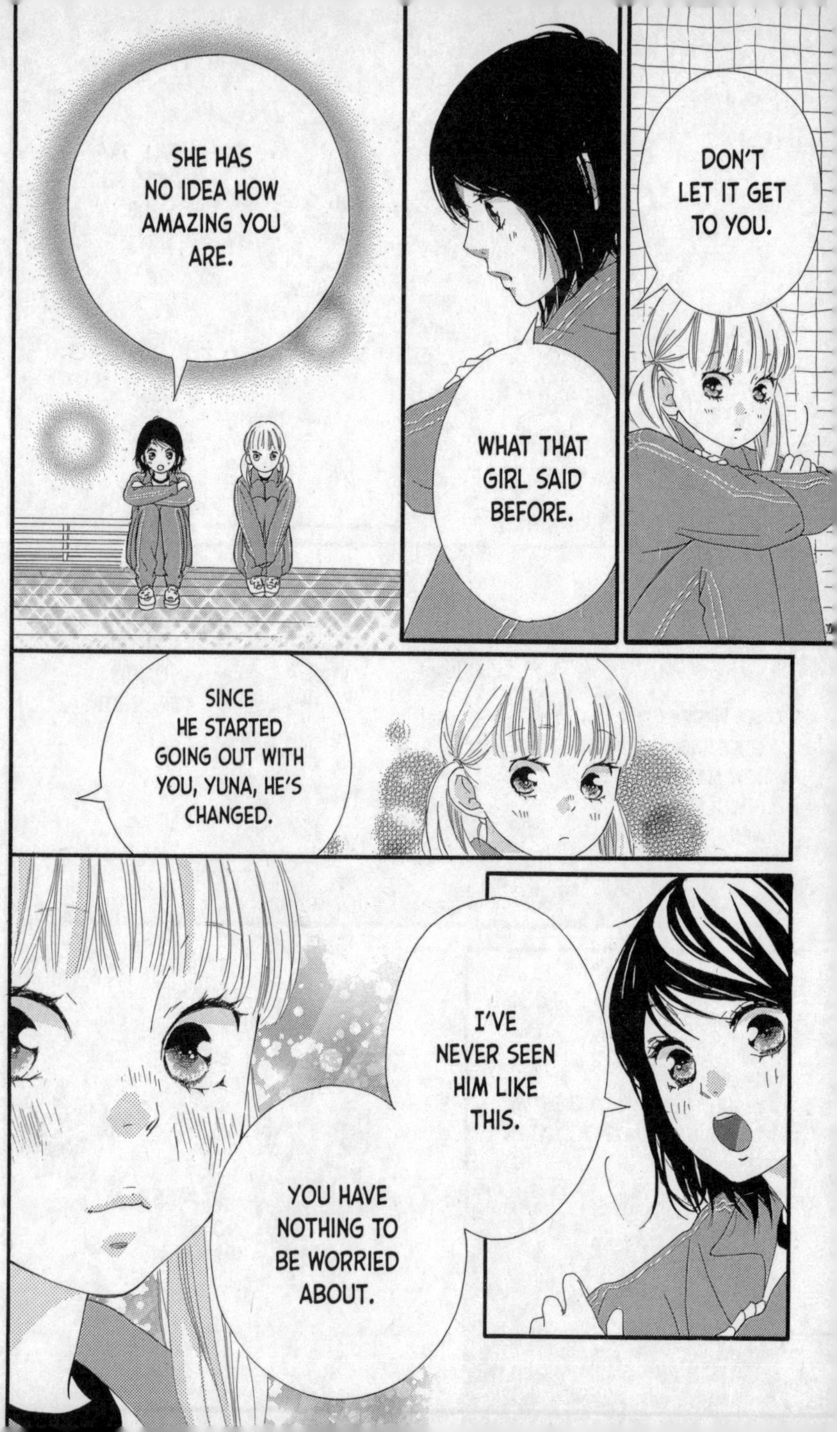
DON'T LET IT GET TO YOU.
WHAT THAT GIRL SAID BEFORE.
SHE HAS NO IDEA HOW AMAZING YOU ARE.
SINCE HE STARTED GOING OUT WITH YOU, YUNA, HE'S CHANGED.
I'VE NEVER SEEN HIM LIKE THIS.
YOU HAVE NOTHING TO BE WORRIED ABOUT.

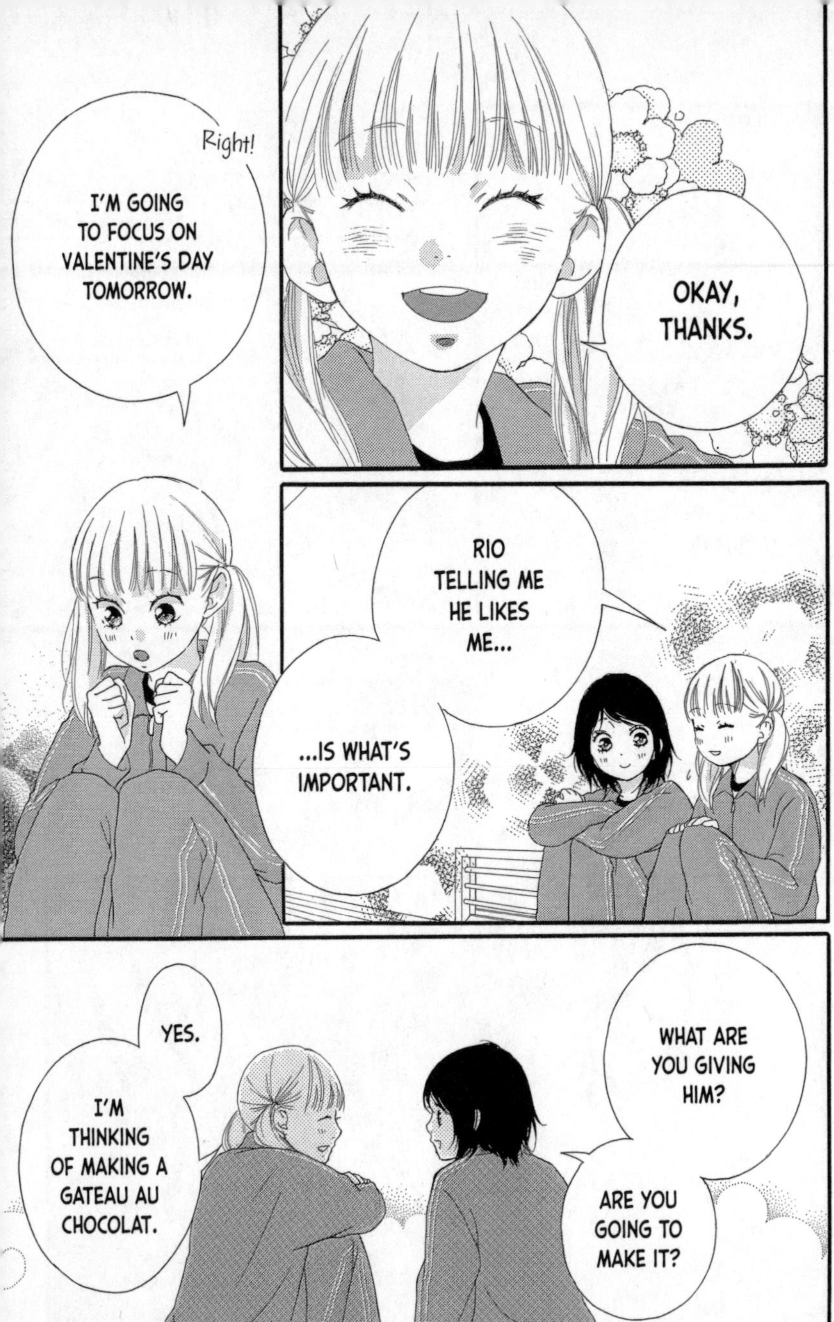
OKAY, THANKS.
RIO TELLING ME HE LIKES ME...
...IS WHAT'S IMPORTANT.
Right!
I'M GOING TO FOCUS ON VALENTINE'S DAY TOMORROW.
WHAT ARE YOU GIVING HIM?
ARE YOU GOING TO MAKE IT?
YES.
I'M THINKING OF MAKING A GATEAU AU CHOCOLAT.

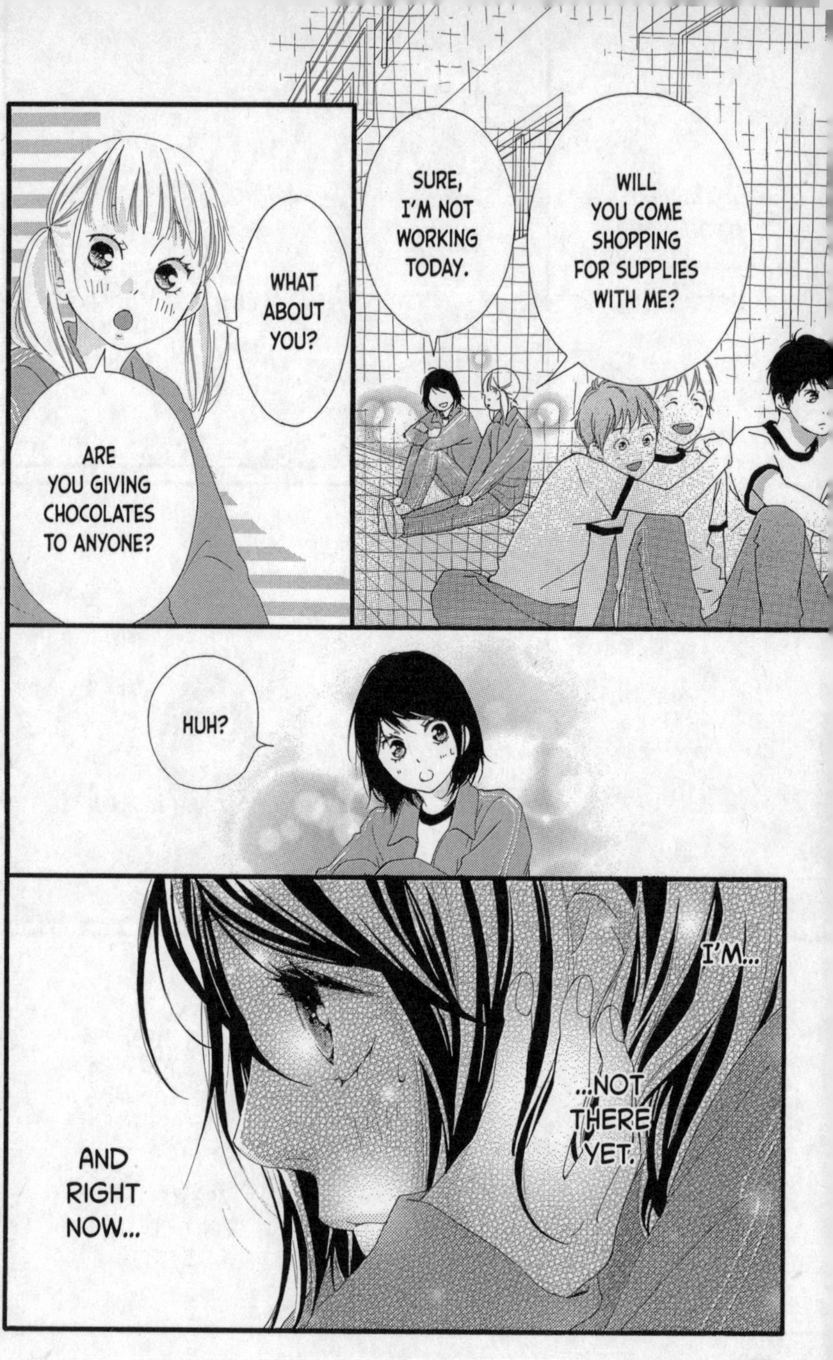
WILL YOU COME SHOPPING FOR SUPPLIES WITH ME?
SURE, I'M NOT WORKING TODAY.
WHAT ABOUT YOU?
ARE YOU GIVING CHOCOLATES TO ANYONE?
HUH?
I'M...
...NOT THERE YET.
AND RIGHT NOW...

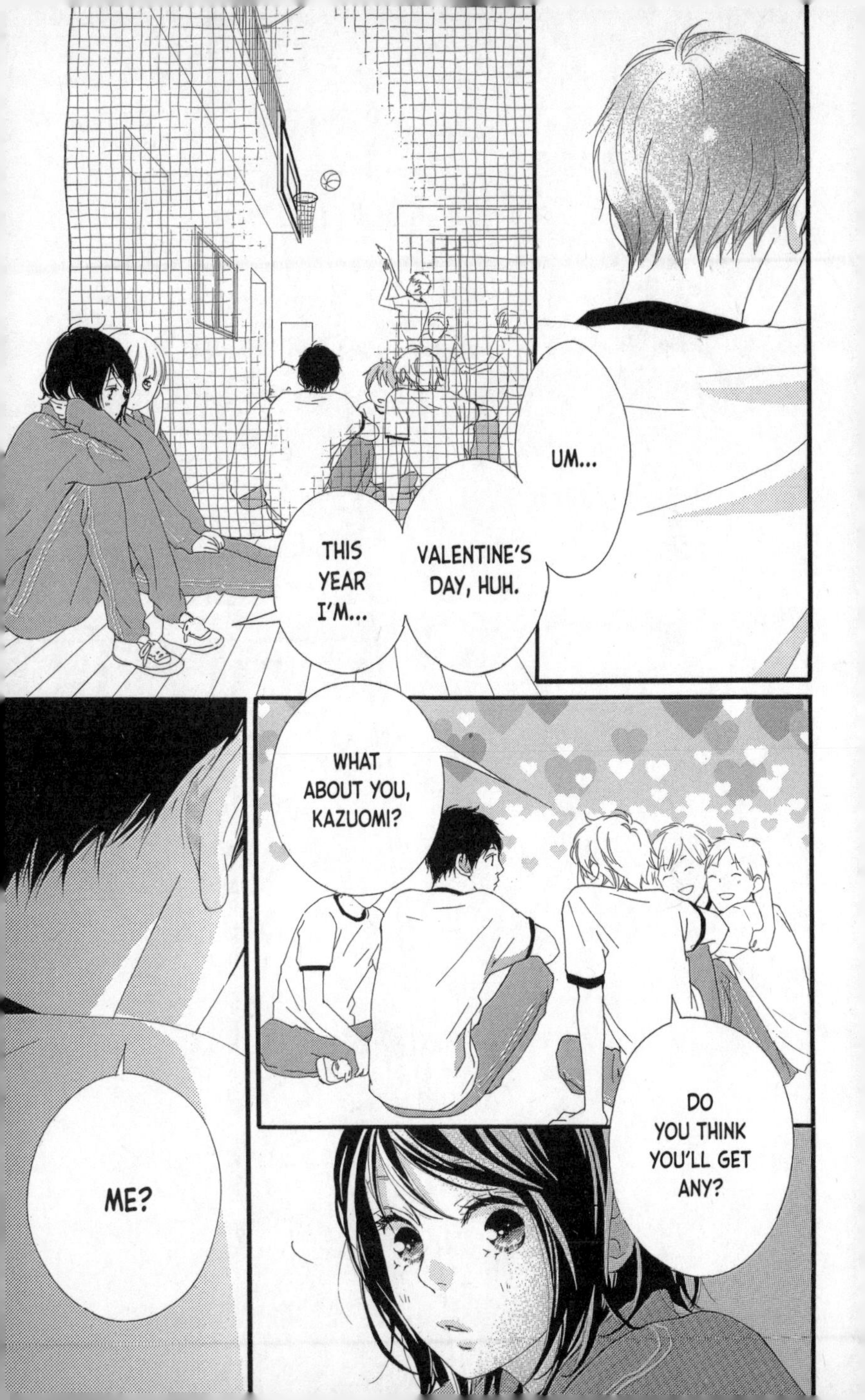
UM...
VALENTINE'S DAY, HUH.
THIS YEAR I'M...
WHAT ABOUT YOU, KAZUOMI?
DO YOU THINK YOU'LL GET ANY?
ME?

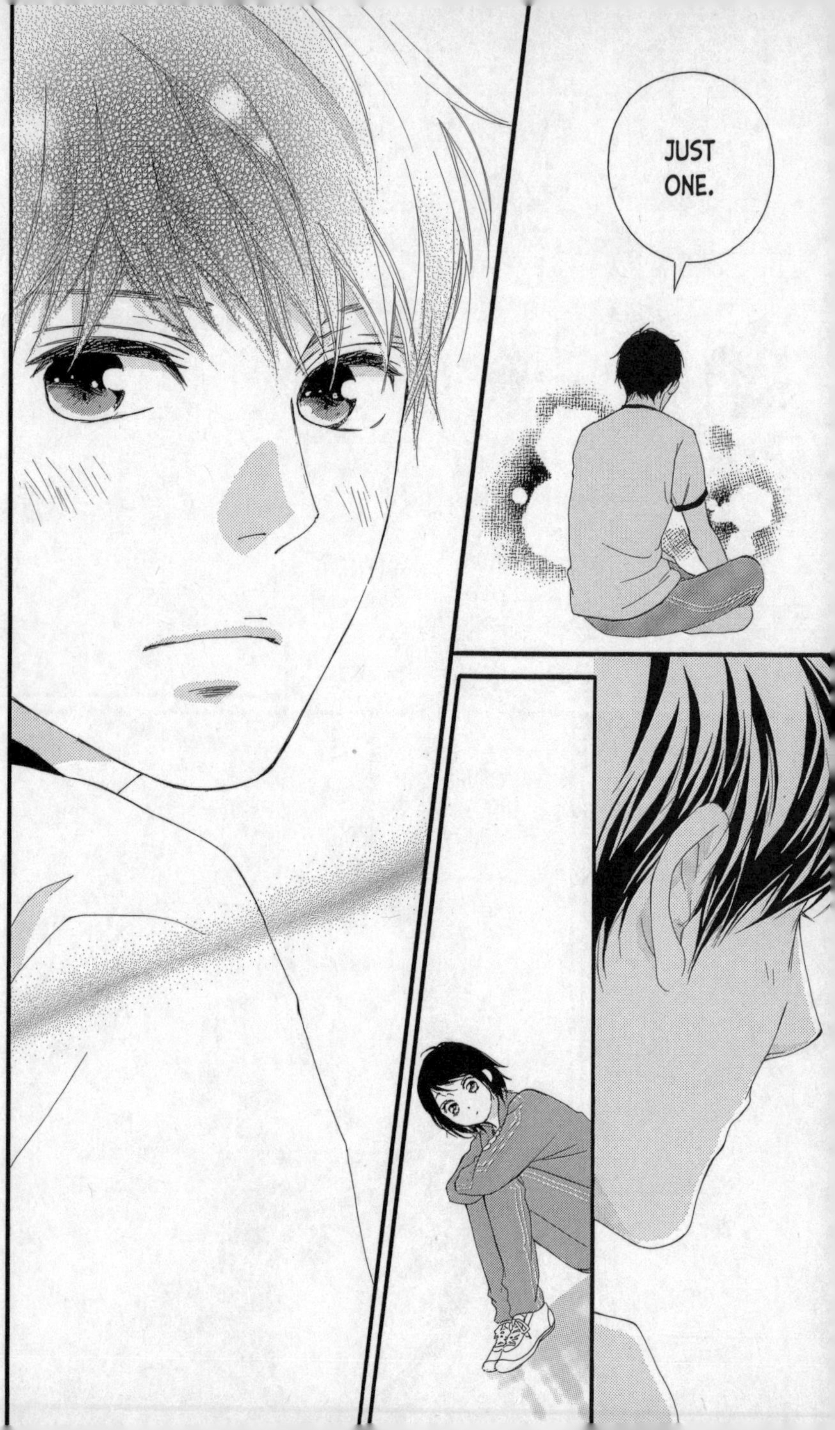
JUST ONE.

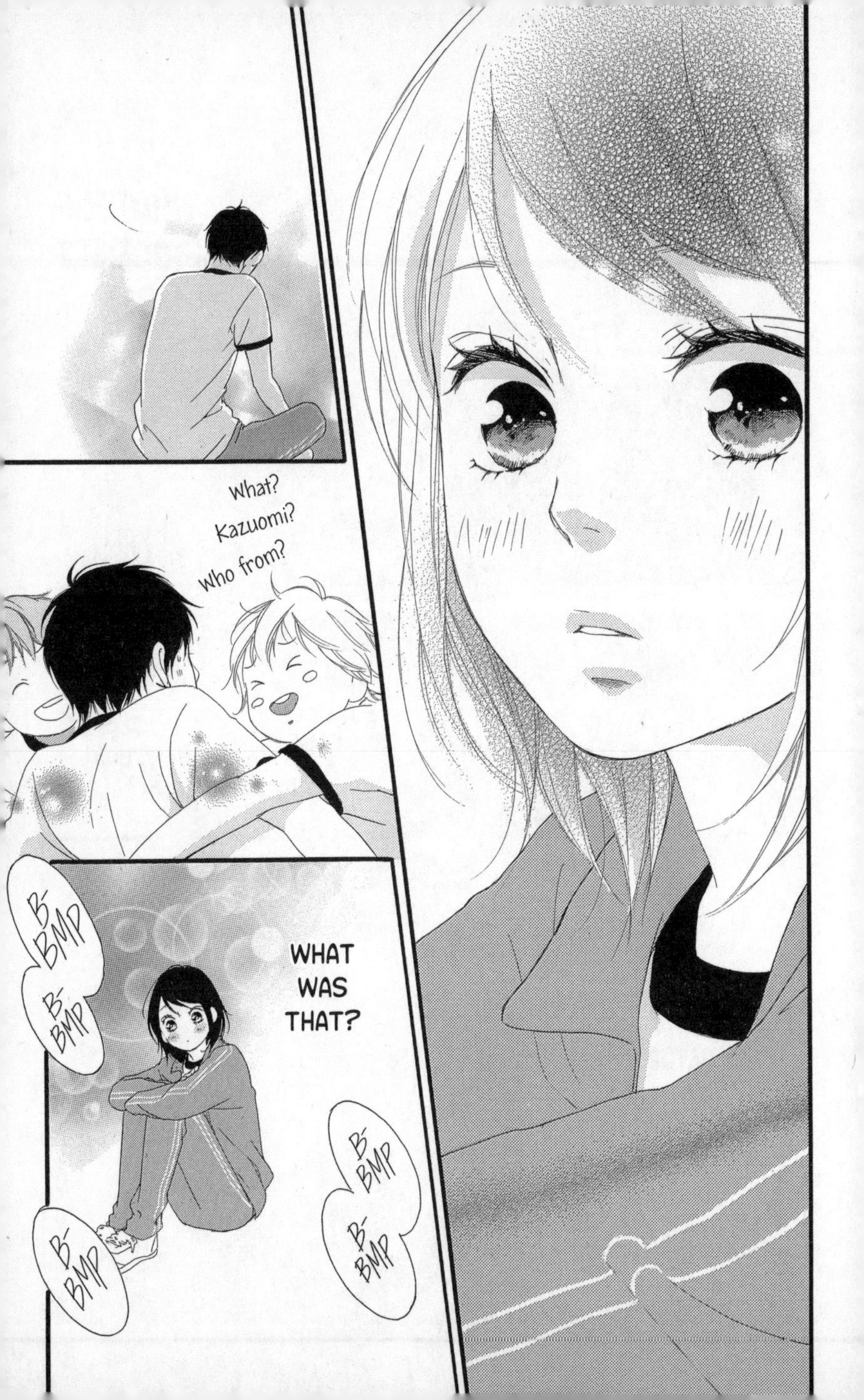
What?
Kazuomi?
Who from?
WHAT WAS THAT?
B-BMP B-BMP
B-BMP B-BMP
B-BMP

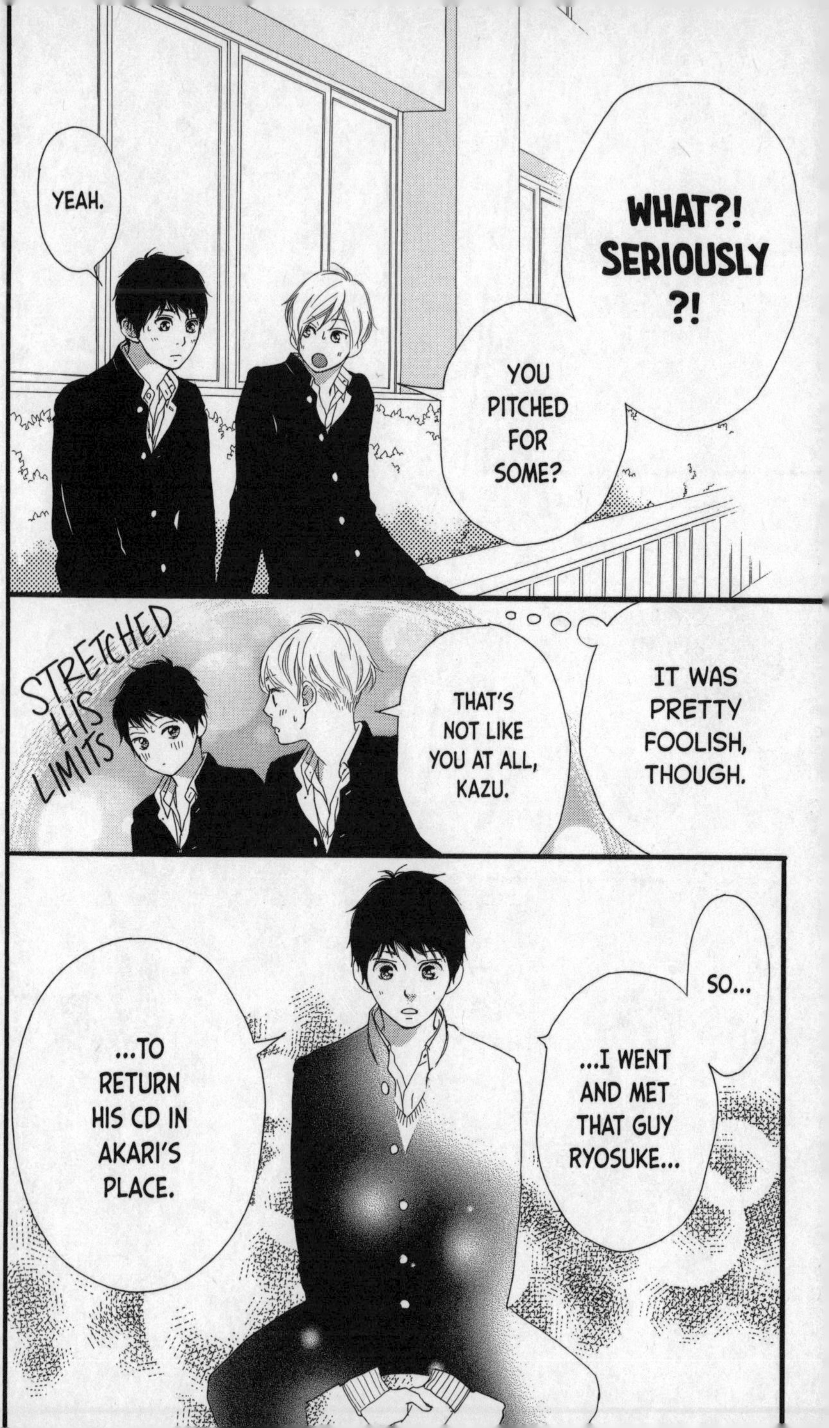
WHAT?! SERIOUSLY ?!
YOU PITCHED FOR SOME?
YEAH.
IT WAS PRETTY FOOLISH, THOUGH.
THAT'S NOT LIKE YOU AT ALL, KAZU.
STRETCHED HIS LIMITS
SO...
...I WENT AND MET THAT GUY RYOSUKE...
...TO RETURN HIS CD IN AKARI'S PLACE.

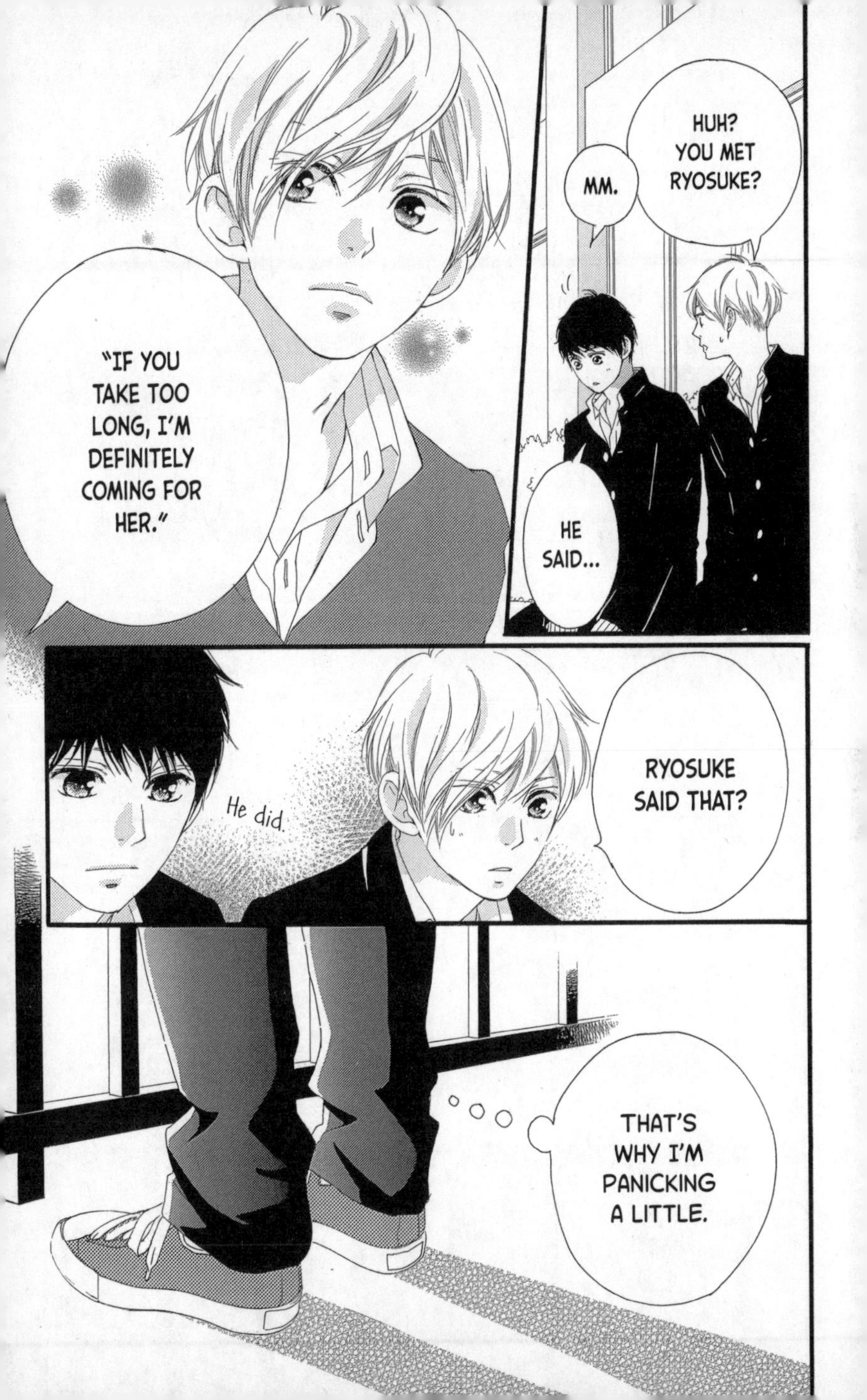
HUH? YOU MET RYOSUKE?
MM.
HE SAID...
"IF YOU TAKE TOO LONG, I'M DEFINITELY COMING FOR HER."
RYOSUKE SAID THAT?
He did.
THAT'S WHY I'M PANICKING A LITTLE.

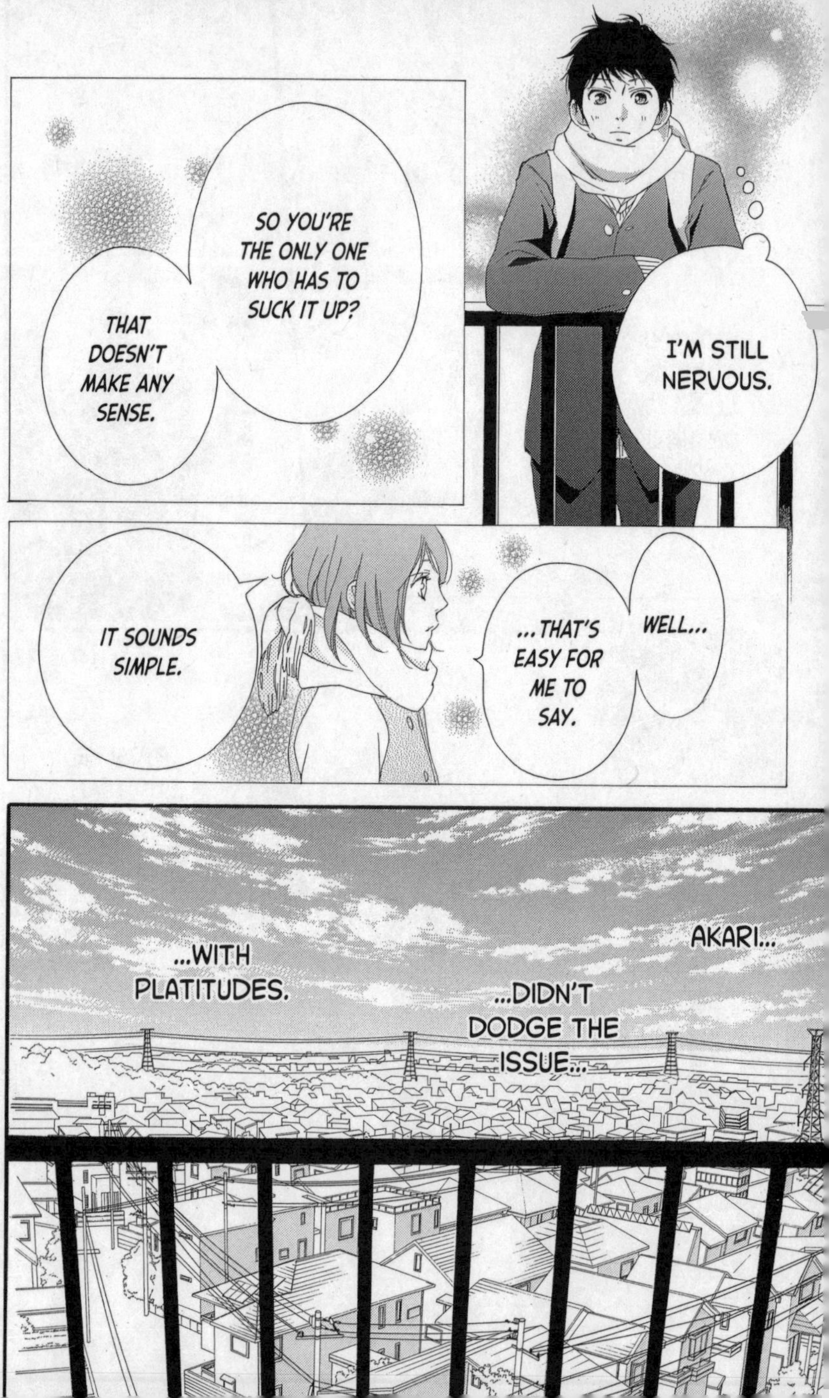
I'M STILL NERVOUS.
SO YOU'RE THE ONLY ONE WHO HAS TO SUCK IT UP?
THAT DOESN'T MAKE ANY SENSE.
WELL...
...THAT'S EASY FOR ME TO SAY.
IT SOUNDS SIMPLE.
AKARI...
...DIDN'T DODGE THE ISSUE...
...WITH PLATITUDES.

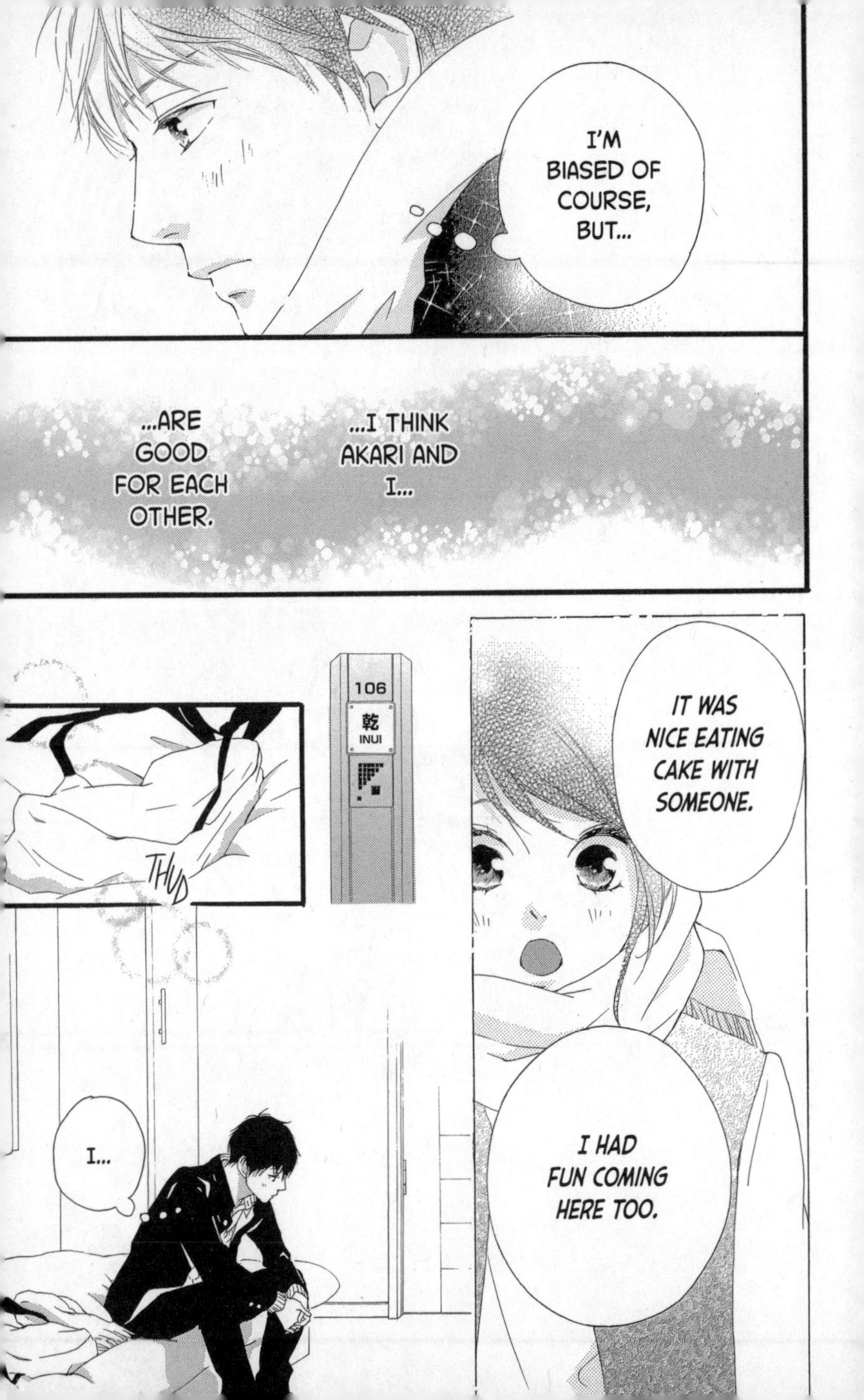
I'M BIASED OF COURSE, BUT...
...I THINK AKARI AND I...
...ARE GOOD FOR EACH OTHER.
IT WAS NICE EATING CAKE WITH SOMEONE.
I HAD FUN COMING HERE TOO.
106
乾
INUI
THUD
I...

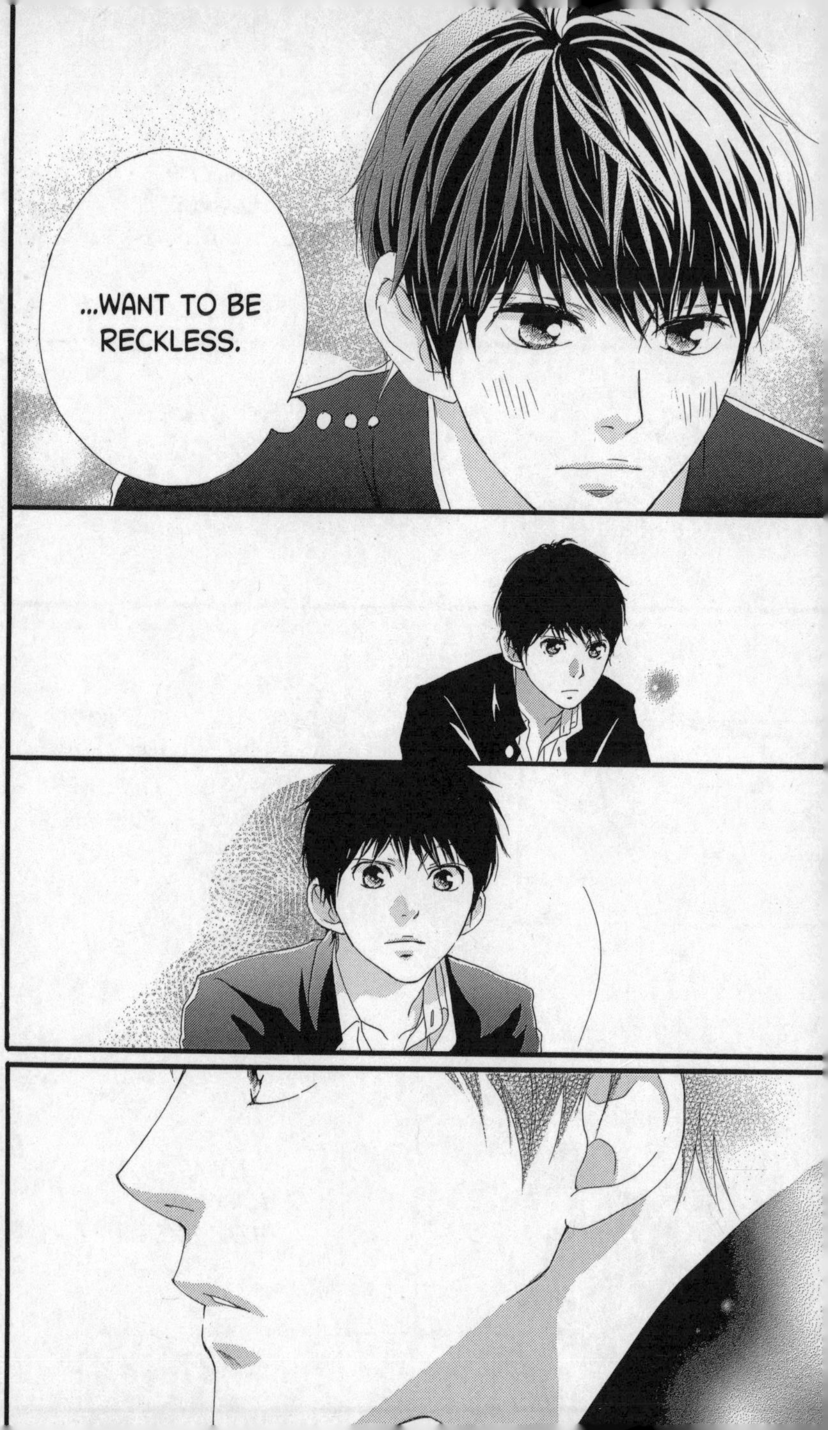
...WANT TO BE RECKLESS.

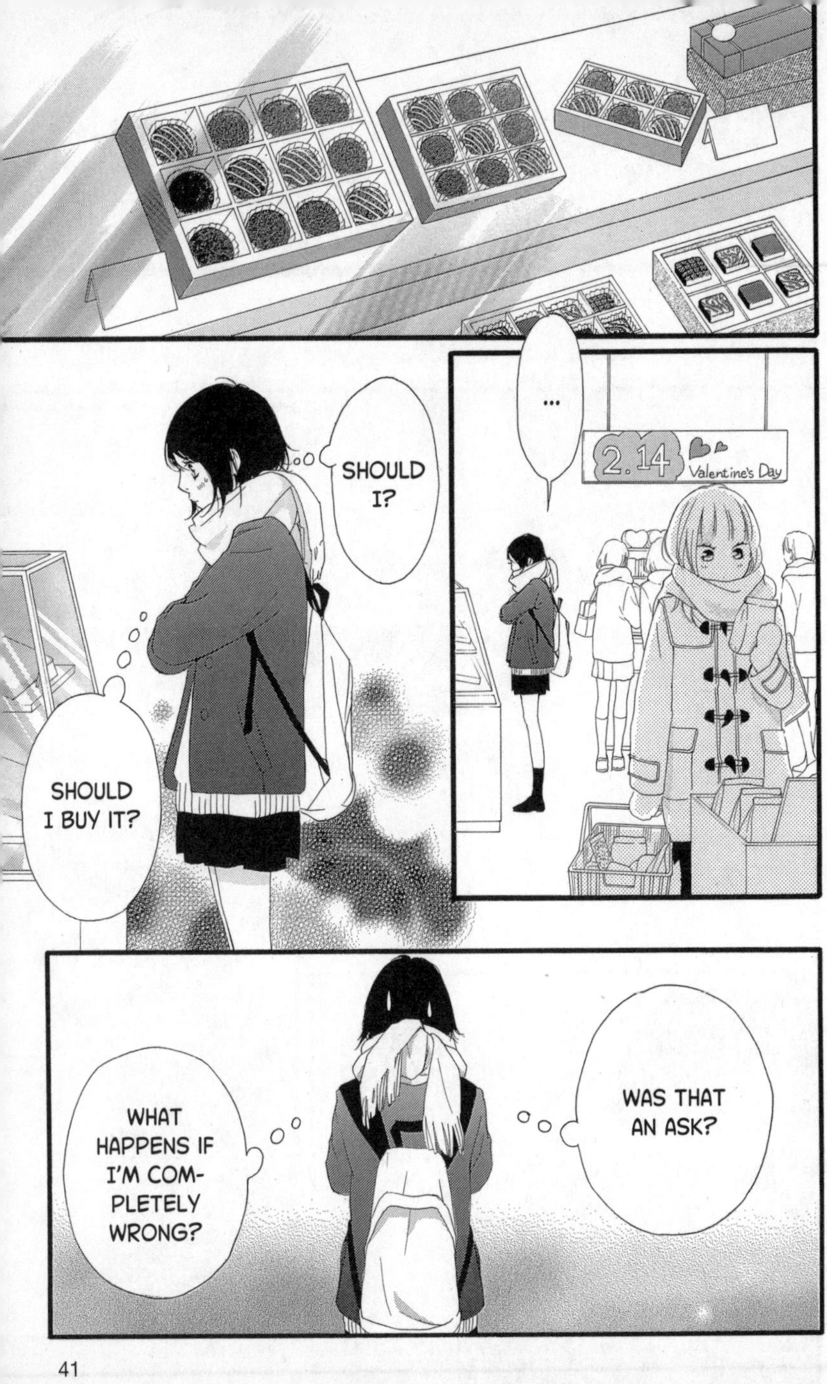
...
2.14
Valentine's Day
SHOULD I?
SHOULD I BUY IT?
WAS THAT AN ASK?
WHAT HAPPENS IF I'M COM-PLETELY WRONG?

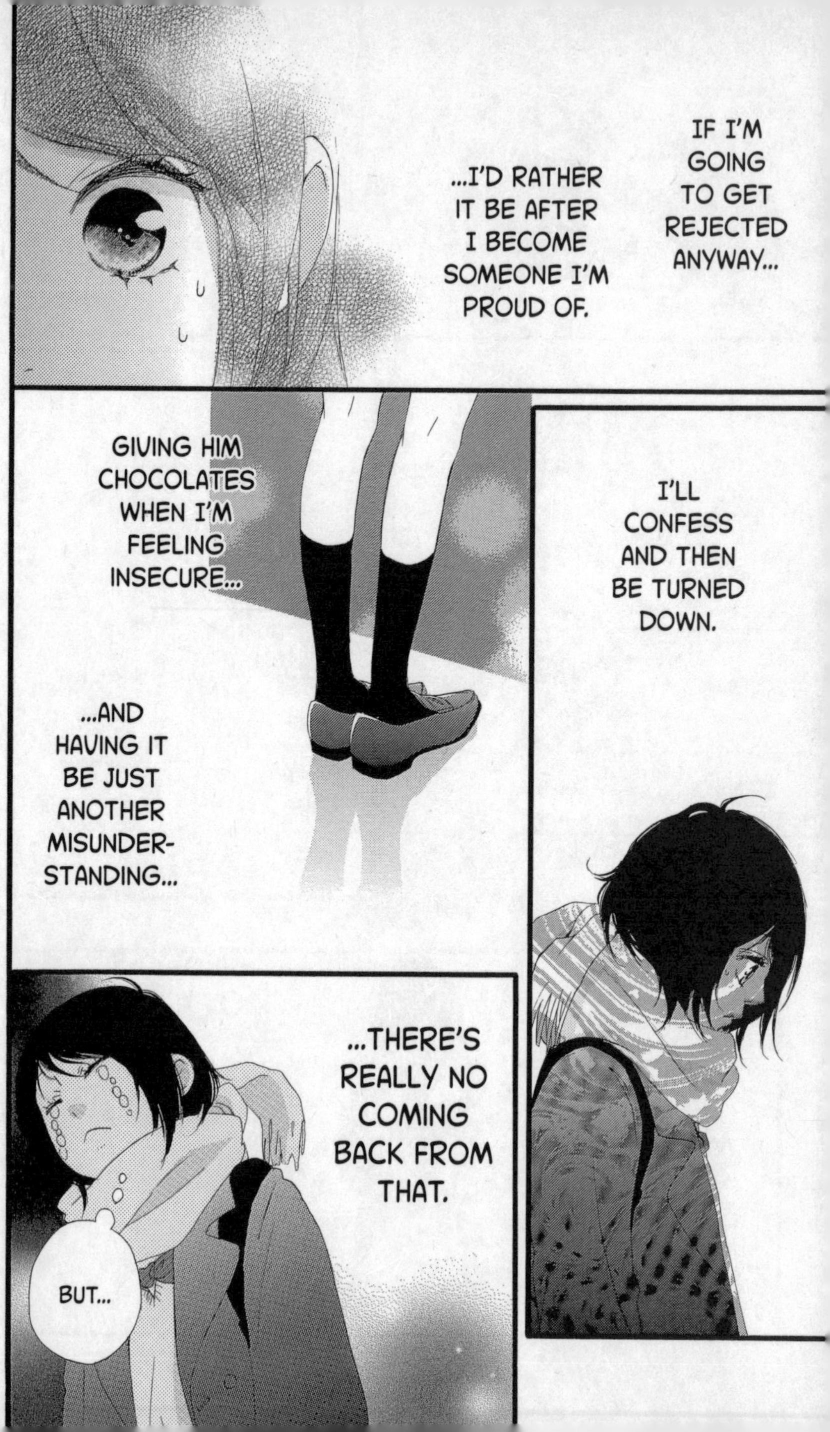
IF I'M GOING TO GET REJECTED ANYWAY...
...I'D RATHER IT BE AFTER I BECOME SOMEONE I'M PROUD OF.
I'LL CONFESS AND THEN BE TURNED DOWN.
GIVING HIM CHOCOLATES WHEN I'M FEELING INSECURE...
...AND HAVING IT BE JUST ANOTHER MISUNDER-STANDING...
...THERE'S REALLY NO COMING BACK FROM THAT.
BUT...

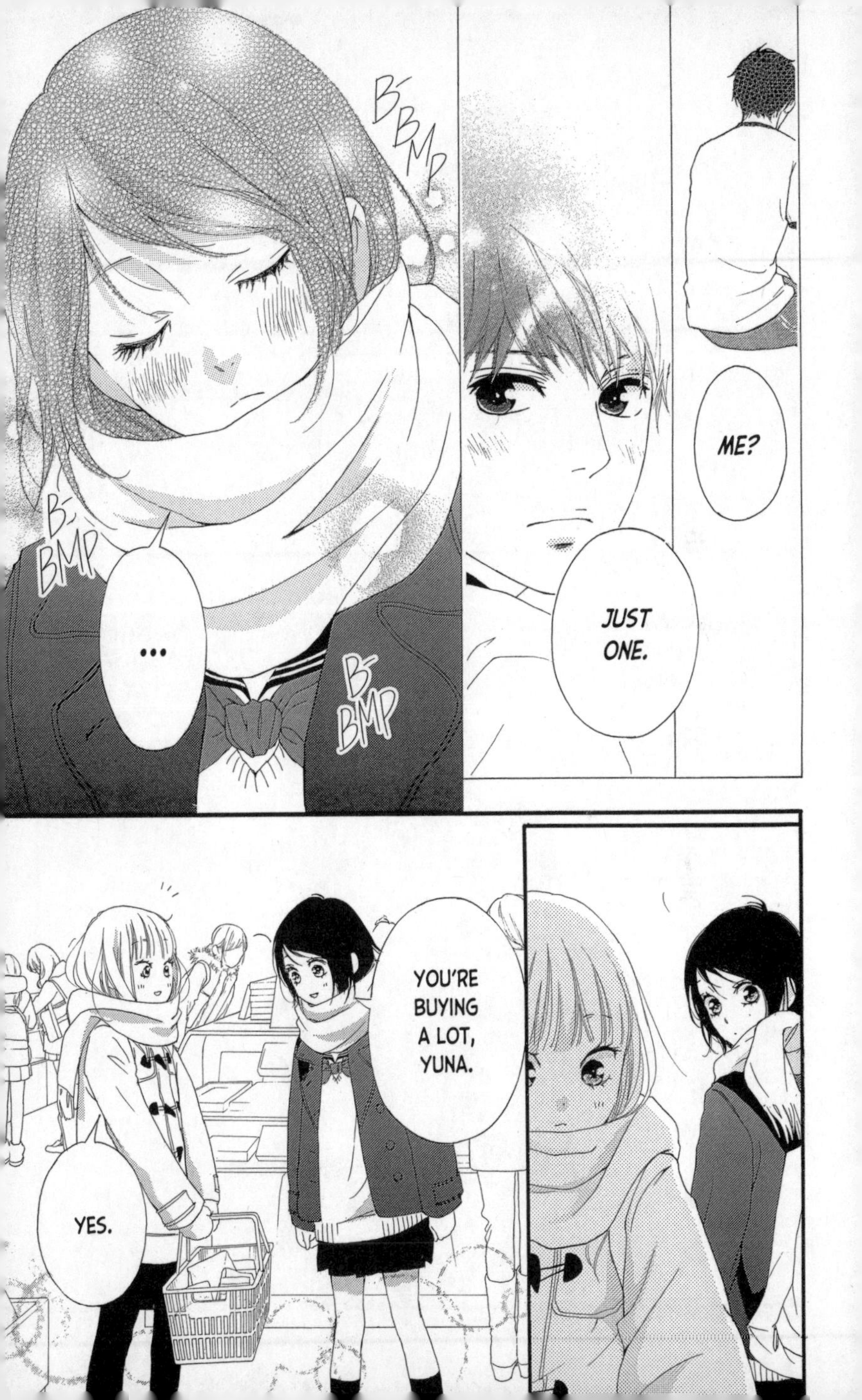
ME?
JUST ONE.
B-BMP
B-BMP
...
B-BMP
YOU'RE BUYING A LOT, YUNA.
YES.

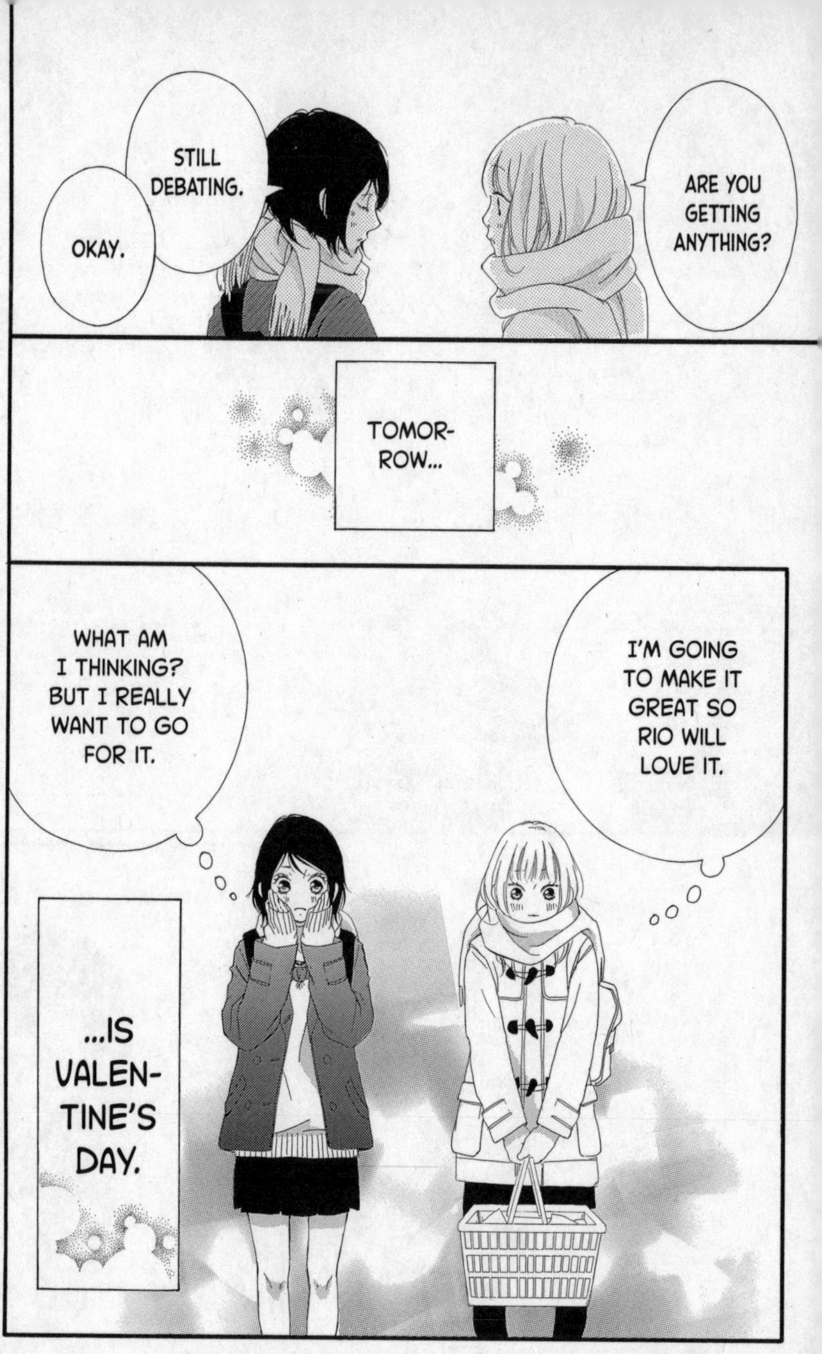
ARE YOU GETTING ANYTHING?
STILL DEBATING.
OKAY.
TOMOR-ROW...
I'M GOING TO MAKE IT GREAT SO RIO WILL LOVE IT.
WHAT AM I THINKING? BUT I REALLY WANT TO GO FOR IT.
...IS VALEN-TINE'S DAY.

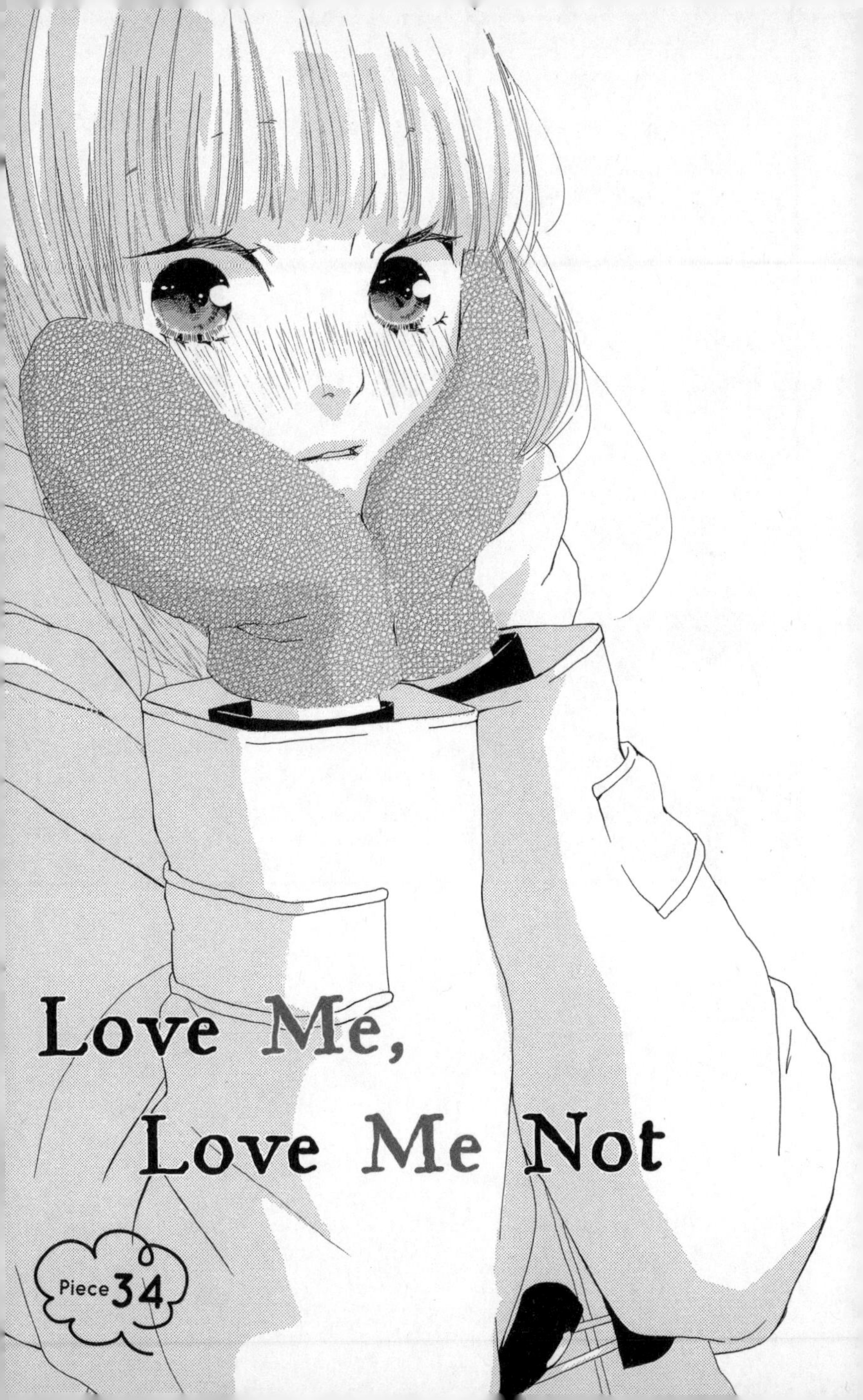
Love Me,
Love Me Not
Piece 34

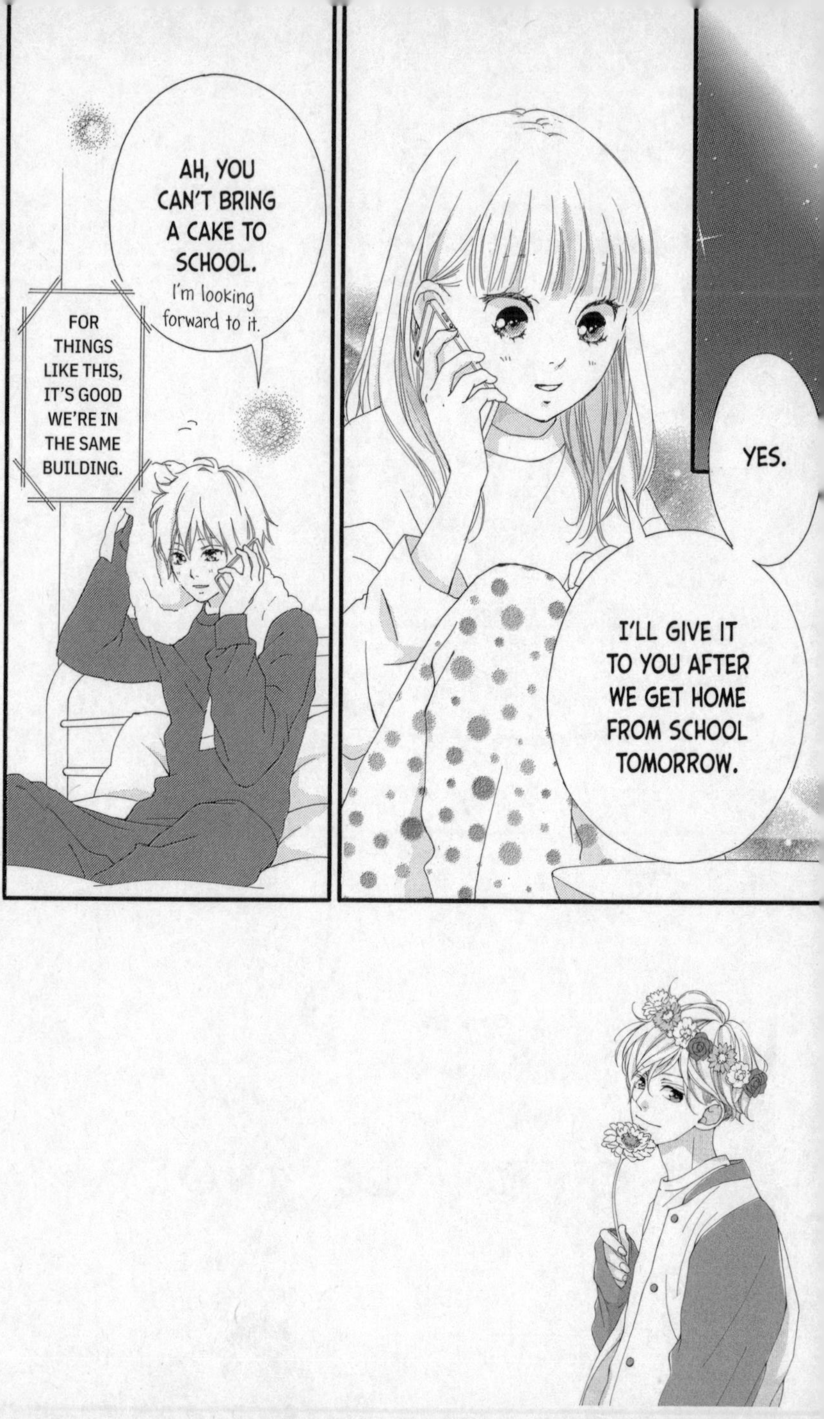
YES.
I'LL GIVE IT TO YOU AFTER WE GET HOME FROM SCHOOL TOMORROW.
AH, YOU CAN'T BRING A CAKE TO SCHOOL. I'm looking forward to it.
FOR THINGS LIKE THIS, IT'S GOOD WE'RE IN THE SAME BUILDING.

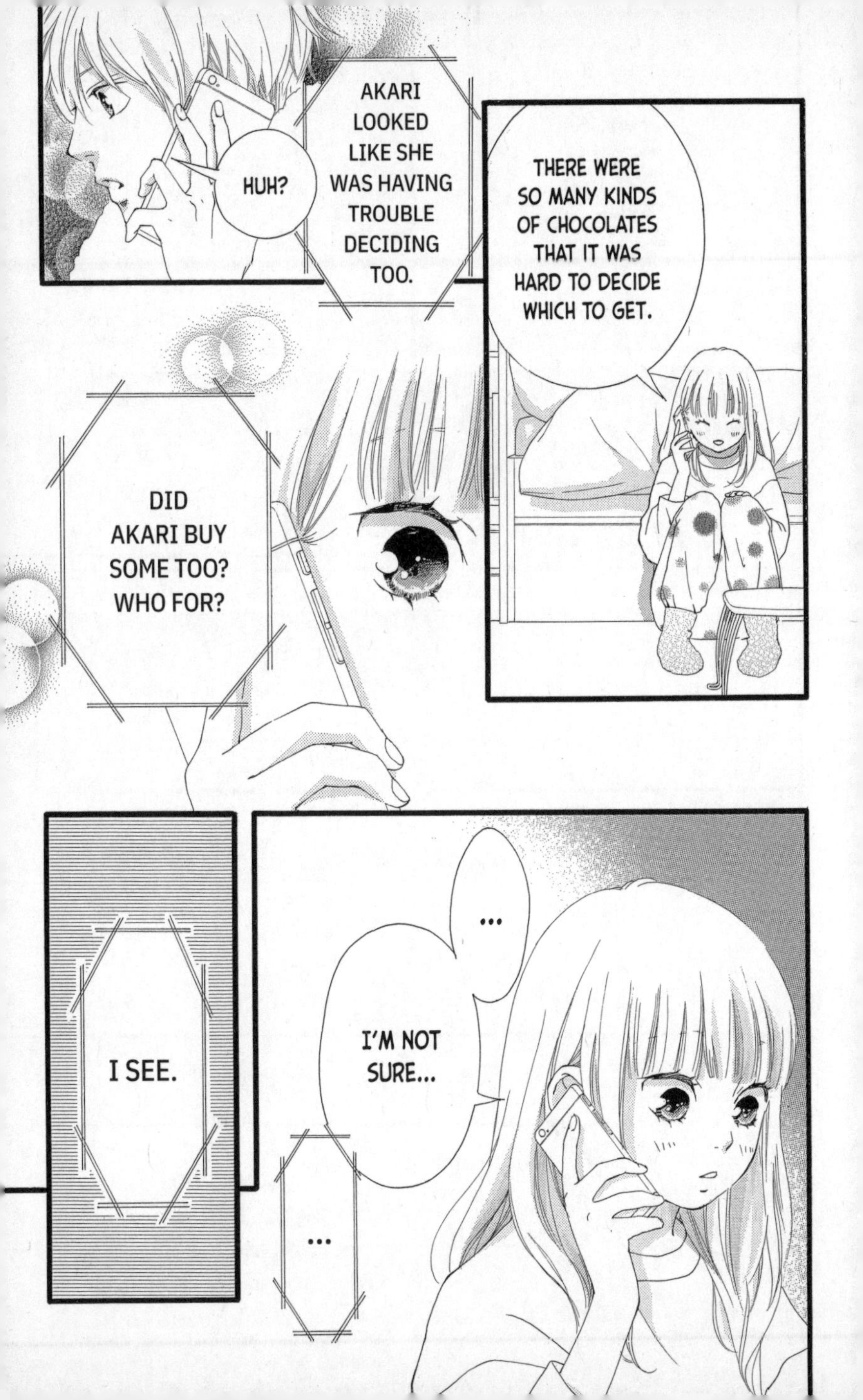
THERE WERE SO MANY KINDS OF CHOCOLATES THAT IT WAS HARD TO DECIDE WHICH TO GET.
AKARI LOOKED LIKE SHE WAS HAVING TROUBLE DECIDING TOO.
HUH?
DID AKARI BUY SOME TOO? WHO FOR?
...
I'M NOT SURE...
...
I SEE.

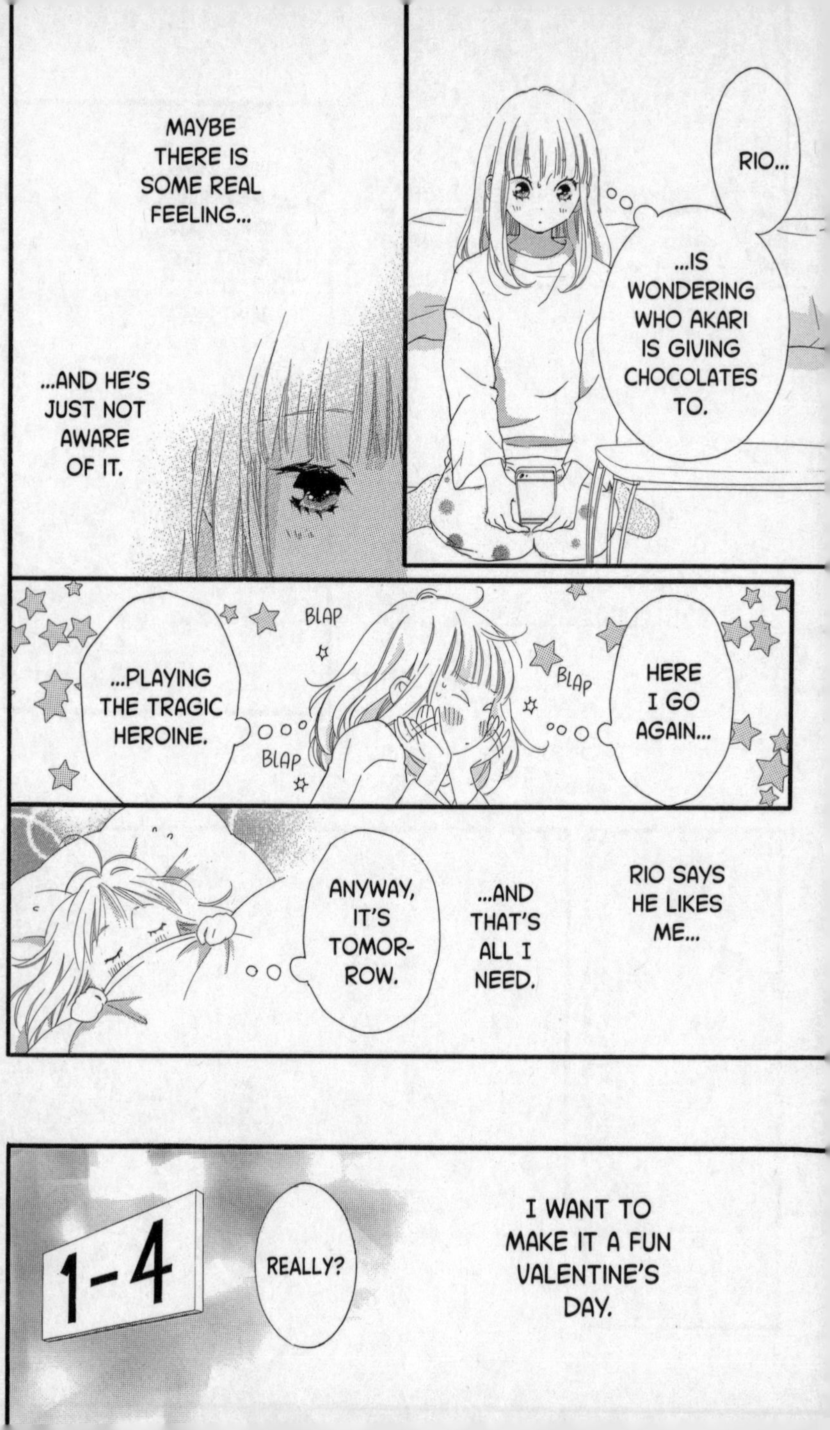
RIO...
...IS WONDERING WHO AKARI IS GIVING CHOCOLATES TO.
MAYBE THERE IS SOME REAL FEELING...
...AND HE'S JUST NOT AWARE OF IT.
HERE I GO AGAIN...
BLAP
BLAP
BLAP
...PLAYING THE TRAGIC HEROINE.
RIO SAYS HE LIKES ME...
...AND THAT'S ALL I NEED.
ANYWAY, IT'S TOMOR-ROW.
I WANT TO MAKE IT A FUN VALENTINE'S DAY.
REALLY?
1-4

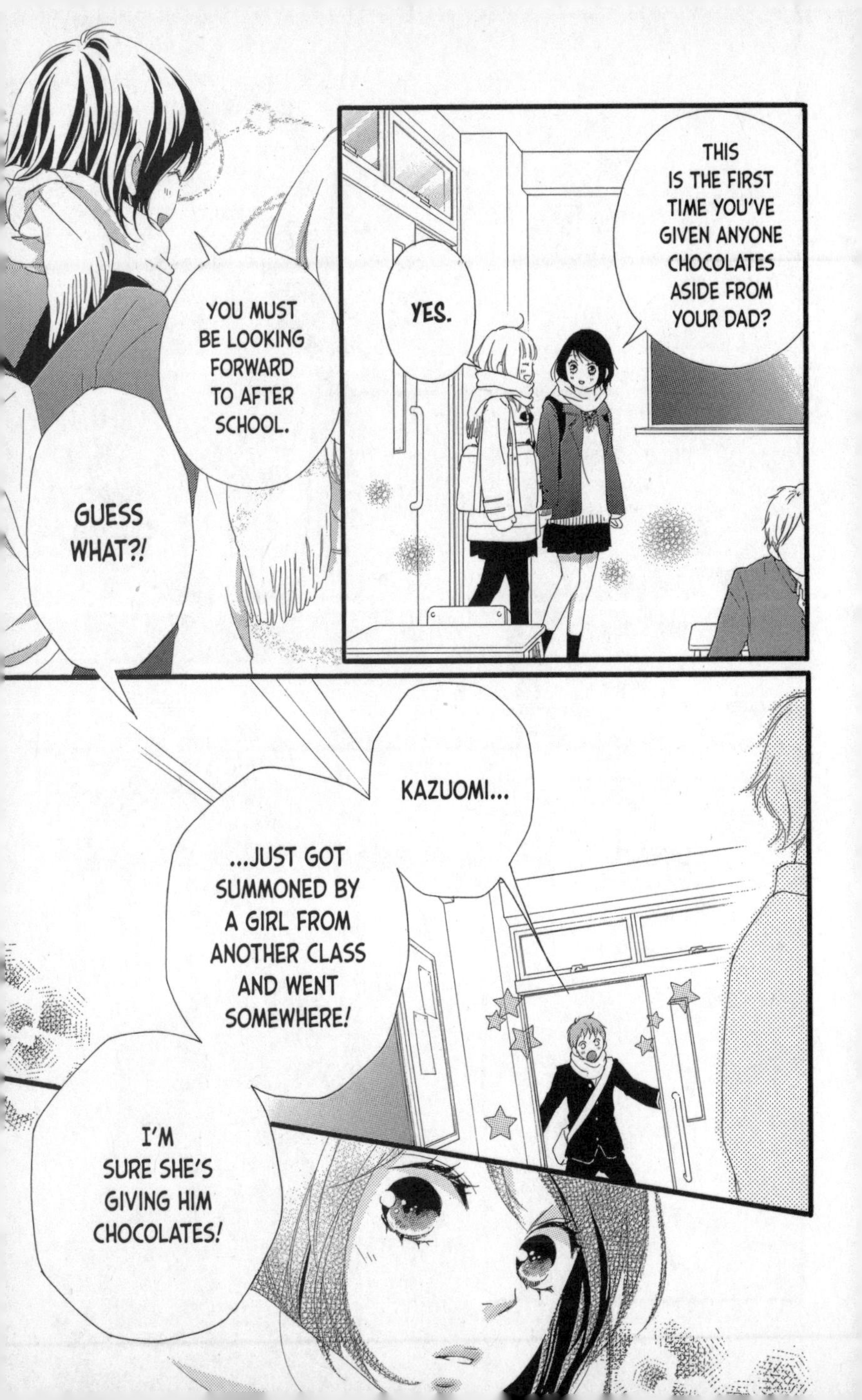
THIS IS THE FIRST TIME YOU'VE GIVEN ANYONE CHOCOLATES ASIDE FROM YOUR DAD?
YES.
YOU MUST BE LOOKING FORWARD TO AFTER SCHOOL.
GUESS WHAT?!
KAZUOMI...
...JUST GOT SUMMONED BY A GIRL FROM ANOTHER CLASS AND WENT SOMEWHERE!
I'M SURE SHE'S GIVING HIM CHOCOLATES!

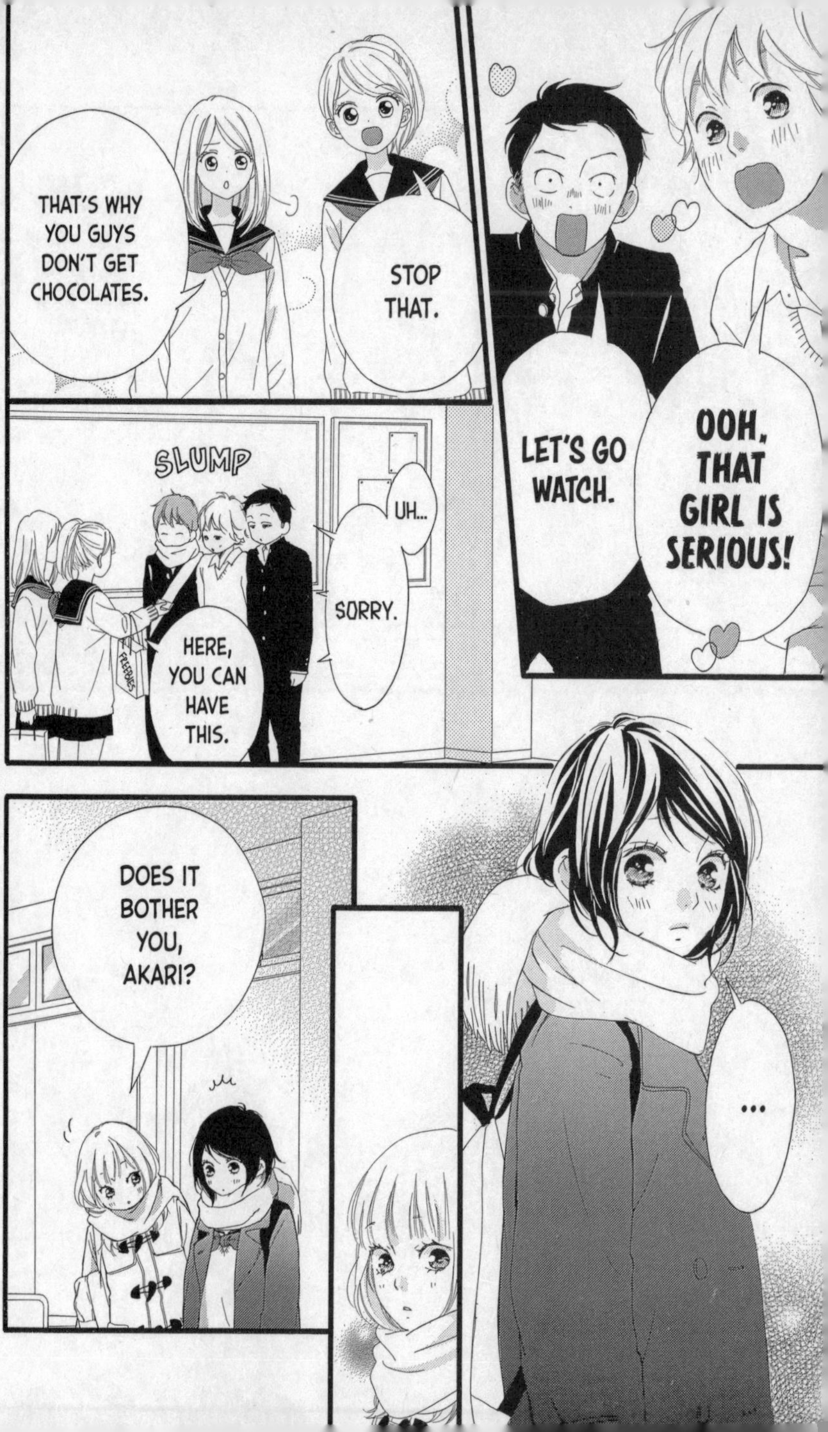
OOH, THAT GIRL IS SERIOUS!
LET'S GO WATCH.
STOP THAT.
THAT'S WHY YOU GUYS DON'T GET CHOCOLATES.
UH...
SORRY.
SLUMP
HERE, YOU CAN HAVE THIS.
...
DOES IT BOTHER YOU, AKARI?

On my assistants' recommendation, I started watching people play video games. I didn't really understand the appeal until I starting watching. Now I know why everyone is obsessed. I don't feel like playing scary games myself—they look tiring—but watching someone else play them is so much fun. Popular games will have lots of different gameplays, so it's fun to see how they all do it differently. Now I have something to listen to while I'm working. Sometimes I can't tear myself away, and my pen stops moving. It's something I need to be careful about. But it is a great accompaniment while I work. Please let me know if there are any that you recommend.

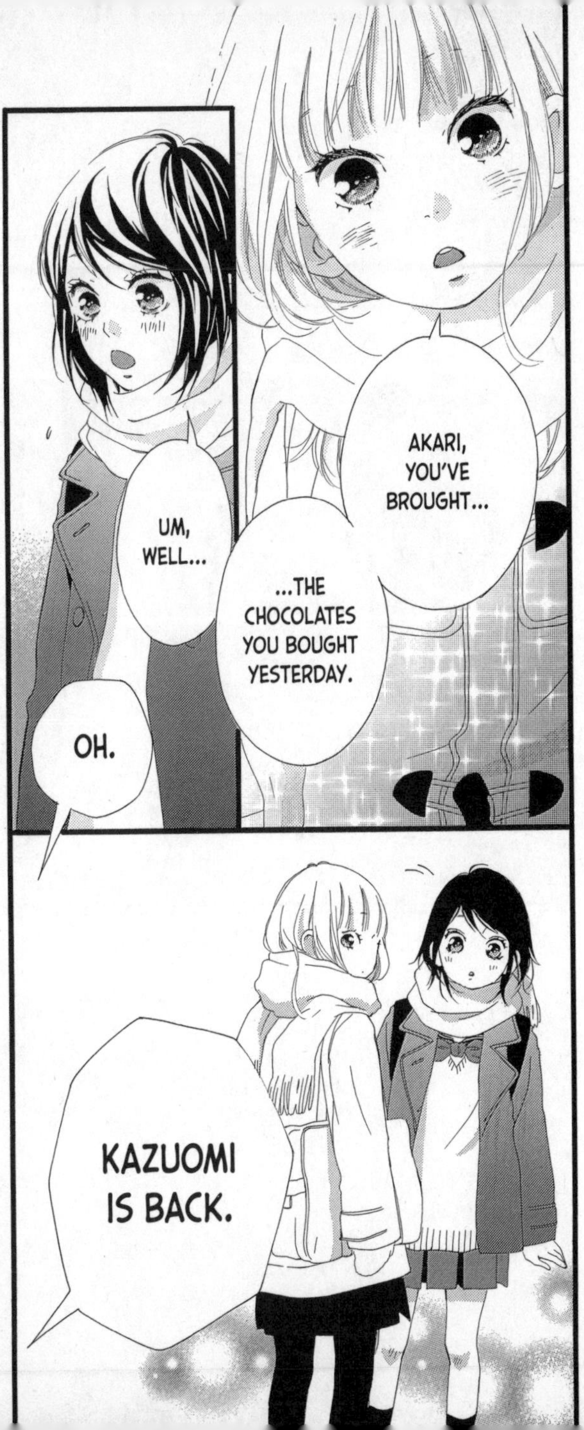
AKARI, YOU'VE BROUGHT...
...THE CHOCOLATES YOU BOUGHT YESTERDAY.
UM, WELL...
OH.
KAZUOMI IS BACK.

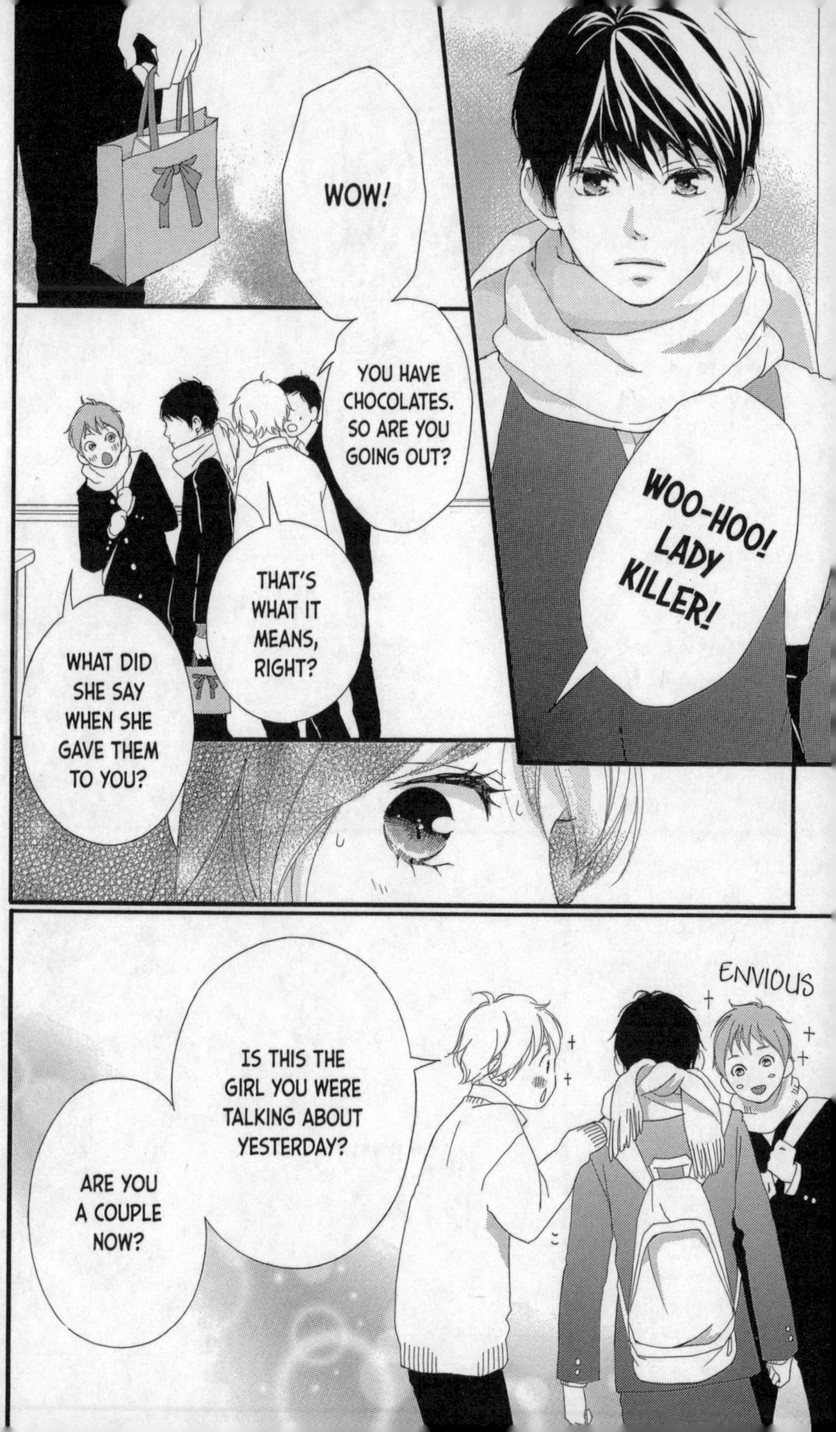
WOO-HOO! LADY KILLER!
WOW!
YOU HAVE CHOCOLATES. SO ARE YOU GOING OUT?
THAT'S WHAT IT MEANS, RIGHT?
WHAT DID SHE SAY WHEN SHE GAVE THEM TO YOU?
ENVIOUS
IS THIS THE GIRL YOU WERE TALKING ABOUT YESTERDAY?
ARE YOU A COUPLE NOW?

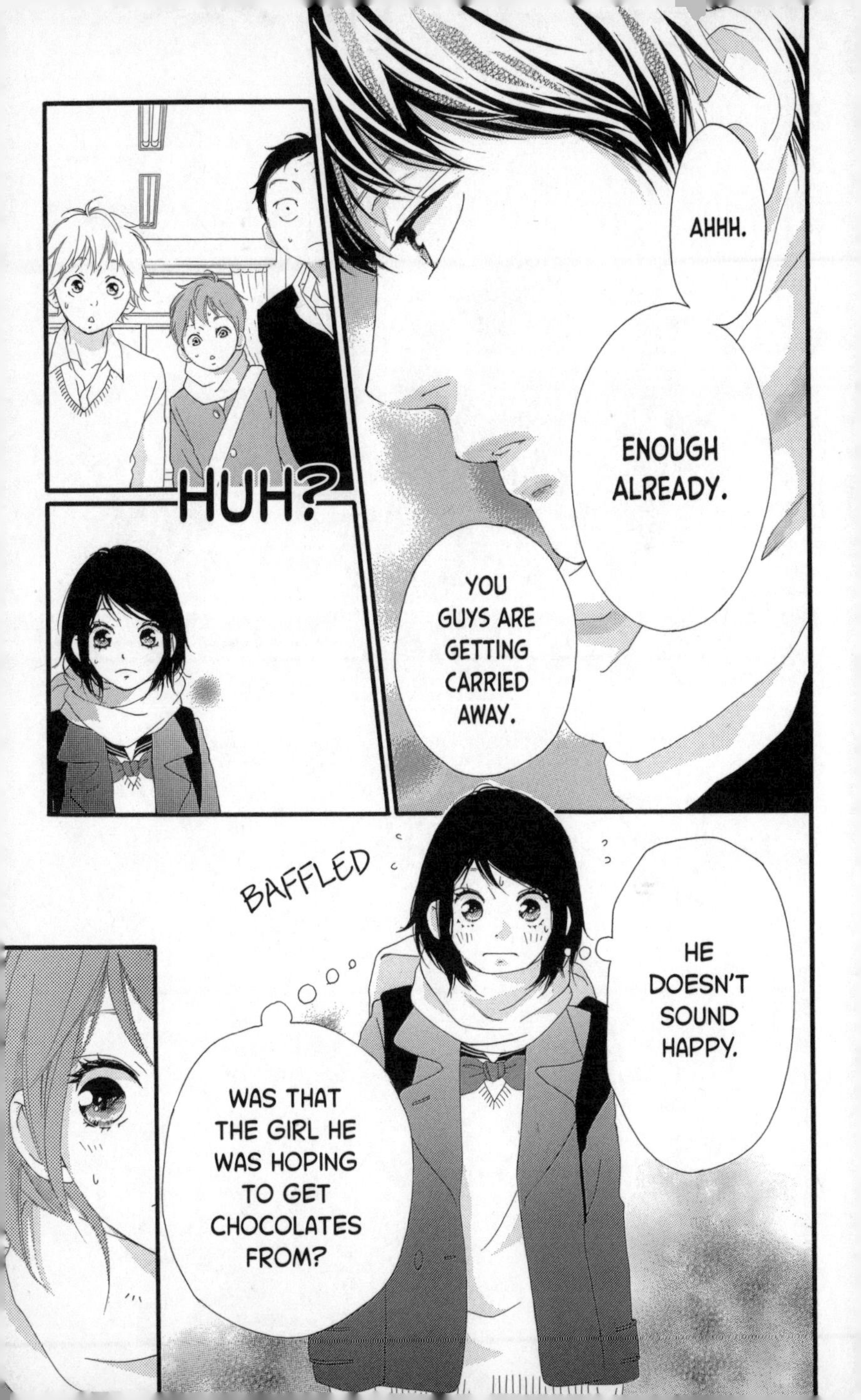
AHHH.
ENOUGH ALREADY.
YOU GUYS ARE GETTING CARRIED AWAY.
HUH?
HE DOESN'T SOUND HAPPY.
BAFFLED
WAS THAT THE GIRL HE WAS HOPING TO GET CHOCOLATES FROM?

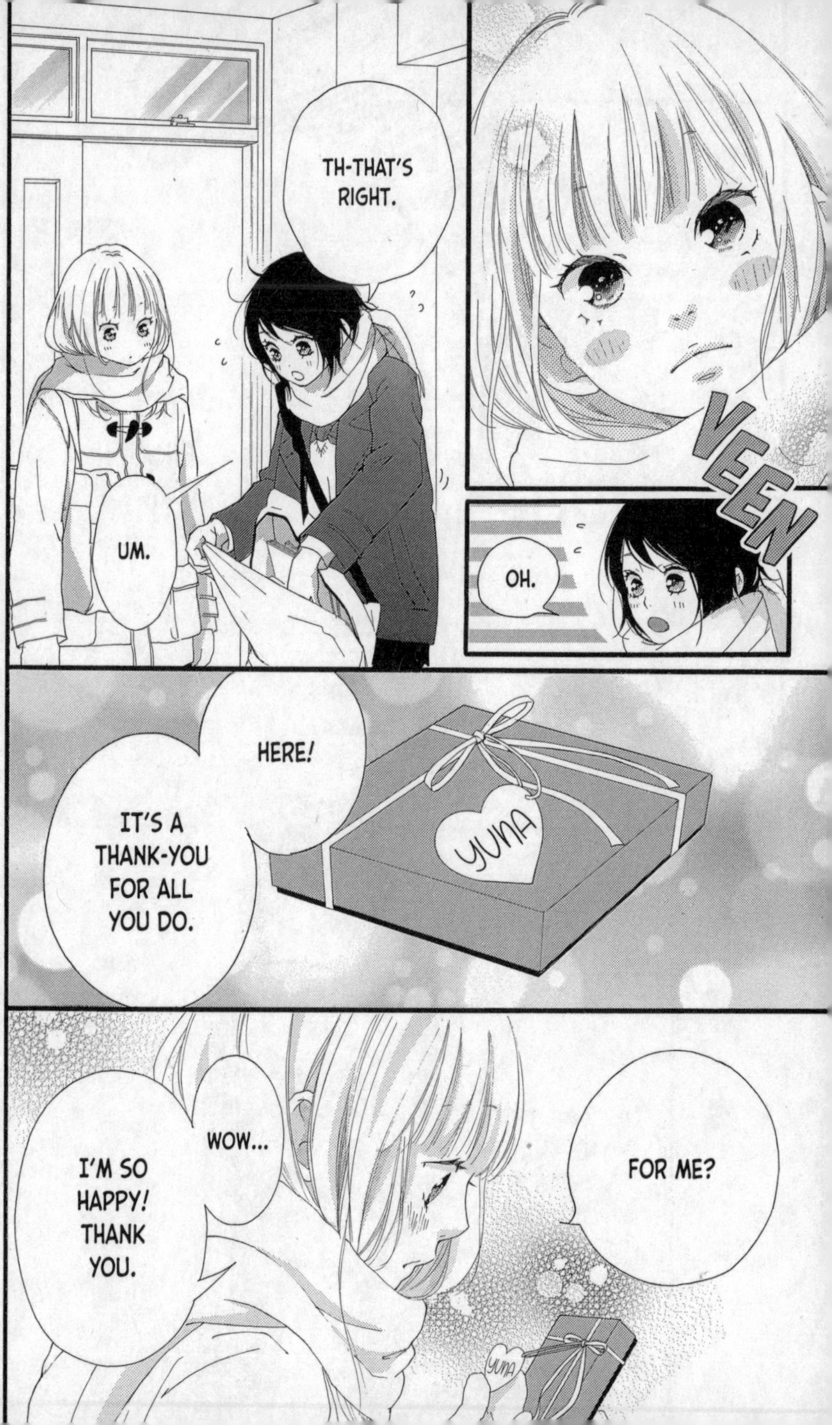

VEEN
OH.
TH-THAT'S RIGHT.
UM.
HERE!
IT'S A THANK-YOU FOR ALL YOU DO.
YUNA
FOR ME?
WOW...
I'M SO HAPPY! THANK YOU.
YUNA

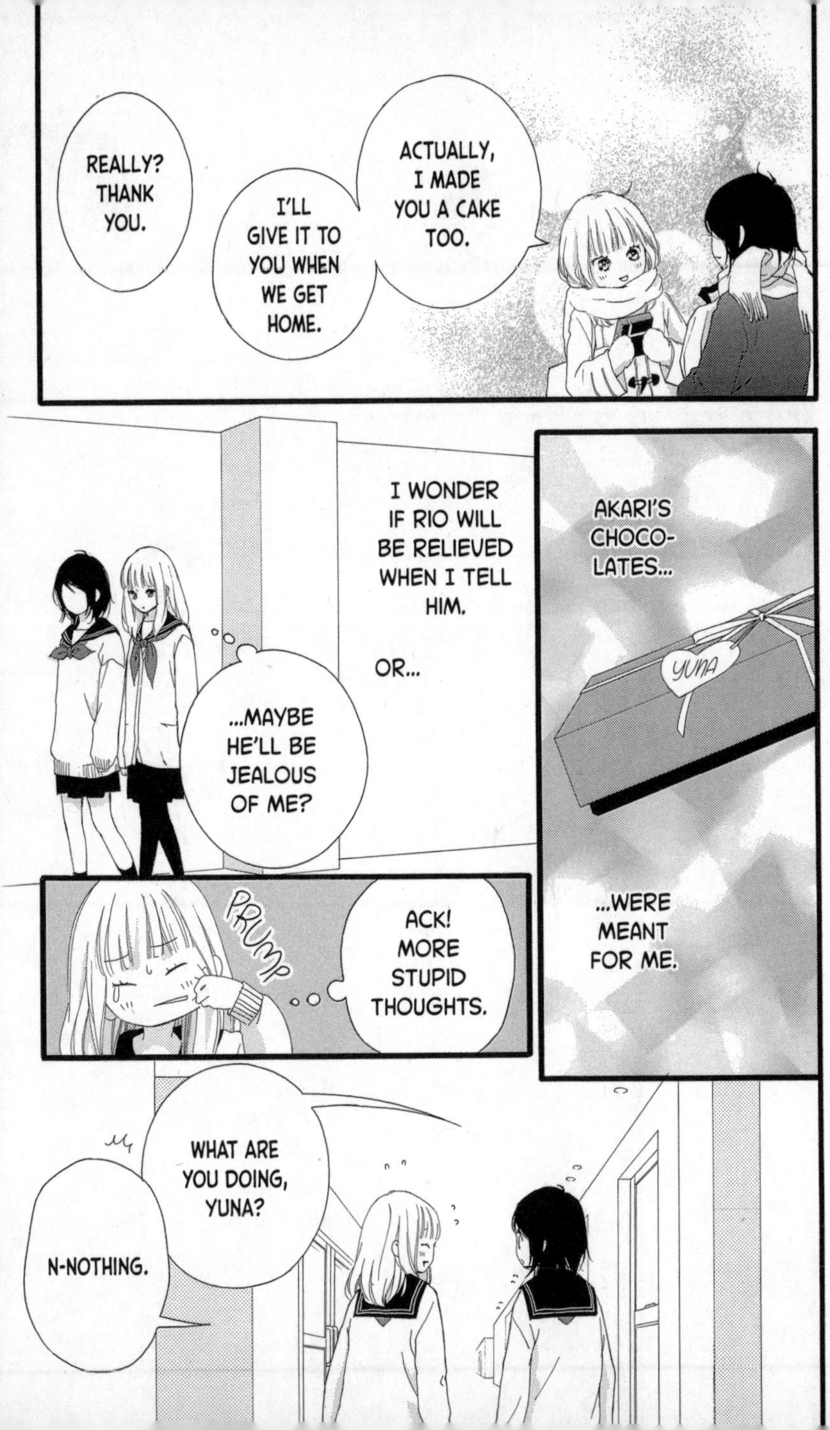
ACTUALLY, I MADE YOU A CAKE TOO.
I'LL GIVE IT TO YOU WHEN WE GET HOME.
REALLY? THANK YOU.
AKARI'S CHOCO-LATES...
YUNA
...WERE MEANT FOR ME.
I WONDER IF RIO WILL BE RELIEVED WHEN I TELL HIM.
OR...
...MAYBE HE'LL BE JEALOUS OF ME?
ACK! MORE STUPID THOUGHTS.
PRUMP
WHAT ARE YOU DOING, YUNA?
N-NOTHING.

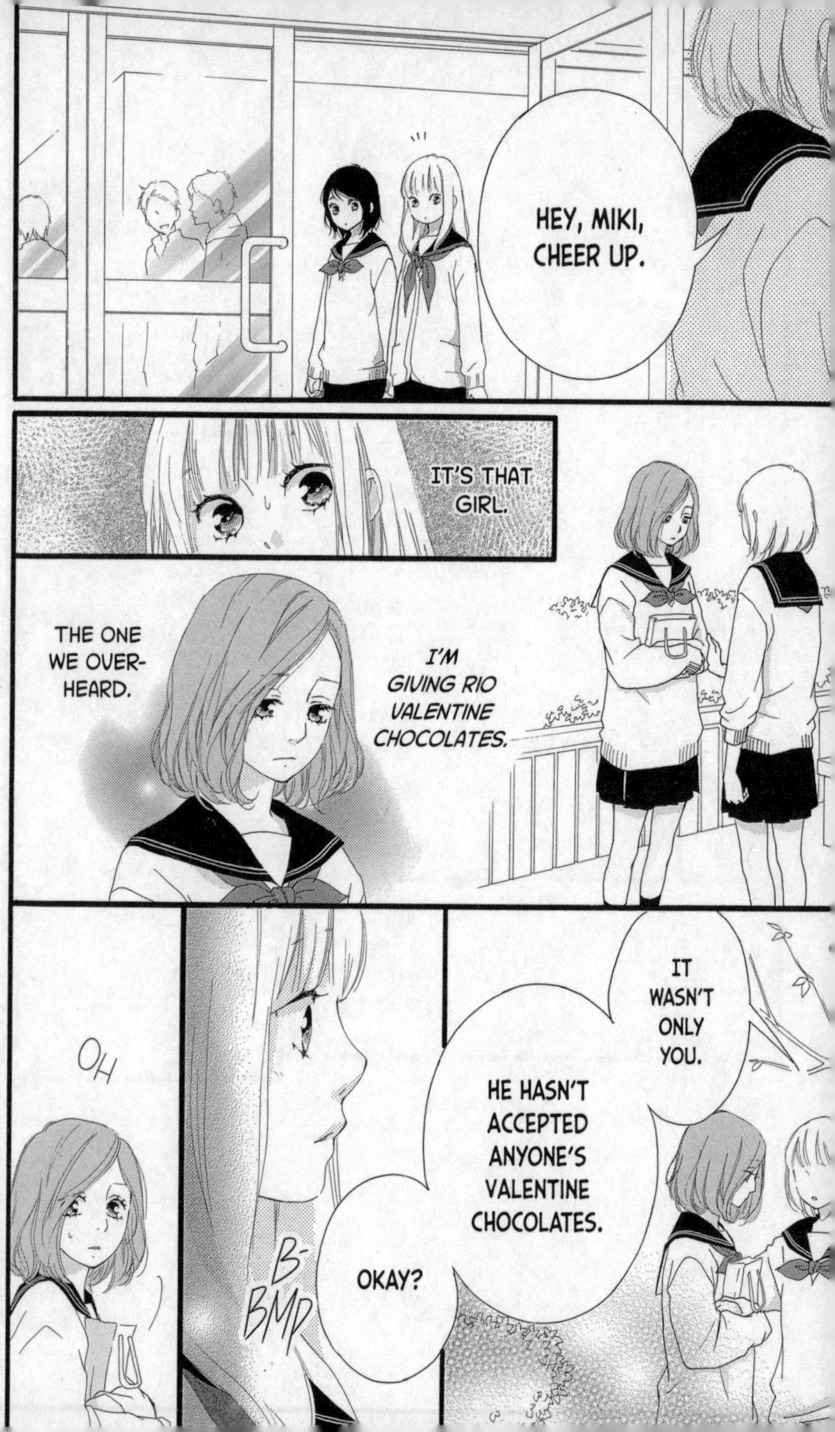
HEY, MIKI, CHEER UP.
IT'S THAT GIRL.
I'M GIVING RIO VALENTINE CHOCOLATES.
THE ONE WE OVER-HEARD.
IT WASN'T ONLY YOU.
HE HASN'T ACCEPTED ANYONE'S VALENTINE CHOCOLATES.
OKAY?
B-BMP
OH

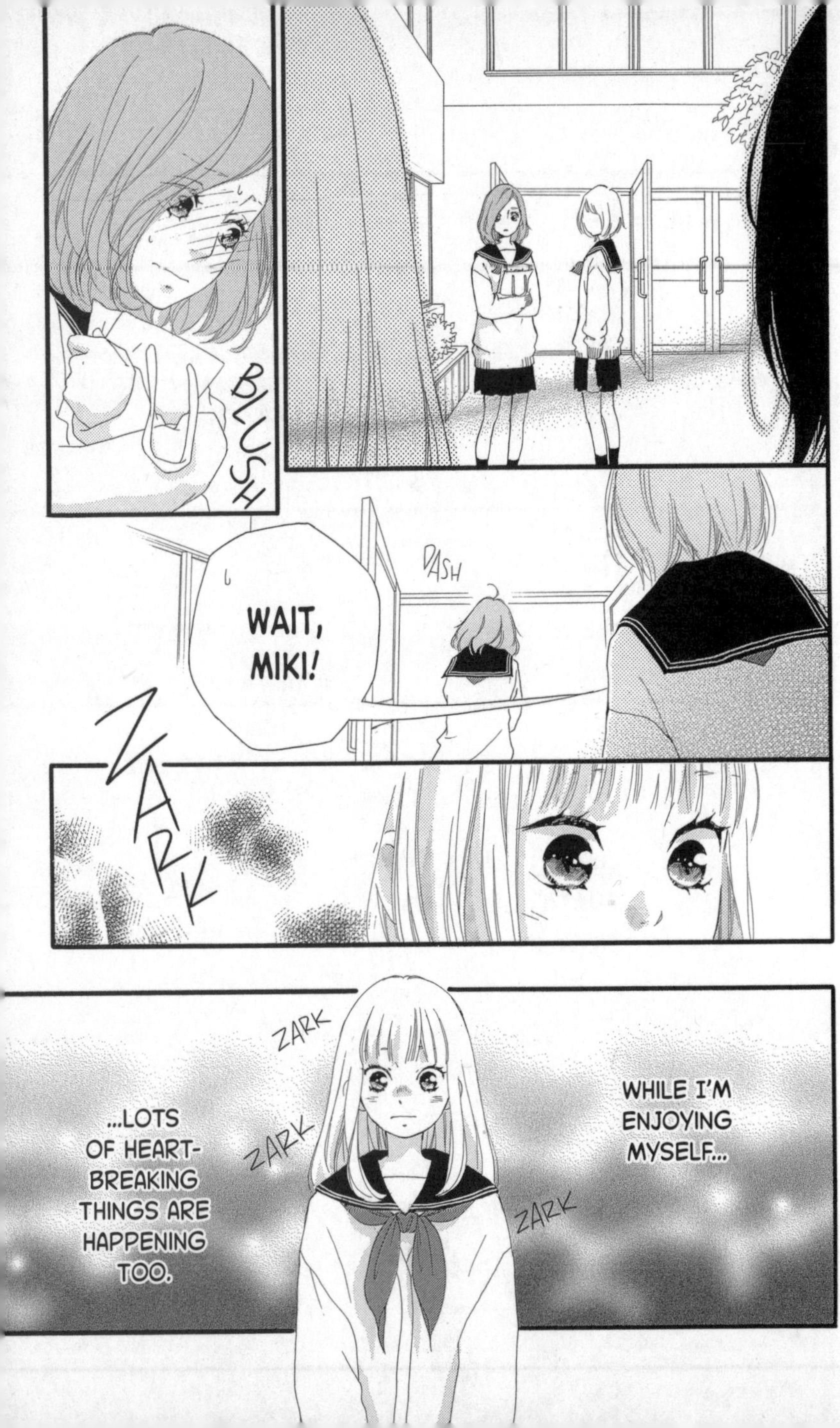
BLUSH
DASH
WAIT, MIKI!
ZARK
WHILE I'M ENJOYING MYSELF...
ZARK
ZARK
ZARK
...LOTS OF HEART-BREAKING THINGS ARE HAPPENING TOO.

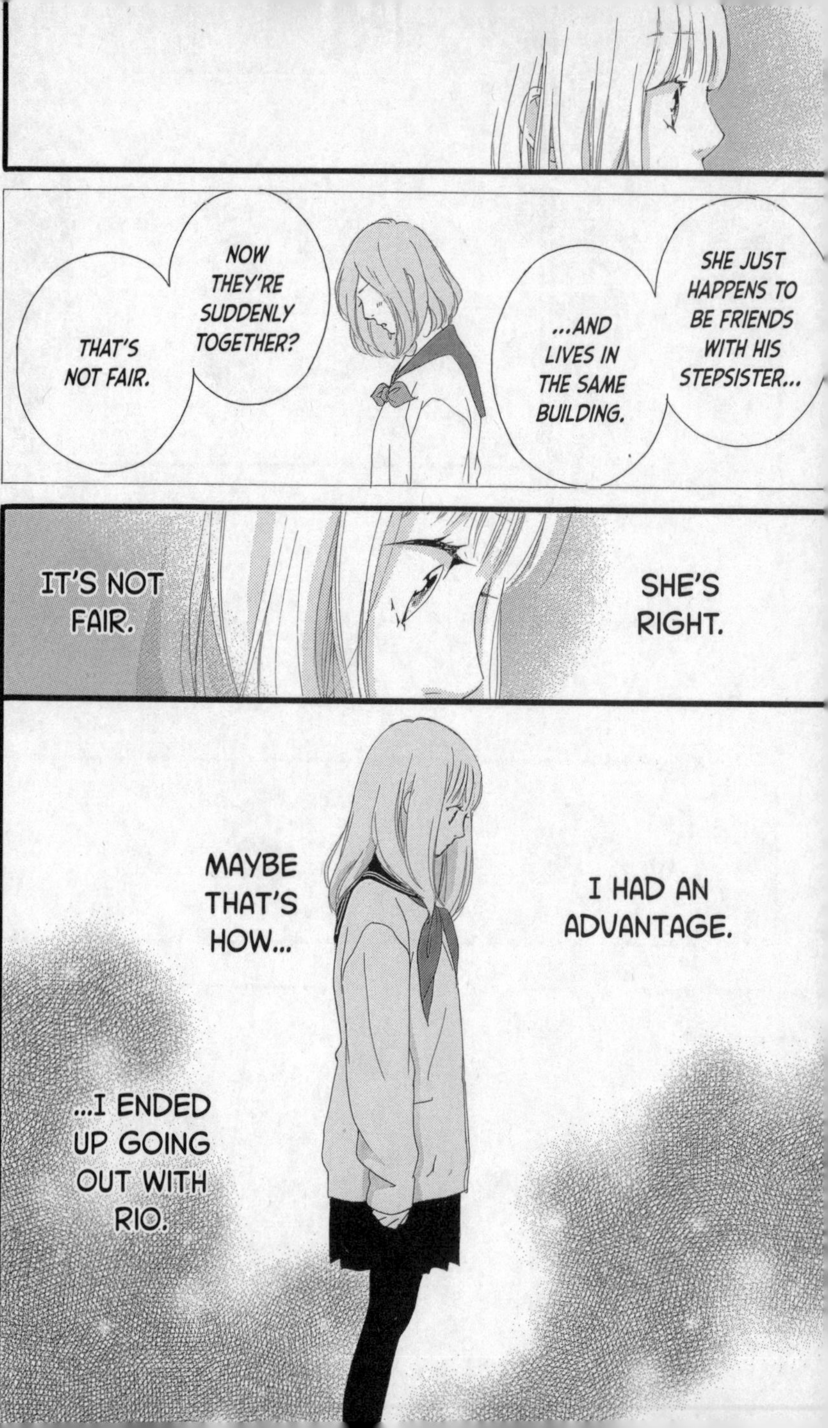
SHE JUST HAPPENS TO BE FRIENDS WITH HIS STEPSISTER...
...AND LIVES IN THE SAME BUILDING.
NOW THEY'RE SUDDENLY TOGETHER?
THAT'S NOT FAIR.
SHE'S RIGHT.
IT'S NOT FAIR.
I HAD AN ADVANTAGE.
MAYBE THAT'S HOW...
...I ENDED UP GOING OUT WITH RIO.

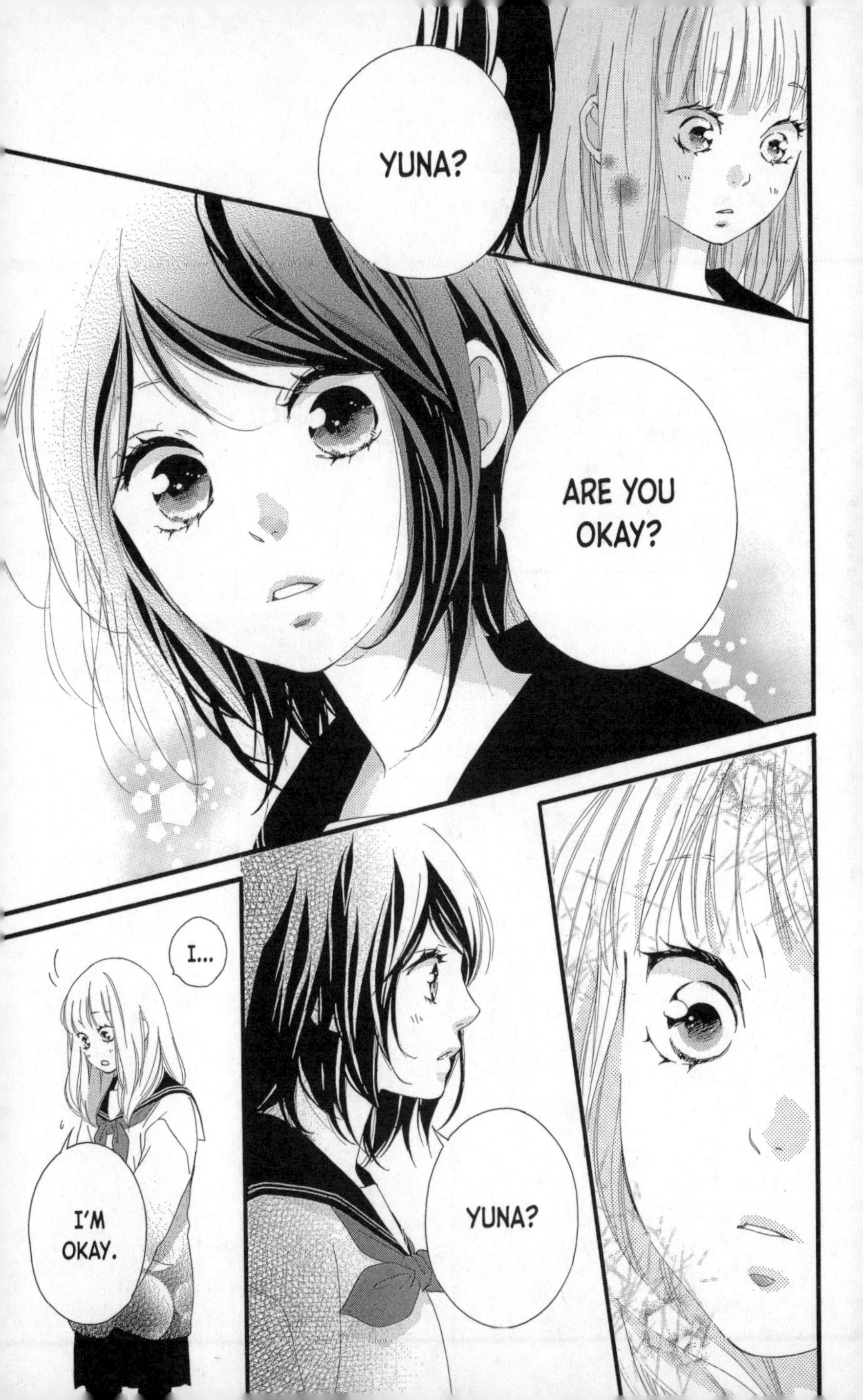
YUNA?
ARE YOU OKAY?
YUNA?
I...
I'M OKAY.

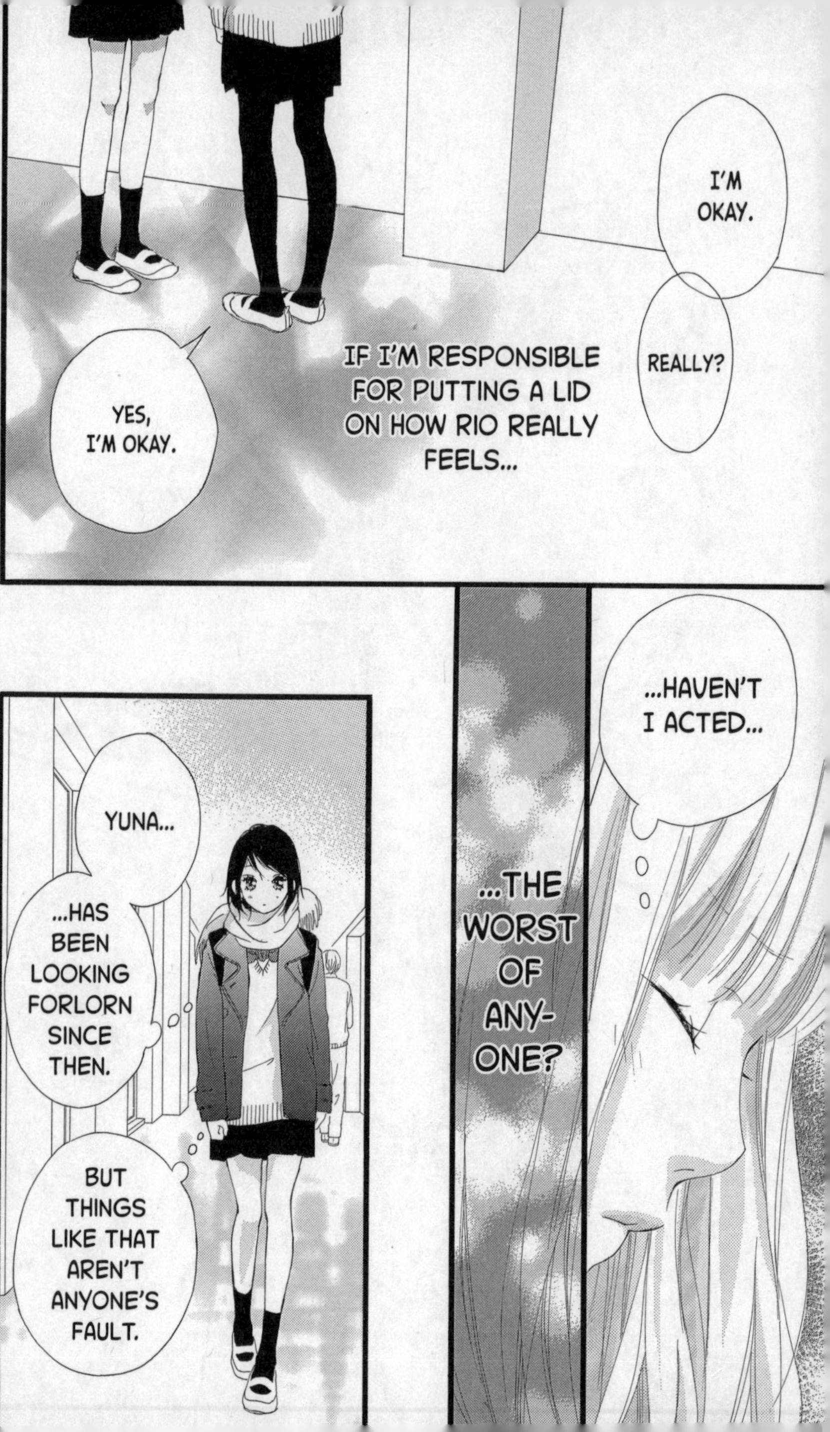
I'M OKAY.
REALLY?
IF I'M RESPONSIBLE FOR PUTTING A LID ON HOW RIO REALLY FEELS...
YES, I'M OKAY.
...HAVEN'T I ACTED...
...THE WORST OF ANY-ONE?
YUNA...
...HAS BEEN LOOKING FORLORN SINCE THEN.
BUT THINGS LIKE THAT AREN'T ANYONE'S FAULT.

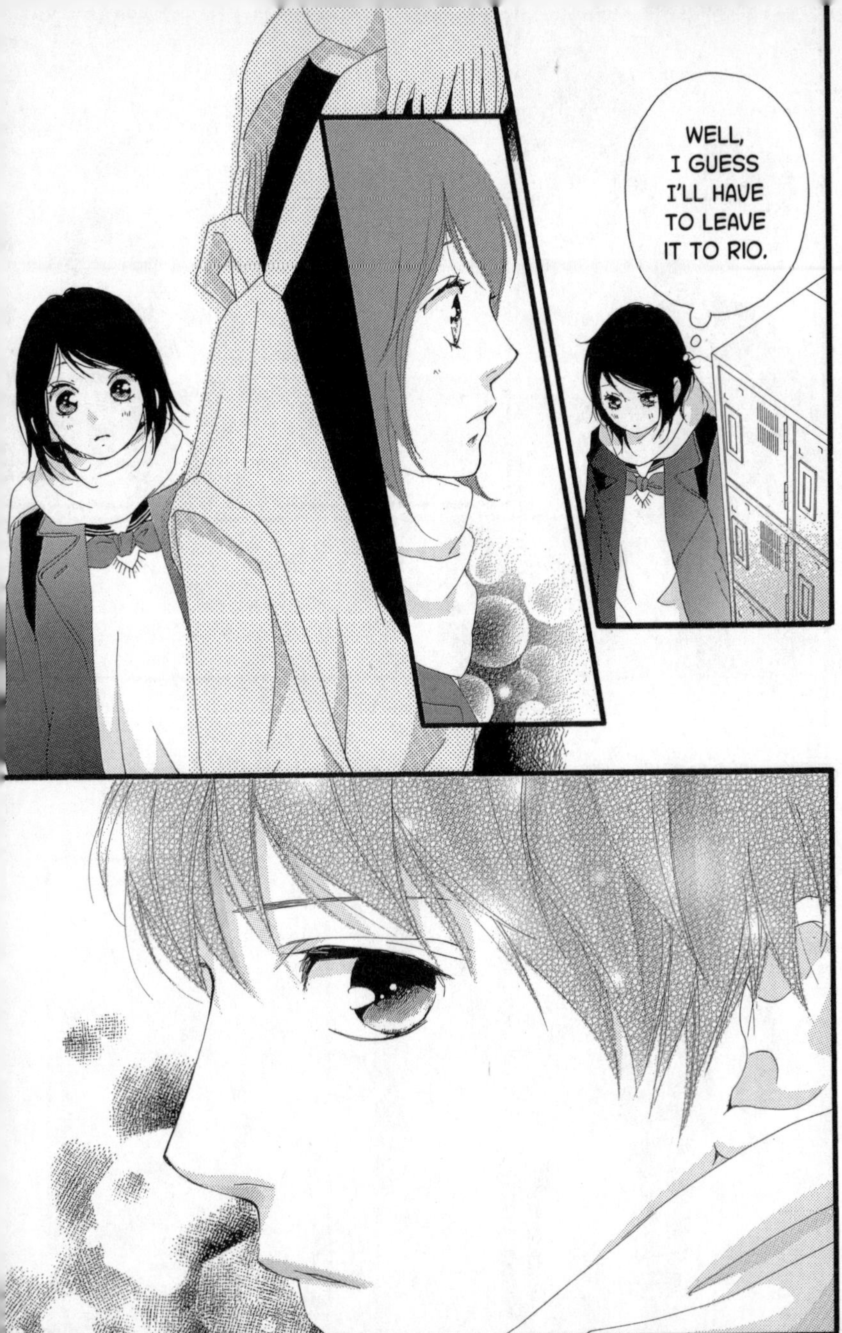
WELL, I GUESS I'LL HAVE TO LEAVE IT TO RIO.

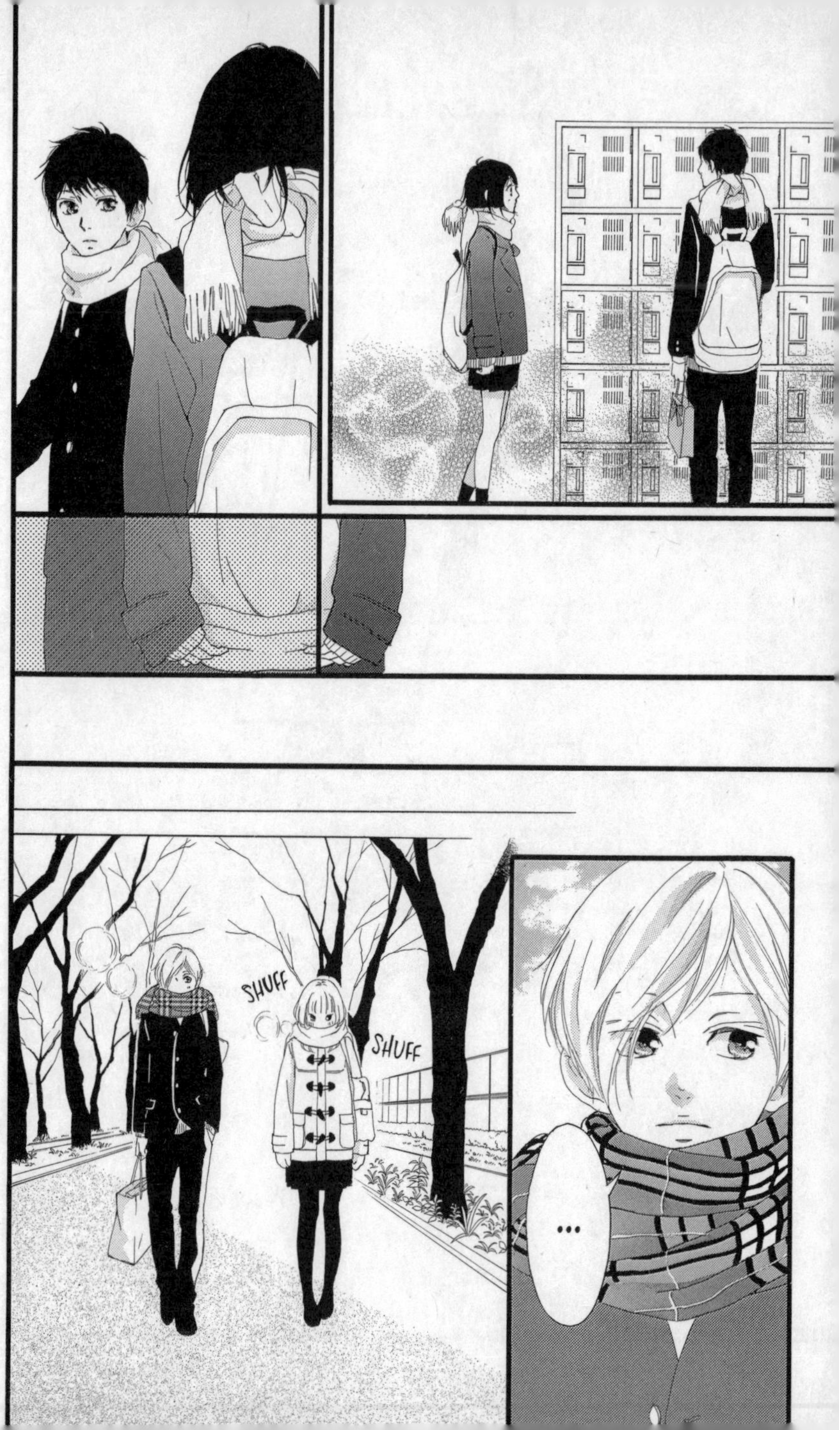
SHUFF
SHUFF
...

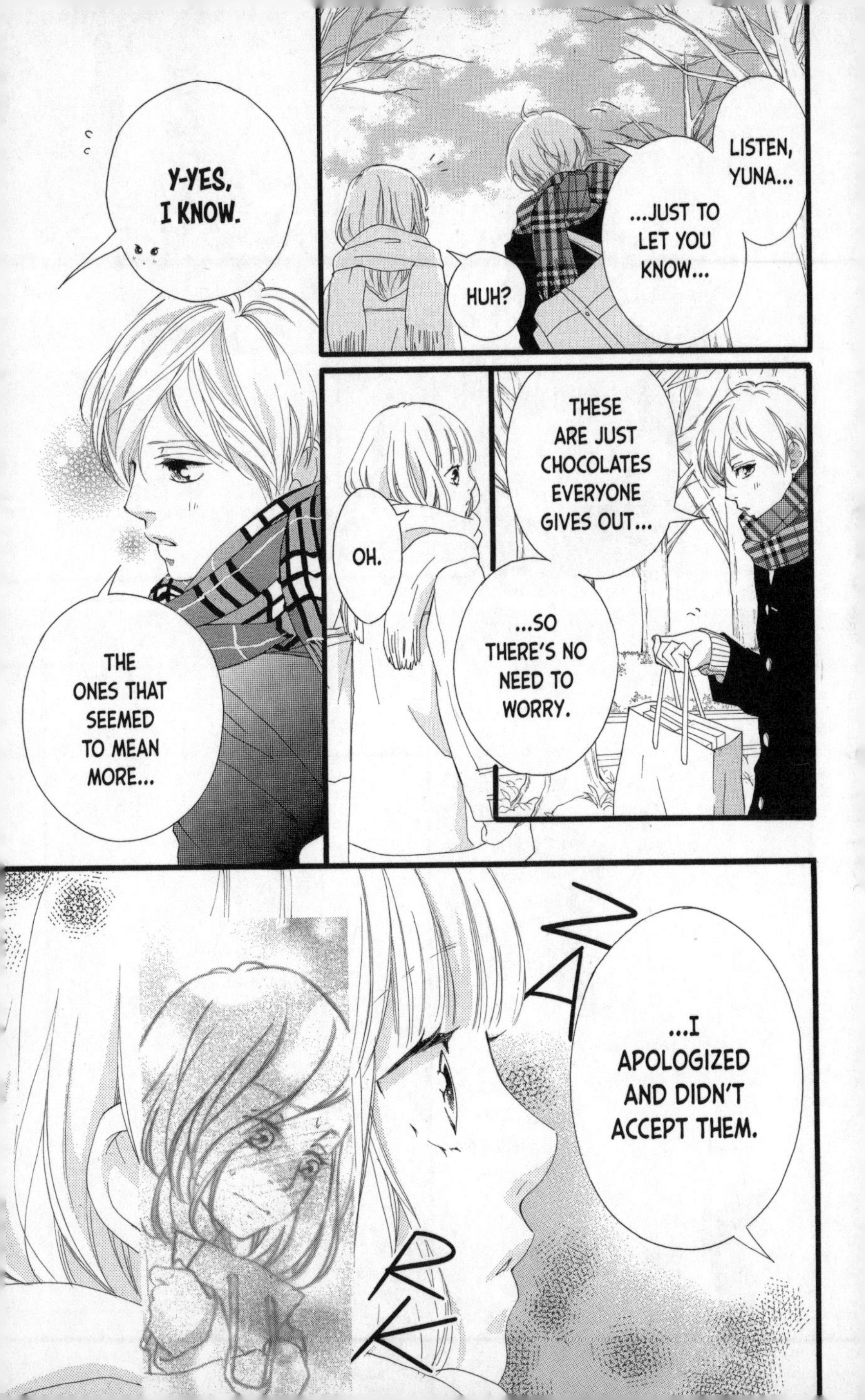
LISTEN, YUNA...
...JUST TO LET YOU KNOW...
HUH?
THESE ARE JUST CHOCOLATES EVERYONE GIVES OUT...
...SO THERE'S NO NEED TO WORRY.
OH.
Y-YES, I KNOW.
THE ONES THAT SEEMED TO MEAN MORE...
...I APOLOGIZED AND DIDN'T ACCEPT THEM.

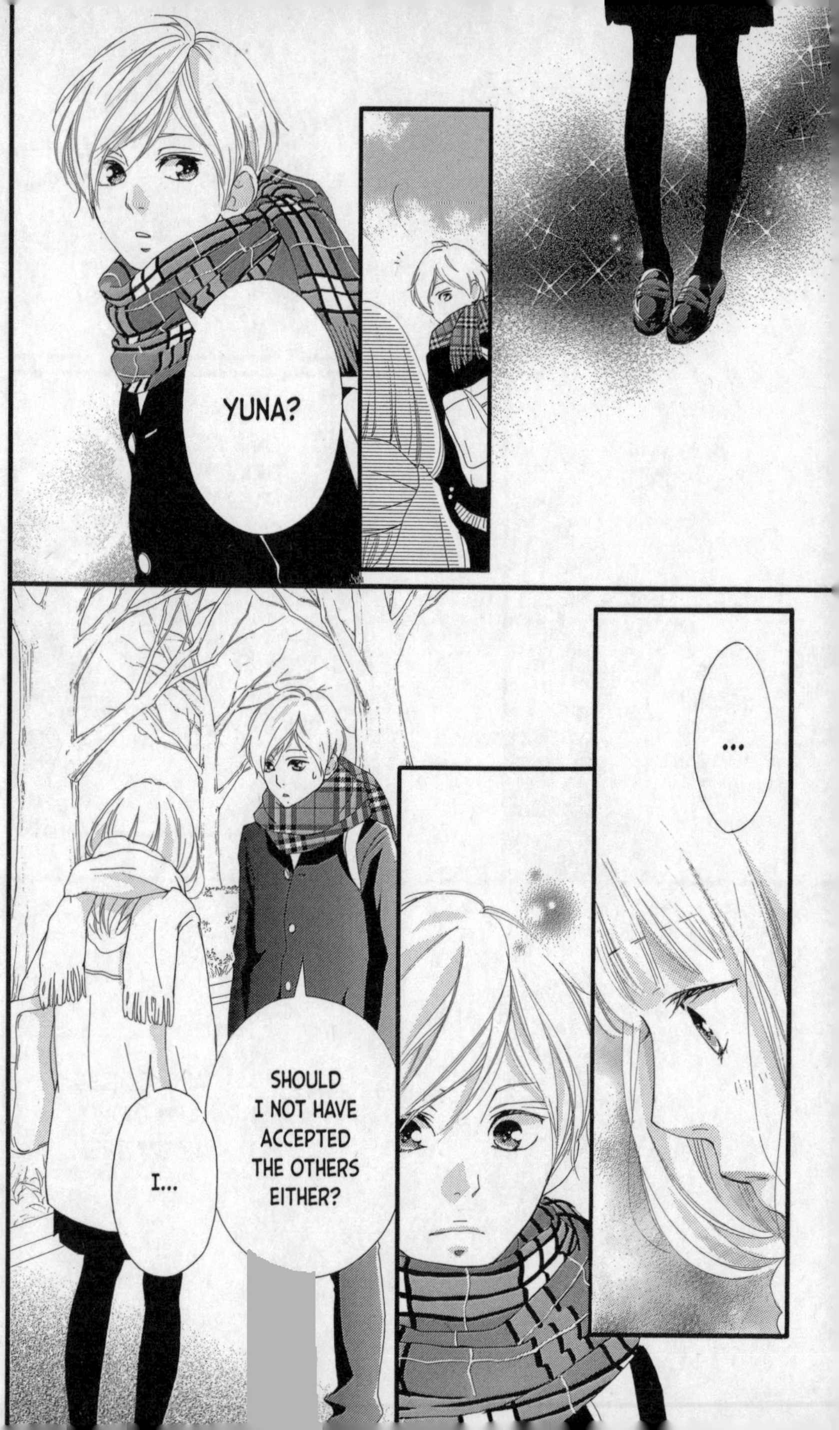
YUNA?
...
SHOULD I NOT HAVE ACCEPTED THE OTHERS EITHER?
I...

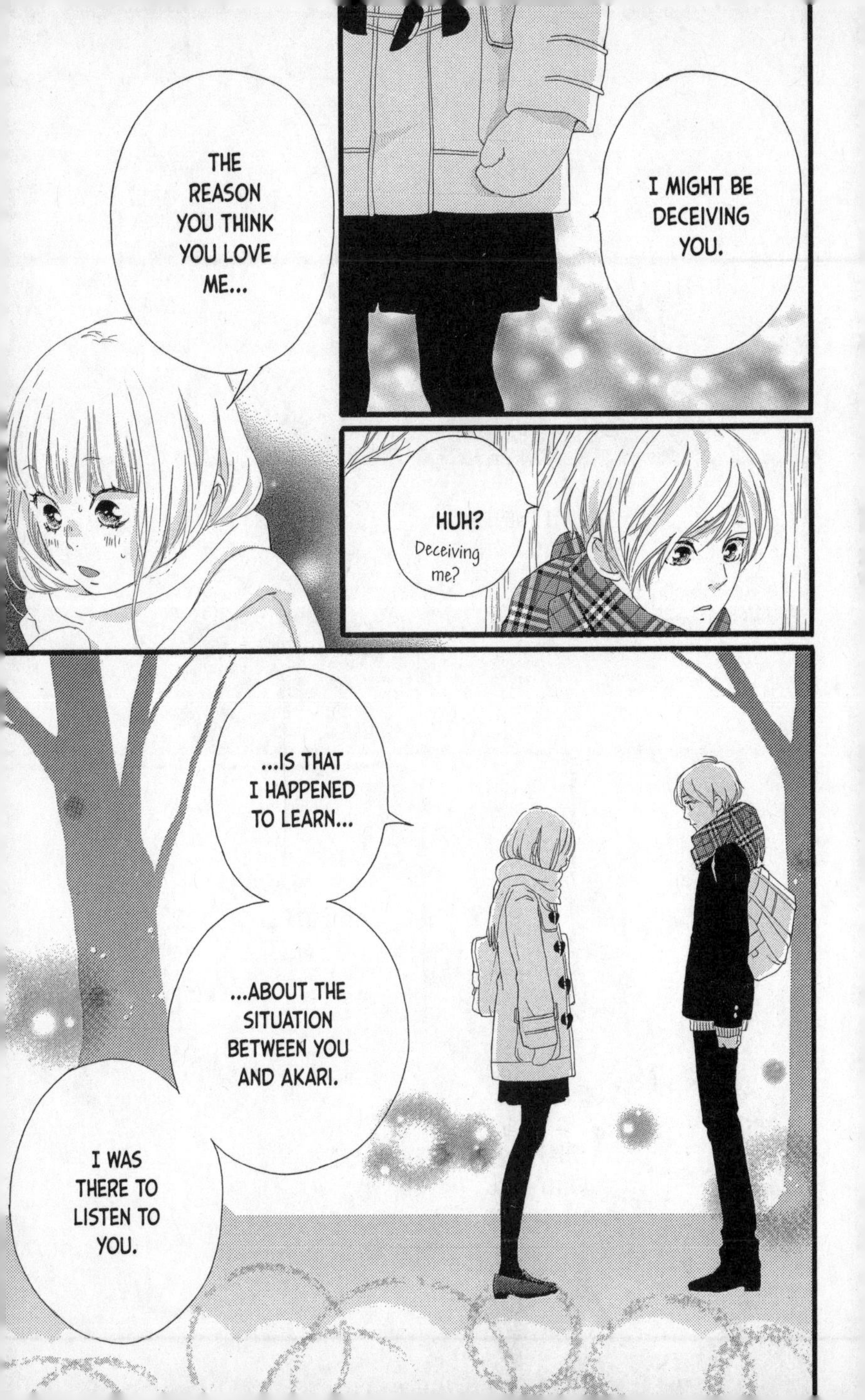
I MIGHT BE DECEIVING YOU.
HUH?
Deceiving me?
THE REASON YOU THINK YOU LOVE ME...
...IS THAT I HAPPENED TO LEARN...
...ABOUT THE SITUATION BETWEEN YOU AND AKARI.
I WAS THERE TO LISTEN TO YOU.

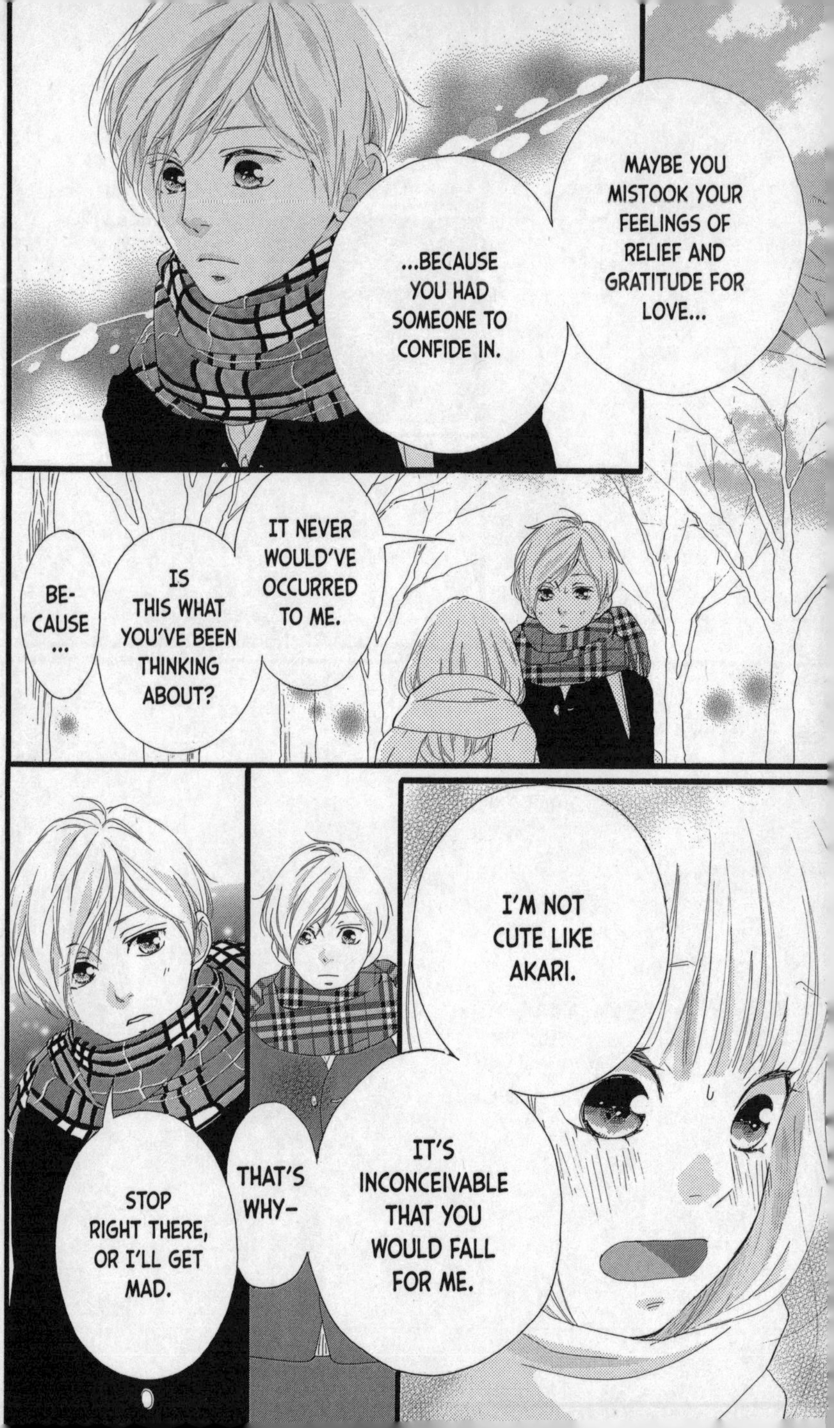
MAYBE YOU MISTOOK YOUR FEELINGS OF RELIEF AND GRATITUDE FOR LOVE...
...BECAUSE YOU HAD SOMEONE TO CONFIDE IN.
IT NEVER WOULD'VE OCCURRED TO ME.
IS THIS WHAT YOU'VE BEEN THINKING ABOUT?
BE-CAUSE...
I'M NOT CUTE LIKE AKARI.
IT'S INCONCEIVABLE THAT YOU WOULD FALL FOR ME.
THAT'S WHY-
STOP RIGHT THERE, OR I'LL GET MAD.

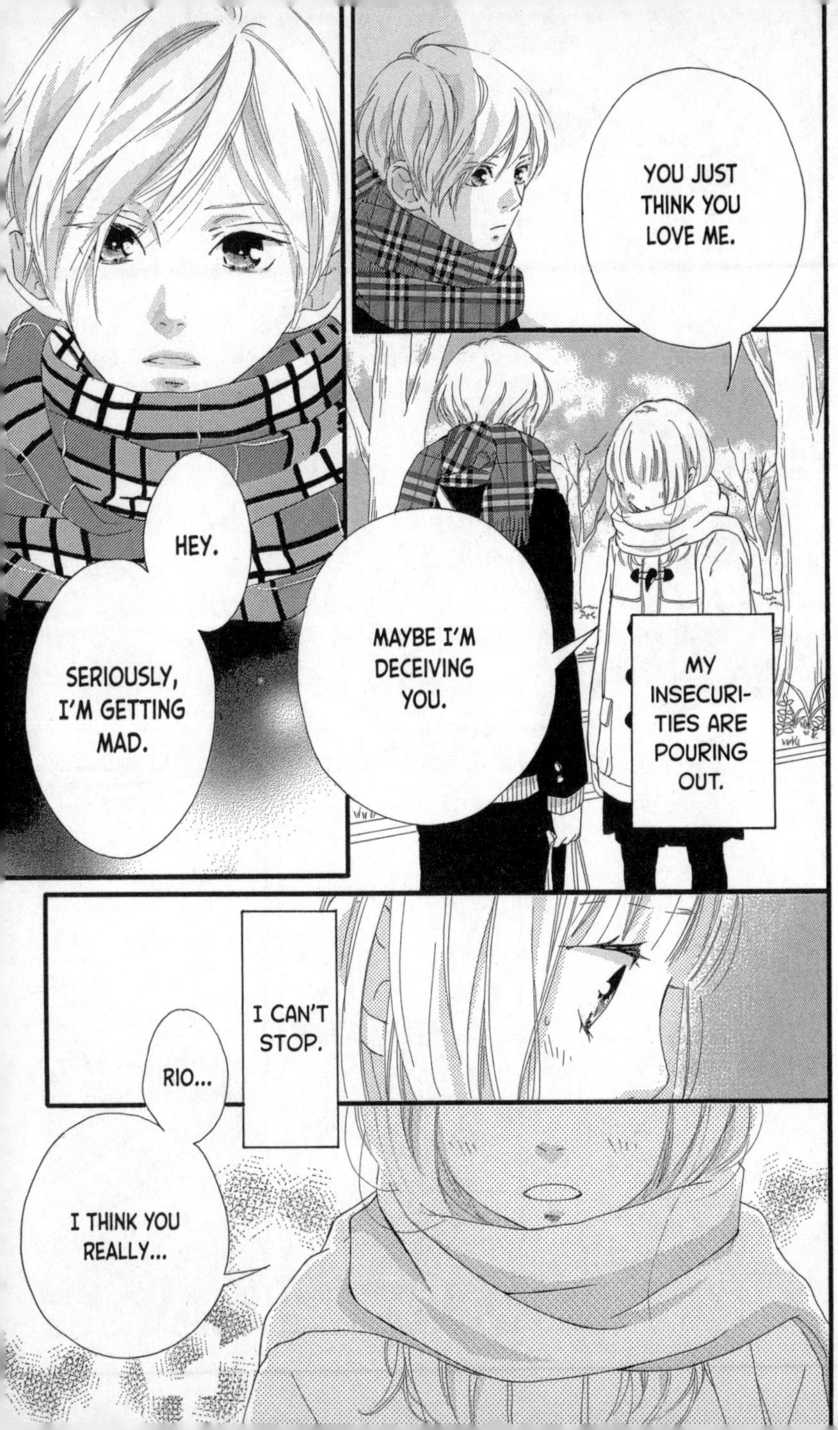
YOU JUST THINK YOU LOVE ME.
MAYBE I'M DECEIVING YOU.
MY INSECURITIES ARE POURING OUT.
HEY.
SERIOUSLY, I'M GETTING MAD.
I CAN'T STOP.
RIO...
I THINK YOU REALLY...

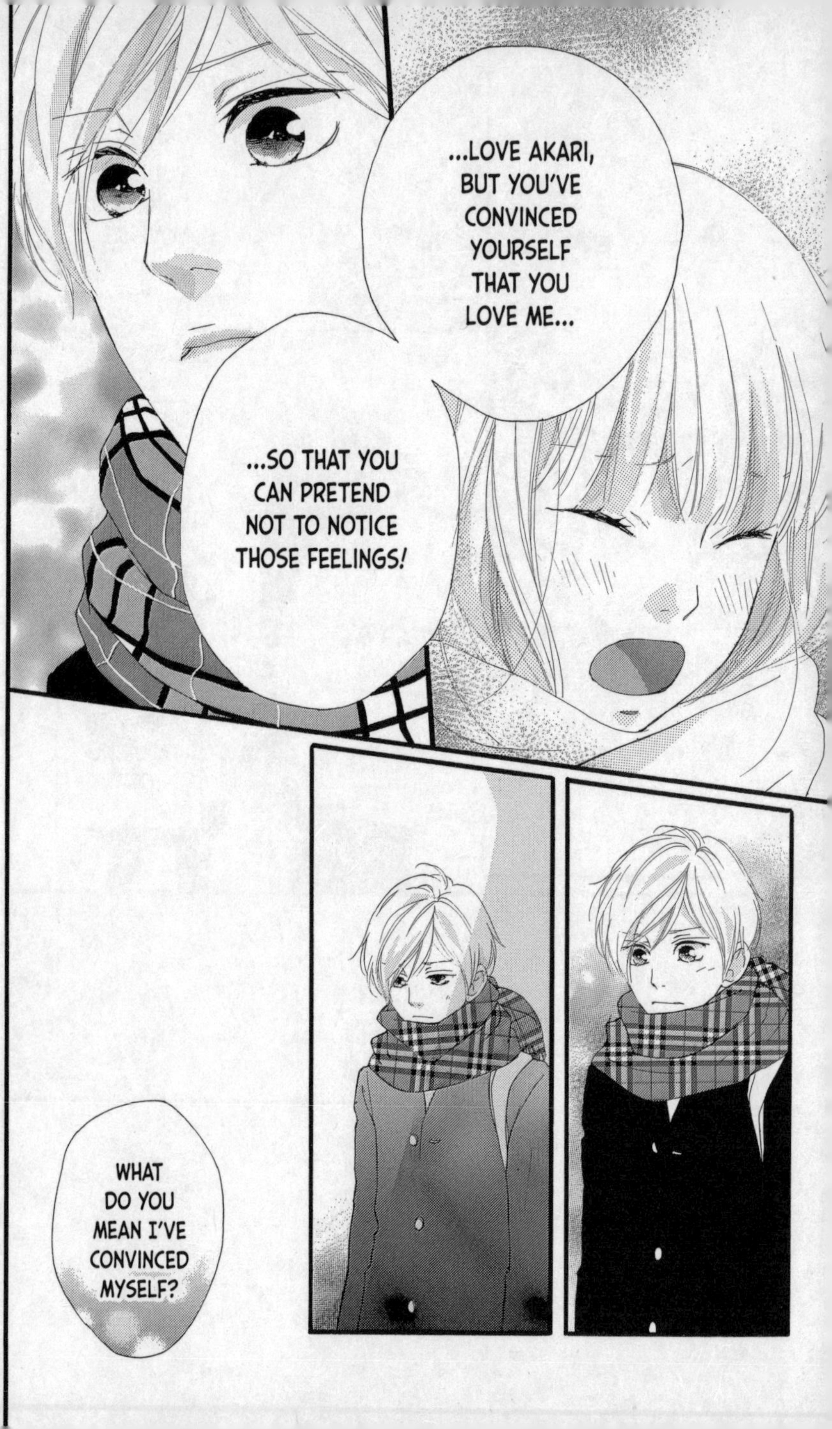
...LOVE AKARI, BUT YOU'VE CONVINCED YOURSELF THAT YOU LOVE ME...
...SO THAT YOU CAN PRETEND NOT TO NOTICE THOSE FEELINGS!
WHAT DO YOU MEAN I'VE CONVINCED MYSELF?

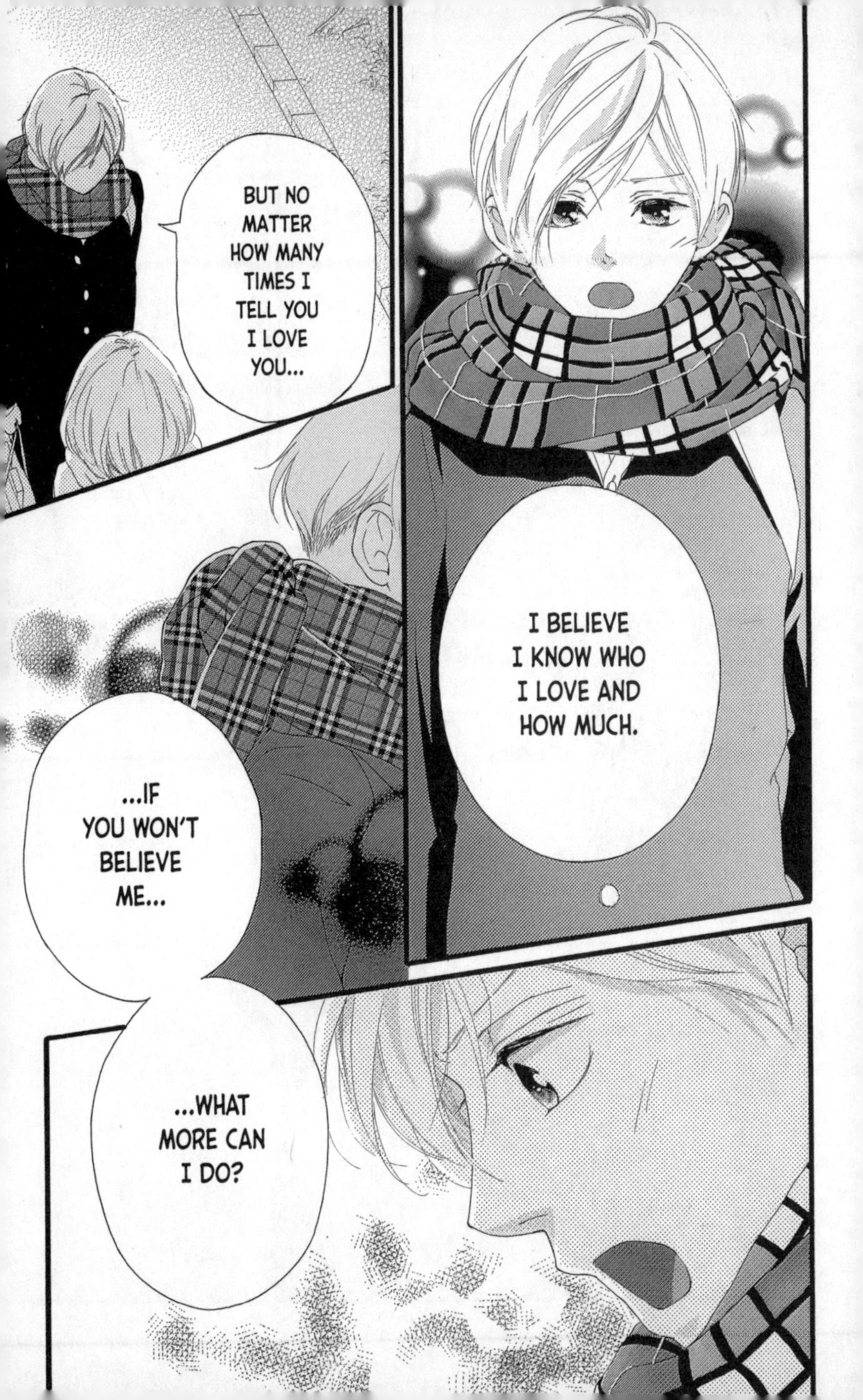
I BELIEVE I KNOW WHO I LOVE AND HOW MUCH.
BUT NO MATTER HOW MANY TIMES I TELL YOU I LOVE YOU...
...IF YOU WON'T BELIEVE ME...
...WHAT MORE CAN I DO?

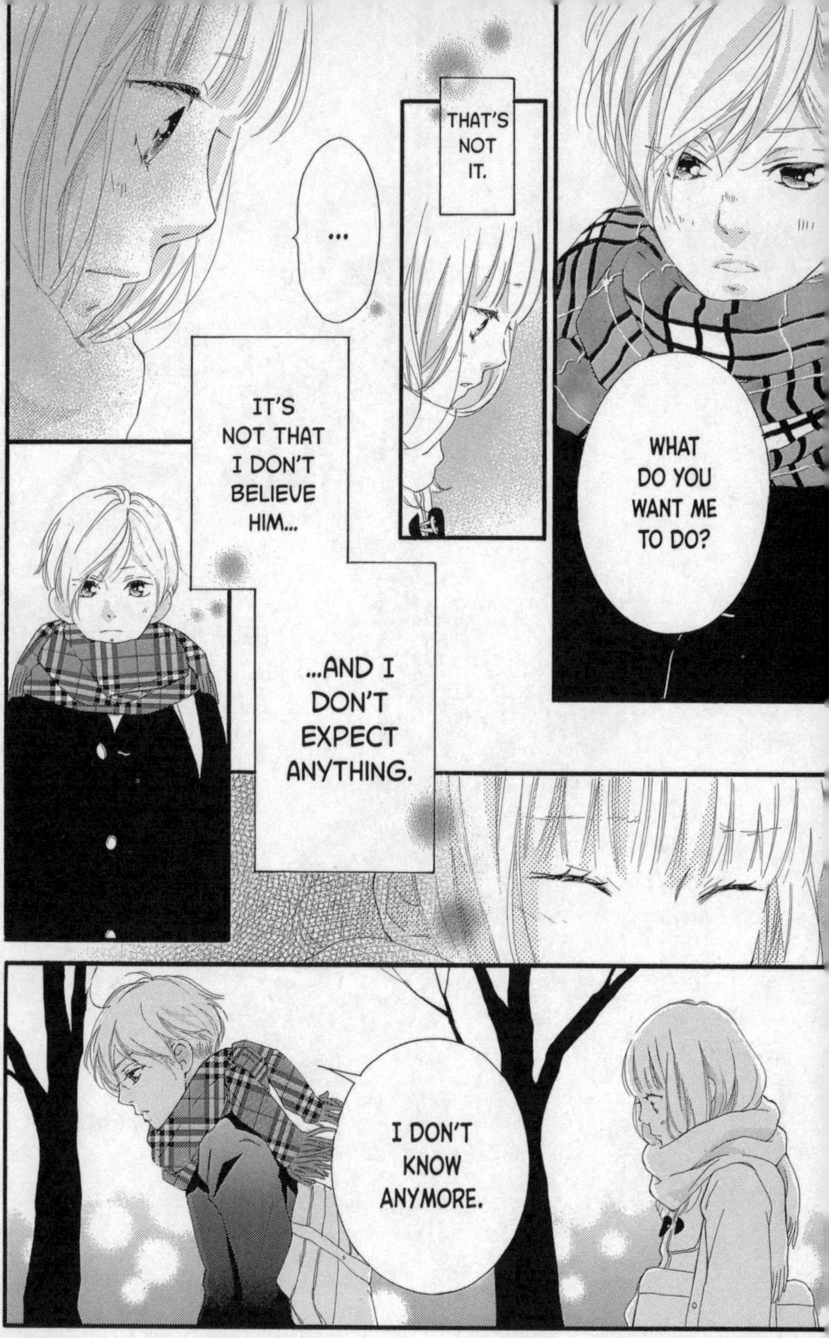
WHAT DO YOU WANT ME TO DO?
THAT'S NOT IT.
...
IT'S NOT THAT I DON'T BELIEVE HIM...
...AND I DON'T EXPECT ANYTHING.
I DON'T KNOW ANYMORE.

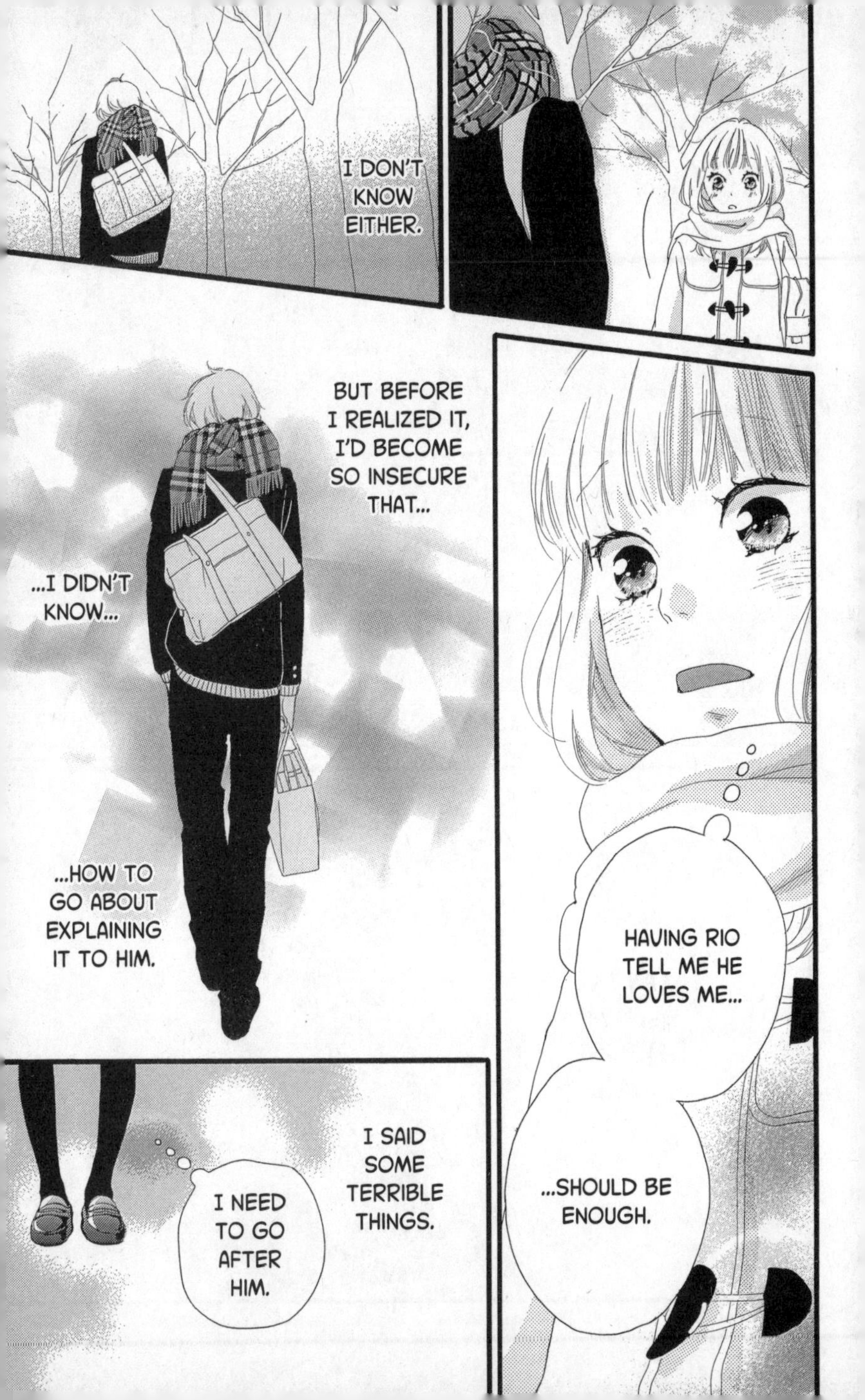
I DON'T KNOW EITHER.
HAVING RIO TELL ME HE LOVES ME...
...SHOULD BE ENOUGH.
BUT BEFORE I REALIZED IT, I'D BECOME SO INSECURE THAT...
...I DIDN'T KNOW...
...HOW TO GO ABOUT EXPLAINING IT TO HIM.
I SAID SOME TERRIBLE THINGS.
I NEED TO GO AFTER HIM.

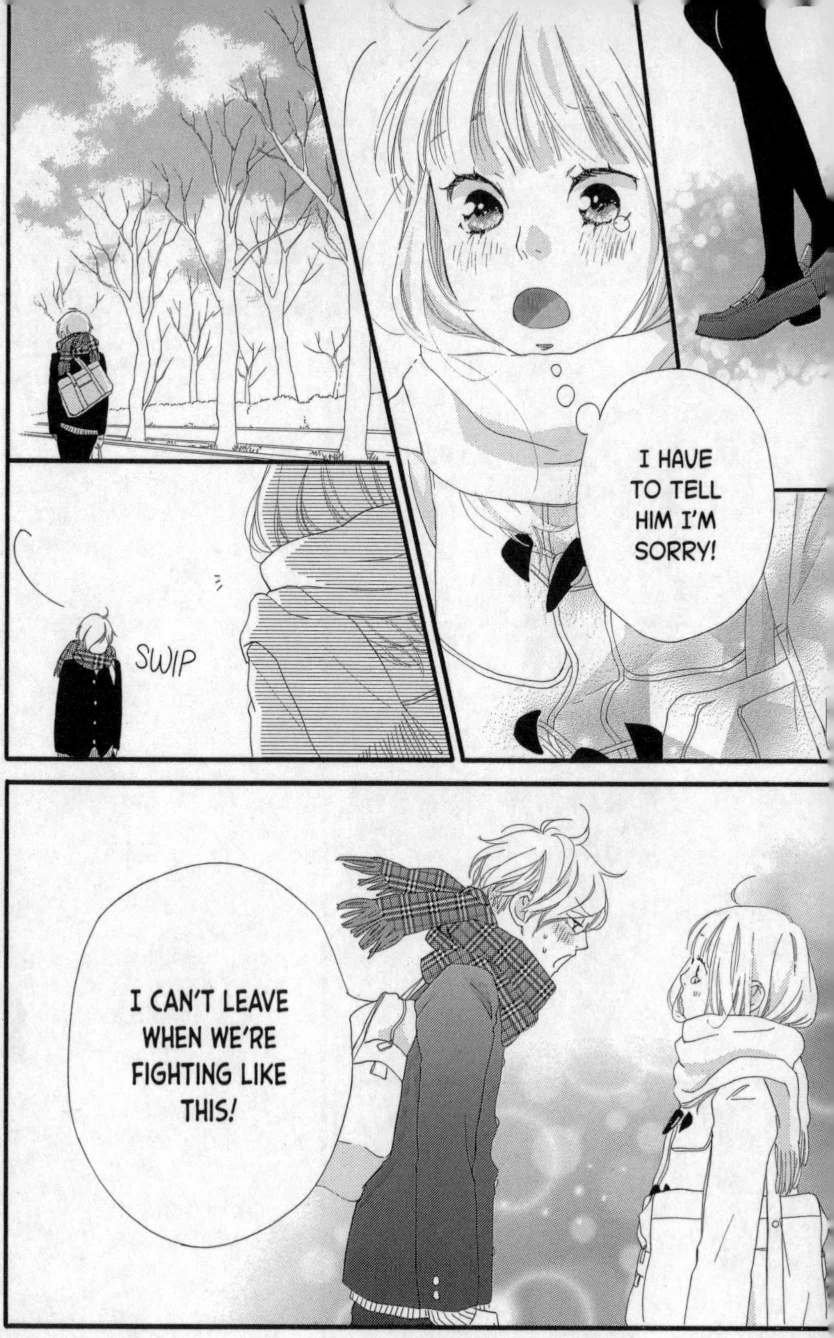
I HAVE TO TELL HIM I'M SORRY!
SWIP
I CAN'T LEAVE WHEN WE'RE FIGHTING LIKE THIS!

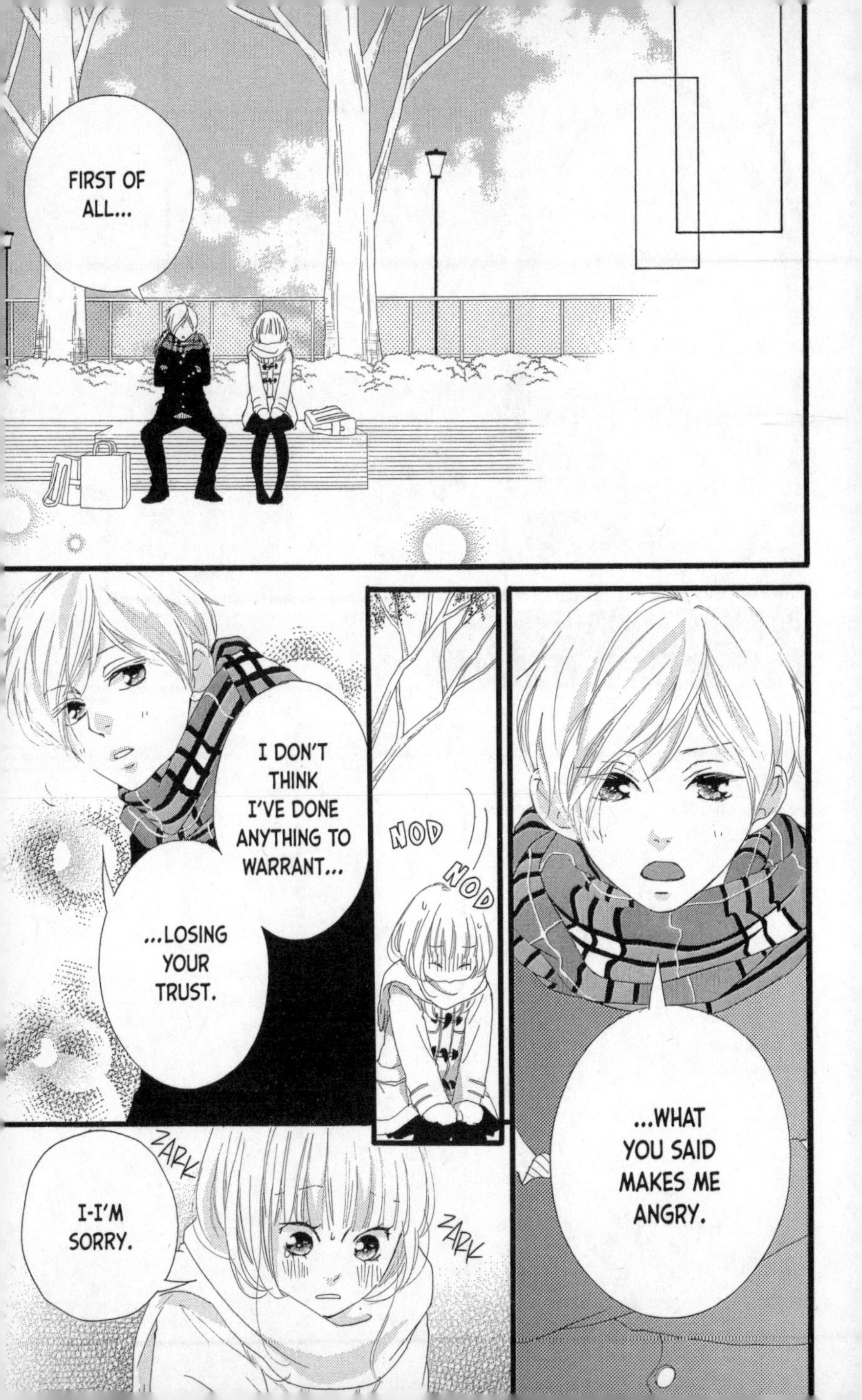
FIRST OF ALL...
...WHAT YOU SAID MAKES ME ANGRY.
NOD
NOD
I DON'T THINK I'VE DONE ANYTHING TO WARRANT...
...LOSING YOUR TRUST.
ZARK
ZARK
I-I'M SORRY.

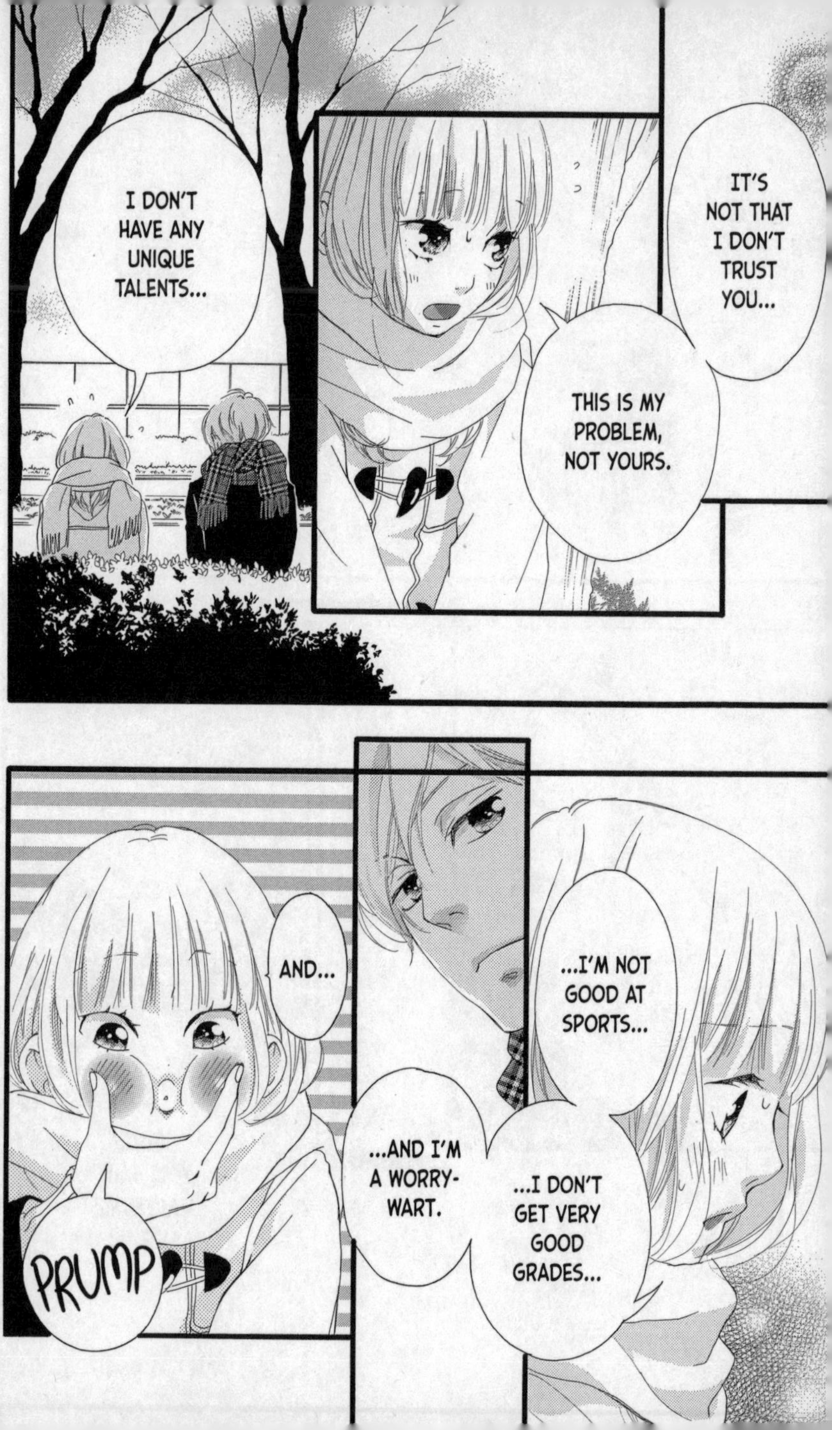
IT'S NOT THAT I DON'T TRUST YOU...
THIS IS MY PROBLEM, NOT YOURS.
I DON'T HAVE ANY UNIQUE TALENTS...
...I'M NOT GOOD AT SPORTS...
...I DON'T GET VERY GOOD GRADES...
...AND I'M A WORRY-WART.
AND...
PRUMP

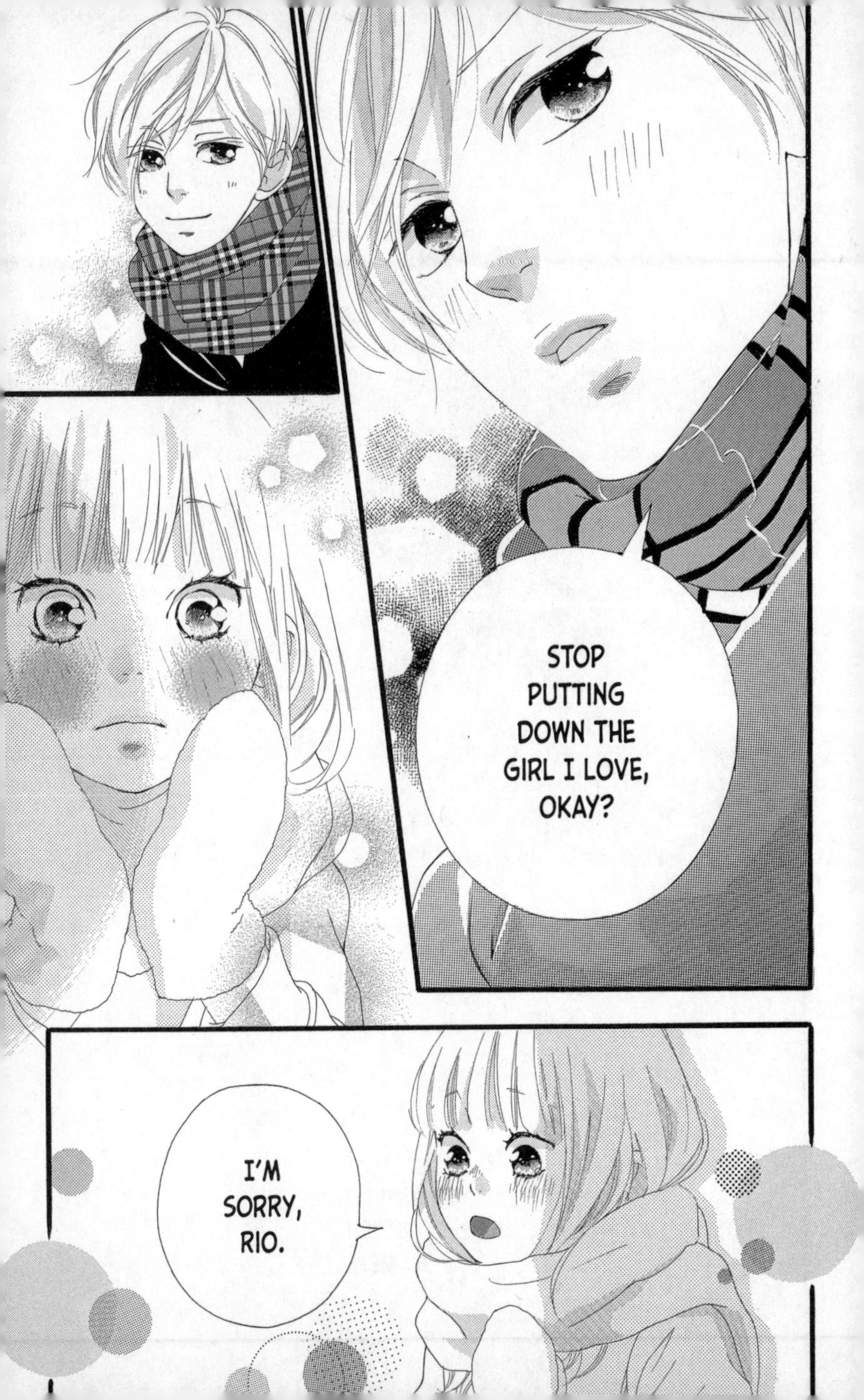
STOP PUTTING DOWN THE GIRL I LOVE, OKAY?
I'M SORRY, RIO.

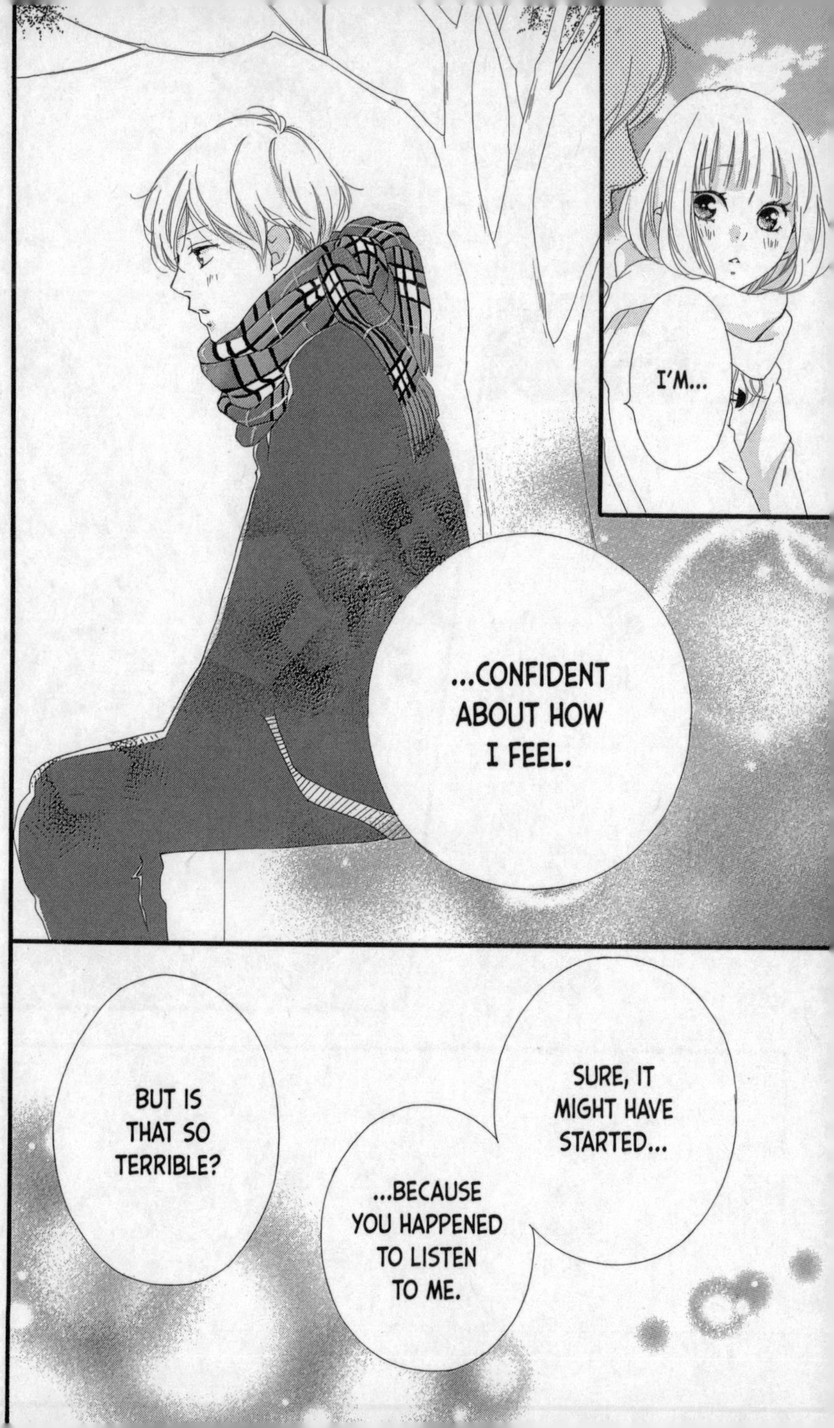
I'M...
...CONFIDENT ABOUT HOW I FEEL.
SURE, IT MIGHT HAVE STARTED...
...BECAUSE YOU HAPPENED TO LISTEN TO ME.
BUT IS THAT SO TERRIBLE?

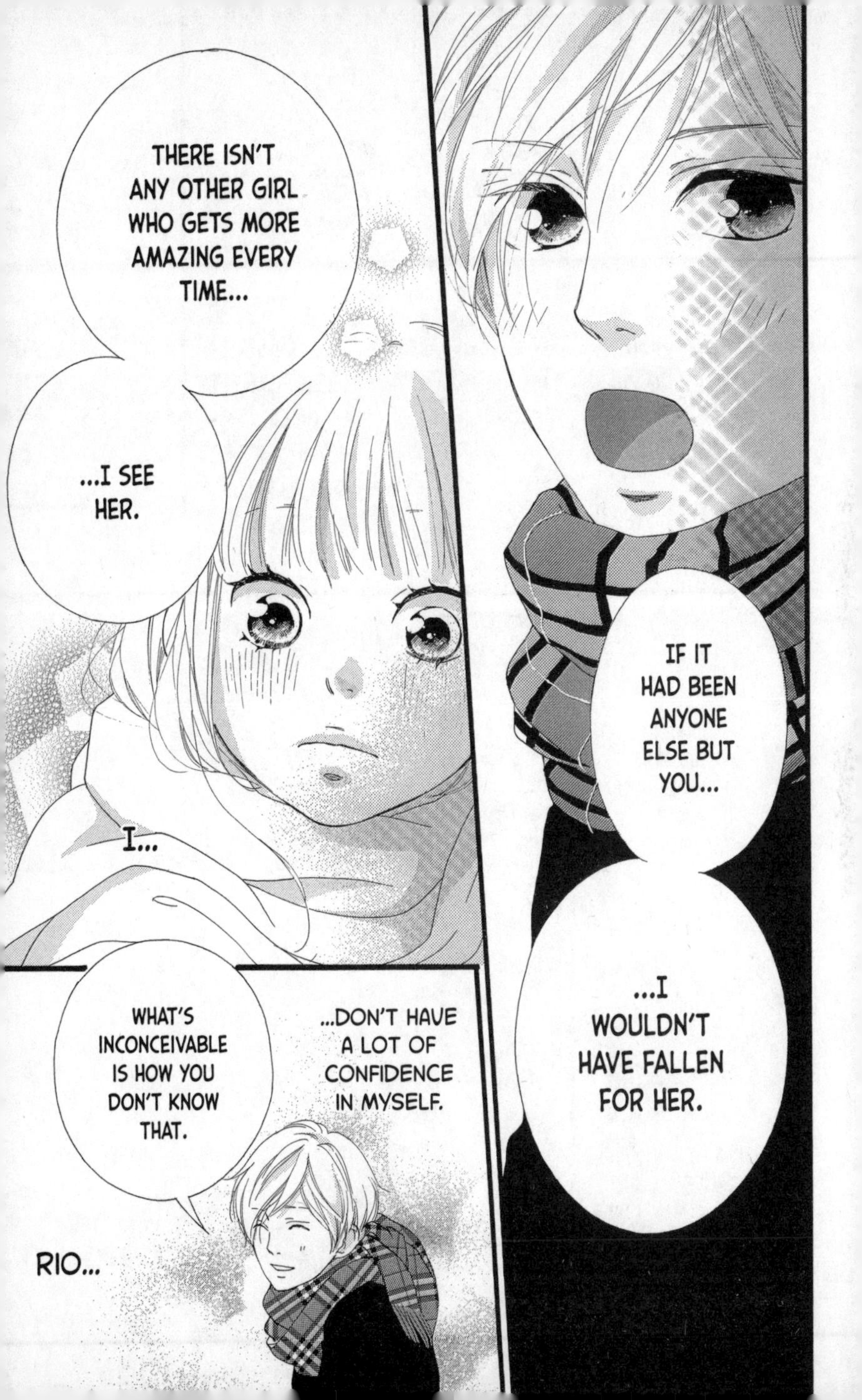
IF IT HAD BEEN ANYONE ELSE BUT YOU...
...I WOULDN'T HAVE FALLEN FOR HER.
THERE ISN'T ANY OTHER GIRL WHO GETS MORE AMAZING EVERY TIME...
...I SEE HER.
I...
...DON'T HAVE A LOT OF CONFIDENCE IN MYSELF.
WHAT'S INCONCEIVABLE IS HOW YOU DON'T KNOW THAT.
RIO...

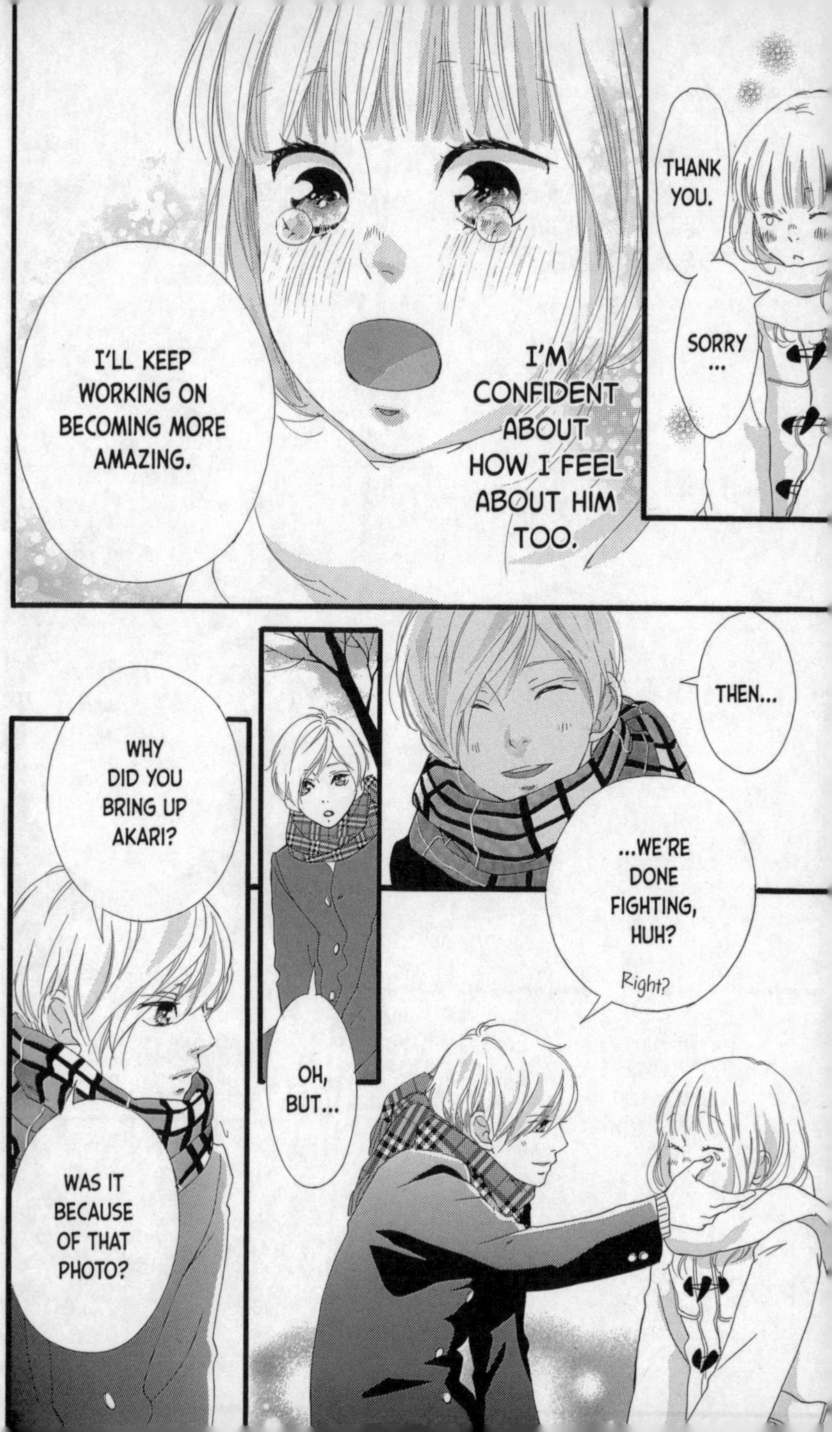
THANK YOU.
SORRY...
I'M CONFIDENT ABOUT HOW I FEEL ABOUT HIM TOO.
I'LL KEEP WORKING ON BECOMING MORE AMAZING.
THEN...
...WE'RE DONE FIGHTING, HUH?
Right?
OH, BUT...
WHY DID YOU BRING UP AKARI?
WAS IT BECAUSE OF THAT PHOTO?

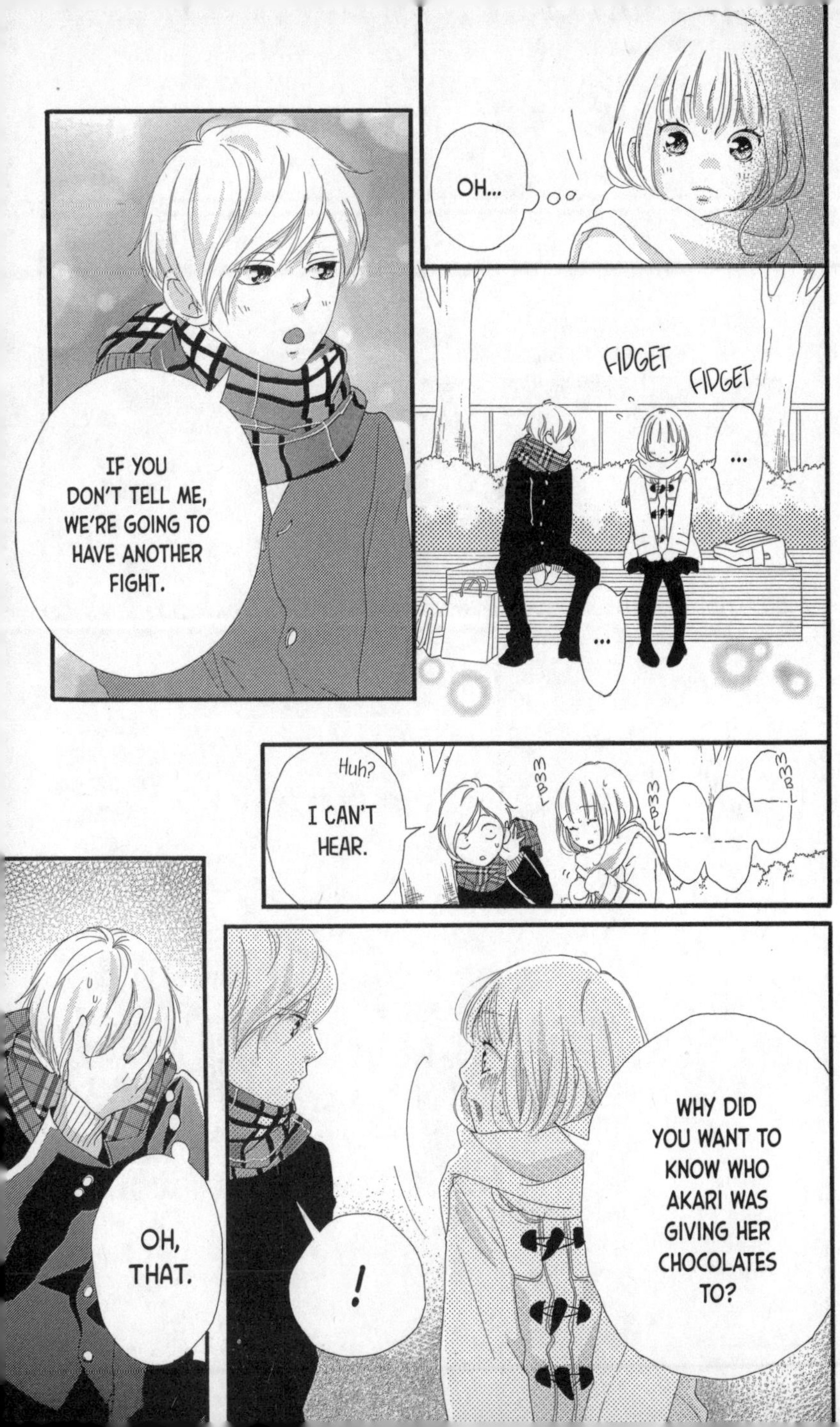
OH...
FIDGET FIDGET
...
...
IF YOU DON'T TELL ME, WE'RE GOING TO HAVE ANOTHER FIGHT.
MMBL
MMBL
MMBL
Huh?
I CAN'T HEAR.
WHY DID YOU WANT TO KNOW WHO AKARI WAS GIVING HER CHOCOLATES TO?
!
OH, THAT.

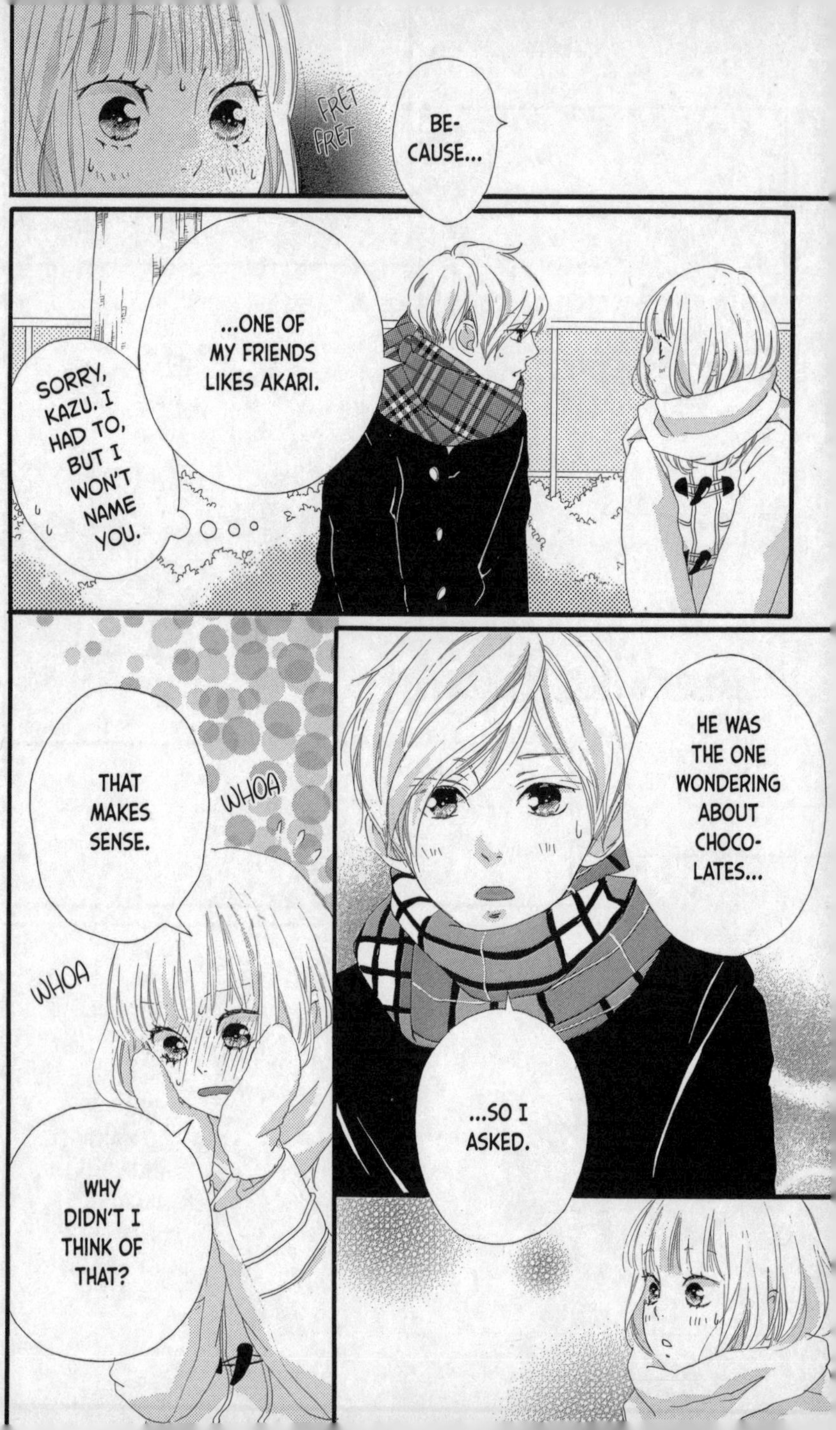
FRET FRET
BE-CAUSE...
...ONE OF MY FRIENDS LIKES AKARI.
SORRY, KAZU. I HAD TO, BUT I WON'T NAME YOU.
HE WAS THE ONE WONDERING ABOUT CHOCO-LATES...
...SO I ASKED.
THAT MAKES SENSE.
WHOA
WHOA
WHY DIDN'T I THINK OF THAT?

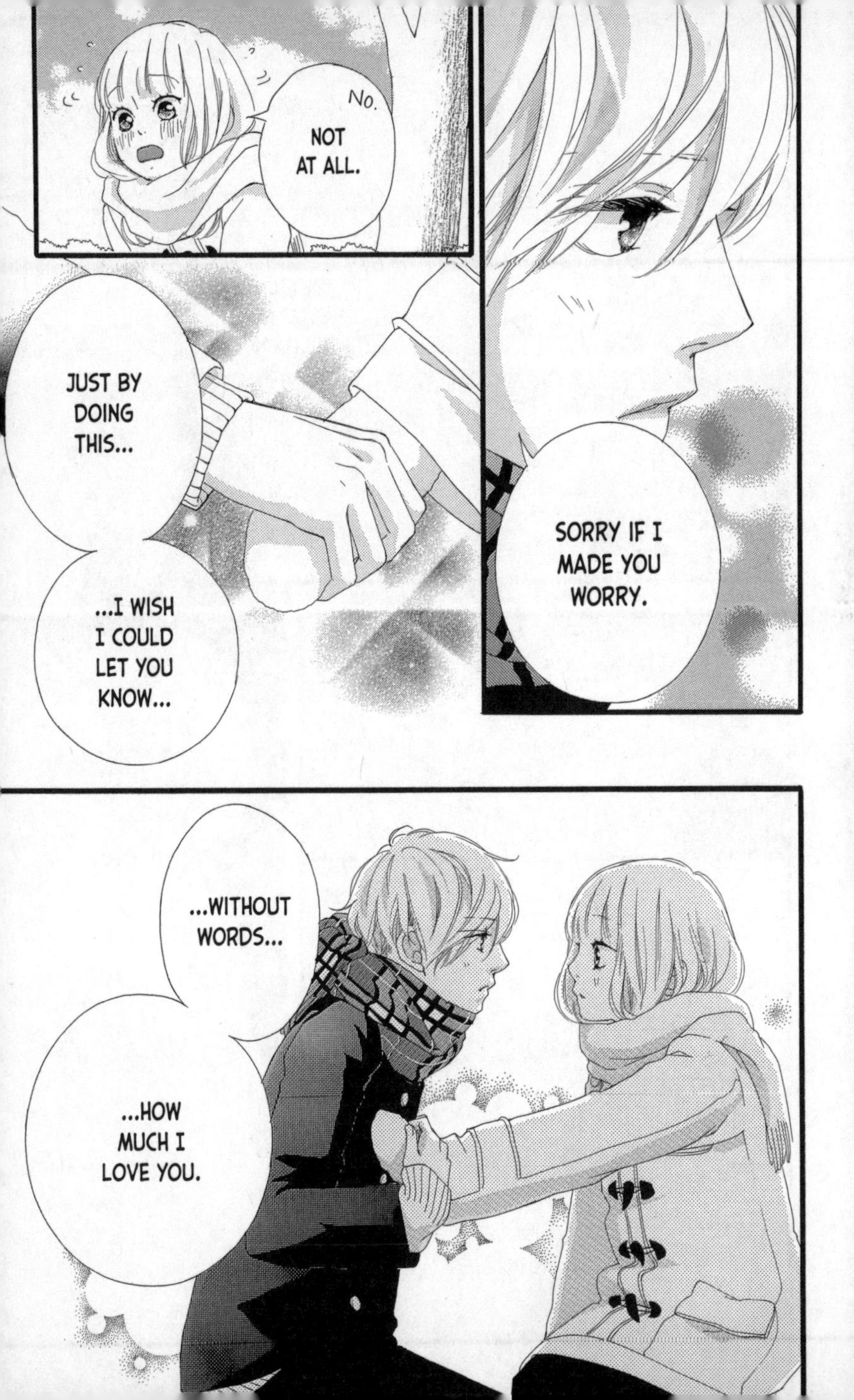
SORRY IF I MADE YOU WORRY.
No.
NOT AT ALL.
JUST BY DOING THIS...
...I WISH I COULD LET YOU KNOW...
...WITHOUT WORDS...
...HOW MUCH I LOVE YOU.

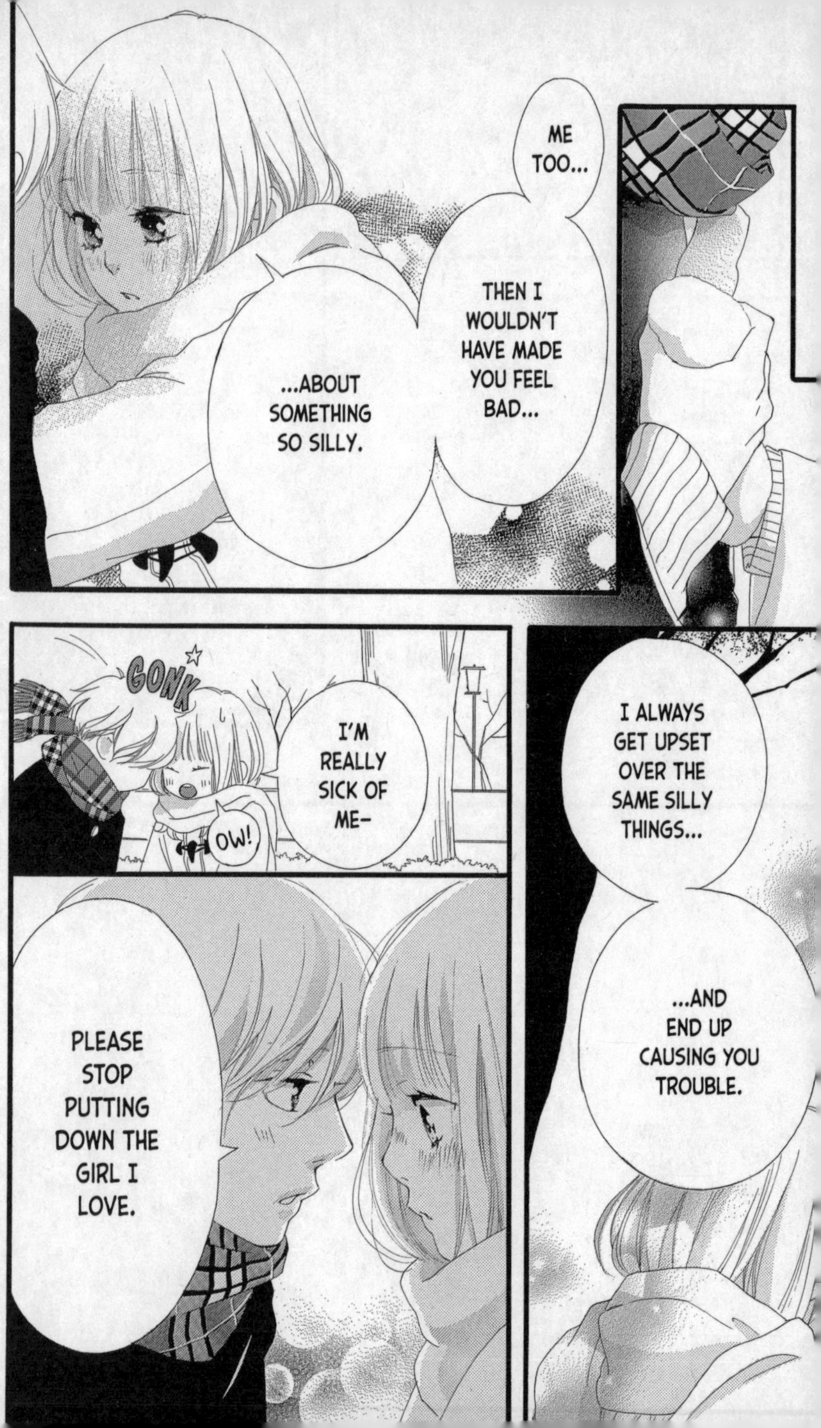
ME TOO...
THEN I WOULDN'T HAVE MADE YOU FEEL BAD...
...ABOUT SOMETHING SO SILLY.
I ALWAYS GET UPSET OVER THE SAME SILLY THINGS...
...AND END UP CAUSING YOU TROUBLE.
I'M REALLY SICK OF ME–
GONK
OW!
PLEASE STOP PUTTING DOWN THE GIRL I LOVE.

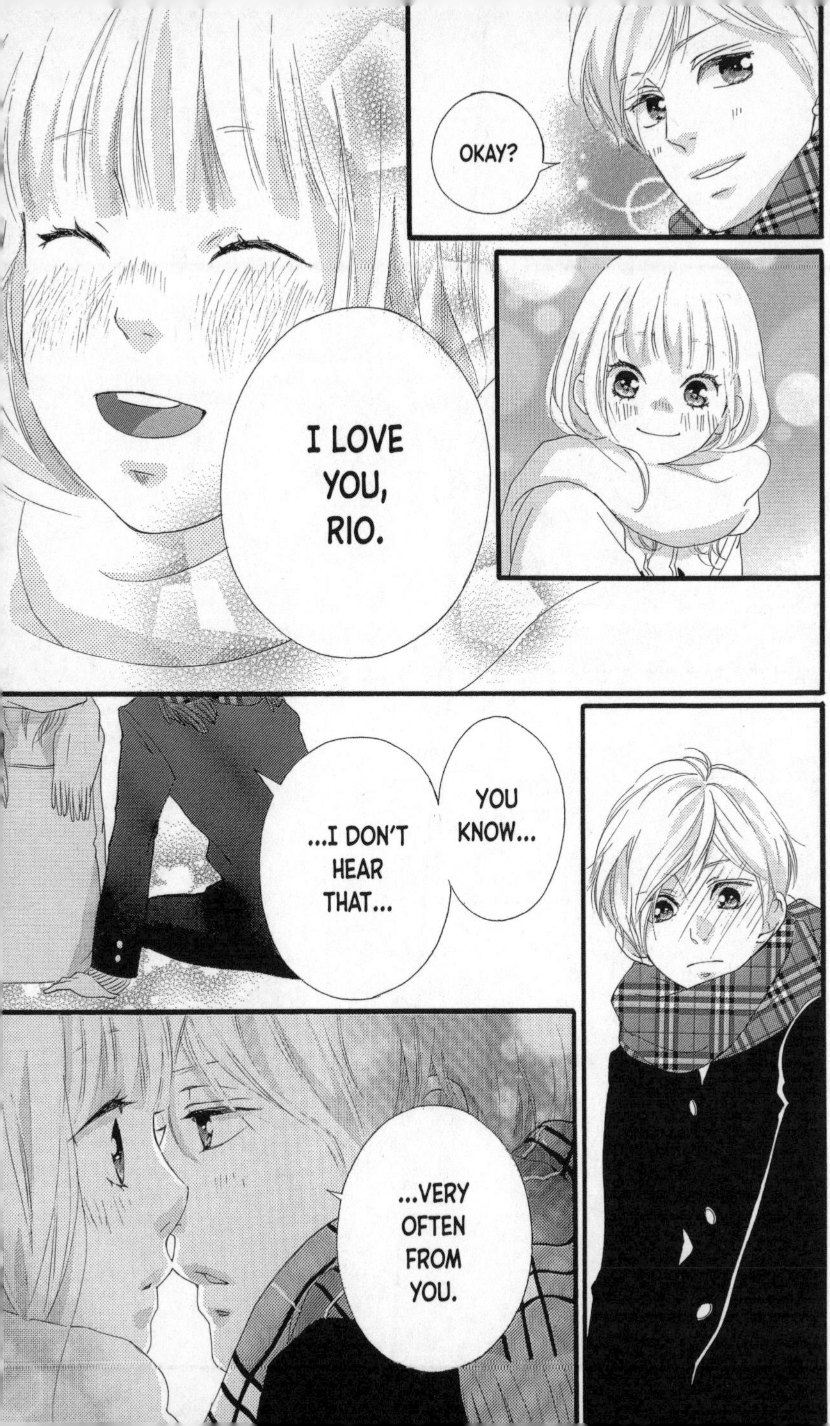
OKAY?
I LOVE YOU, RIO.
YOU KNOW...
...I DON'T HEAR THAT...
...VERY OFTEN FROM YOU.

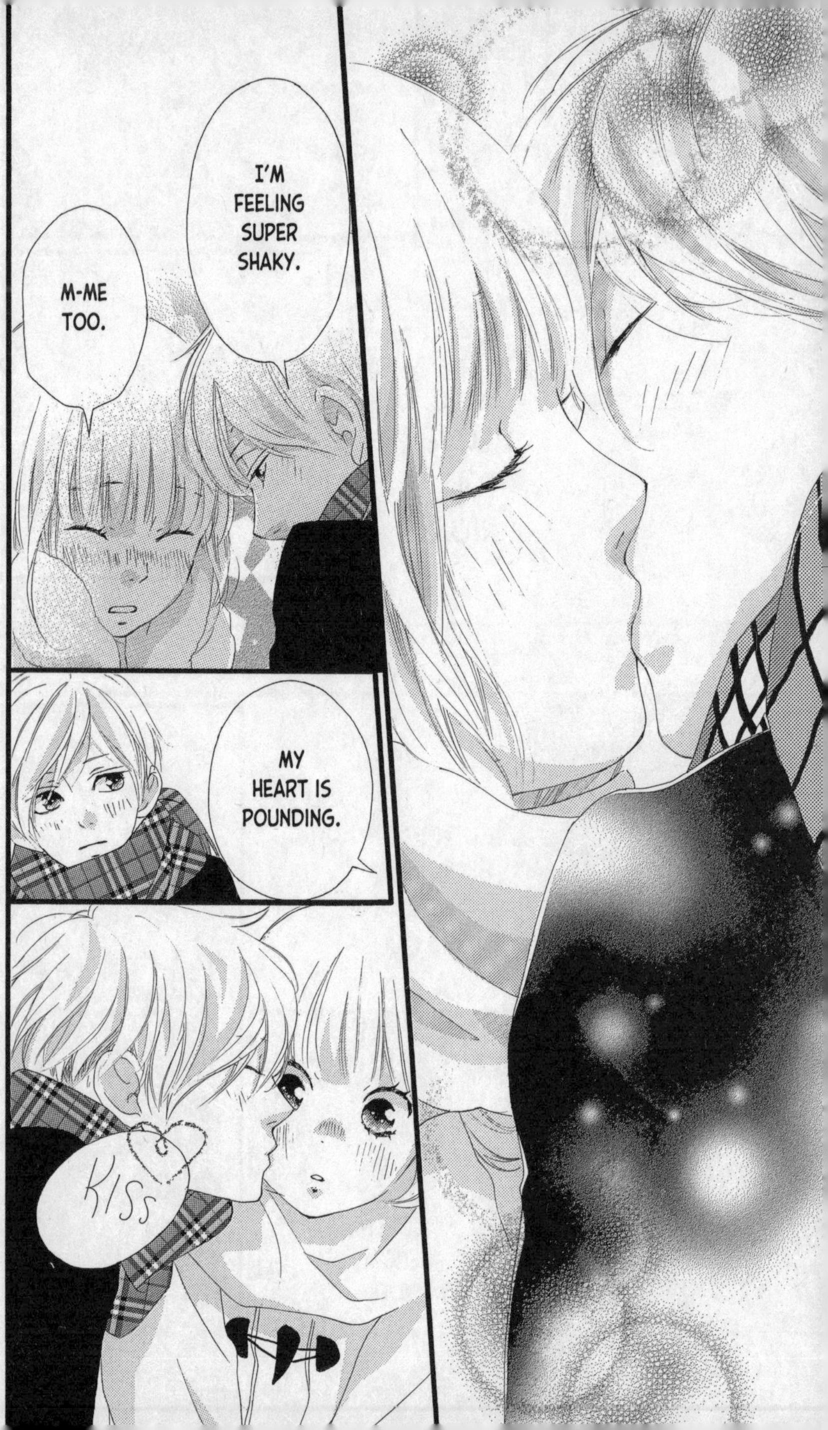
I'M FEELING SUPER SHAKY.
M-ME TOO.
MY HEART IS POUNDING.
KISS

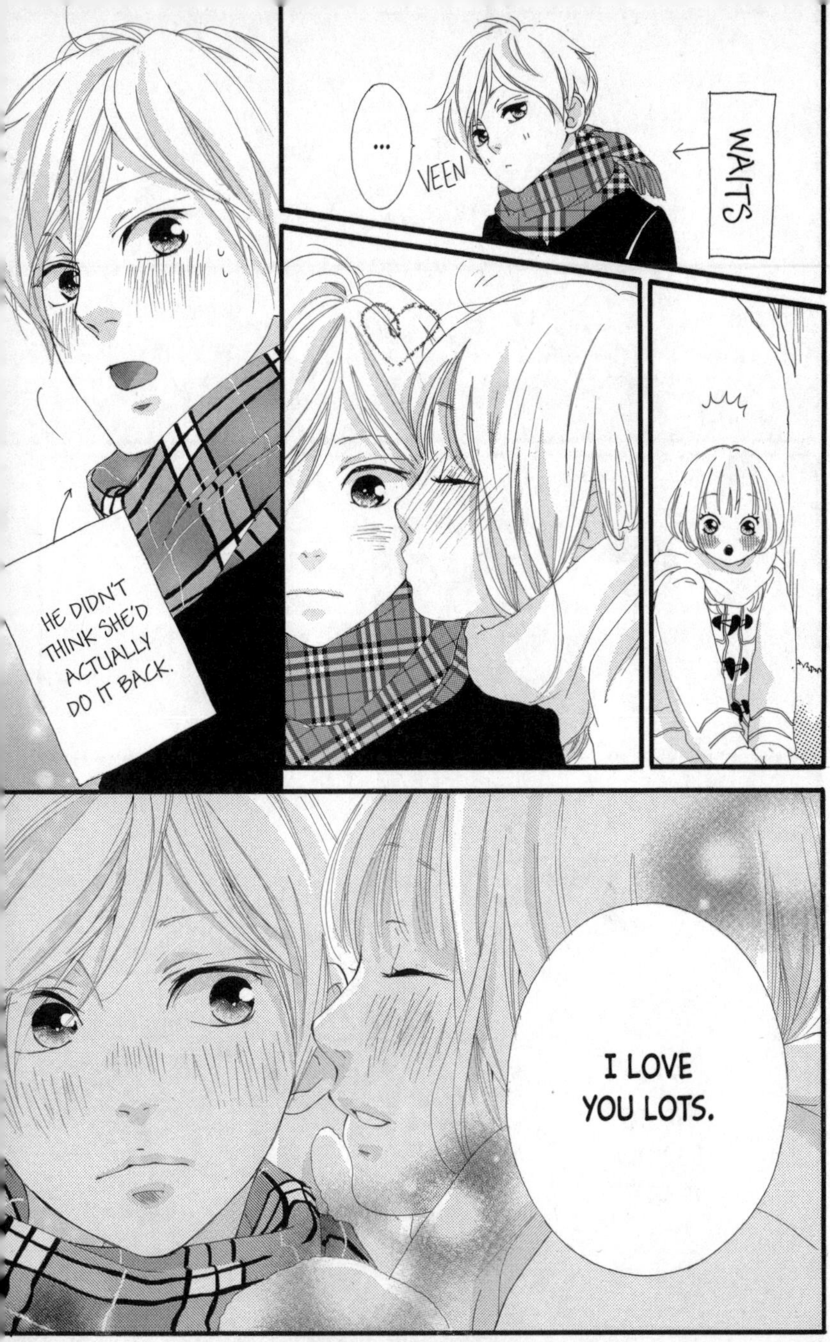
WAITS
...
VEEN
HE DIDN'T THINK SHE'D ACTUALLY DO IT BACK.
I LOVE YOU LOTS.

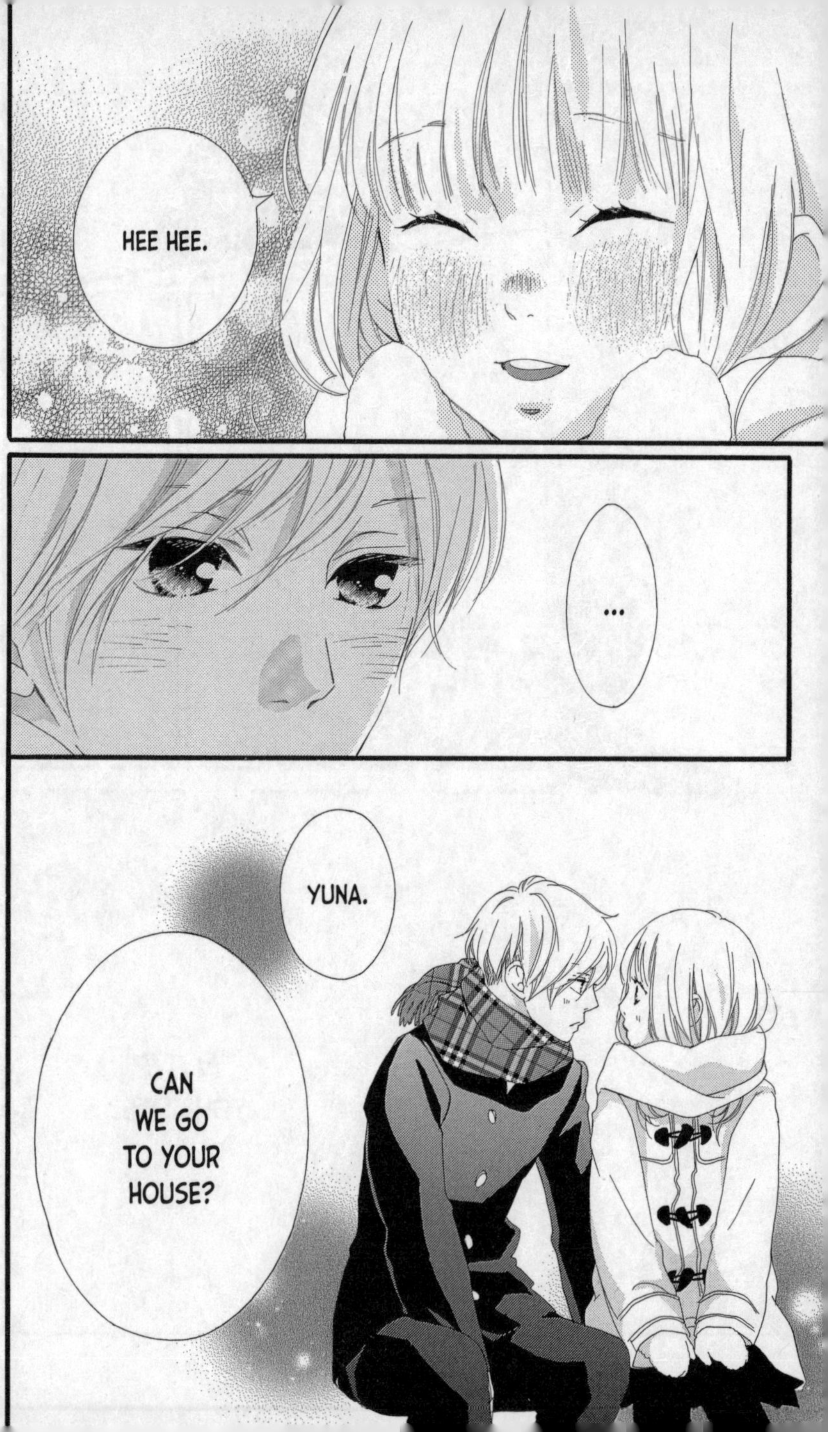
HEE HEE.
...
YUNA.
CAN WE GO TO YOUR HOUSE?

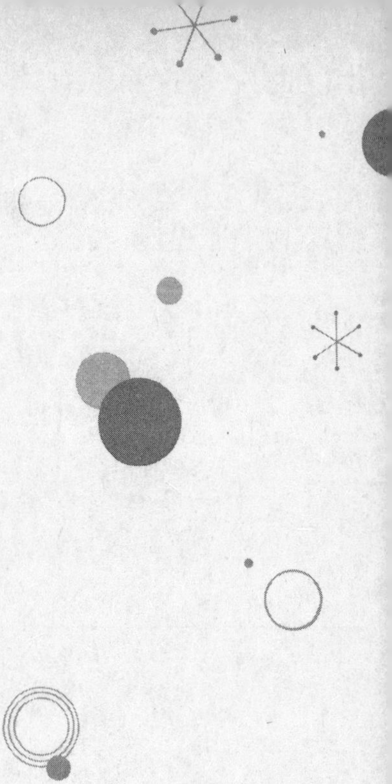

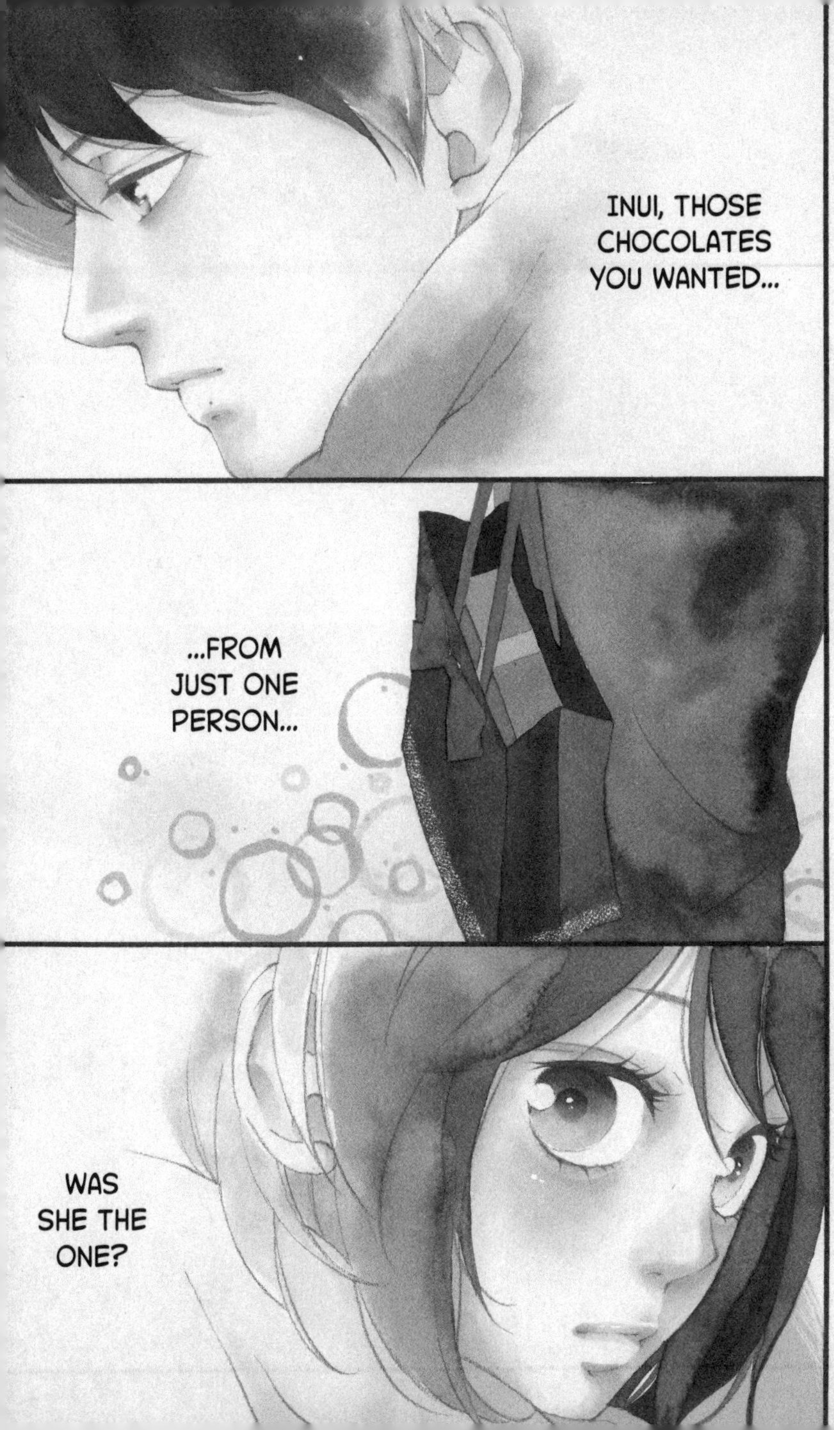
INUI, THOSE CHOCOLATES YOU WANTED...
...FROM JUST ONE PERSON...
WAS SHE THE ONE?

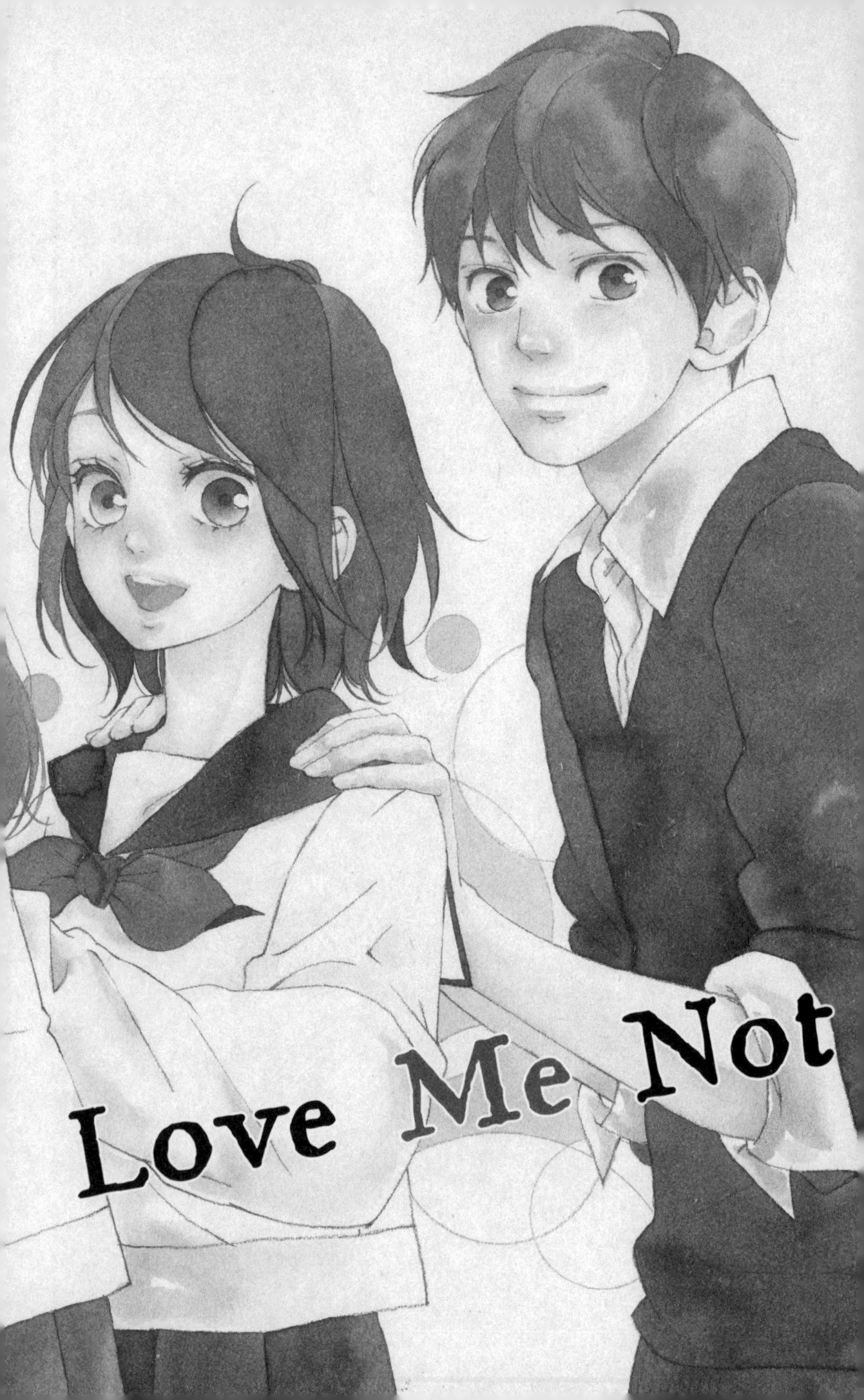
Love Me Not

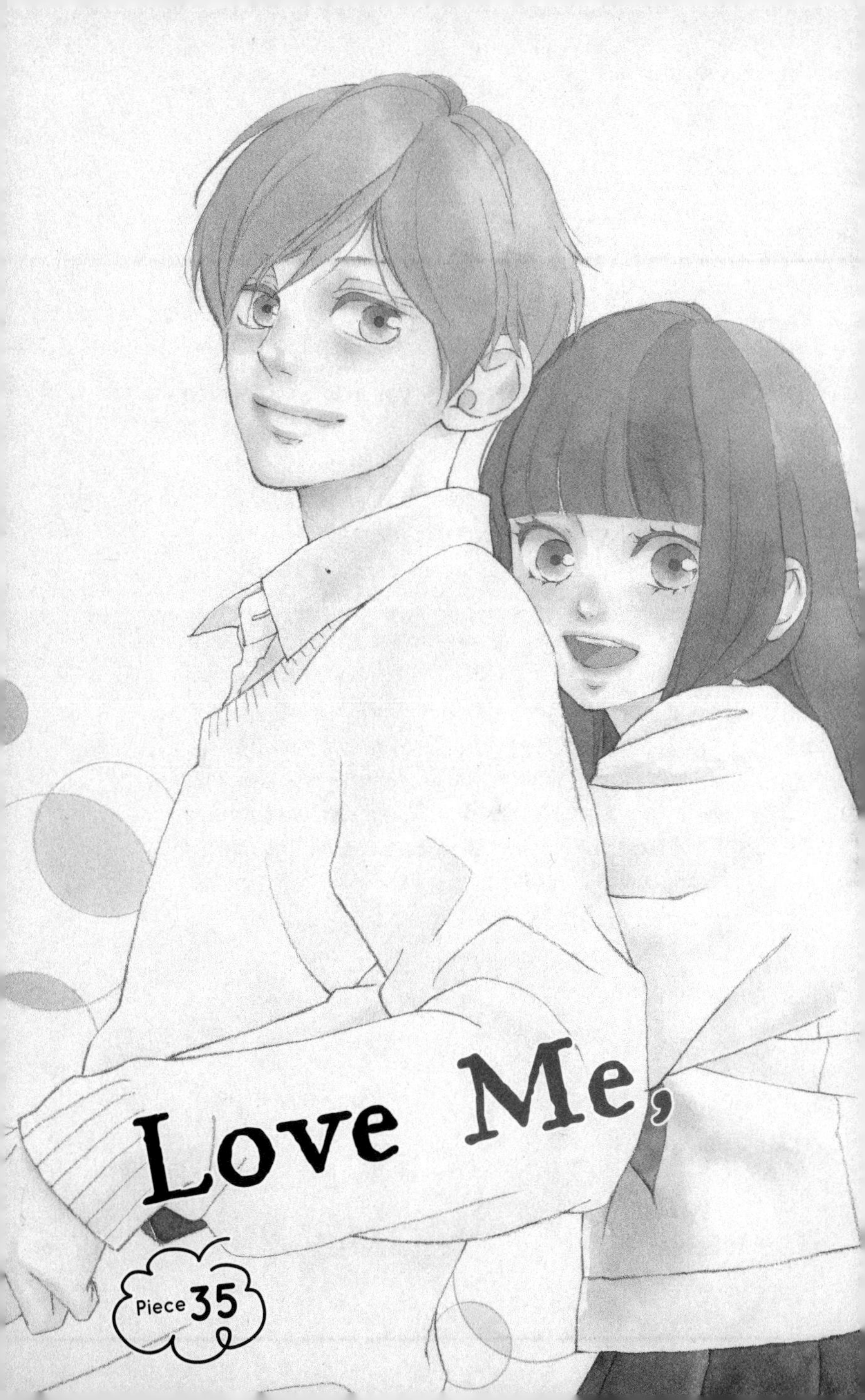
Love Me,
Piece 35

GREETINGS

Hello. I'm Io Sakisaka.
Thank you so much for picking up volume 9 of *Love Me, Love Me Not*.

I changed the mood of the illustration on the cover with this volume. This is the "Yuna and Rio as a couple" version. I went back to my old watercolor paper because it's easy to use and very adaptable. No matter how long I do this, I am always very nervous about creating color drawings. I never get used to it. I tend to self-destruct by putting undue pressure on myself. I think, "I need to get this right. I need to color properly." When I work on paper, I think, "There's no saving it once I make a mistake," which makes me even more nervous. If there's no pressure, that's no fun either, but I'd like to relax just a little bit more while working. Will that day ever come? I'd like to have more guts.

Io Sakisaka

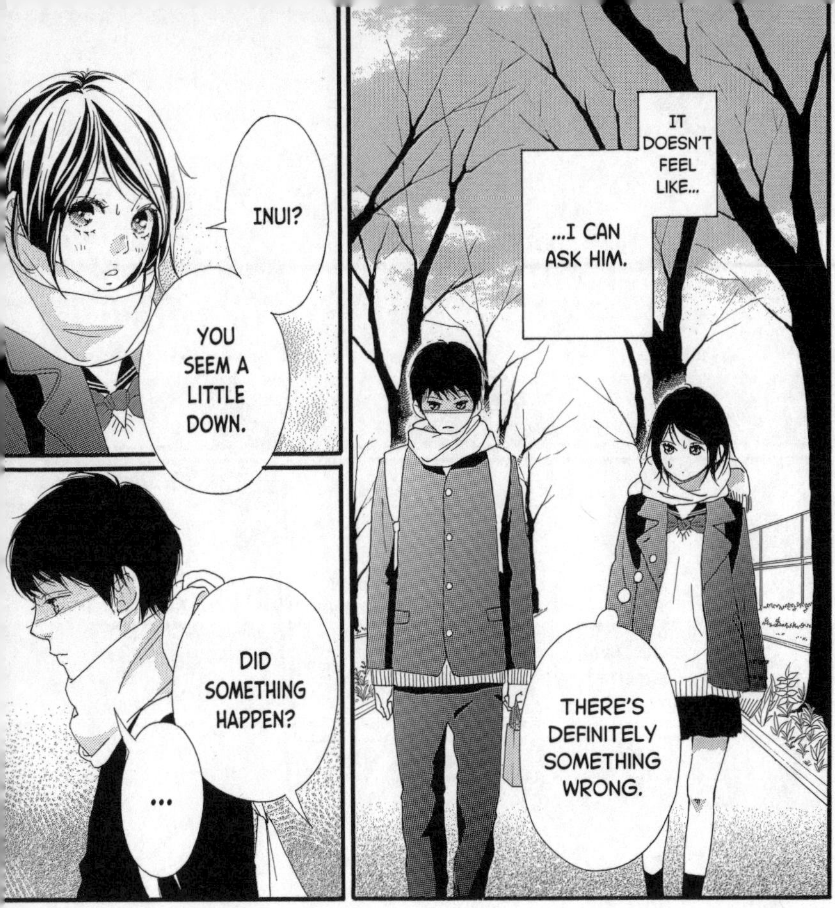
IT DOESN'T FEEL LIKE...
...I CAN ASK HIM.
THERE'S DEFINITELY SOMETHING WRONG.
INUI?
YOU SEEM A LITTLE DOWN.
DID SOMETHING HAPPEN?
...

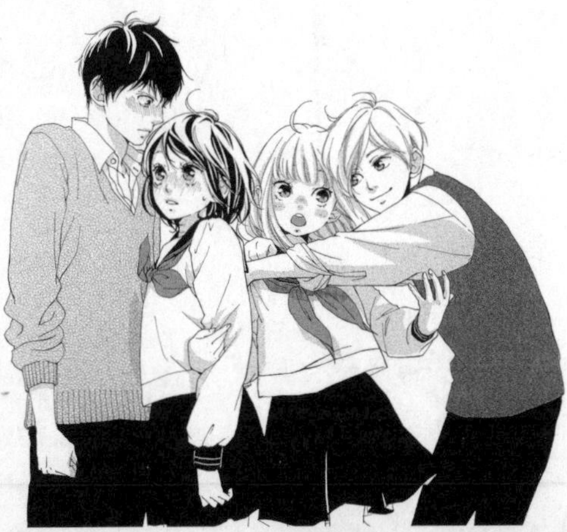

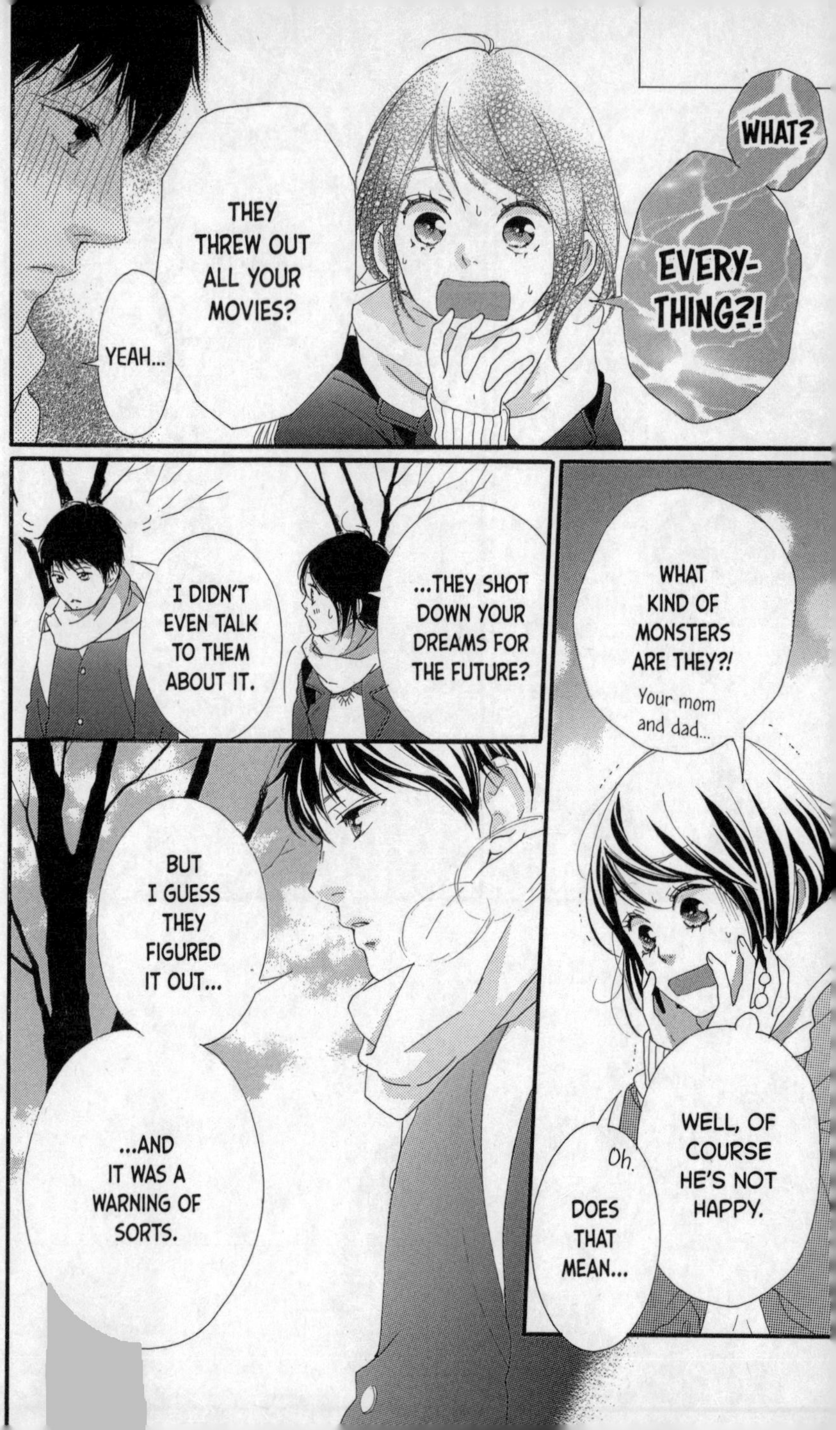
WHAT?
EVERY-THING?!
THEY THREW OUT ALL YOUR MOVIES?
YEAH...
WHAT KIND OF MONSTERS ARE THEY?! Your mom and dad...
WELL, OF COURSE HE'S NOT HAPPY.
Oh.
DOES THAT MEAN...
...THEY SHOT DOWN YOUR DREAMS FOR THE FUTURE?
I DIDN'T EVEN TALK TO THEM ABOUT IT.
BUT I GUESS THEY FIGURED IT OUT...
...AND IT WAS A WARNING OF SORTS.

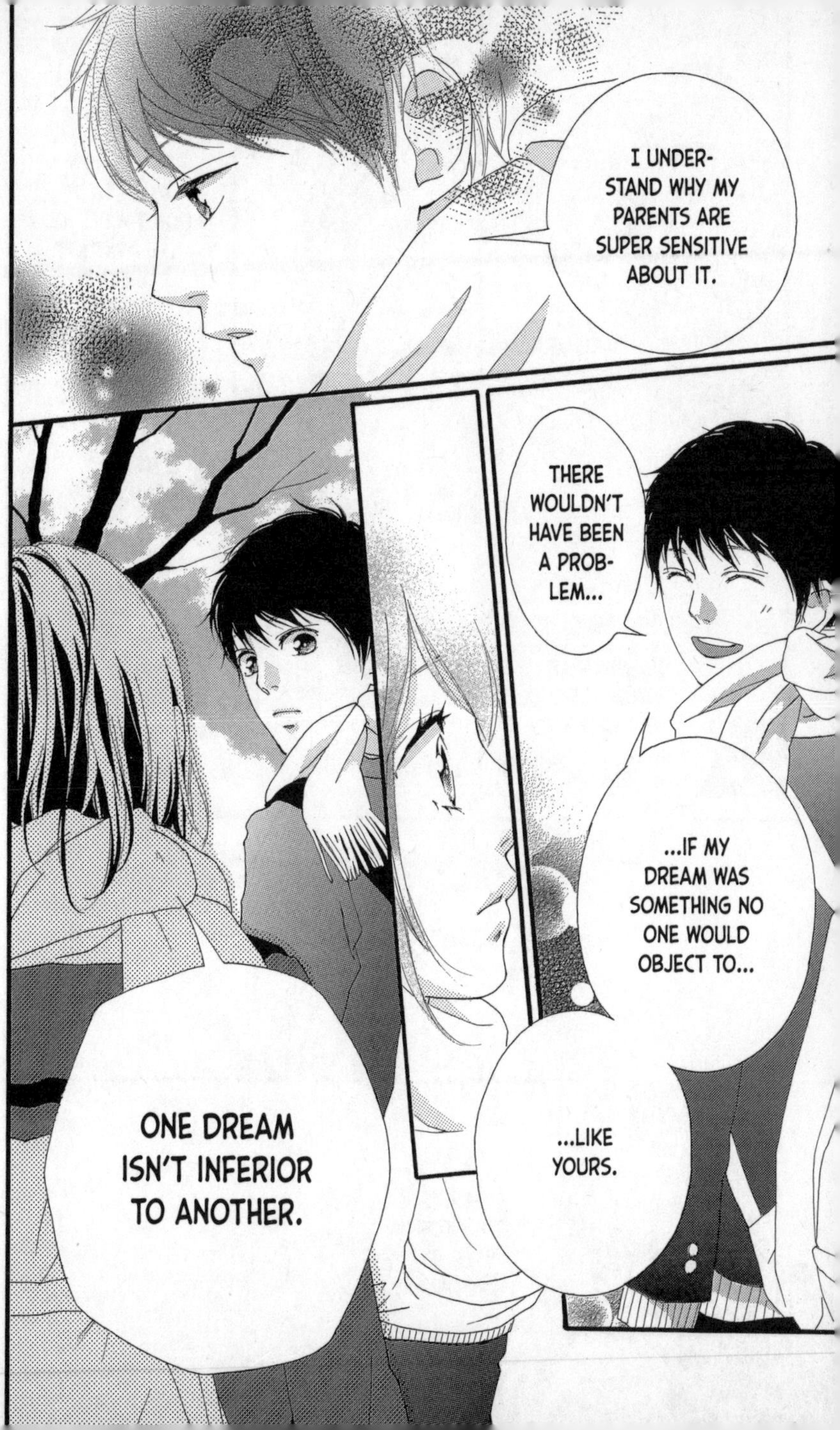
I UNDER-STAND WHY MY PARENTS ARE SUPER SENSITIVE ABOUT IT.
THERE WOULDN'T HAVE BEEN A PROB-LEM...
...IF MY DREAM WAS SOMETHING NO ONE WOULD OBJECT TO...
...LIKE YOURS.
ONE DREAM ISN'T INFERIOR TO ANOTHER.

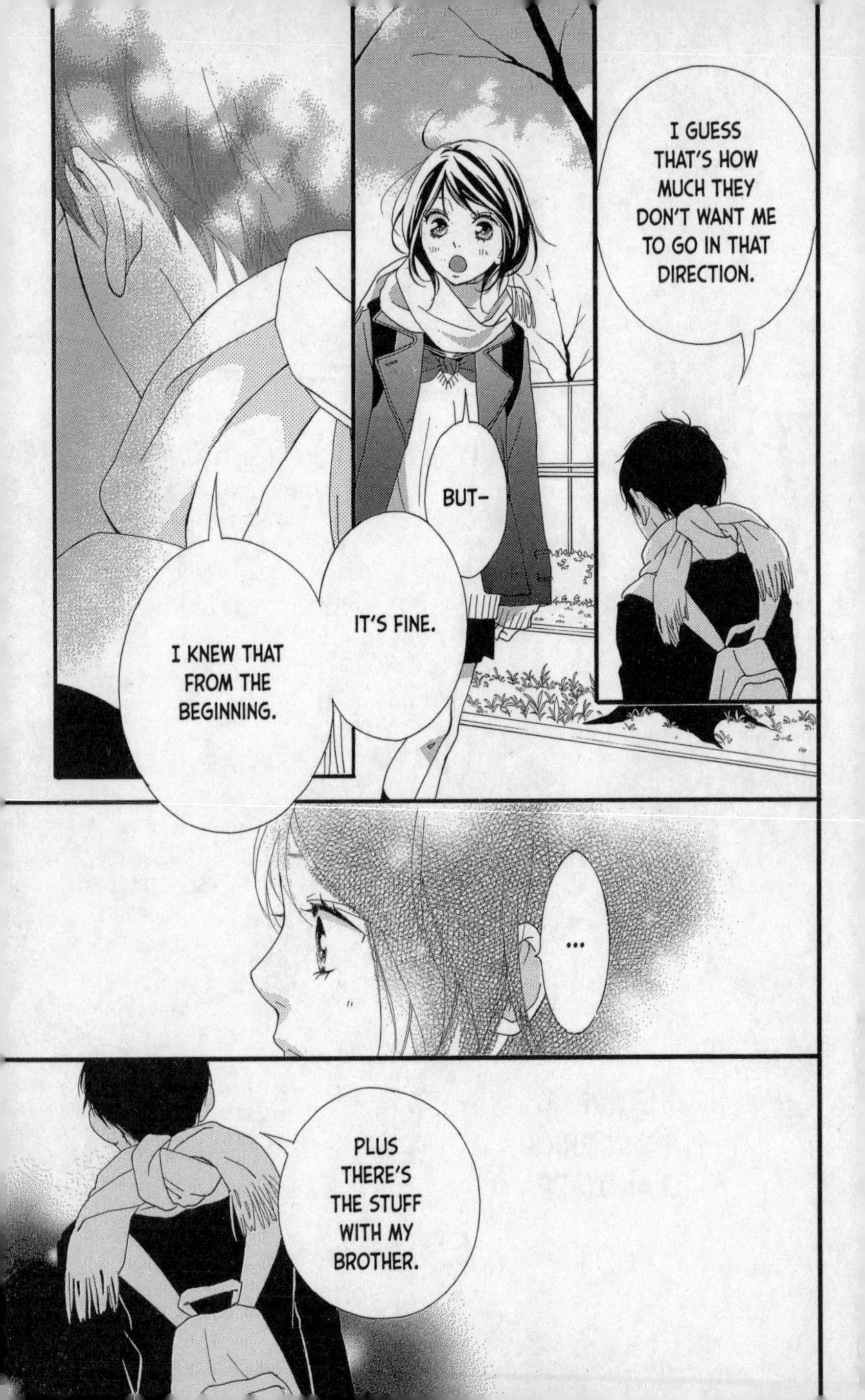
I GUESS THAT'S HOW MUCH THEY DON'T WANT ME TO GO IN THAT DIRECTION.
BUT-
IT'S FINE.
I KNEW THAT FROM THE BEGINNING.
...
PLUS THERE'S THE STUFF WITH MY BROTHER.

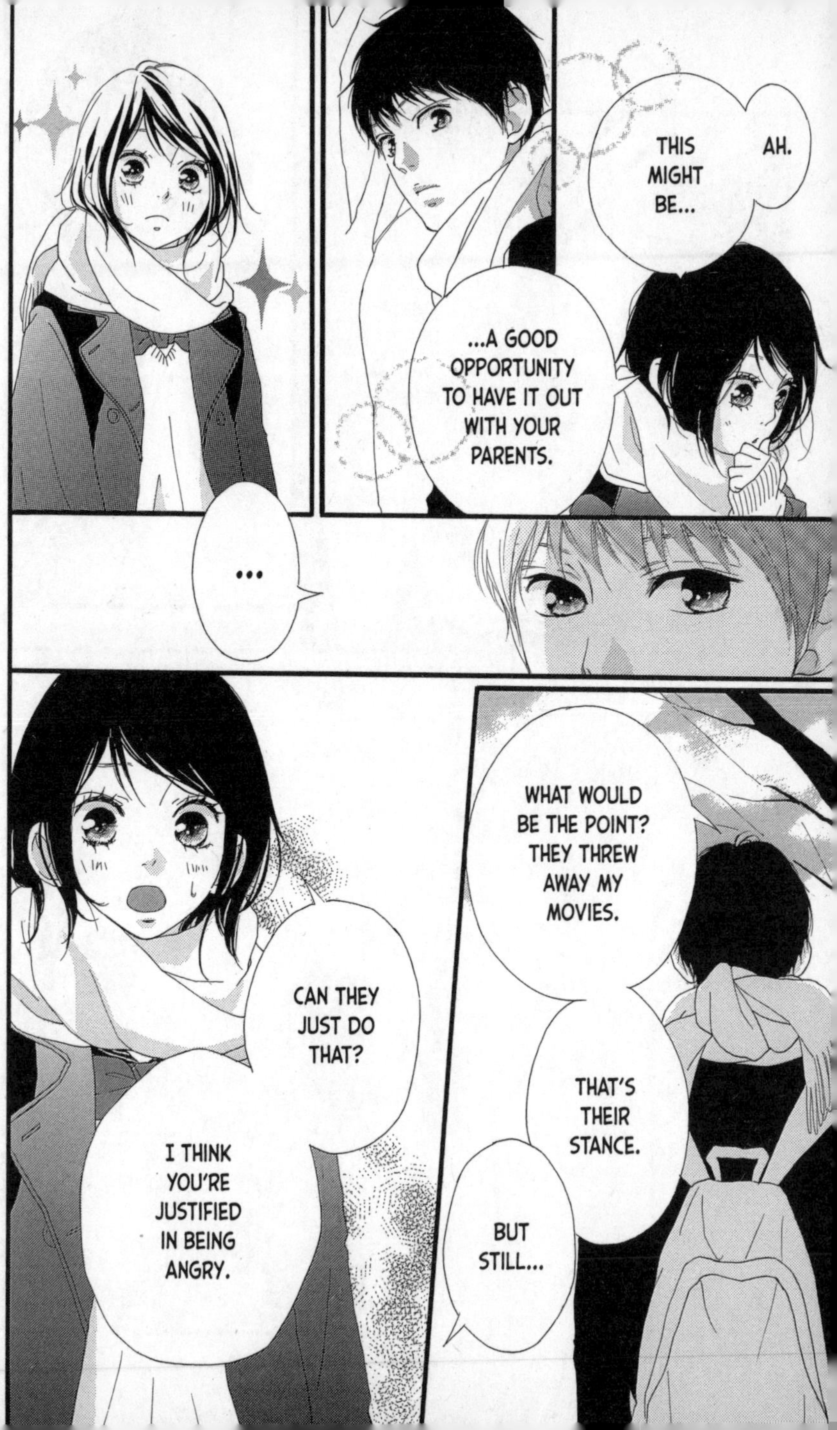
AH.
THIS MIGHT BE...
...A GOOD OPPORTUNITY TO HAVE IT OUT WITH YOUR PARENTS.
...
WHAT WOULD BE THE POINT? THEY THREW AWAY MY MOVIES.
THAT'S THEIR STANCE.
BUT STILL...
CAN THEY JUST DO THAT?
I THINK YOU'RE JUSTIFIED IN BEING ANGRY.

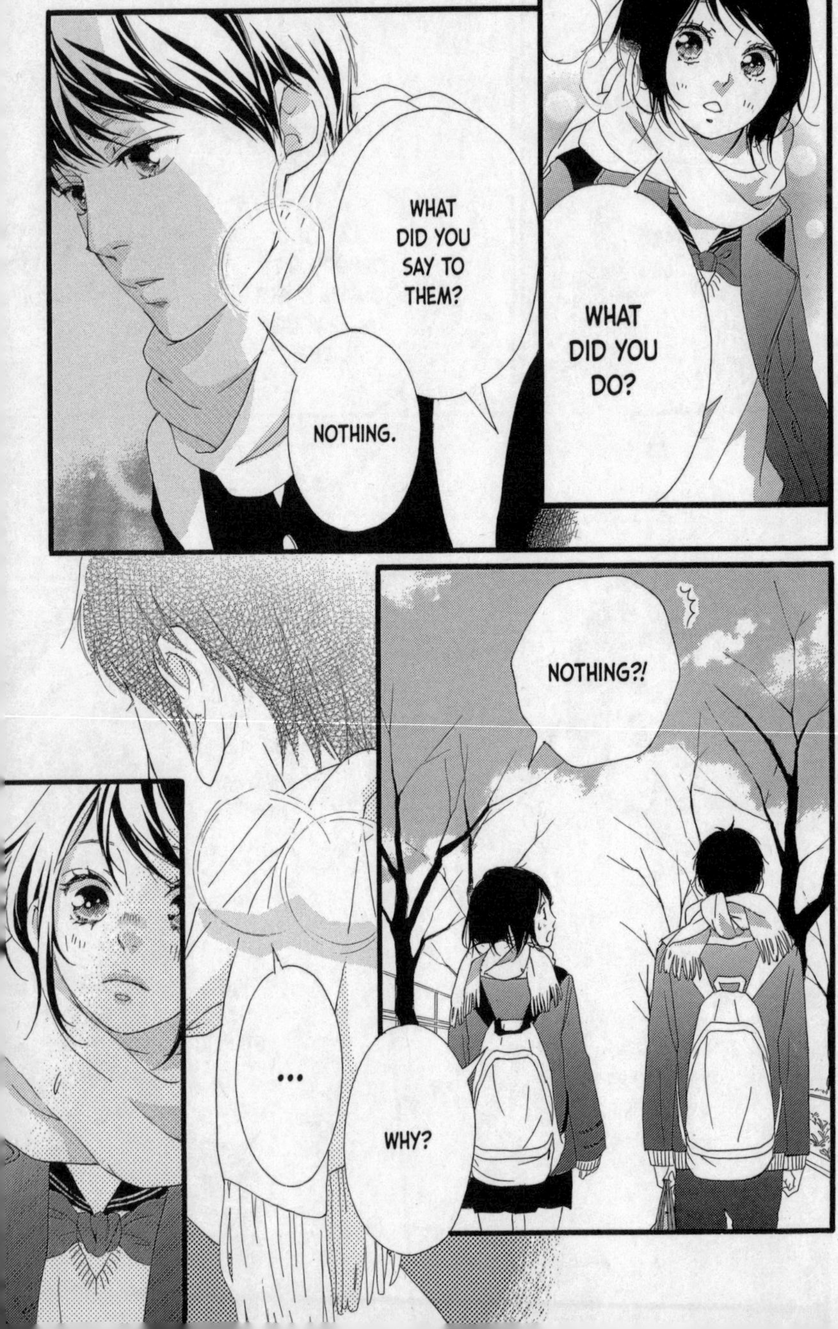
WHAT DID YOU DO?
WHAT DID YOU SAY TO THEM?
NOTHING.
NOTHING?!
WHY?
...

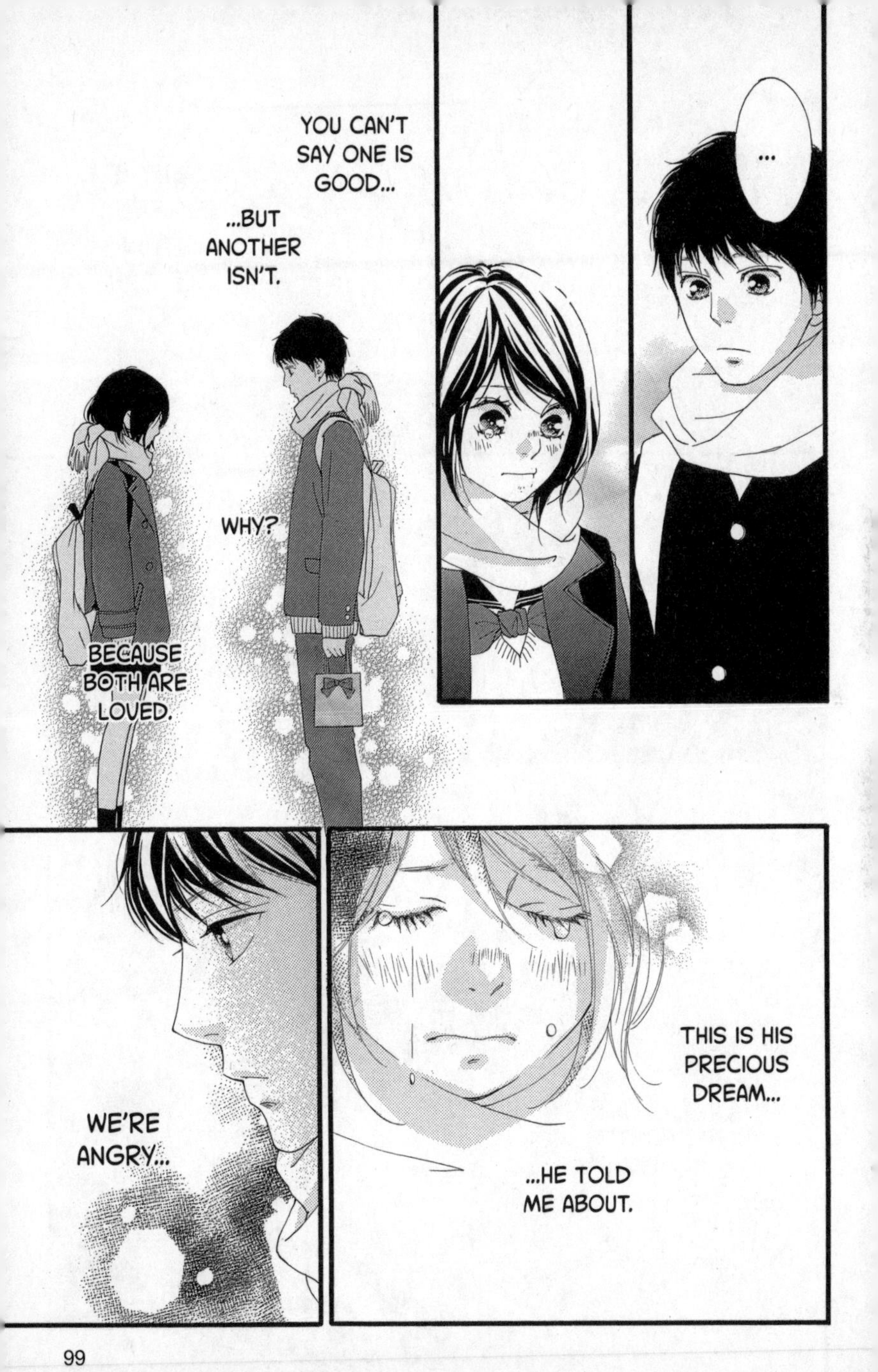
...
YOU CAN'T SAY ONE IS GOOD...
...BUT ANOTHER ISN'T.
WHY?
BECAUSE BOTH ARE LOVED.
THIS IS HIS PRECIOUS DREAM...
...HE TOLD ME ABOUT.
WE'RE ANGRY...

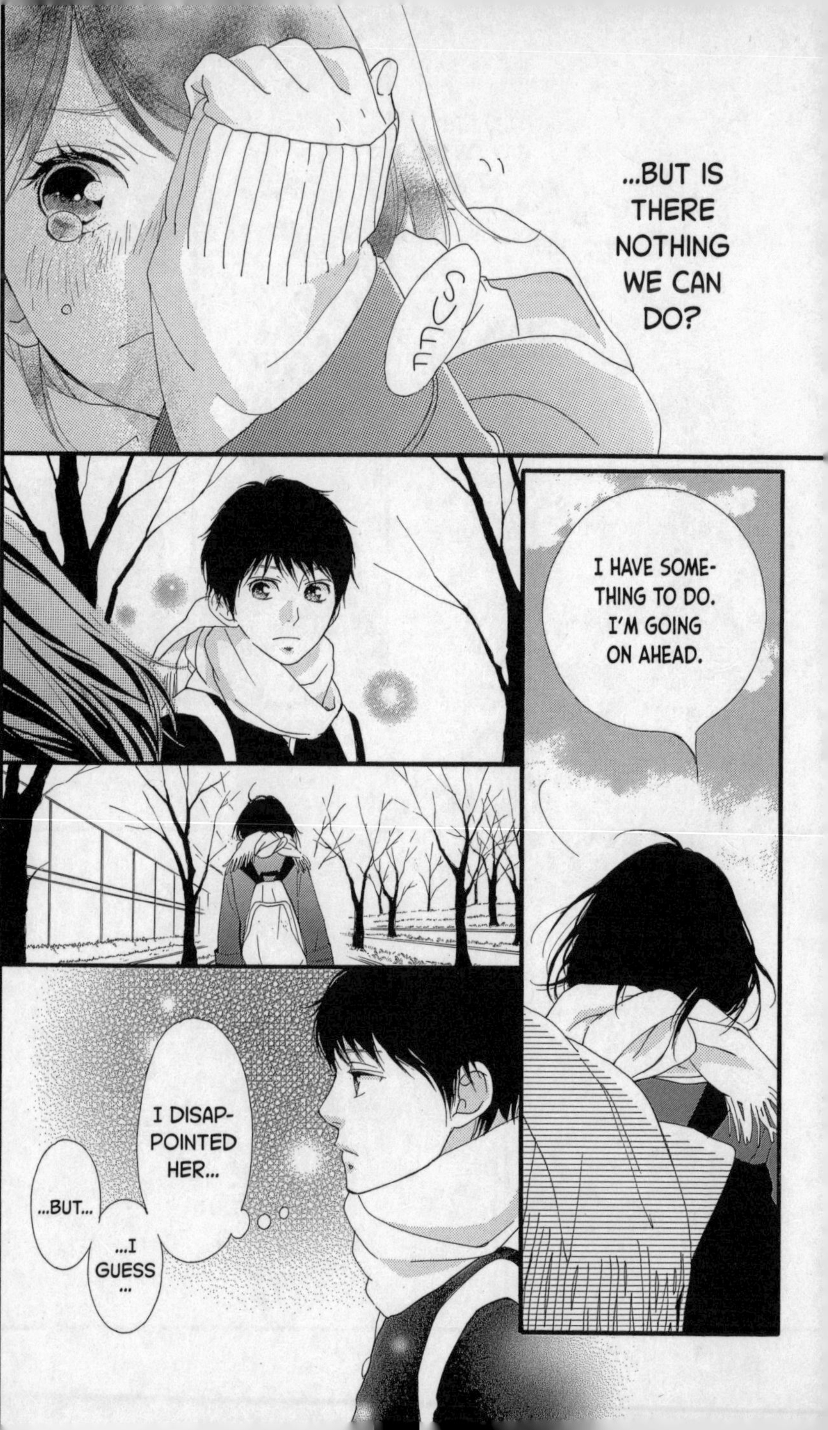
...BUT IS THERE NOTHING WE CAN DO?
SUFF
I HAVE SOME-THING TO DO. I'M GOING ON AHEAD.
I DISAP-POINTED HER...
...BUT...
...I GUESS ...

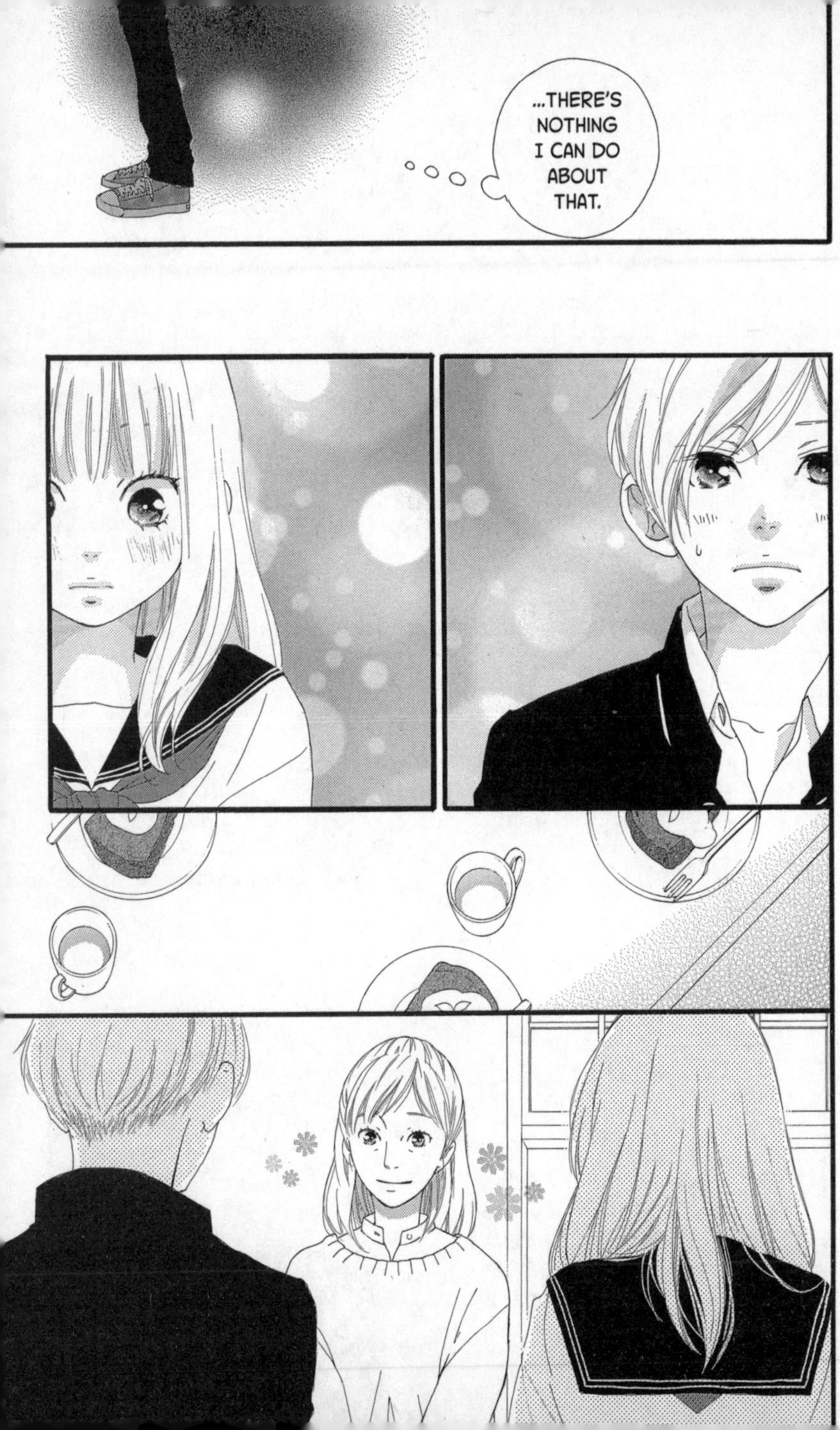
...THERE'S NOTHING I CAN DO ABOUT THAT.

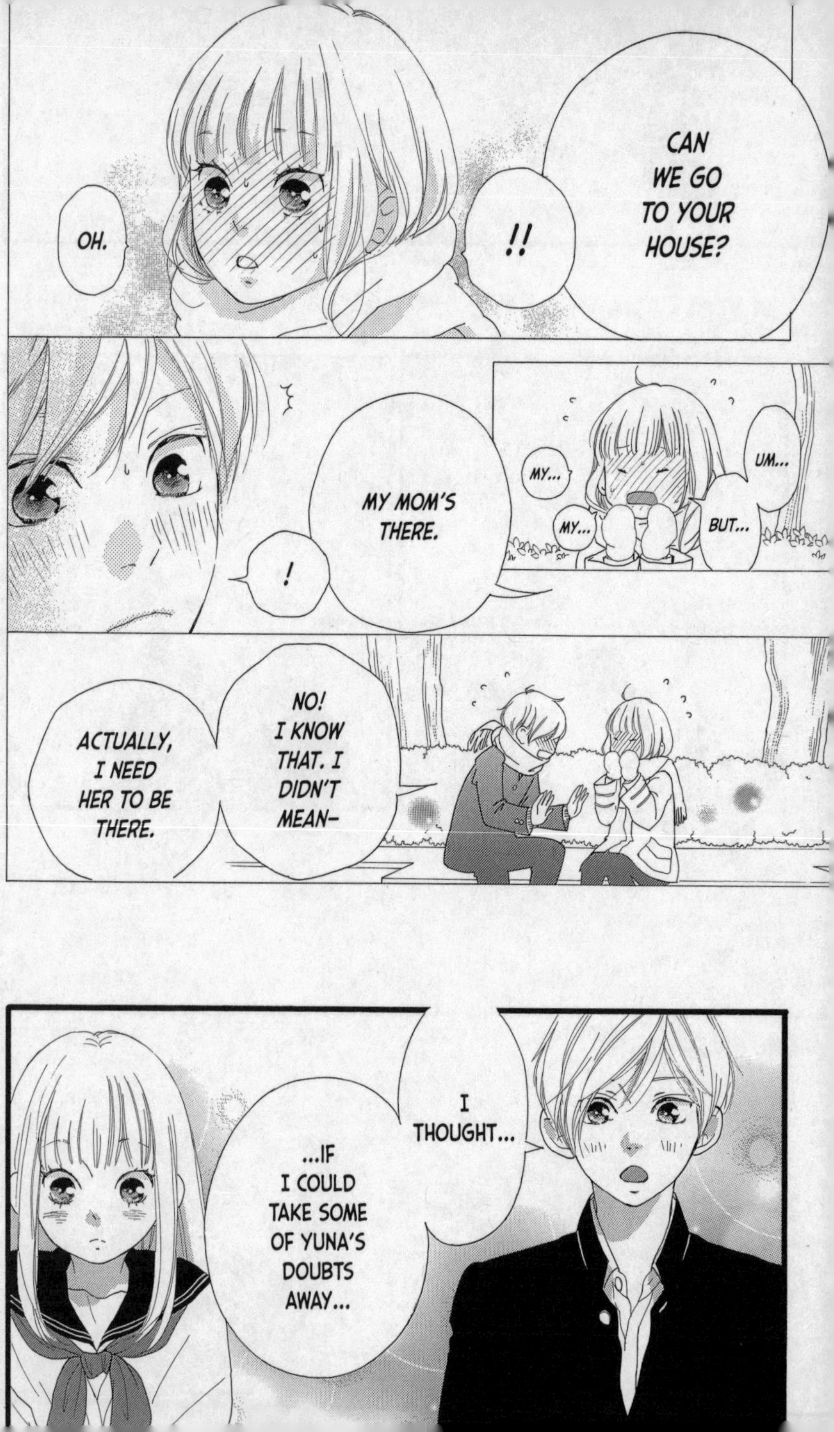
CAN WE GO TO YOUR HOUSE?
!!
OH.
UM...
BUT...
MY...
MY...
MY MOM'S THERE.
!
NO! I KNOW THAT. I DIDN'T MEAN–
ACTUALLY, I NEED HER TO BE THERE.
I THOUGHT...
...IF I COULD TAKE SOME OF YUNA'S DOUBTS AWAY...

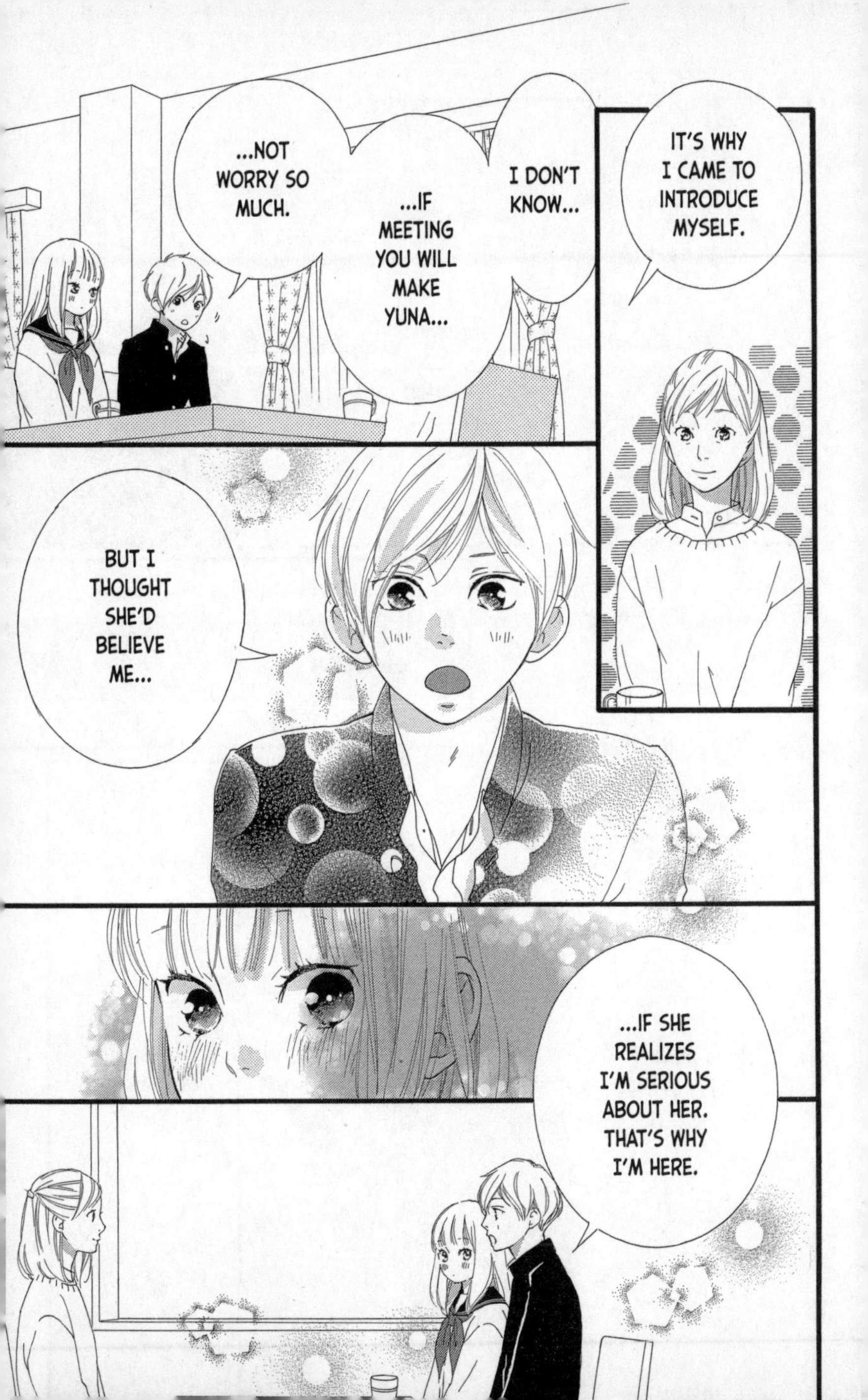
IT'S WHY I CAME TO INTRODUCE MYSELF.
I DON'T KNOW...
...IF MEETING YOU WILL MAKE YUNA...
...NOT WORRY SO MUCH.
BUT I THOUGHT SHE'D BELIEVE ME...
...IF SHE REALIZES I'M SERIOUS ABOUT HER. THAT'S WHY I'M HERE.

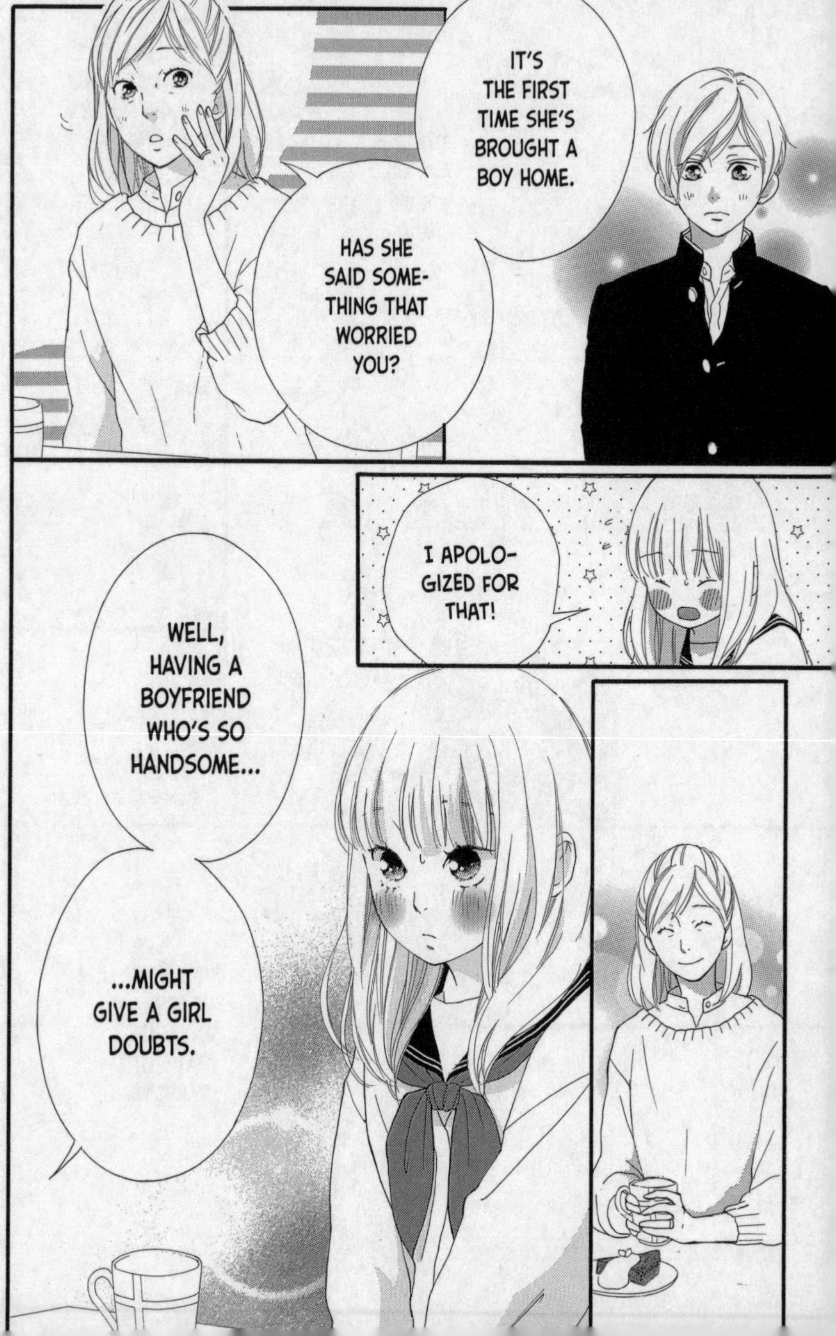
IT'S THE FIRST TIME SHE'S BROUGHT A BOY HOME.
HAS SHE SAID SOME-THING THAT WORRIED YOU?
I APOLO-GIZED FOR THAT!
WELL, HAVING A BOYFRIEND WHO'S SO HANDSOME...
...MIGHT GIVE A GIRL DOUBTS.

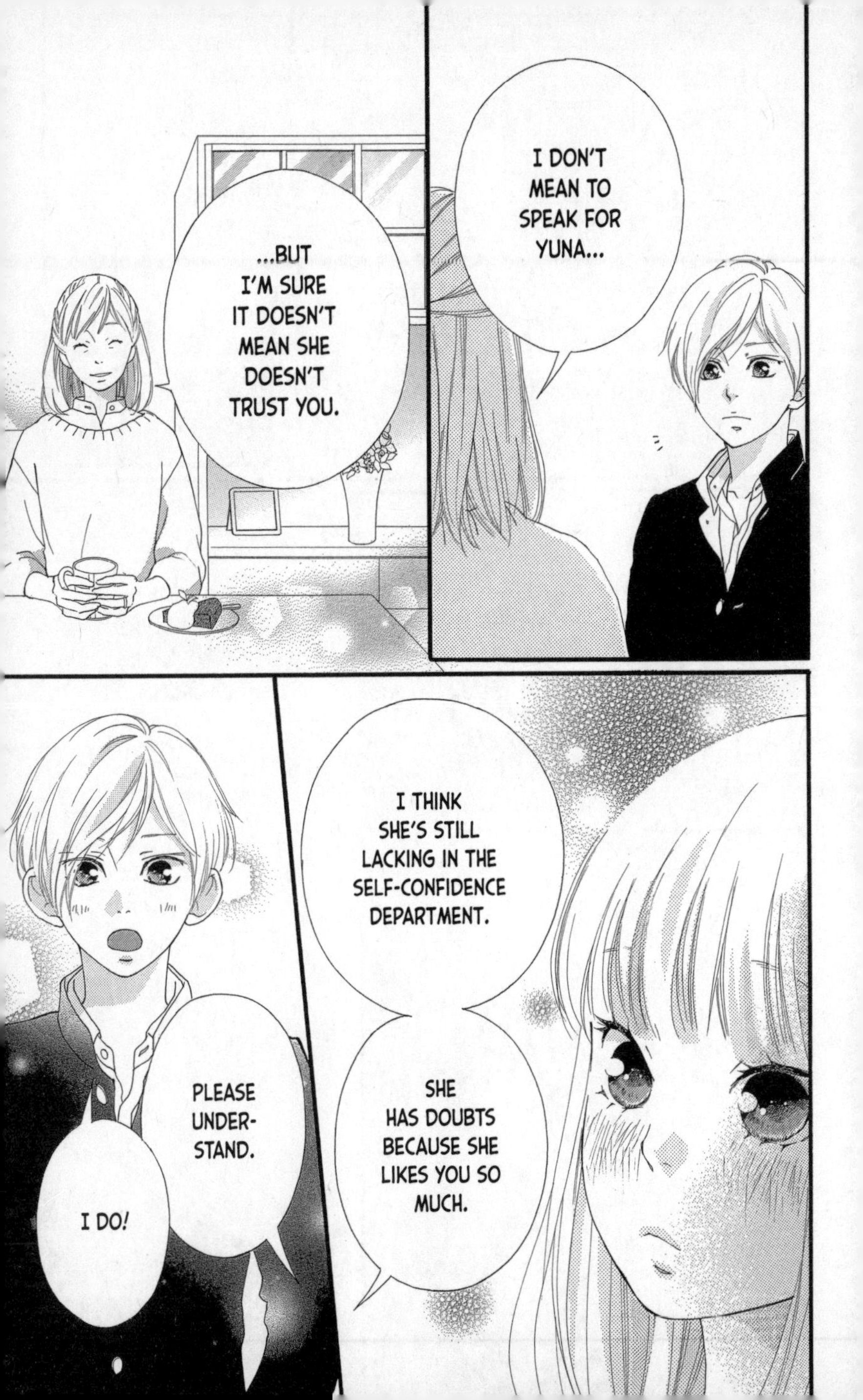
I DON'T MEAN TO SPEAK FOR YUNA...
...BUT I'M SURE IT DOESN'T MEAN SHE DOESN'T TRUST YOU.
I THINK SHE'S STILL LACKING IN THE SELF-CONFIDENCE DEPARTMENT.
SHE HAS DOUBTS BECAUSE SHE LIKES YOU SO MUCH.
PLEASE UNDER-STAND.
I DO!

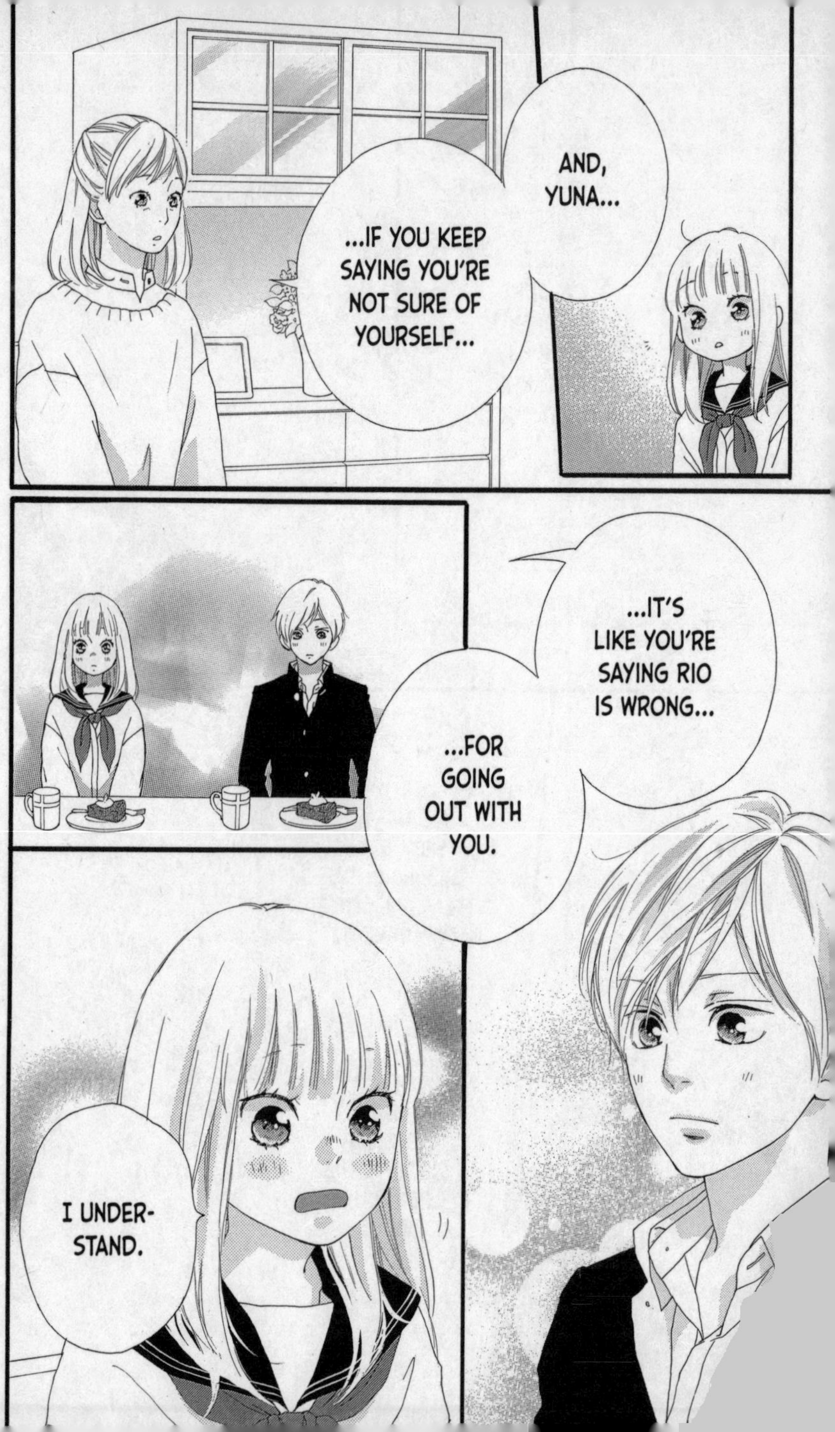
AND, YUNA...
...IF YOU KEEP SAYING YOU'RE NOT SURE OF YOURSELF...
...IT'S LIKE YOU'RE SAYING RIO IS WRONG...
...FOR GOING OUT WITH YOU.
I UNDER-STAND.

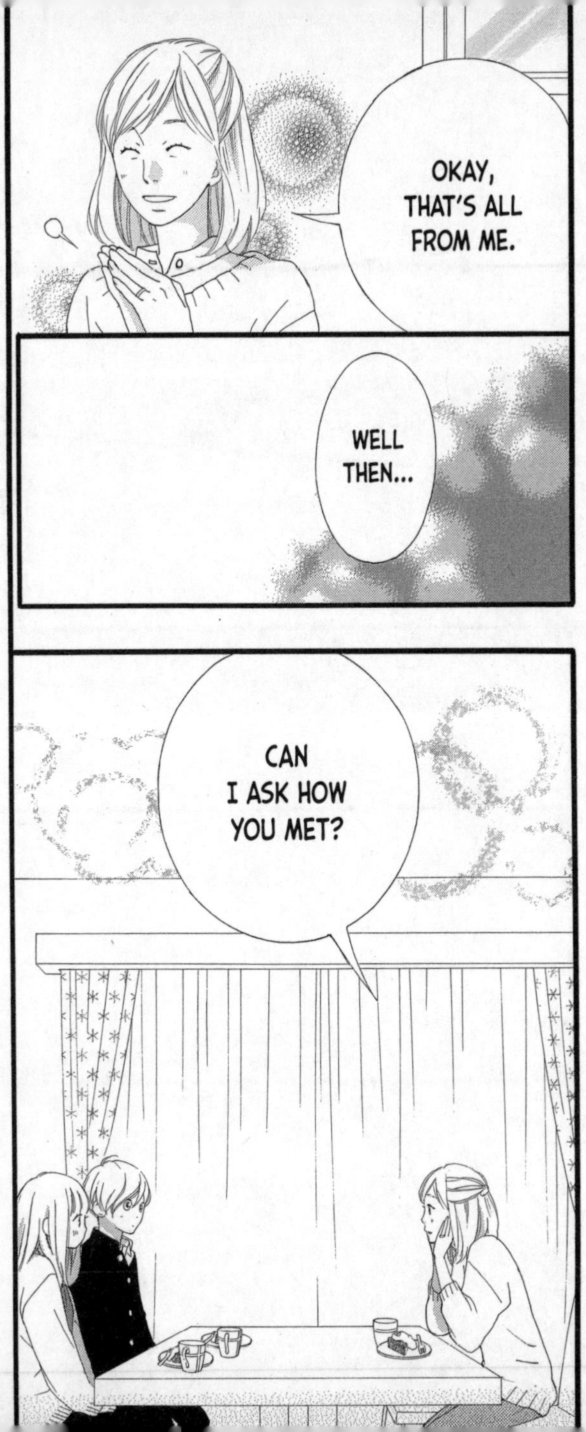
OKAY, THAT'S ALL FROM ME.
WELL THEN...
CAN I ASK HOW YOU MET?

I like Riverdance, the Irish dance group. They performed several times before in Japan, and I saw them then. I remember the music and dance having a huge impact on me. Dancing in a sharp straight line, doing their unique steps—it made me practically swoon because they were so cool. I've always been infatuated with uniform movements and formations, so Riverdance is the perfect entertainment for me. Back then I even bought the DVD and watched it over and over again. A couple of years ago, for their 20th anniversary tour, they came to Japan for the first time in a long while. I didn't see the information about it, so I was sad to discover it was over before I knew about it. I hope they perform again in Japan one day.

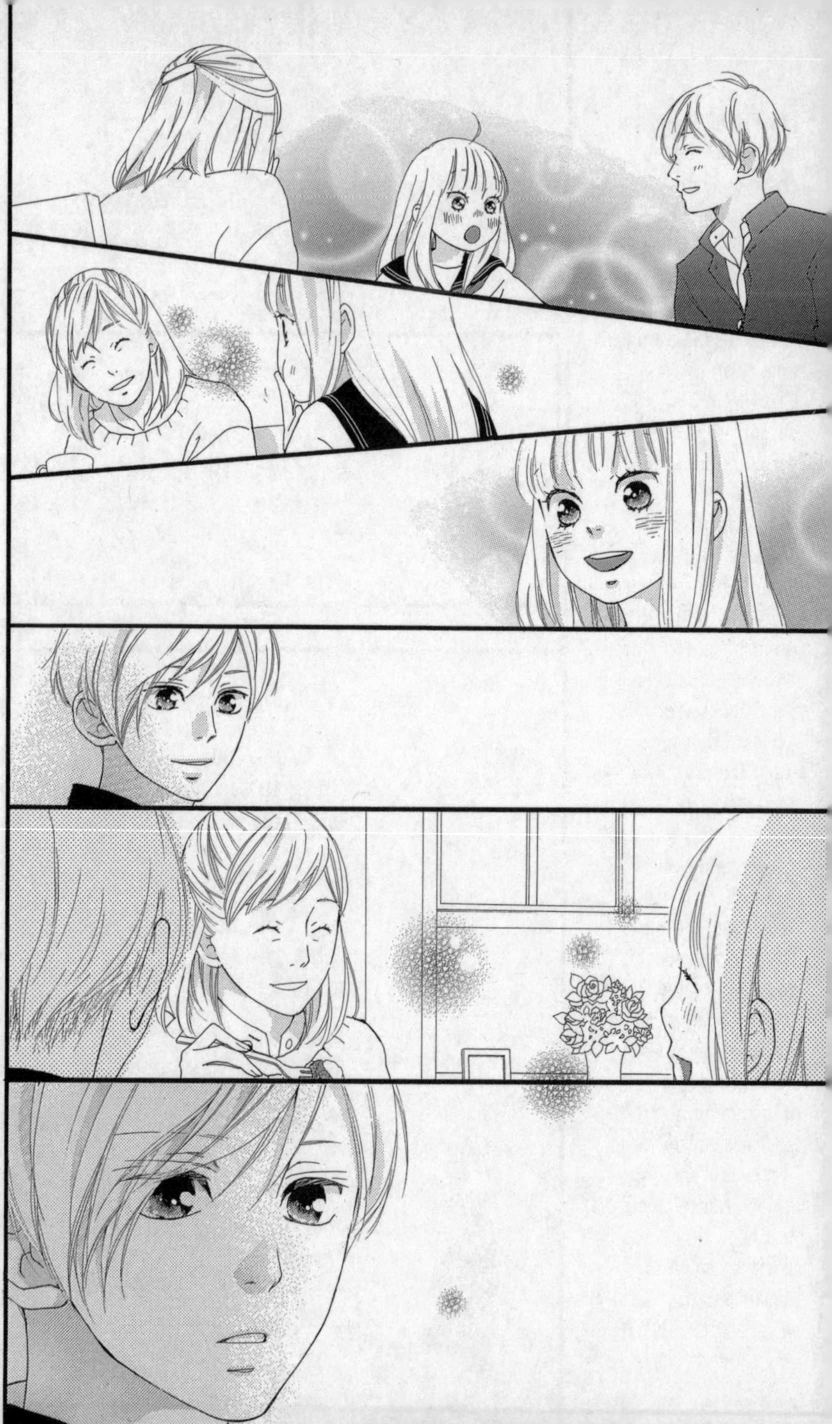

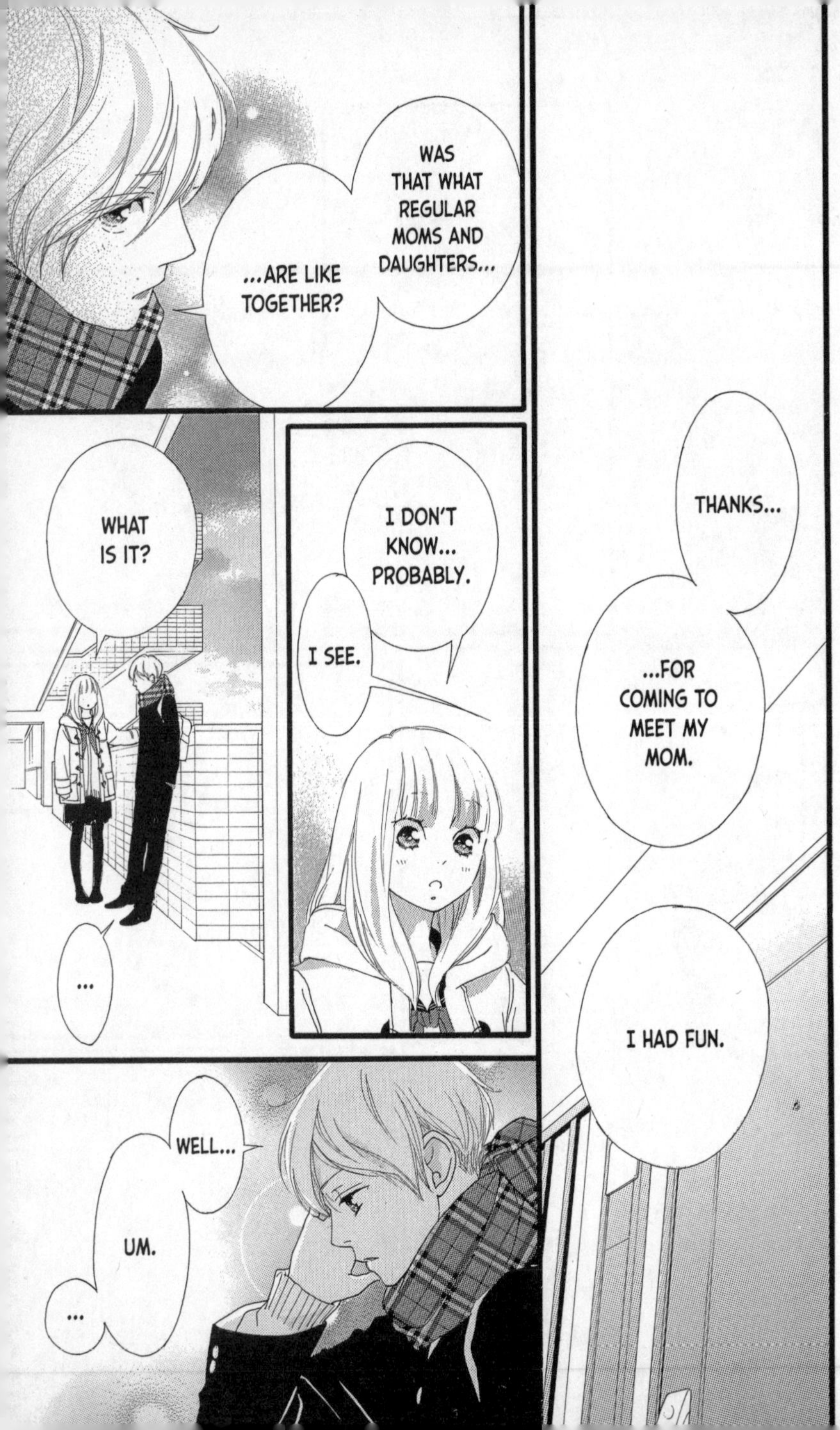
THANKS...
...FOR COMING TO MEET MY MOM.
I HAD FUN.
WAS THAT WHAT REGULAR MOMS AND DAUGHTERS...
...ARE LIKE TOGETHER?
I DON'T KNOW... PROBABLY.
I SEE.
WHAT IS IT?
...
WELL...
UM.
...

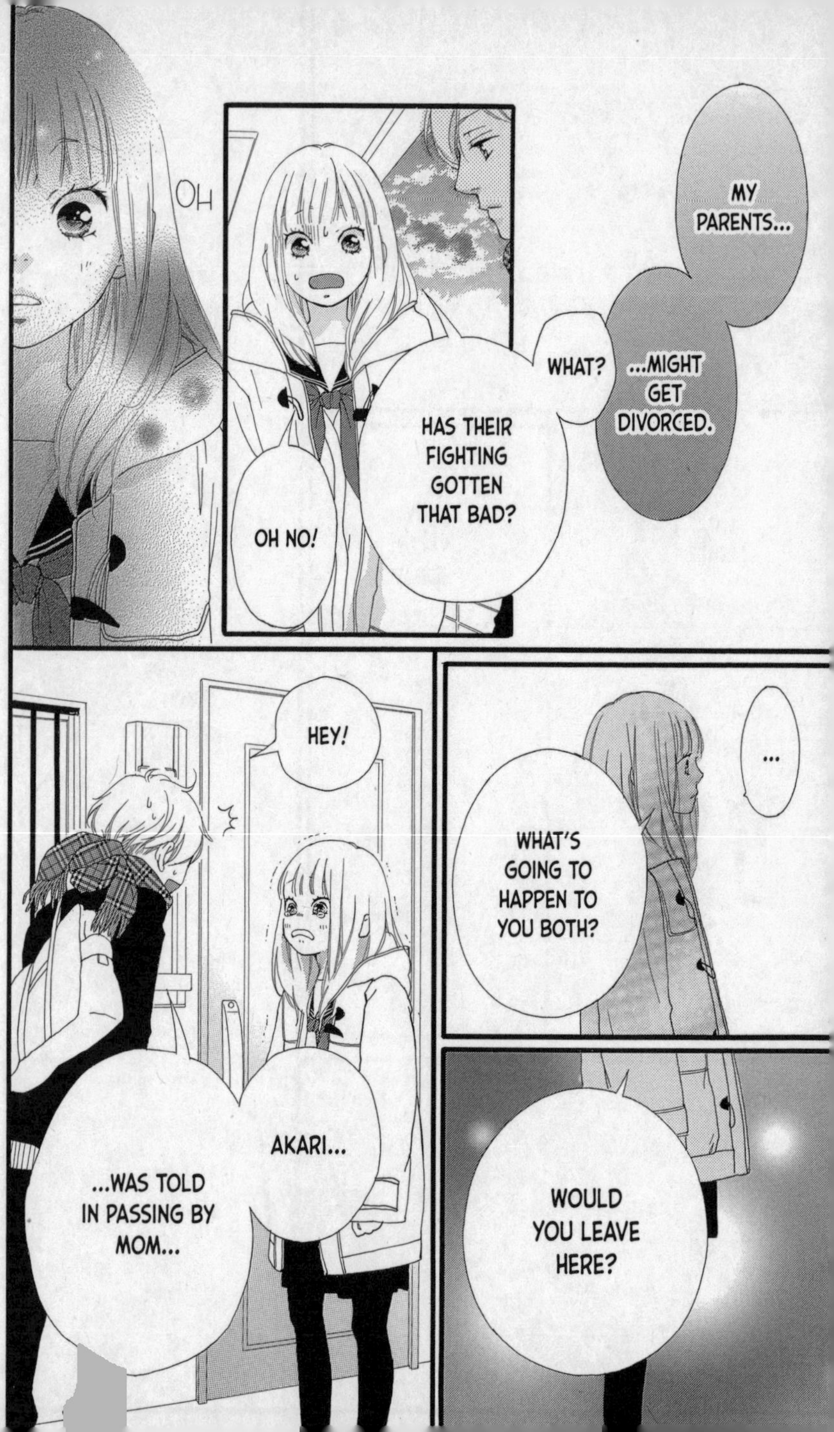
MY PARENTS...
...MIGHT GET DIVORCED.
WHAT?
HAS THEIR FIGHTING GOTTEN THAT BAD?
OH NO!
OH
...
WHAT'S GOING TO HAPPEN TO YOU BOTH?
WOULD YOU LEAVE HERE?
HEY!
AKARI...
...WAS TOLD IN PASSING BY MOM...

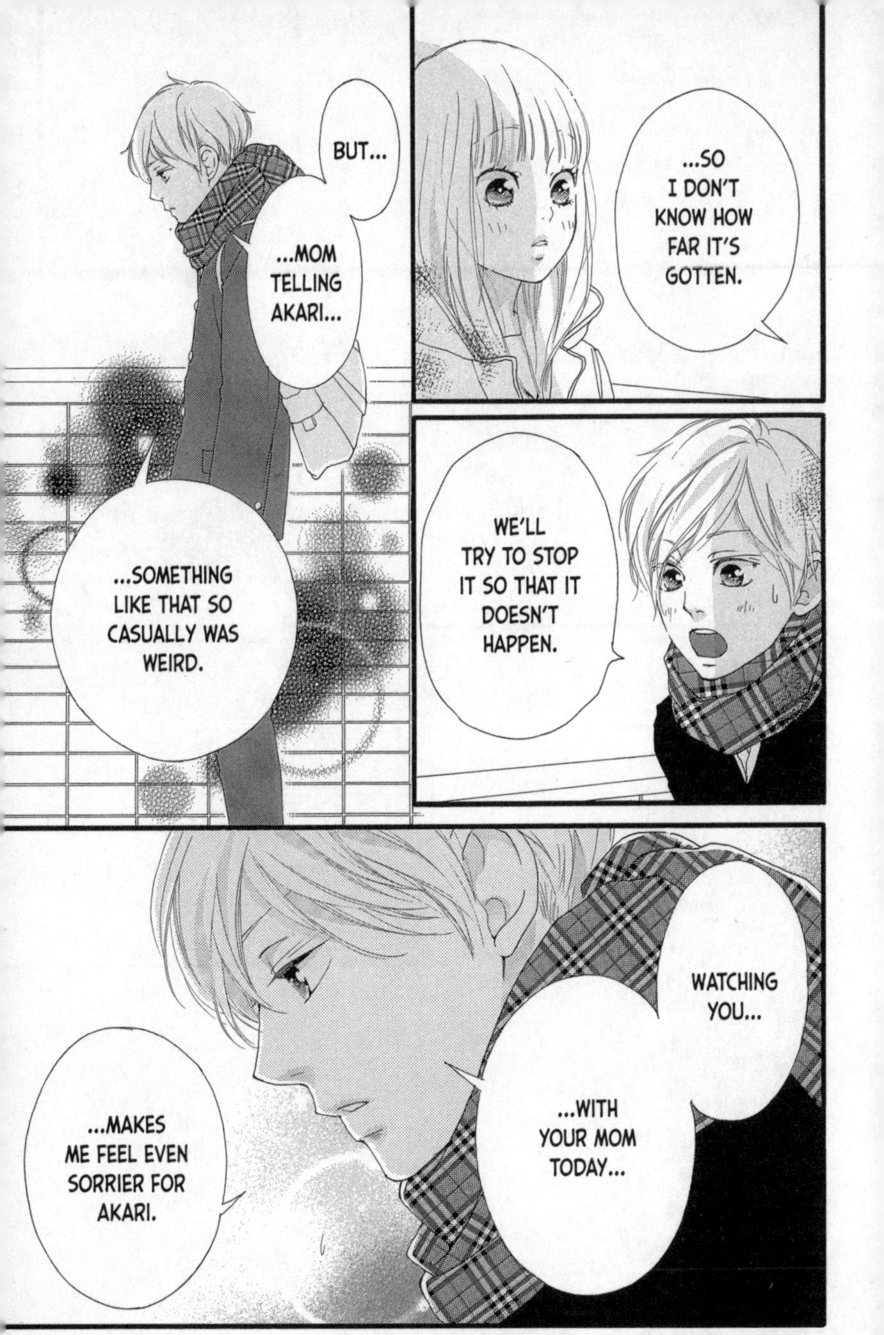
...SO I DON'T KNOW HOW FAR IT'S GOTTEN.
WE'LL TRY TO STOP IT SO THAT IT DOESN'T HAPPEN.
BUT...
...MOM TELLING AKARI...
...SOMETHING LIKE THAT SO CASUALLY WAS WEIRD.
WATCHING YOU...
...WITH YOUR MOM TODAY...
...MAKES ME FEEL EVEN SORRIER FOR AKARI.

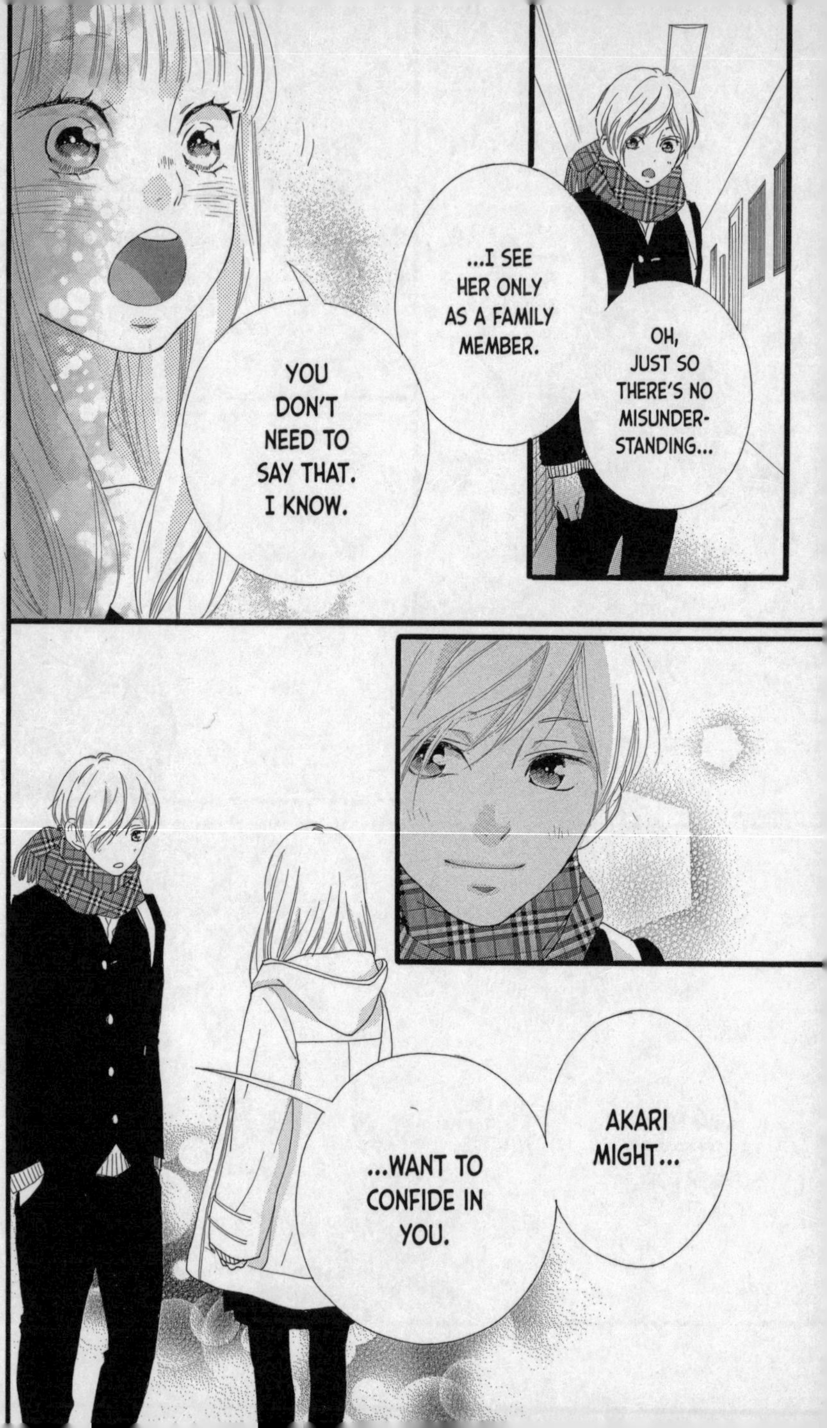
OH, JUST SO THERE'S NO MISUNDER-STANDING...
...I SEE HER ONLY AS A FAMILY MEMBER.
YOU DON'T NEED TO SAY THAT. I KNOW.
AKARI MIGHT...
...WANT TO CONFIDE IN YOU.

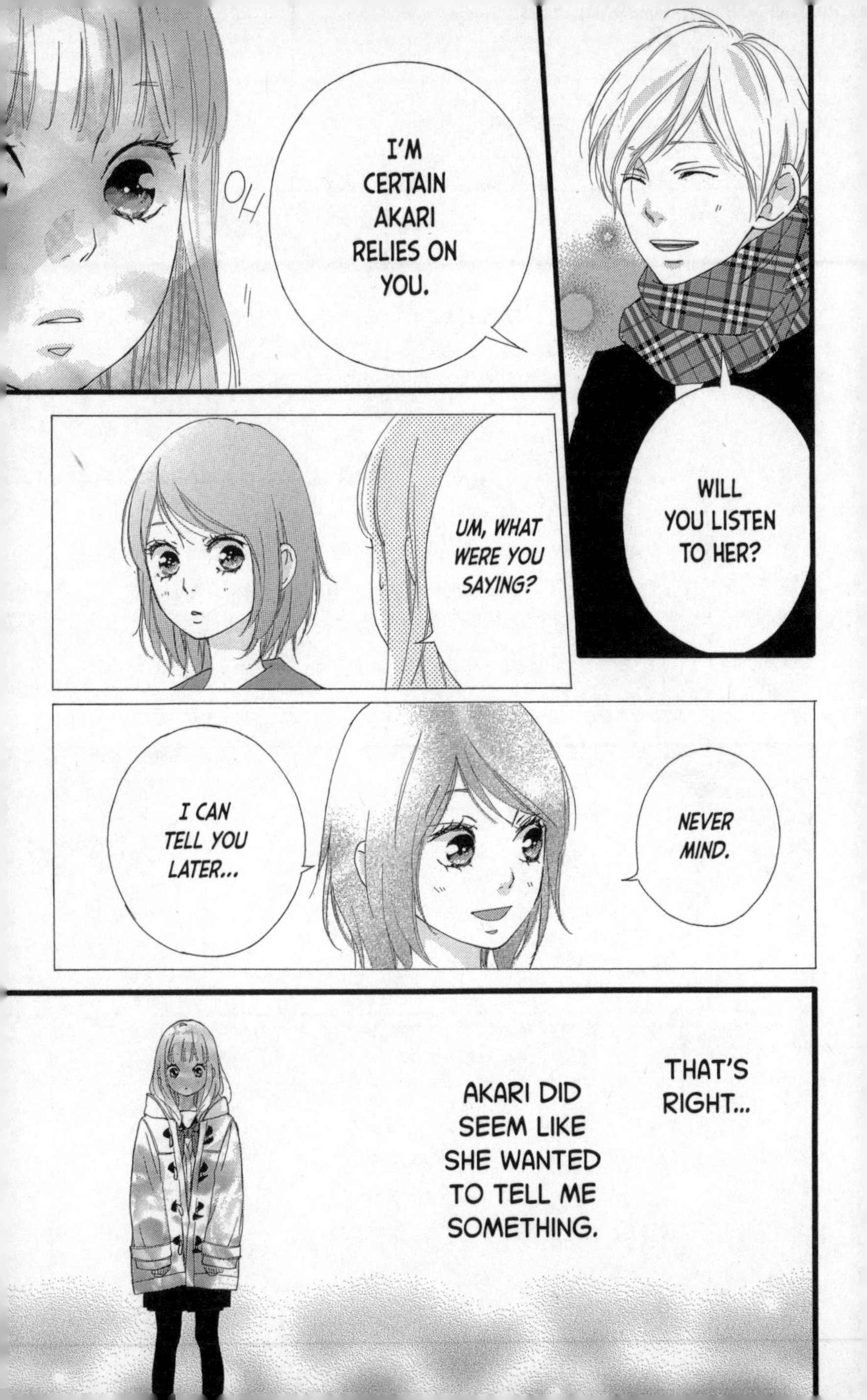
WILL YOU LISTEN TO HER?
I'M CERTAIN AKARI RELIES ON YOU.
OH
UM, WHAT WERE YOU SAYING?
NEVER MIND.
I CAN TELL YOU LATER...
THAT'S RIGHT...
AKARI DID SEEM LIKE SHE WANTED TO TELL ME SOMETHING.

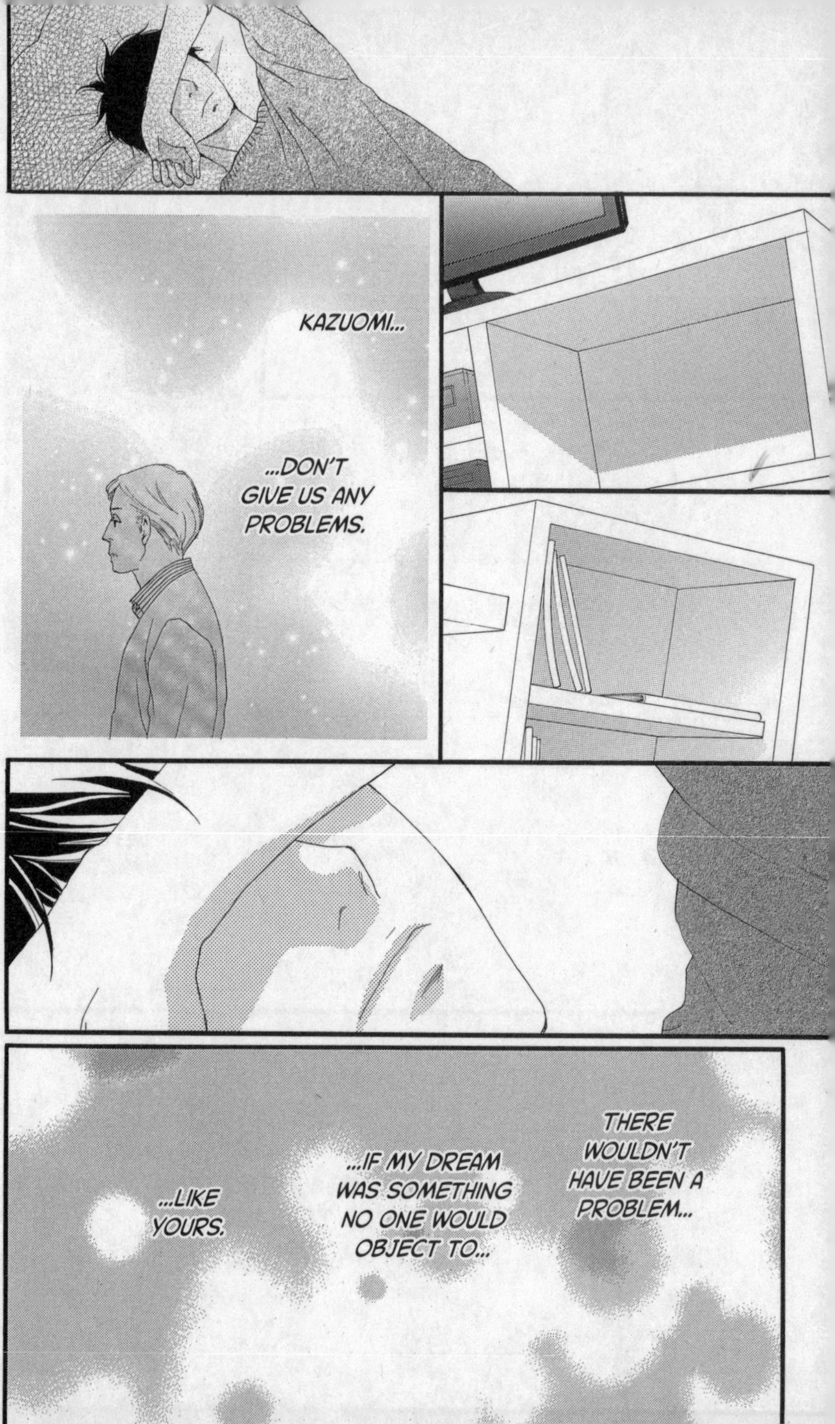
KAZUOMI...
...DON'T GIVE US ANY PROBLEMS.
THERE WOULDN'T HAVE BEEN A PROBLEM...
...IF MY DREAM WAS SOMETHING NO ONE WOULD OBJECT TO...
...LIKE YOURS.

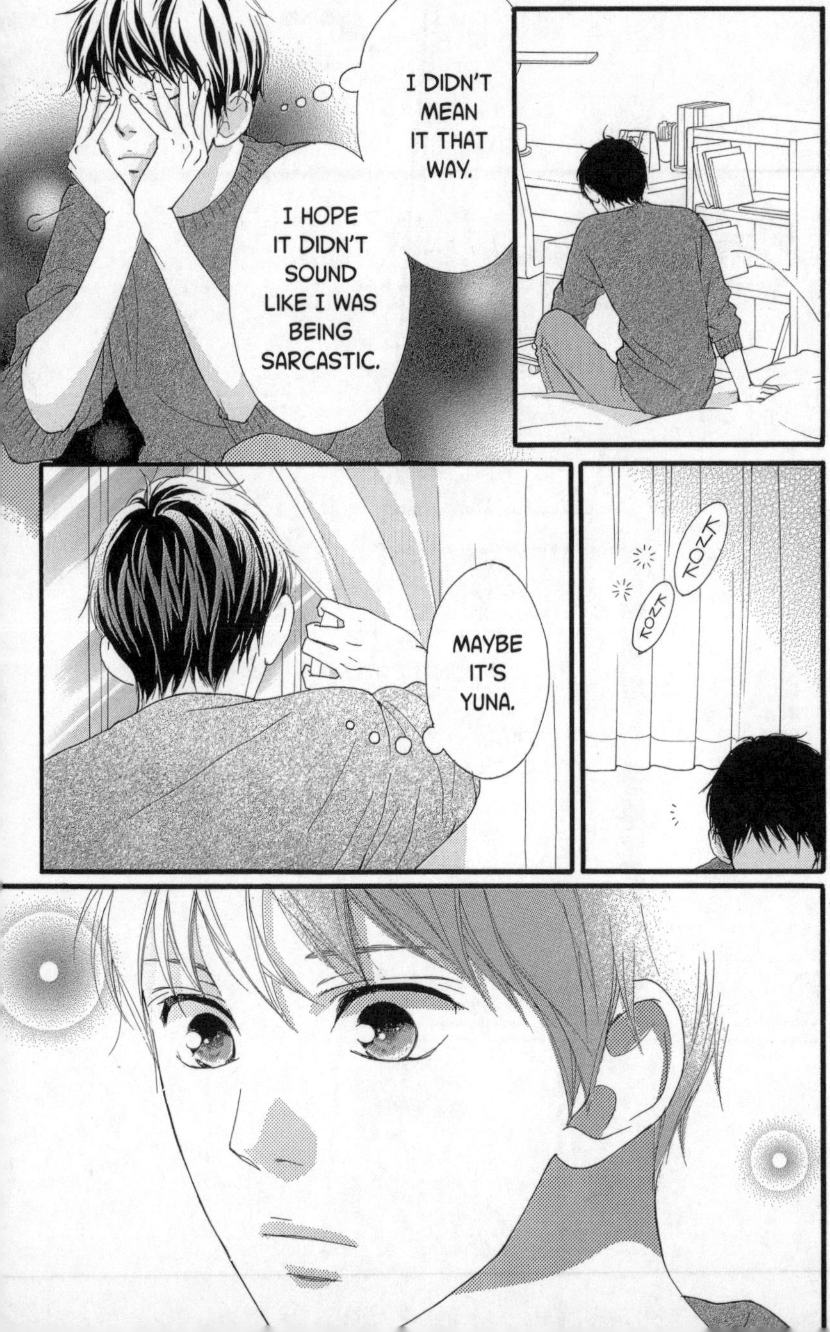
I DIDN'T MEAN IT THAT WAY.
I HOPE IT DIDN'T SOUND LIKE I WAS BEING SARCASTIC.
KONK
KONK
MAYBE IT'S YUNA.

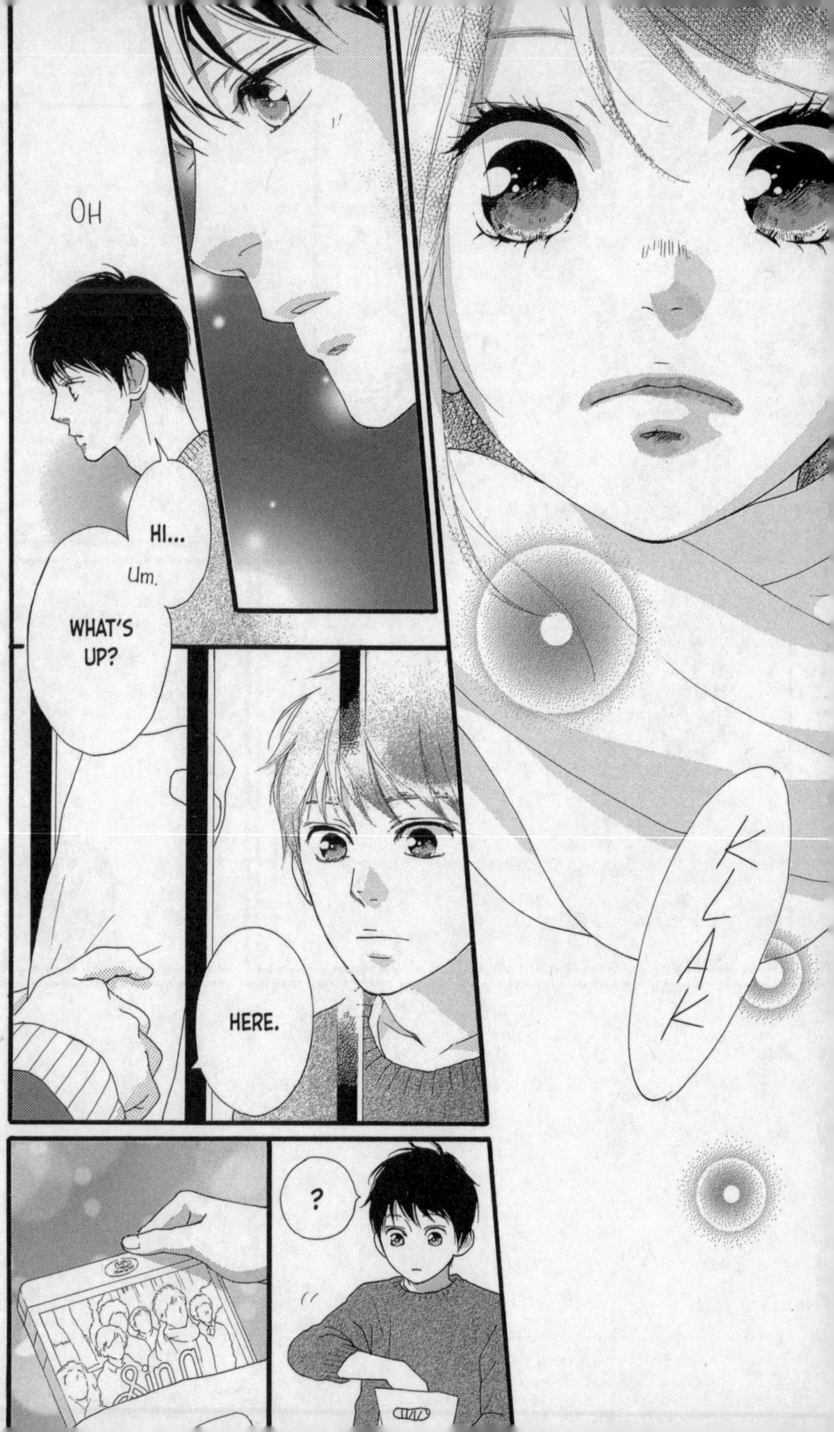
KLAK
OH
HI...
Um.
WHAT'S UP?
HERE.
?

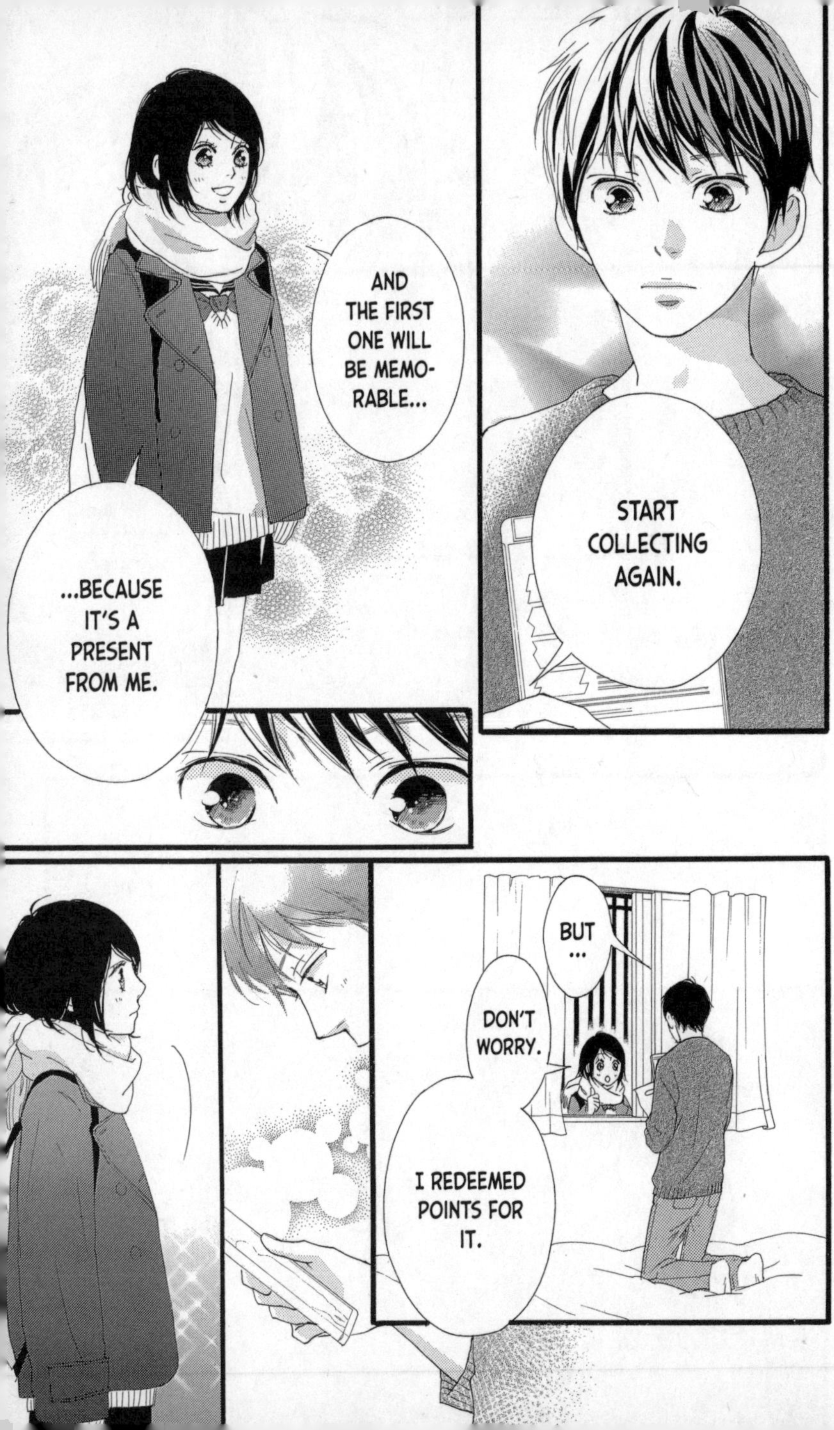
START COLLECTING AGAIN.
AND THE FIRST ONE WILL BE MEMO-RABLE...
...BECAUSE IT'S A PRESENT FROM ME.
BUT ...
DON'T WORRY.
I REDEEMED POINTS FOR IT.

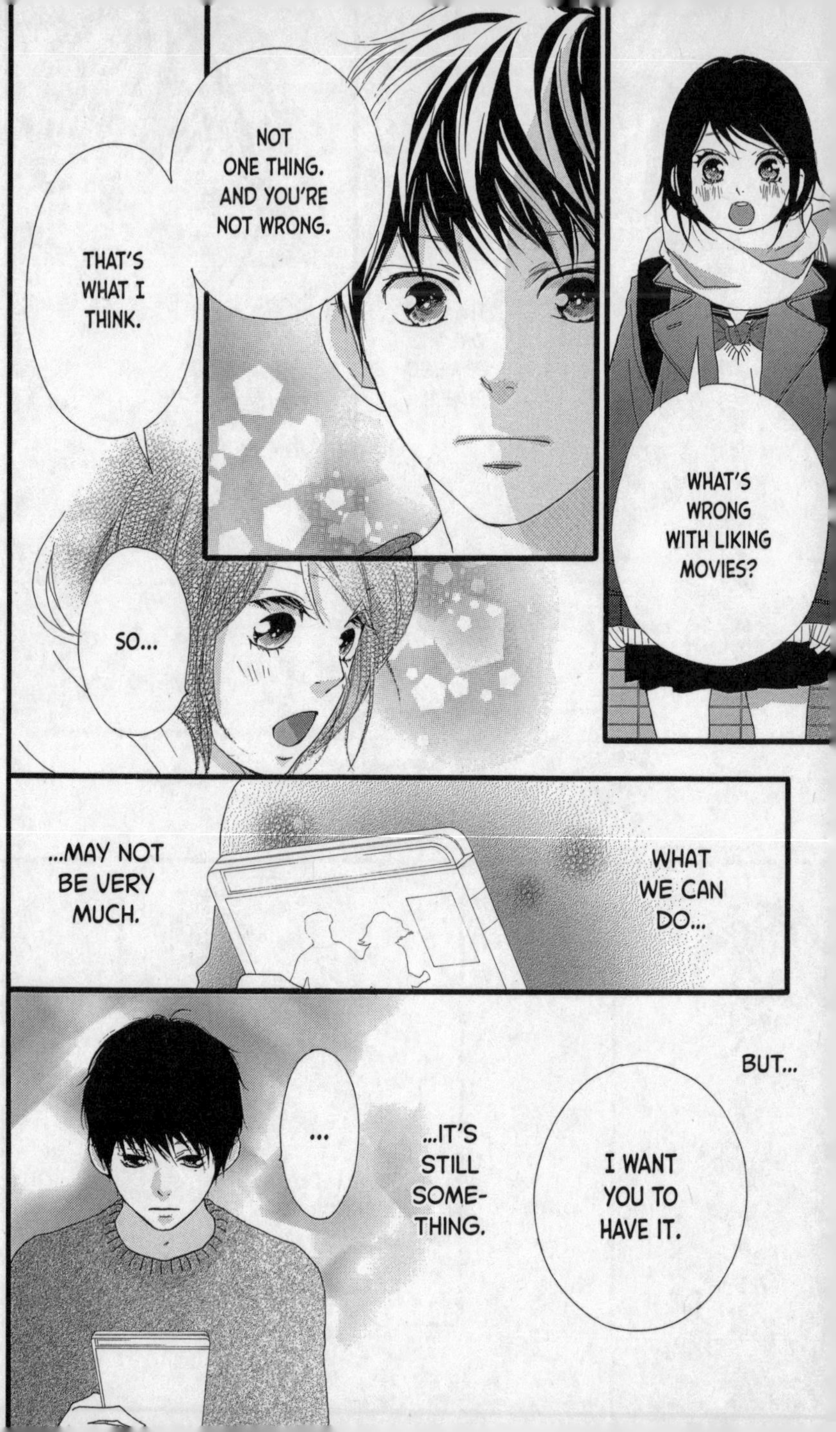
WHAT'S WRONG WITH LIKING MOVIES?
NOT ONE THING. AND YOU'RE NOT WRONG.
THAT'S WHAT I THINK.
SO...
WHAT WE CAN DO...
...MAY NOT BE VERY MUCH.
BUT...
I WANT YOU TO HAVE IT.
...IT'S STILL SOMETHING.
...

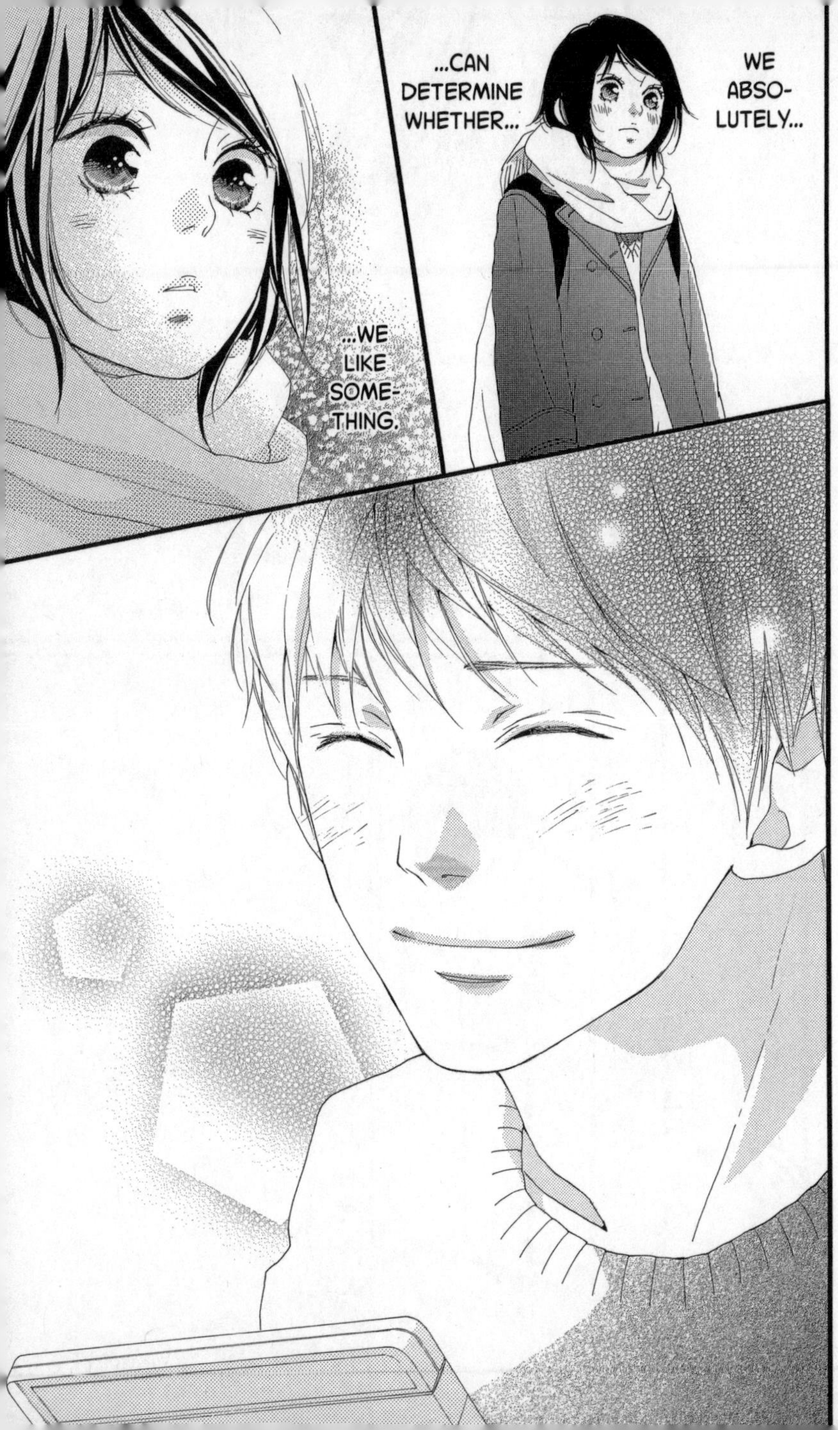
WE ABSO-LUTELY...
...CAN DETERMINE WHETHER...
...WE LIKE SOME-THING.

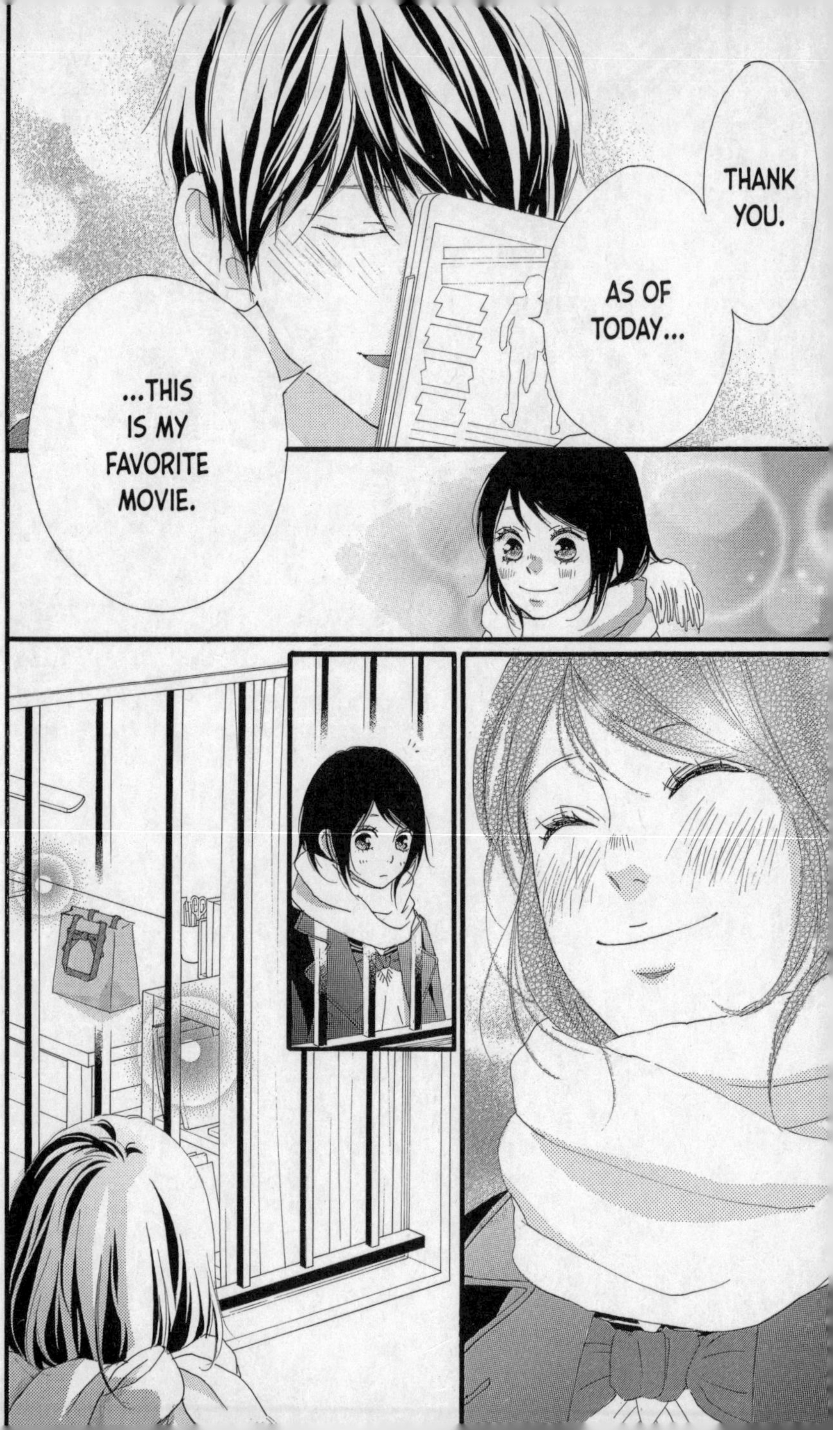
THANK YOU.
AS OF TODAY...
...THIS IS MY FAVORITE MOVIE.

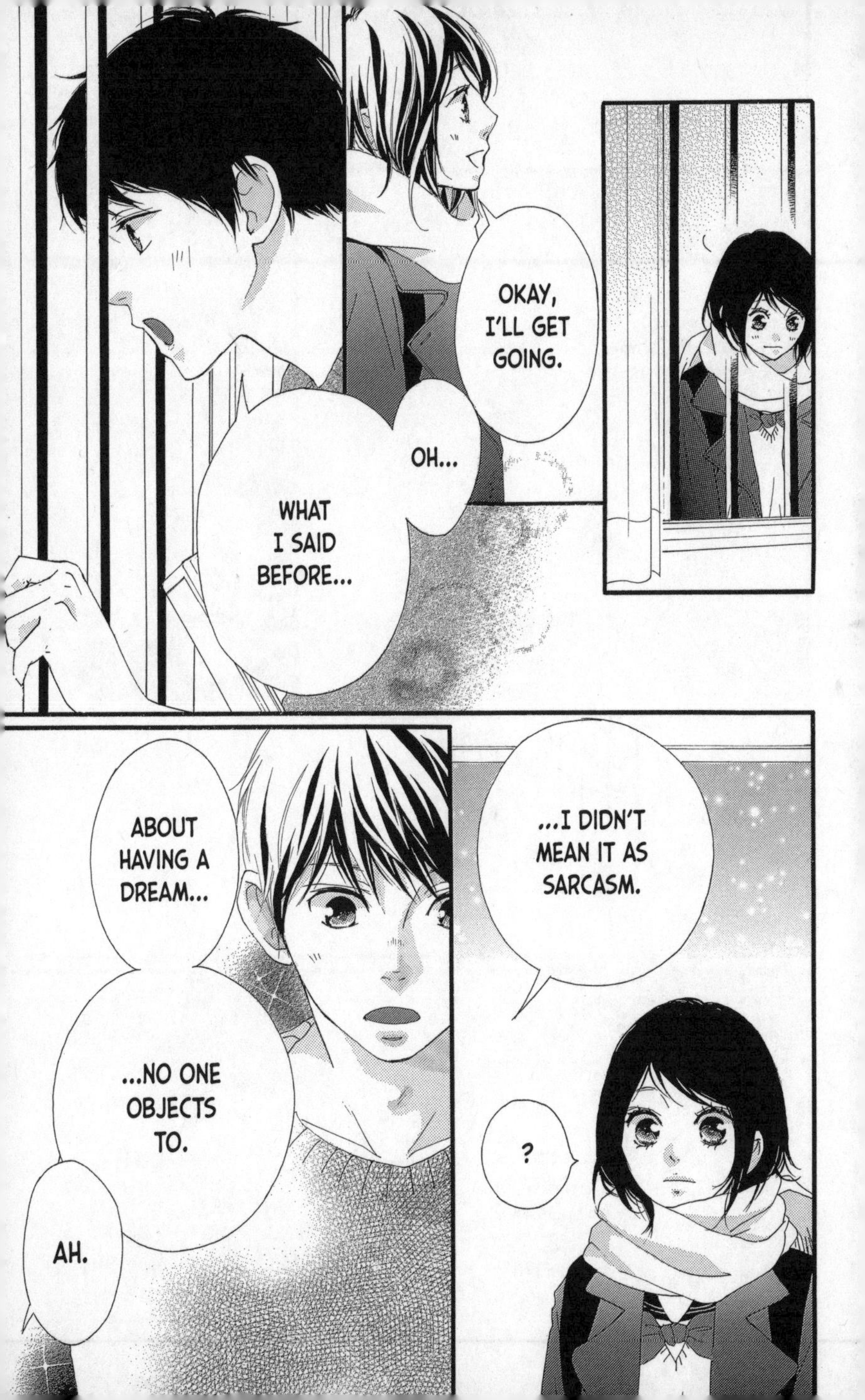
OKAY, I'LL GET GOING.
OH...
WHAT I SAID BEFORE...
...I DIDN'T MEAN IT AS SARCASM.
?
ABOUT HAVING A DREAM...
...NO ONE OBJECTS TO.
AH.

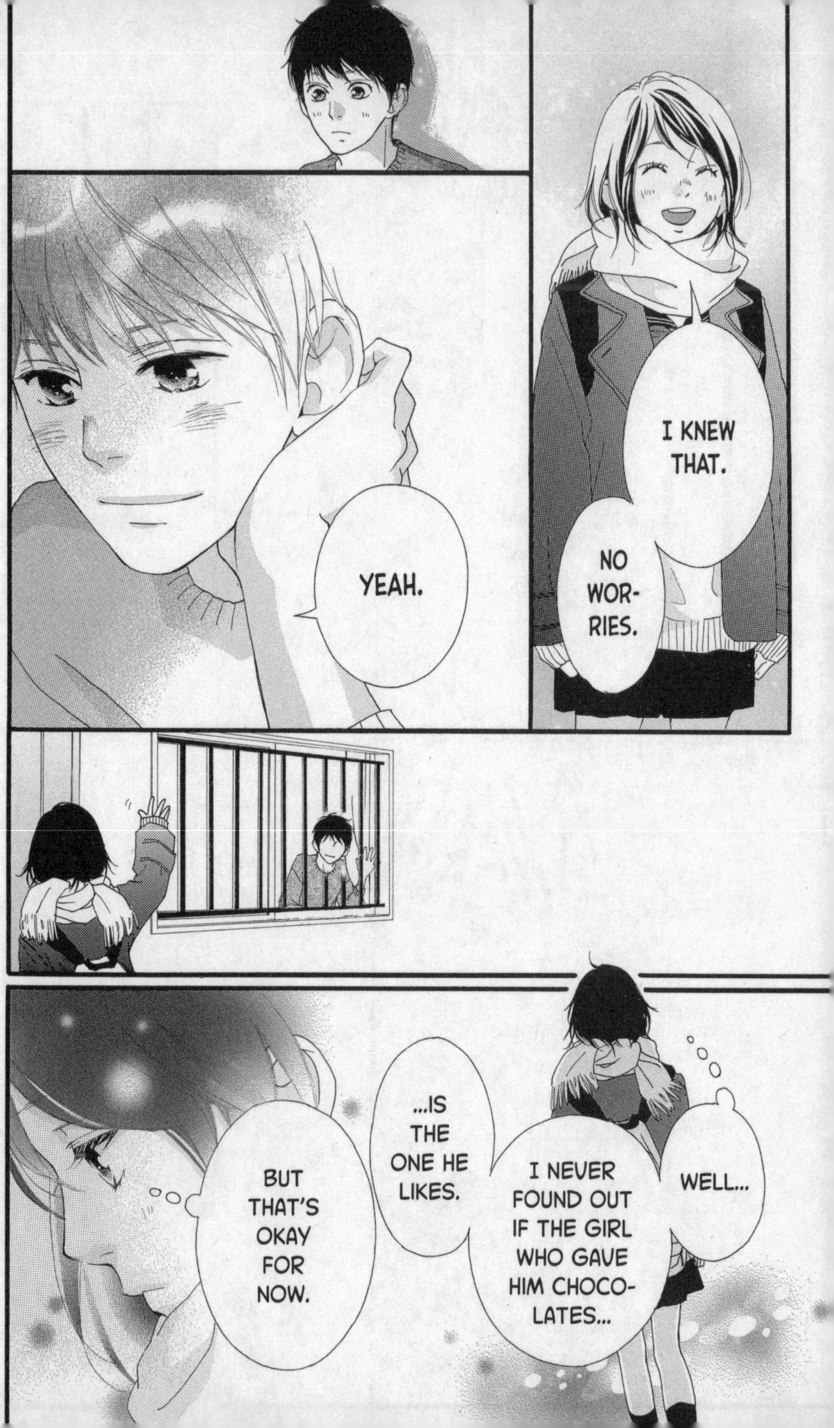
I KNEW THAT.
NO WORRIES.
YEAH.
WELL...
I NEVER FOUND OUT IF THE GIRL WHO GAVE HIM CHOCOLATES...
...IS THE ONE HE LIKES.
BUT THAT'S OKAY FOR NOW.

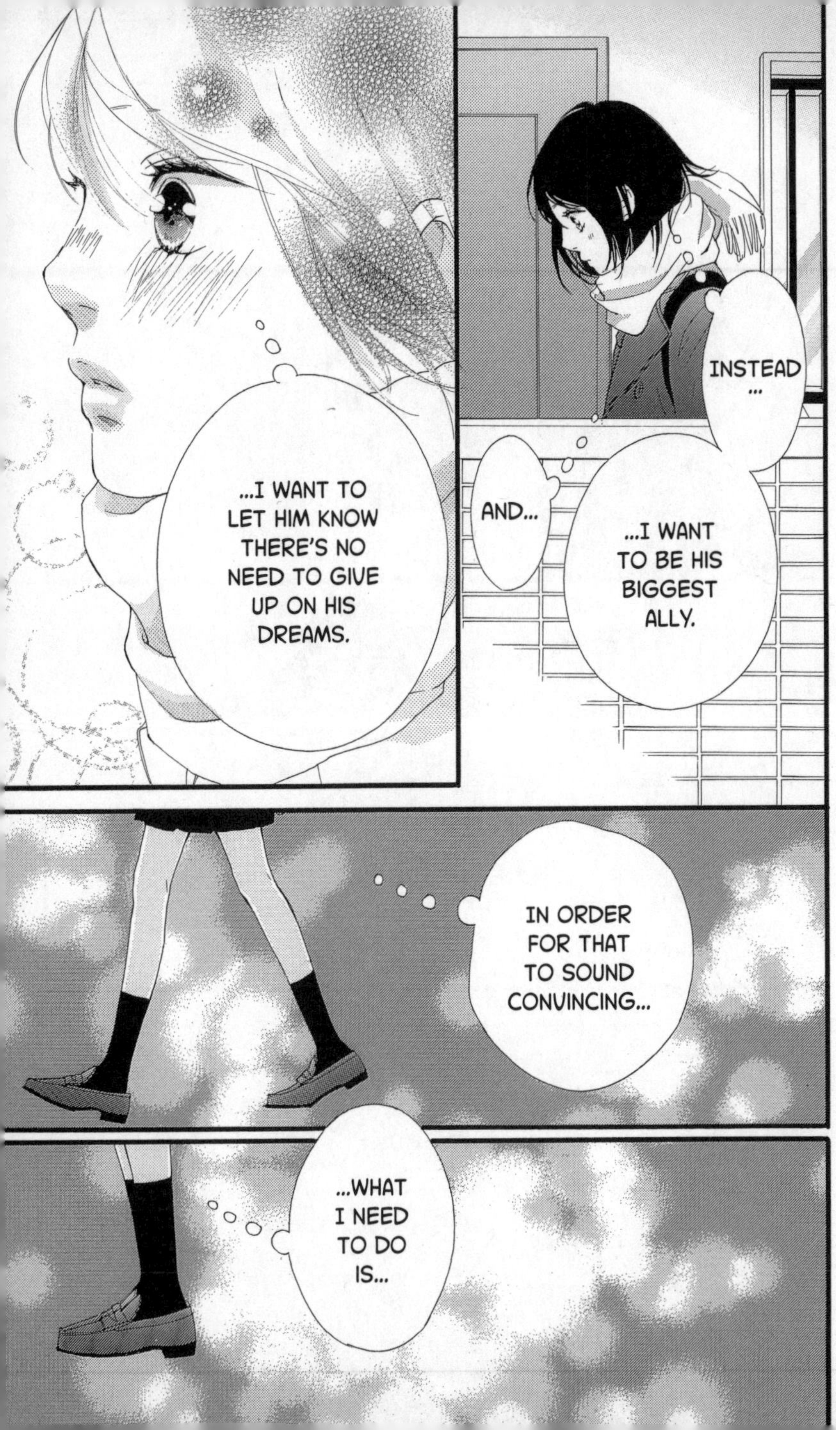
INSTEAD...
...I WANT TO BE HIS BIGGEST ALLY.
AND...
...I WANT TO LET HIM KNOW THERE'S NO NEED TO GIVE UP ON HIS DREAMS.
IN ORDER FOR THAT TO SOUND CONVINCING...
...WHAT I NEED TO DO IS...

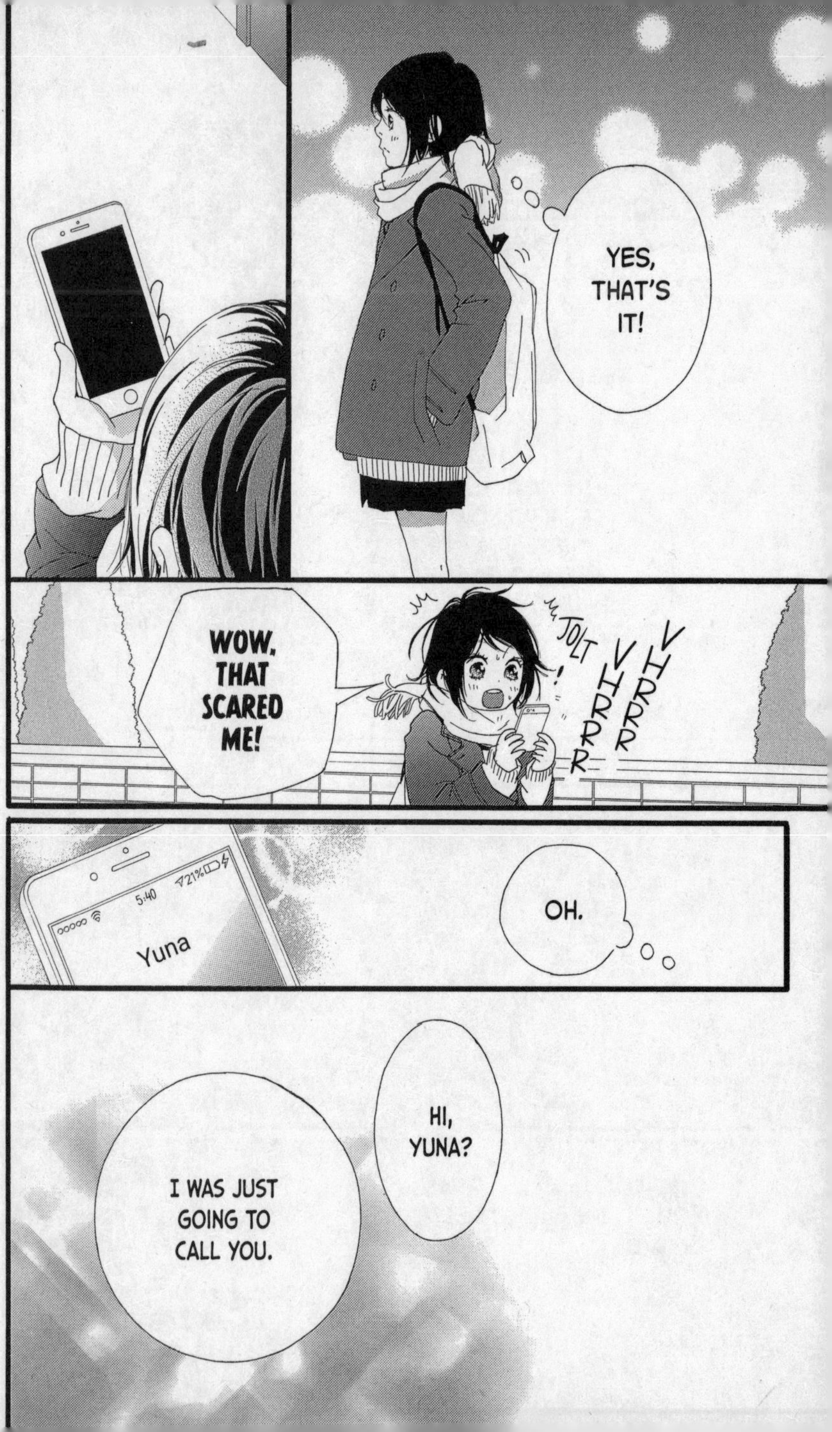

YES, THAT'S IT!
WOW. THAT SCARED ME!
VHRRR
VHRRR
JOLT
OH.
21%
5:40
Yuna
HI, YUNA?
I WAS JUST GOING TO CALL YOU.

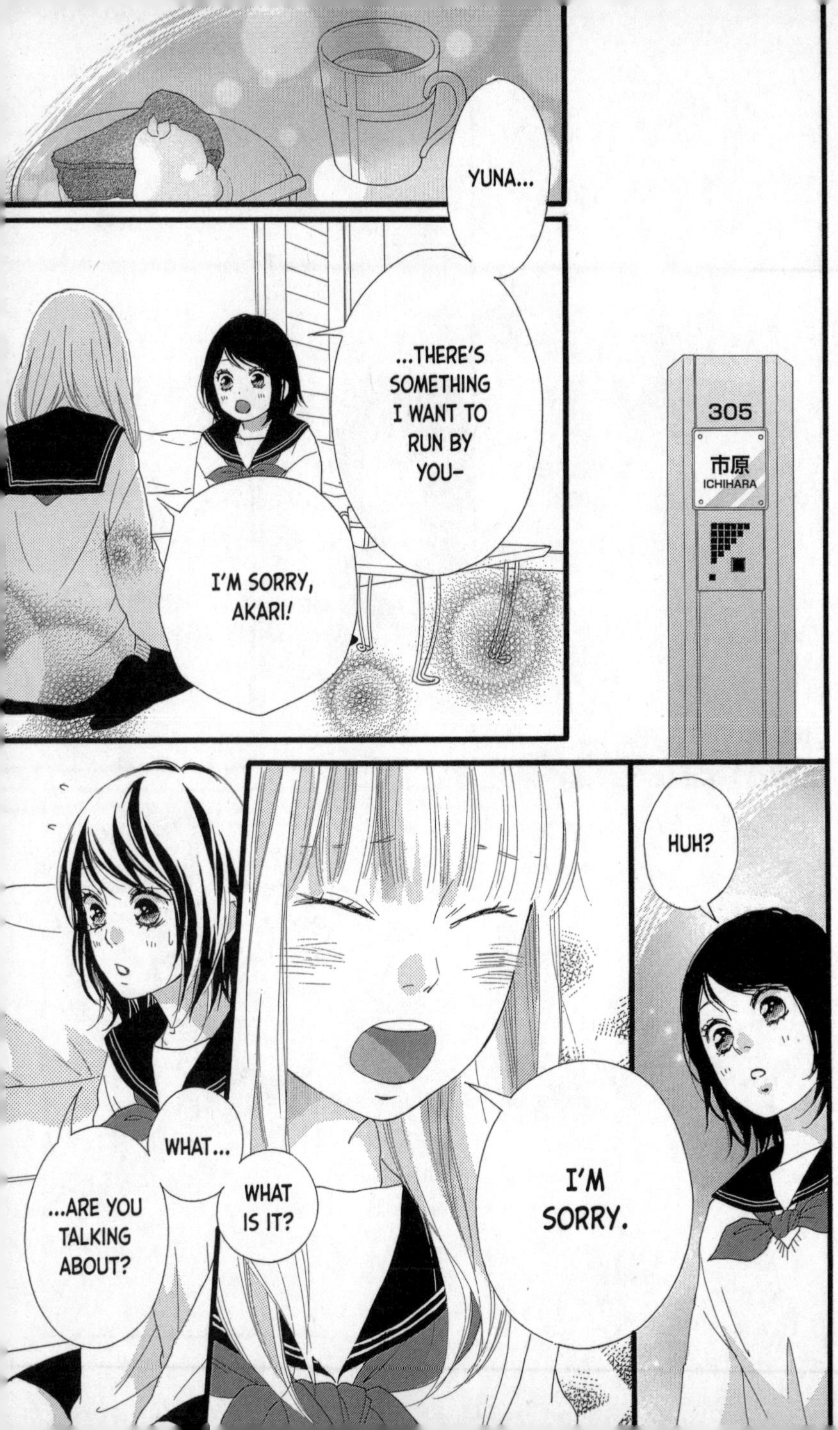

305
市原
ICHIHARA
YUNA...
...THERE'S SOMETHING I WANT TO RUN BY YOU–
I'M SORRY, AKARI!
HUH?
I'M SORRY.
WHAT IS IT?
WHAT...
...ARE YOU TALKING ABOUT?

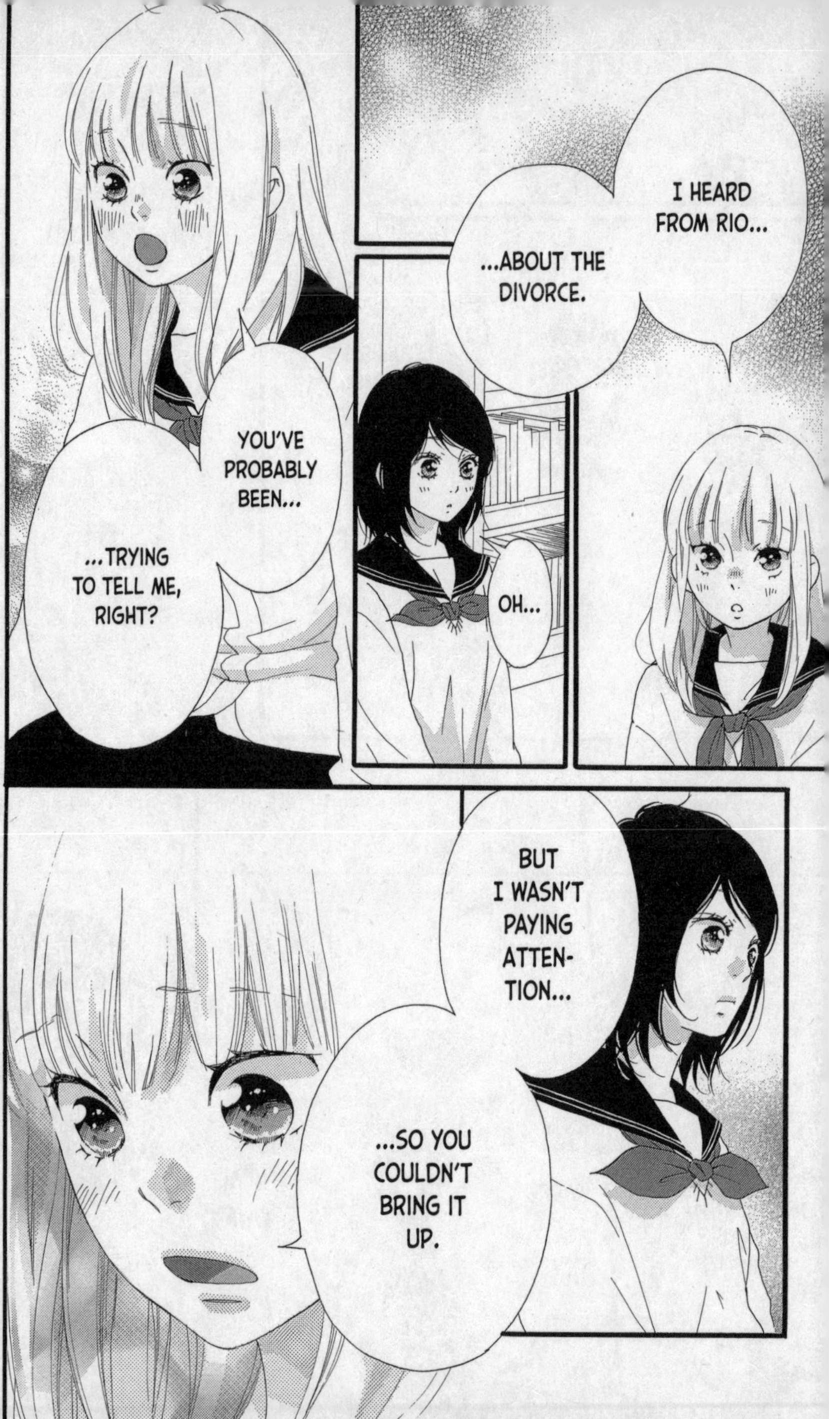
I HEARD FROM RIO...
...ABOUT THE DIVORCE.
OH...
YOU'VE PROBABLY BEEN...
...TRYING TO TELL ME, RIGHT?
BUT I WASN'T PAYING ATTEN-TION...
...SO YOU COULDN'T BRING IT UP.

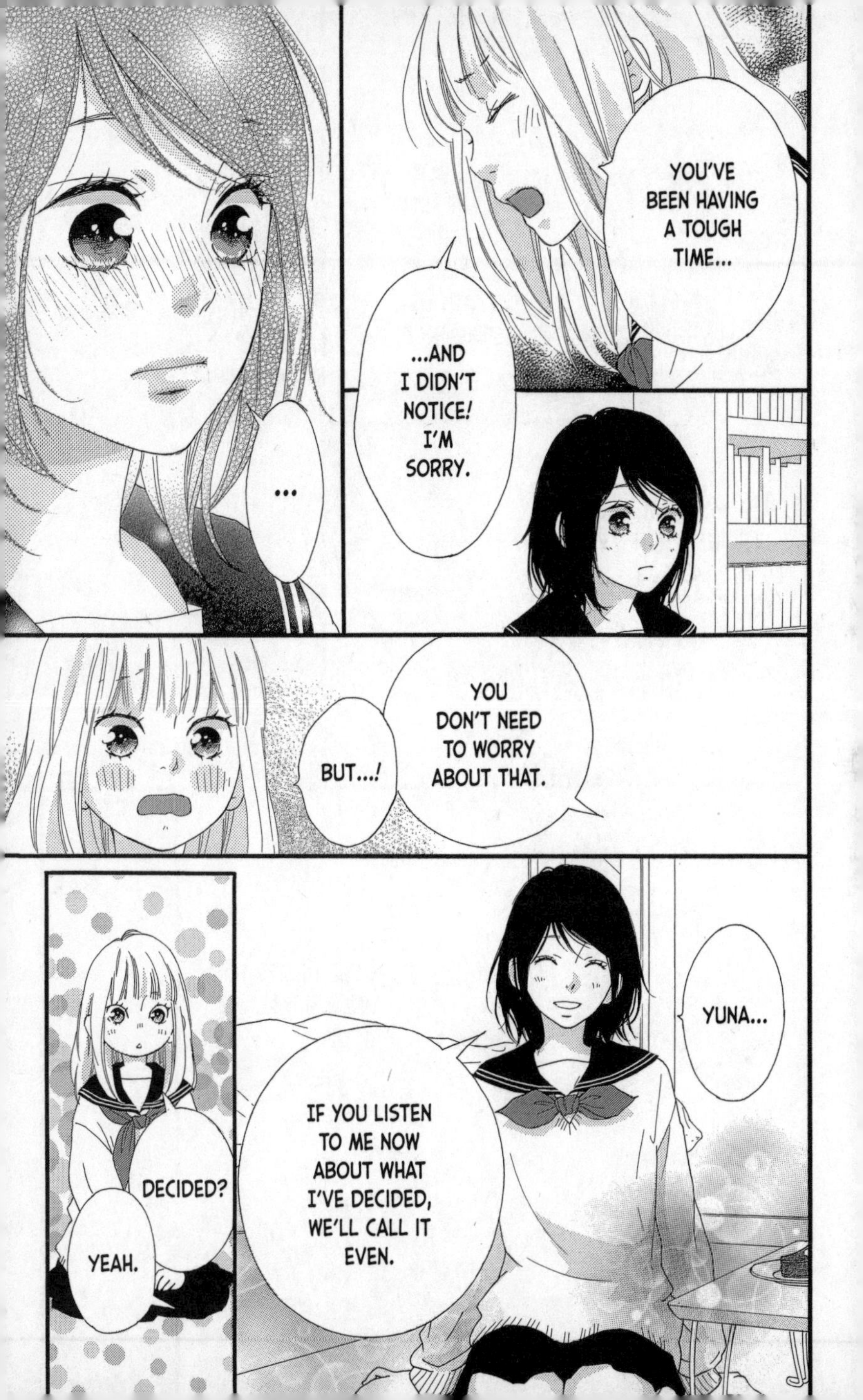
YOU'VE BEEN HAVING A TOUGH TIME...
...AND I DIDN'T NOTICE! I'M SORRY.
...
YOU DON'T NEED TO WORRY ABOUT THAT.
BUT...!
YUNA...
IF YOU LISTEN TO ME NOW ABOUT WHAT I'VE DECIDED, WE'LL CALL IT EVEN.
DECIDED?
YEAH.

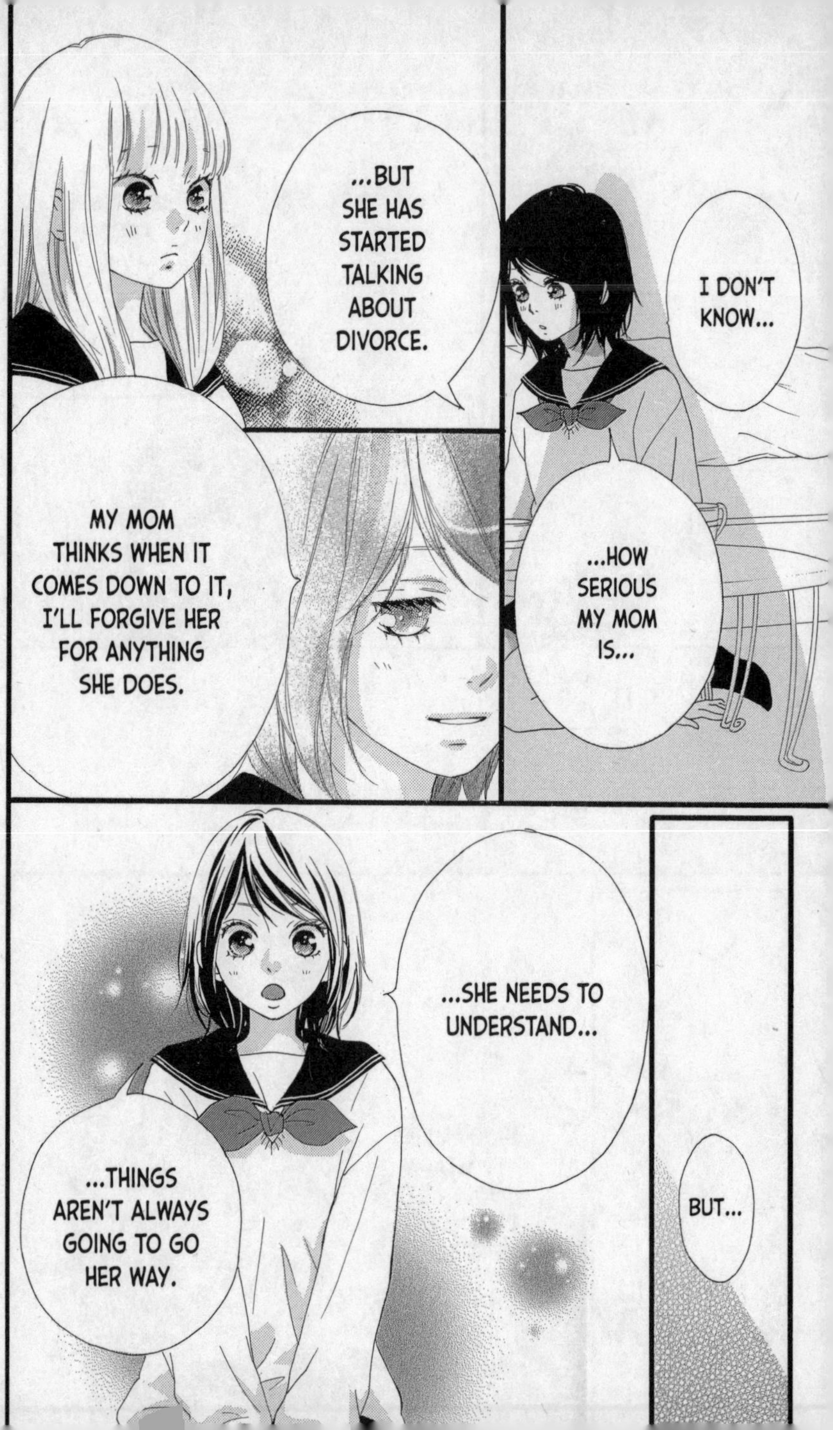
I DON'T KNOW...
...HOW SERIOUS MY MOM IS...
...BUT SHE HAS STARTED TALKING ABOUT DIVORCE.
MY MOM THINKS WHEN IT COMES DOWN TO IT, I'LL FORGIVE HER FOR ANYTHING SHE DOES.
BUT...
...SHE NEEDS TO UNDERSTAND...
...THINGS AREN'T ALWAYS GOING TO GO HER WAY.

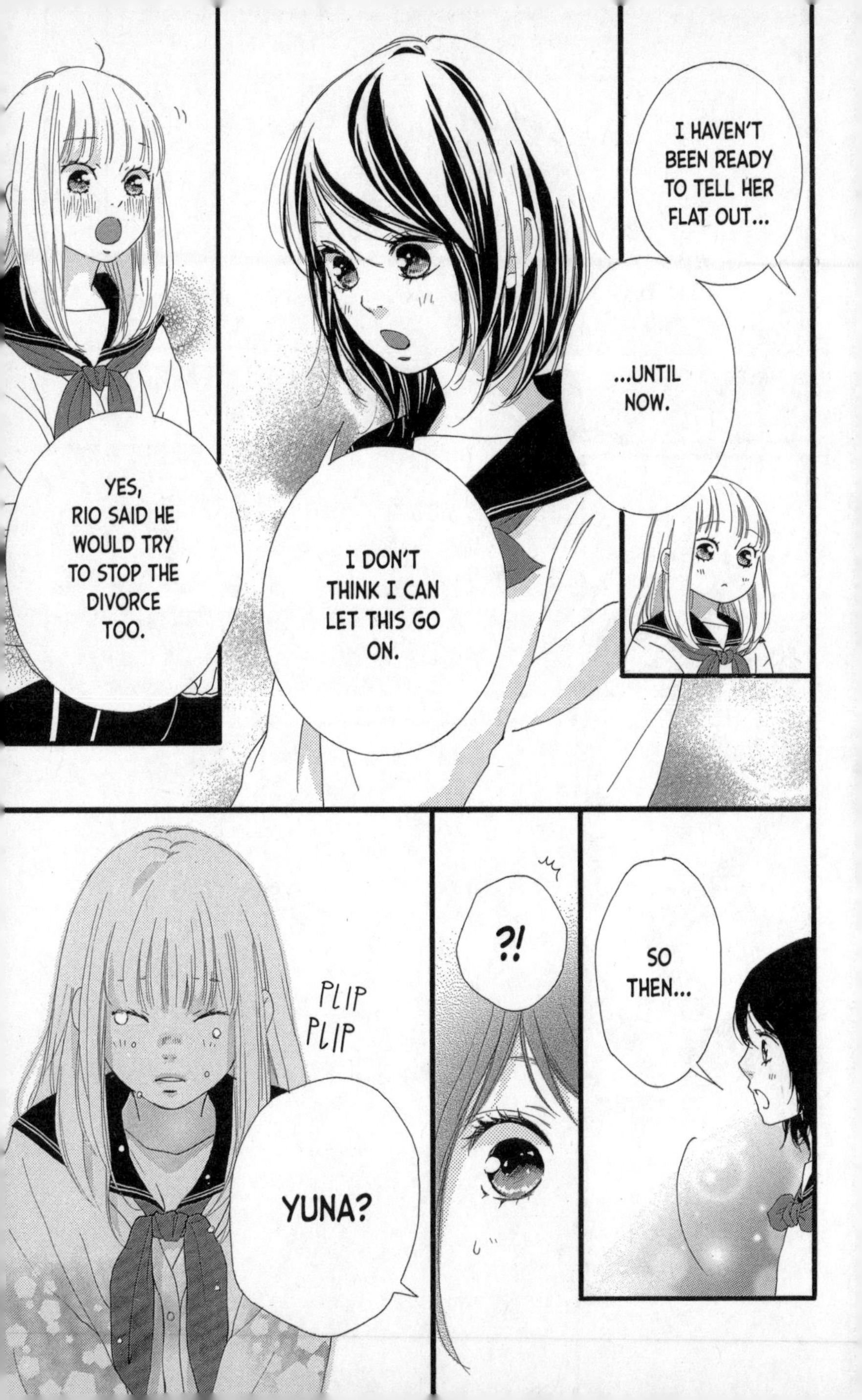
I HAVEN'T BEEN READY TO TELL HER FLAT OUT...
...UNTIL NOW.
I DON'T THINK I CAN LET THIS GO ON.
YES, RIO SAID HE WOULD TRY TO STOP THE DIVORCE TOO.
SO THEN...
?!
PLIP PLIP
YUNA?

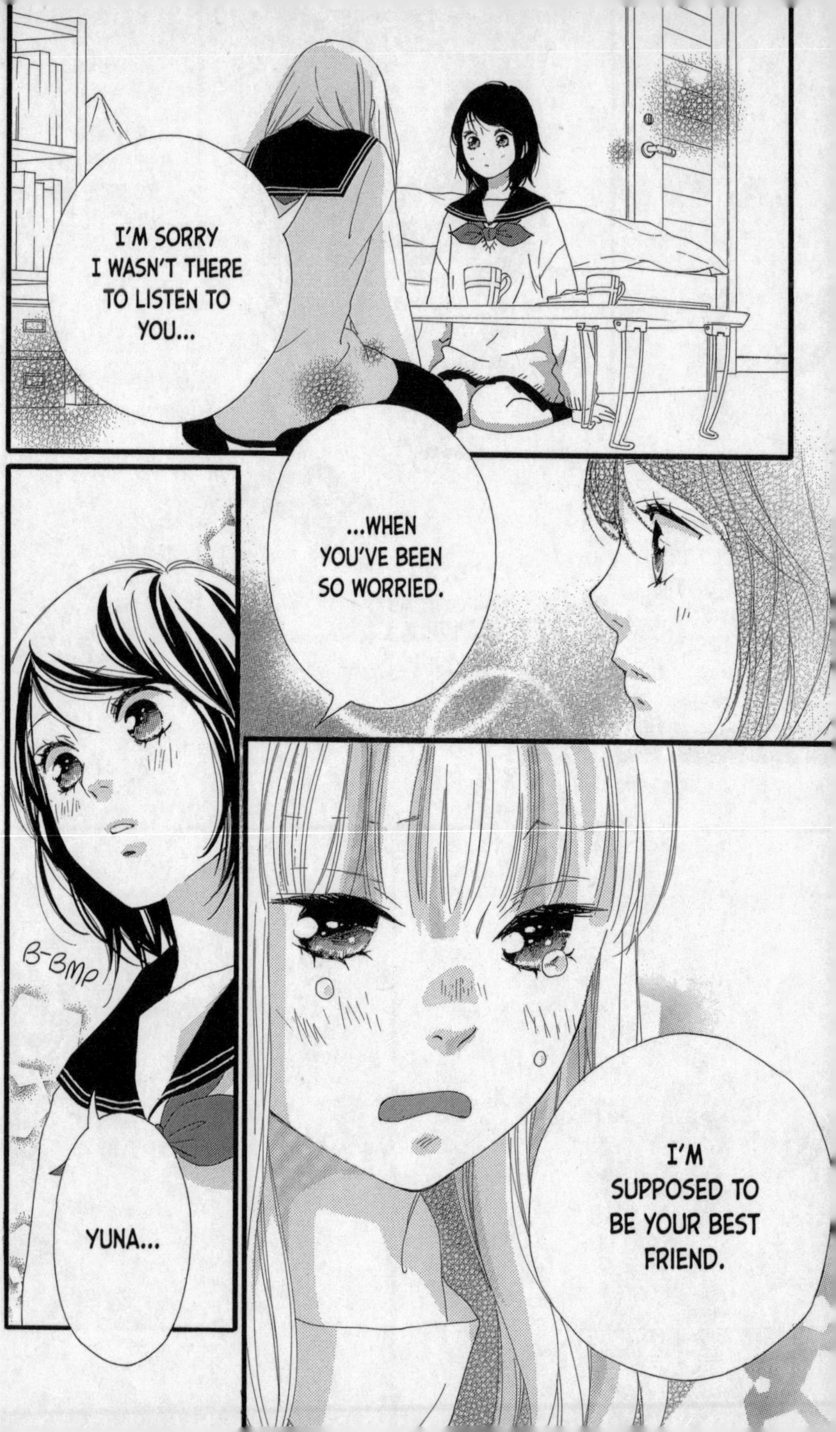
I'M SORRY I WASN'T THERE TO LISTEN TO YOU...
...WHEN YOU'VE BEEN SO WORRIED.
I'M SUPPOSED TO BE YOUR BEST FRIEND.
B-BMP
YUNA...

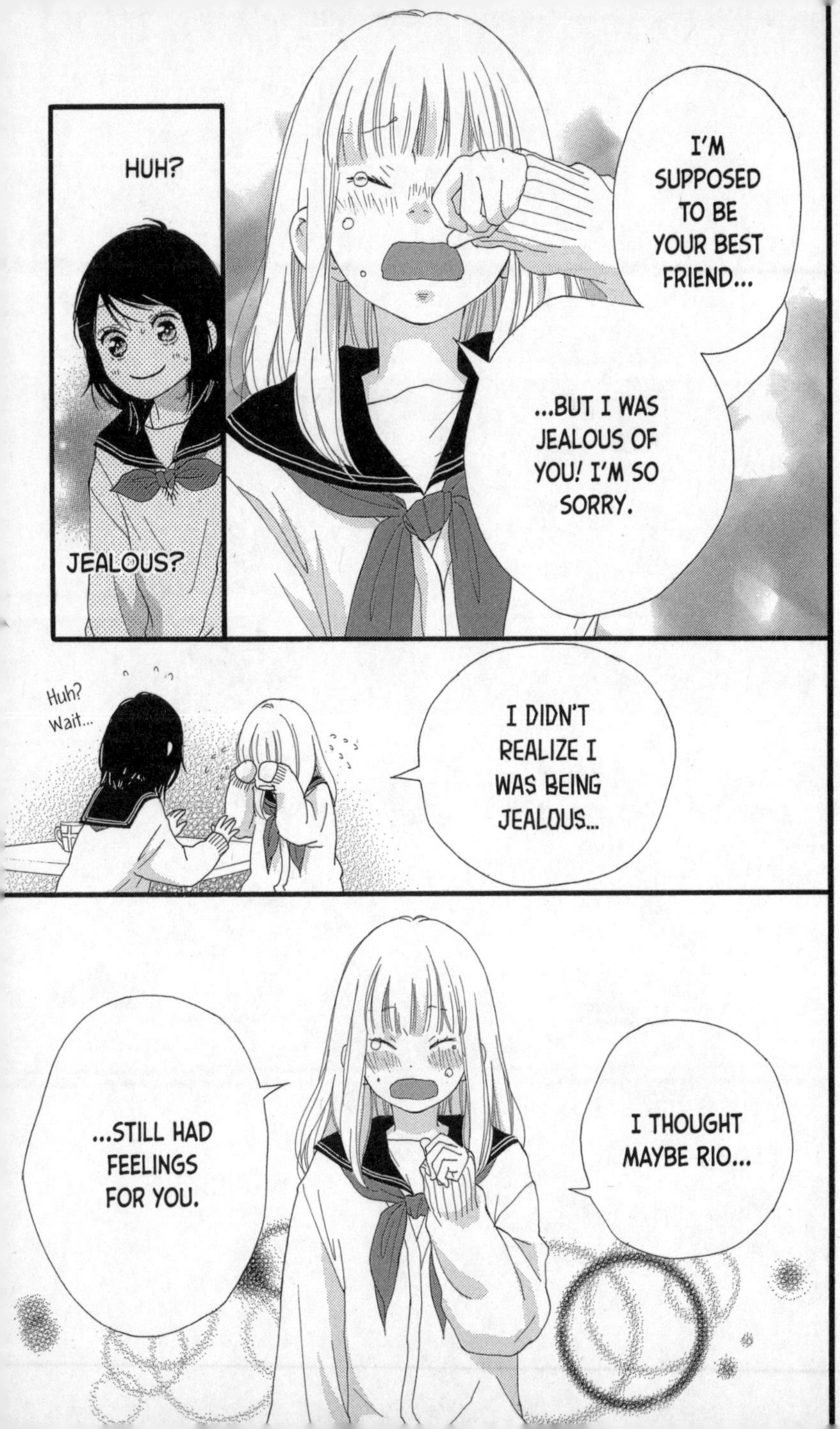
I'M SUPPOSED TO BE YOUR BEST FRIEND...
...BUT I WAS JEALOUS OF YOU! I'M SO SORRY.
HUH?
JEALOUS?
I DIDN'T REALIZE I WAS BEING JEALOUS...
Huh? Wait...
I THOUGHT MAYBE RIO...
...STILL HAD FEELINGS FOR YOU.

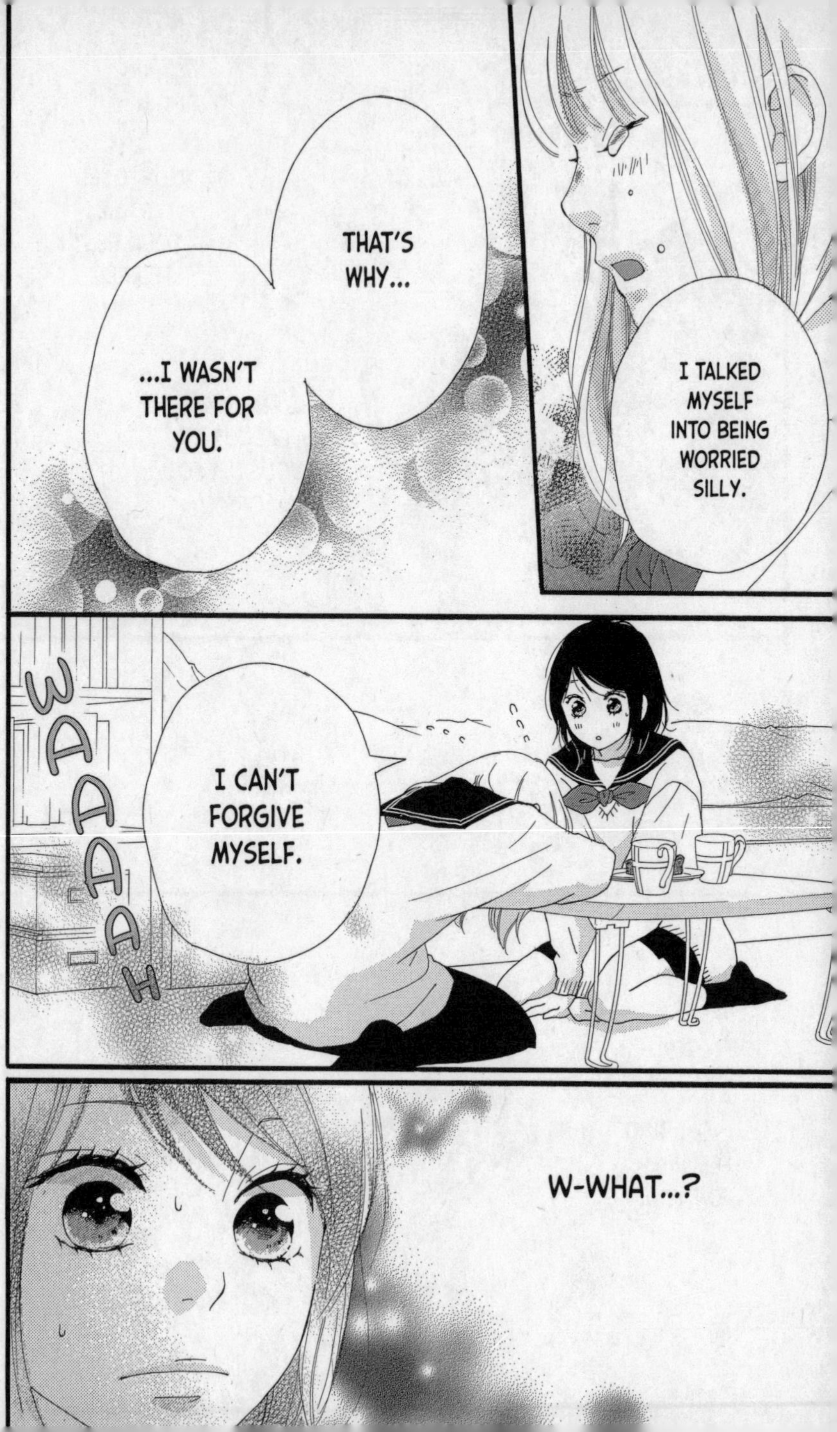
I TALKED MYSELF INTO BEING WORRIED SILLY.
THAT'S WHY...
...I WASN'T THERE FOR YOU.
I CAN'T FORGIVE MYSELF.
WAAAAH
W-WHAT...?

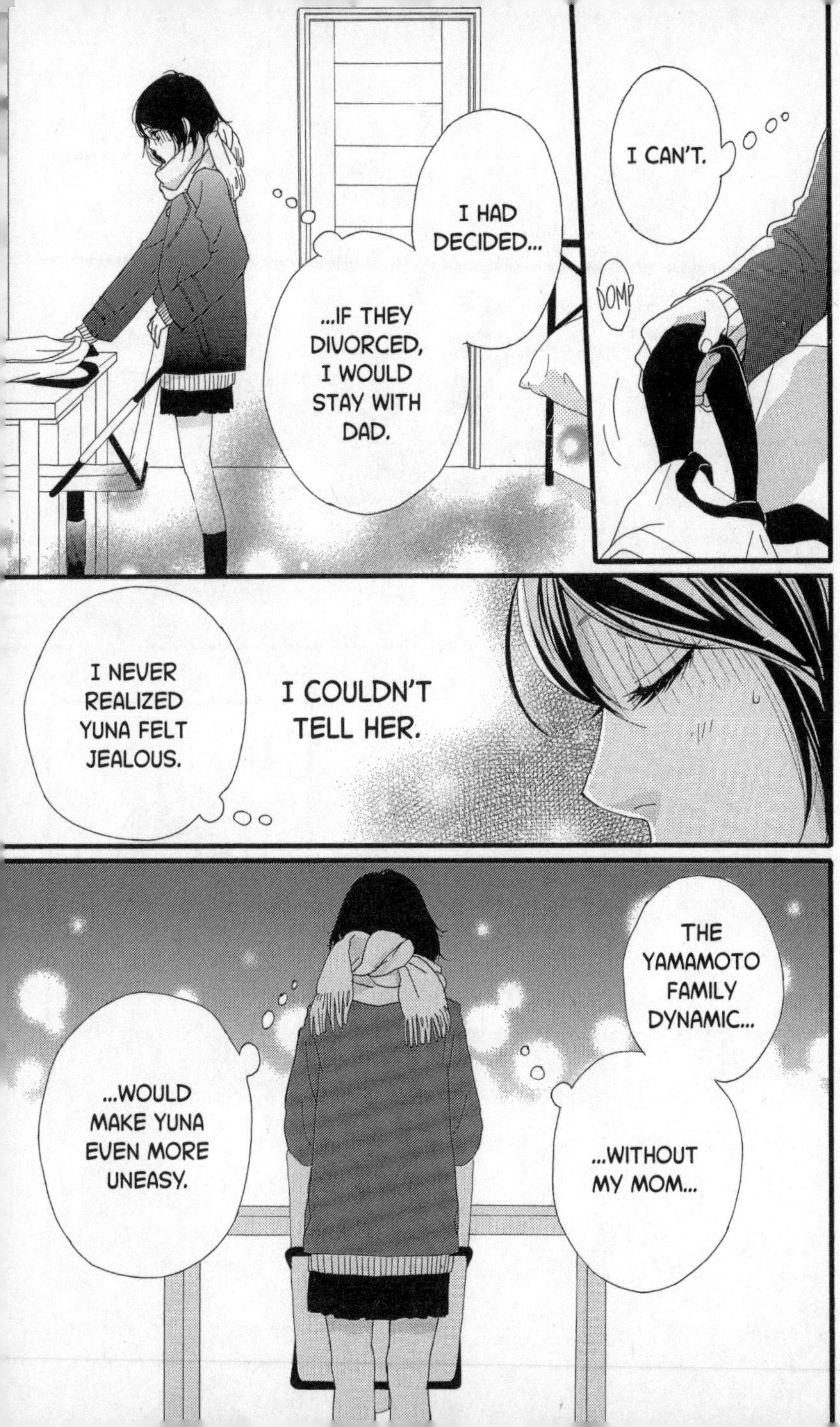
I CAN'T.
DOMP
I HAD DECIDED...
...IF THEY DIVORCED, I WOULD STAY WITH DAD.
I COULDN'T TELL HER.
I NEVER REALIZED YUNA FELT JEALOUS.
THE YAMAMOTO FAMILY DYNAMIC...
...WITHOUT MY MOM...
...WOULD MAKE YUNA EVEN MORE UNEASY.

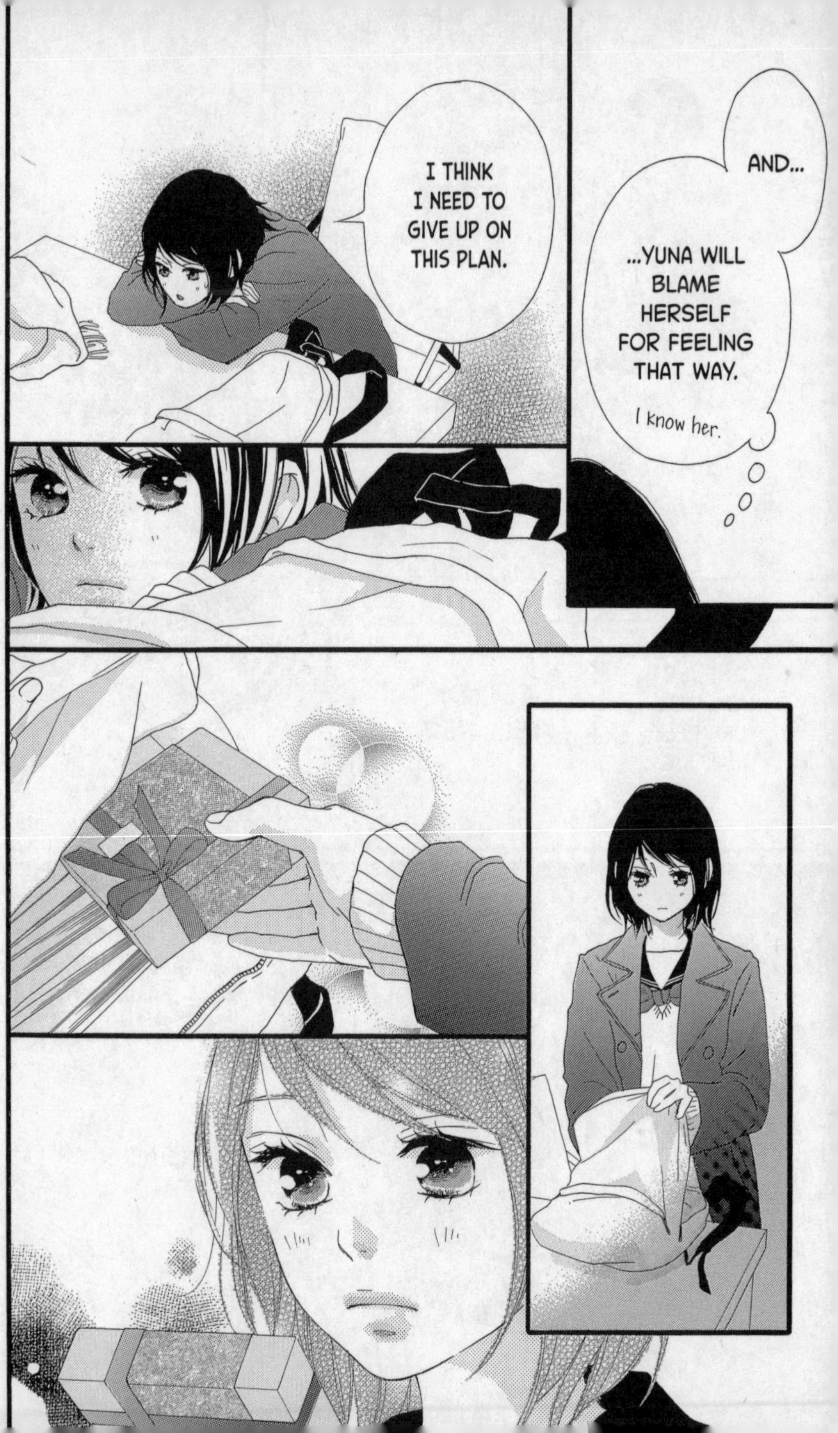
AND...
...YUNA WILL BLAME HERSELF FOR FEELING THAT WAY.
I know her.
I THINK I NEED TO GIVE UP ON THIS PLAN.

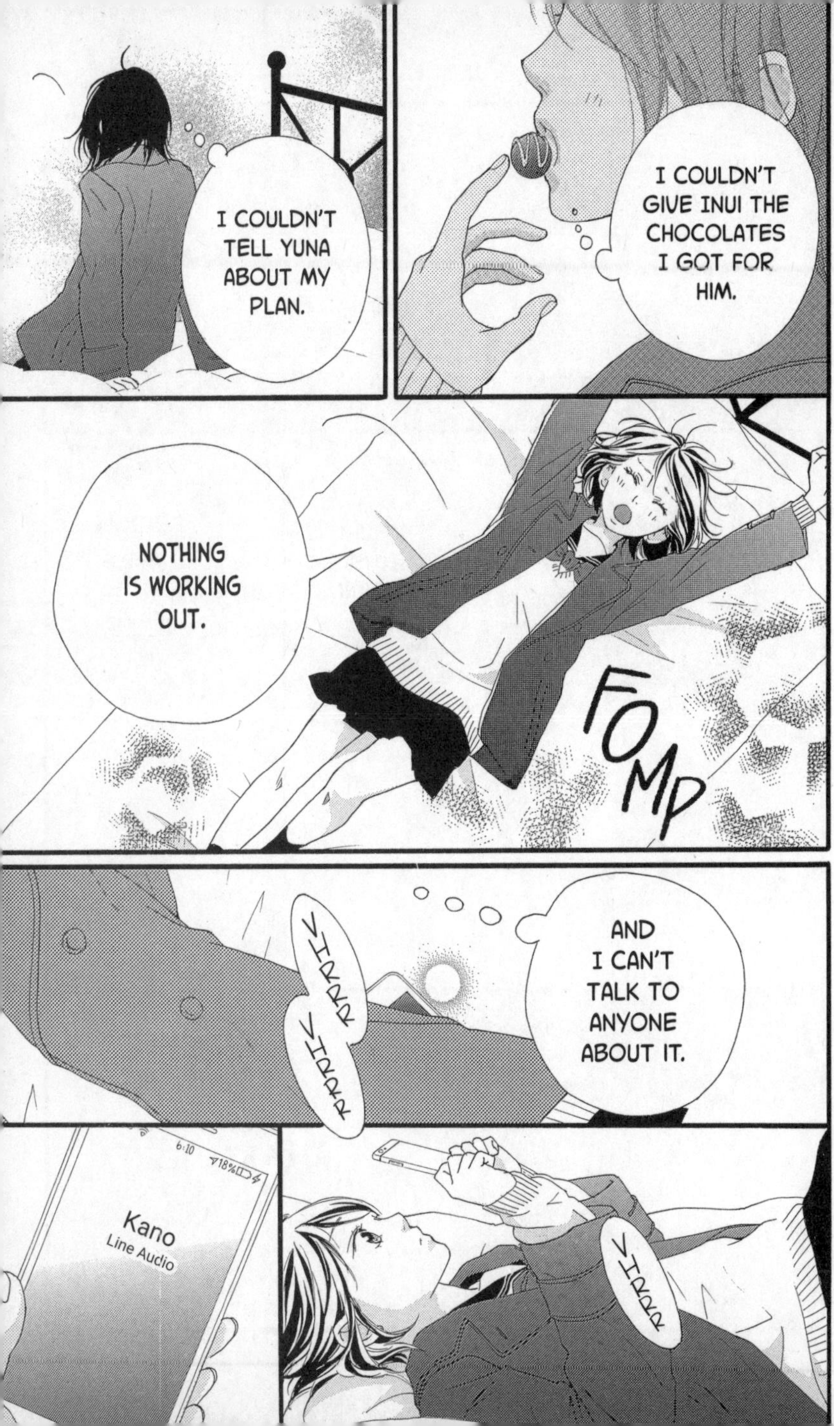
I COULDN'T GIVE INUI THE CHOCOLATES I GOT FOR HIM.
I COULDN'T TELL YUNA ABOUT MY PLAN.
NOTHING IS WORKING OUT.
FOMP
AND I CAN'T TALK TO ANYONE ABOUT IT.
VIRRRR
VIRRRR
VIRRRR
6:10
18%
Kano
Line Audio

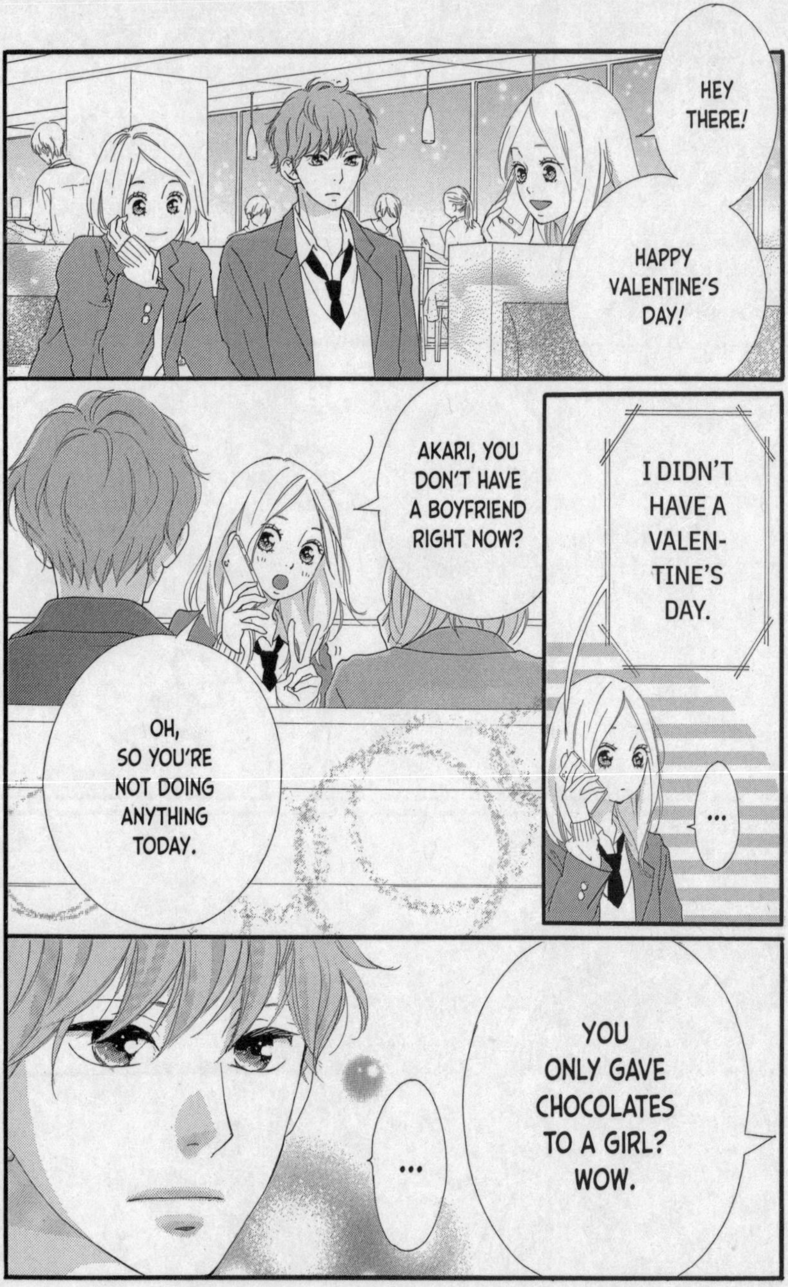
HEY THERE!
HAPPY VALENTINE'S DAY!
I DIDN'T HAVE A VALEN-TINE'S DAY.
...
AKARI, YOU DON'T HAVE A BOYFRIEND RIGHT NOW?
OH, SO YOU'RE NOT DOING ANYTHING TODAY.
YOU ONLY GAVE CHOCOLATES TO A GIRL? WOW.
...

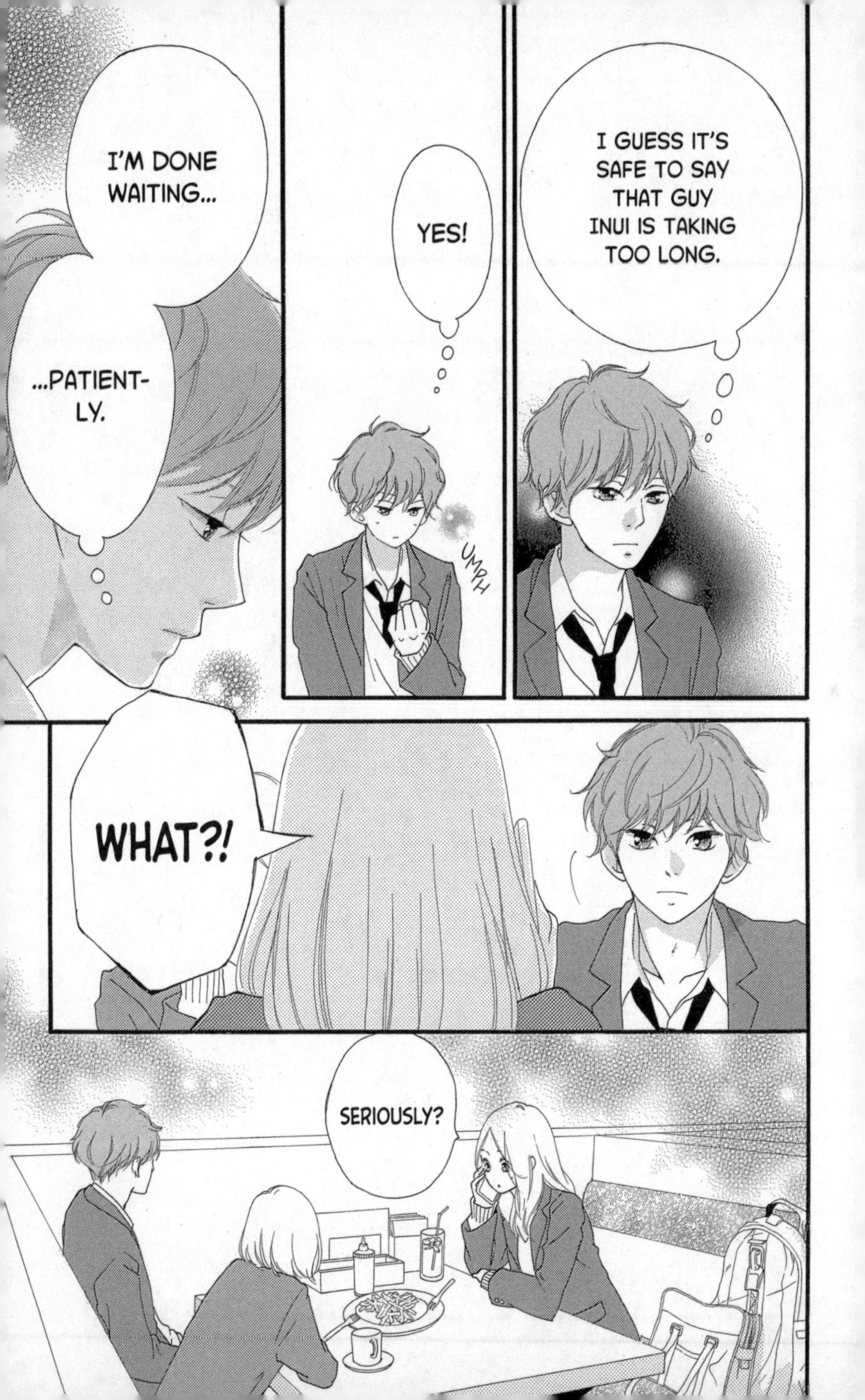
I GUESS IT'S SAFE TO SAY THAT GUY INUI IS TAKING TOO LONG.
YES!
UMPH
I'M DONE WAITING...
...PATIENT-LY.
WHAT?!
SERIOUSLY?

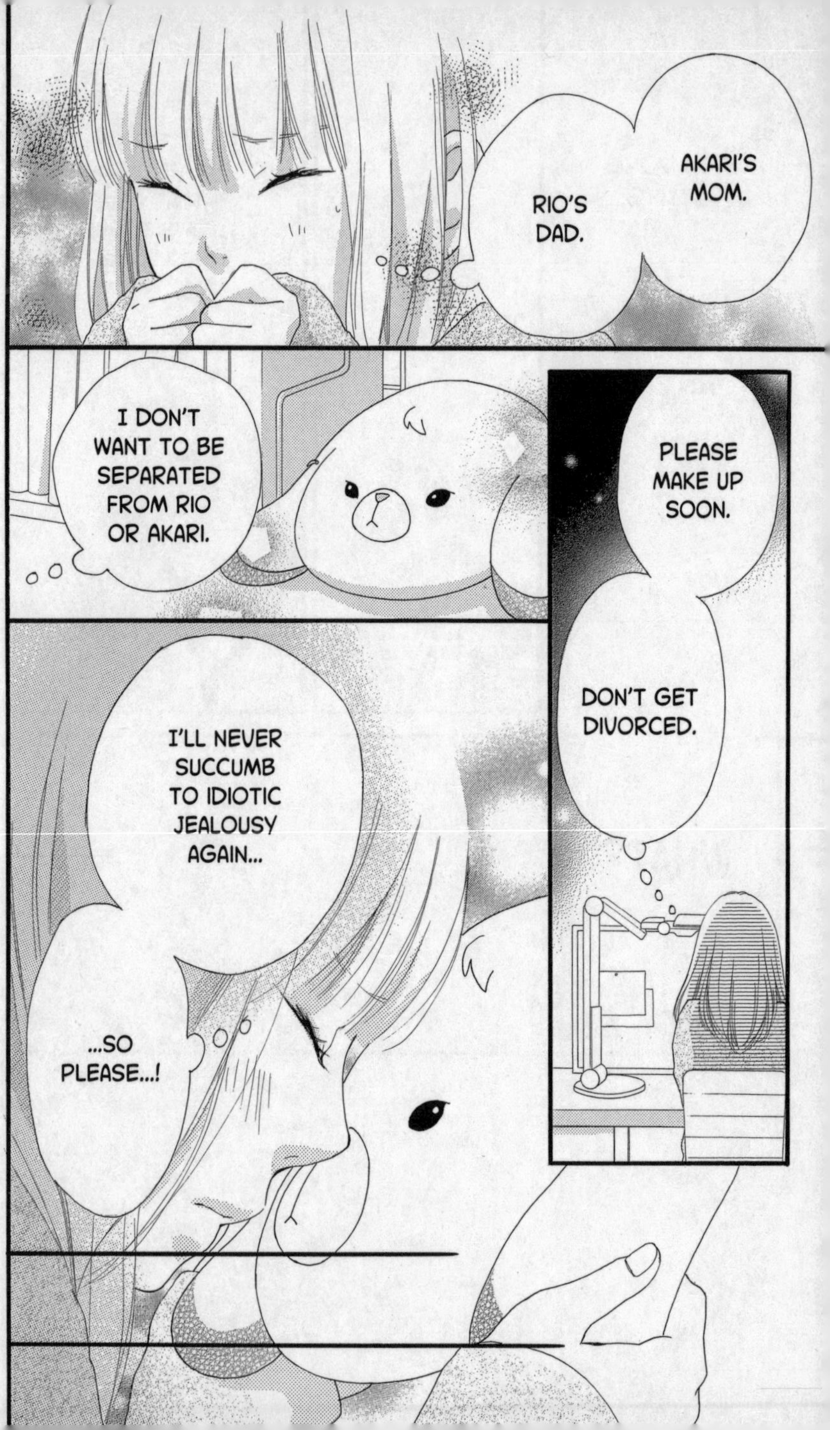
AKARI'S MOM.
RIO'S DAD.
PLEASE MAKE UP SOON.
DON'T GET DIVORCED.
I DON'T WANT TO BE SEPARATED FROM RIO OR AKARI.
I'LL NEVER SUCCUMB TO IDIOTIC JEALOUSY AGAIN...
...SO PLEASE...!

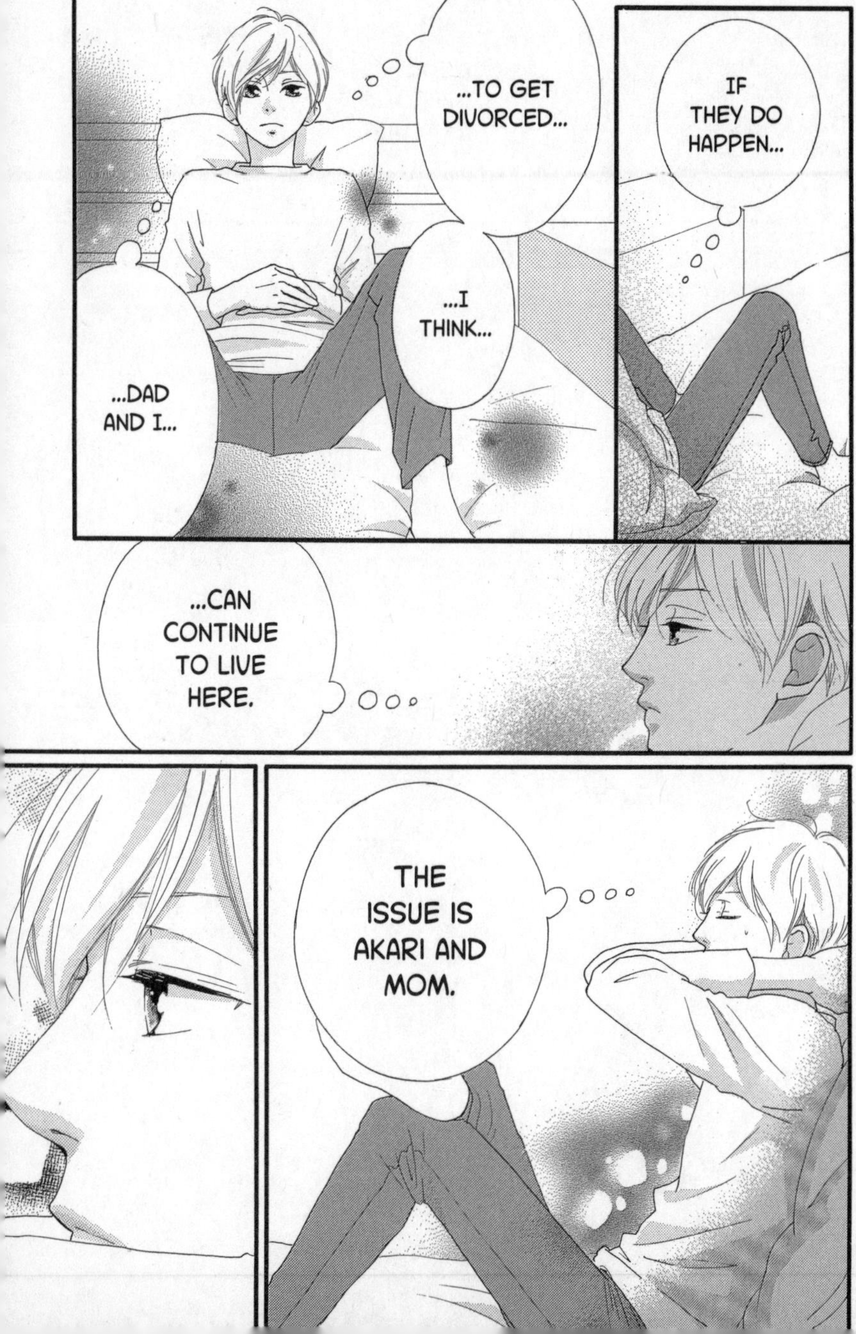
IF THEY DO HAPPEN...
...TO GET DIVORCED...
...I THINK...
...DAD AND I...
...CAN CONTINUE TO LIVE HERE.
THE ISSUE IS AKARI AND MOM.

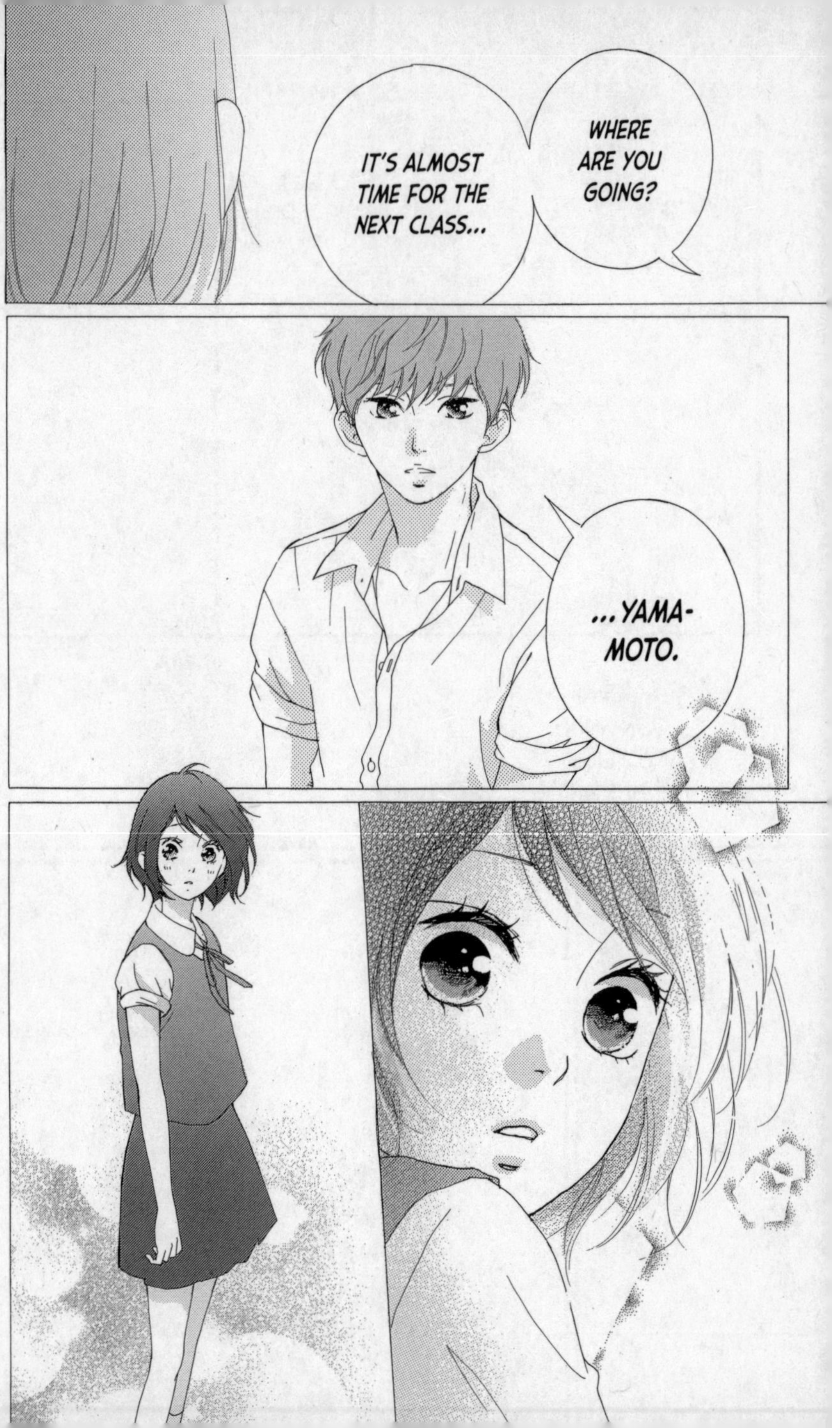
WHERE ARE YOU GOING?
IT'S ALMOST TIME FOR THE NEXT CLASS...
...YAMA-MOTO.

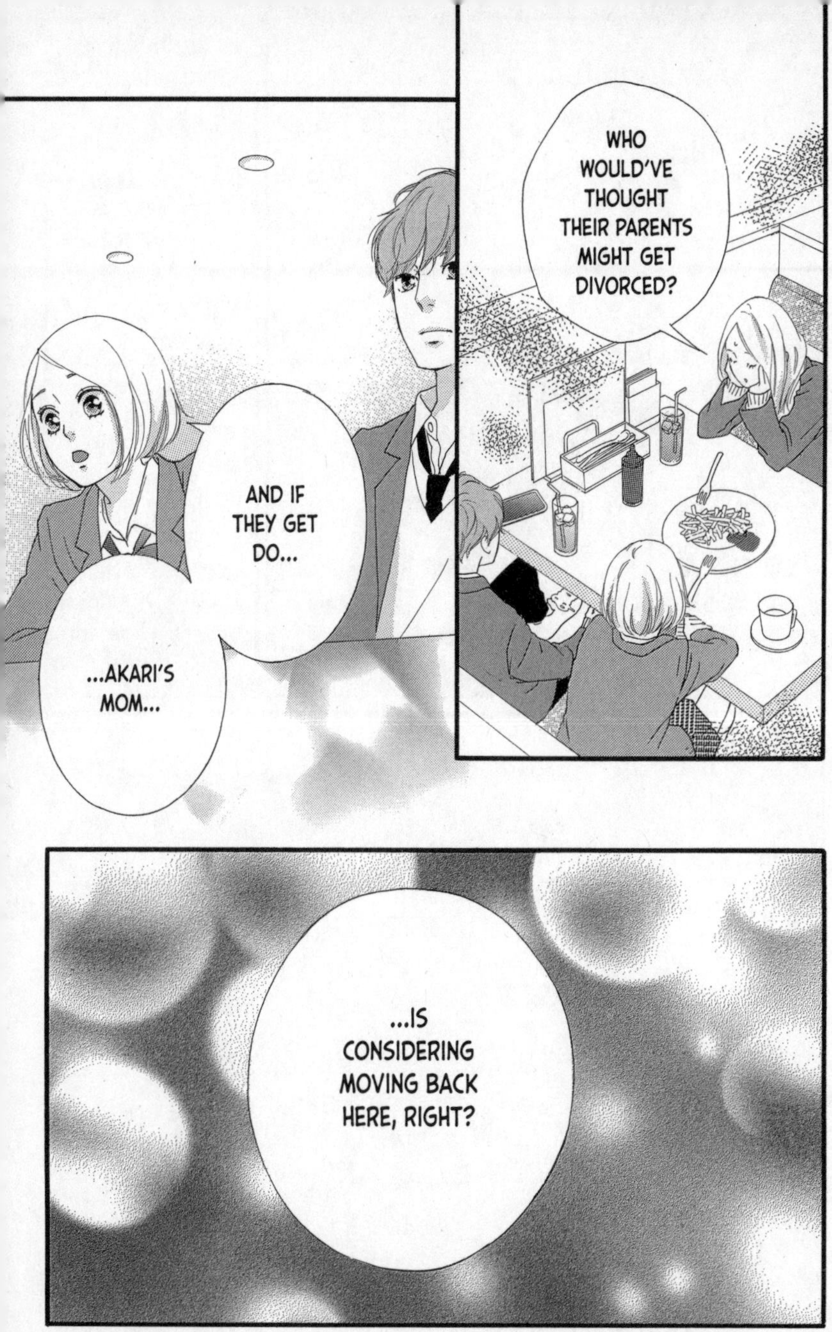
WHO WOULD'VE THOUGHT THEIR PARENTS MIGHT GET DIVORCED?
AND IF THEY GET DO...
...AKARI'S MOM...
...IS CONSIDERING MOVING BACK HERE, RIGHT?

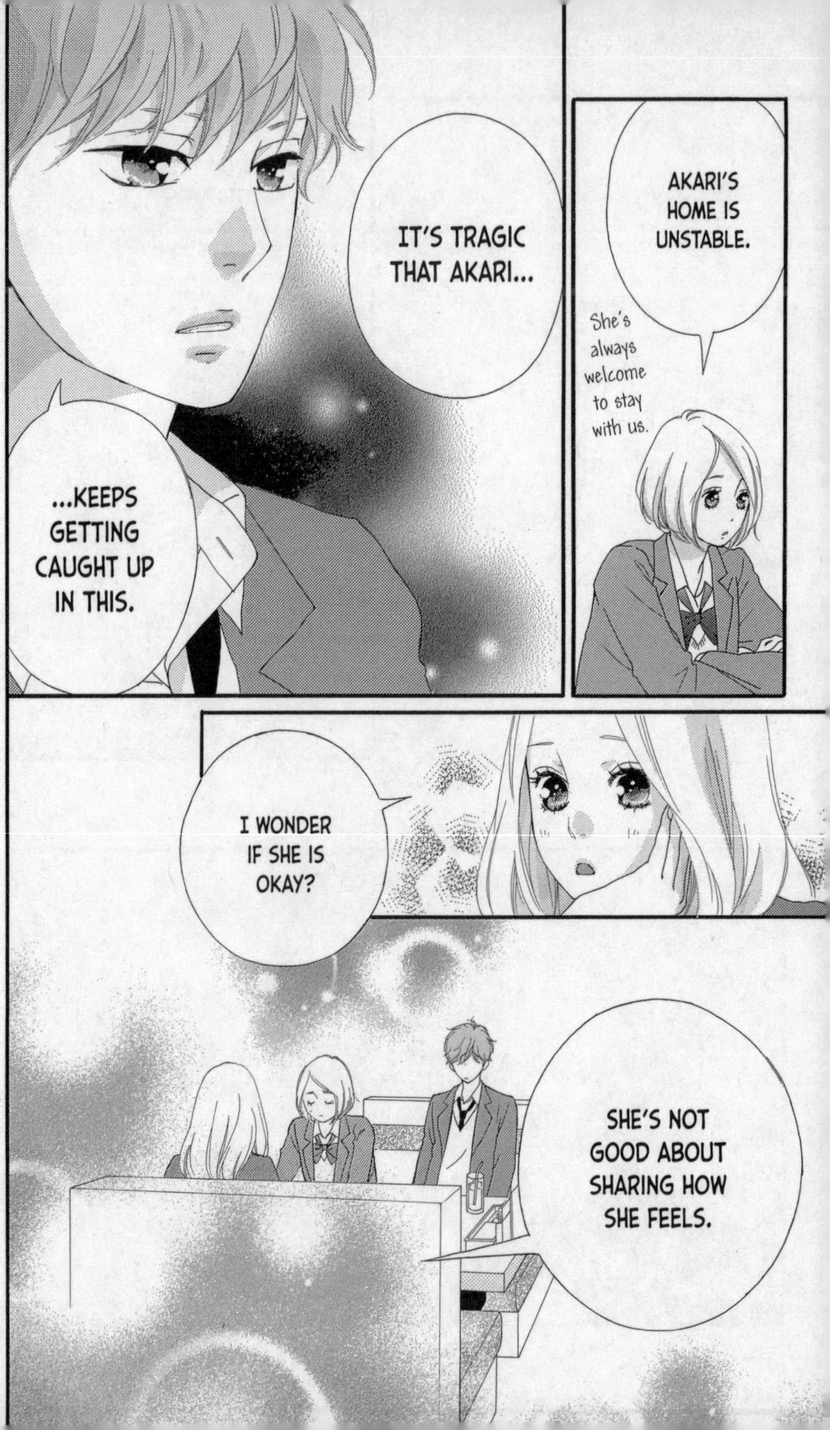
AKARI'S HOME IS UNSTABLE.
She's always welcome to stay with us.
IT'S TRAGIC THAT AKARI...
...KEEPS GETTING CAUGHT UP IN THIS.
I WONDER IF SHE IS OKAY?
SHE'S NOT GOOD ABOUT SHARING HOW SHE FEELS.

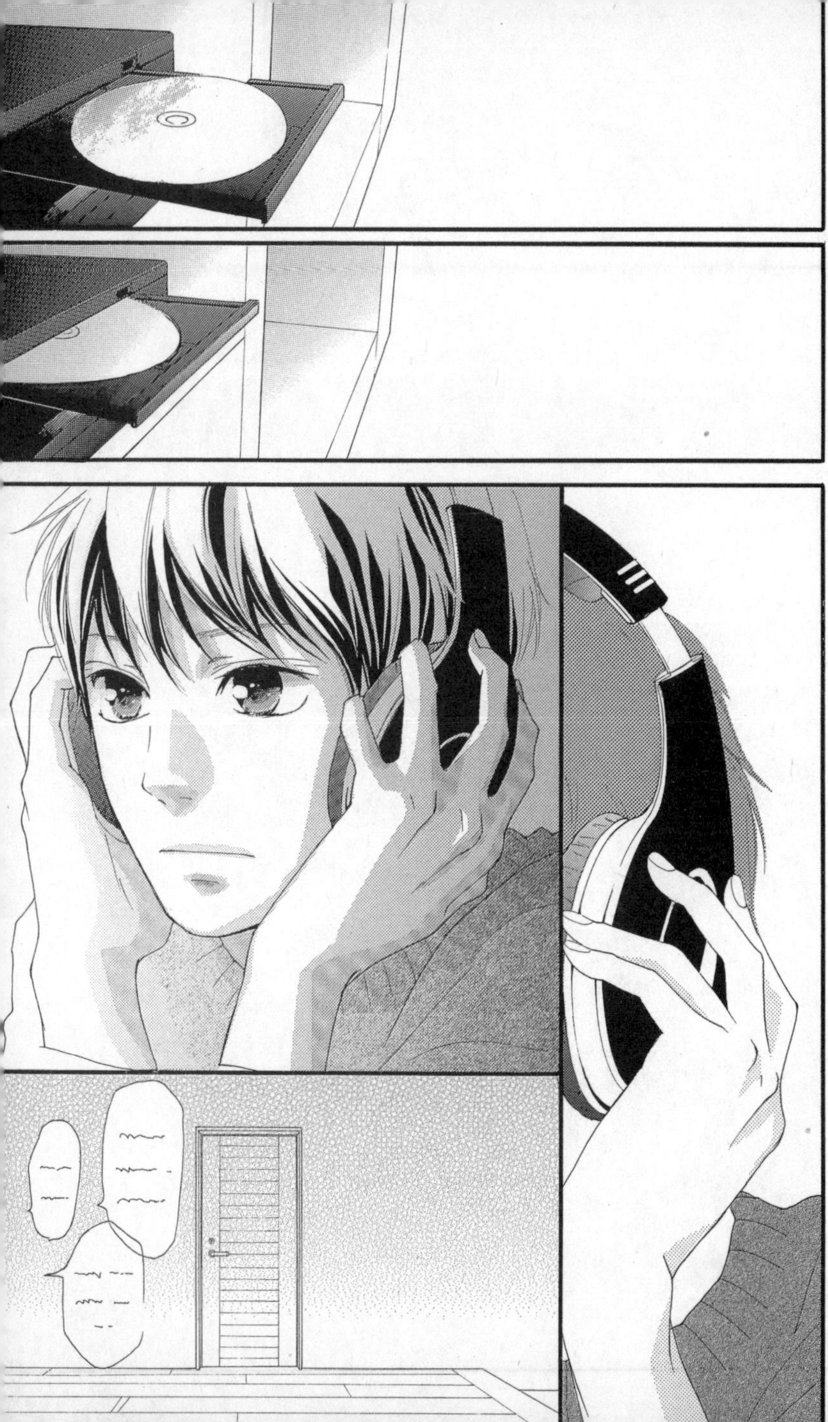

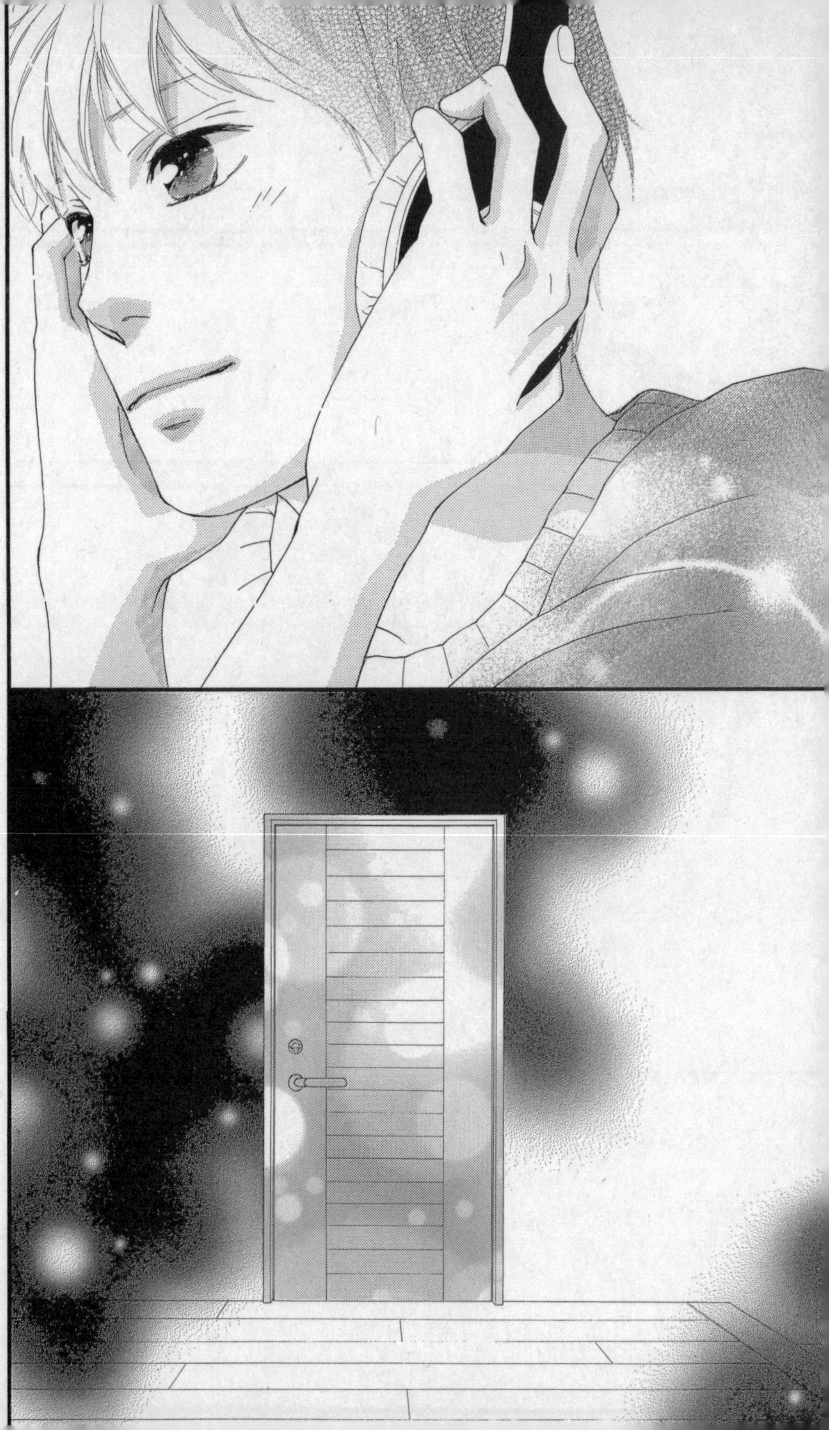

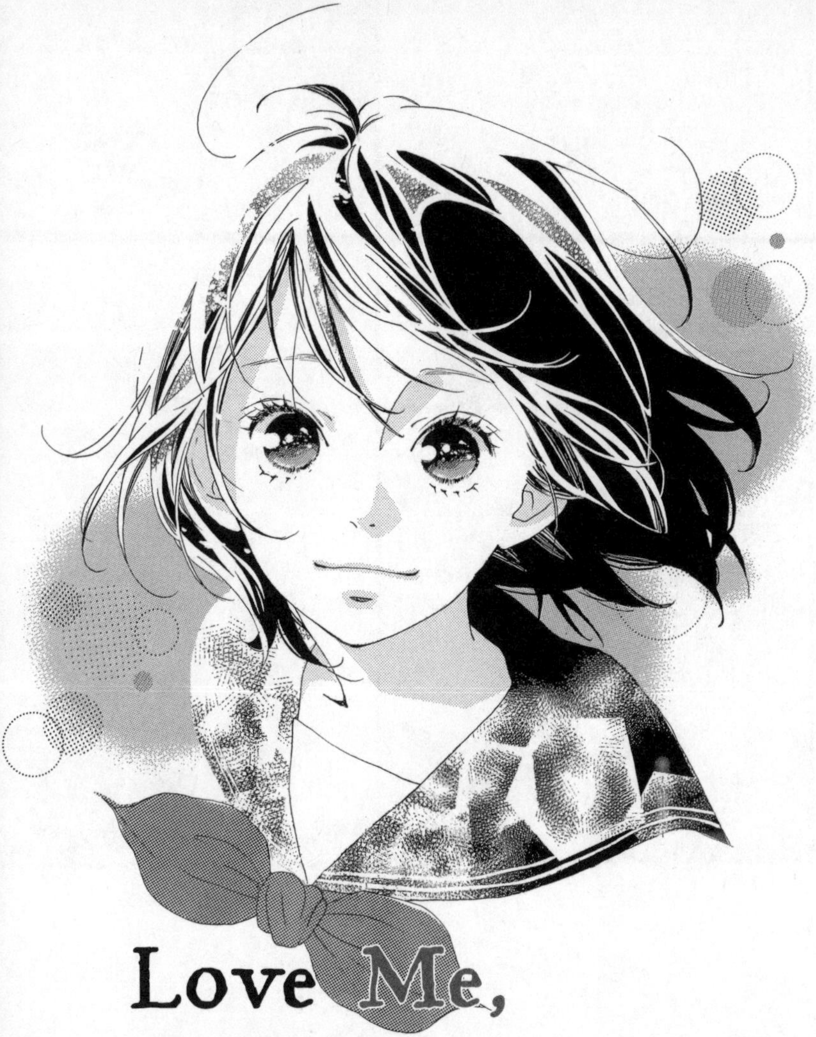

Love Me, Love Me Not

Piece 36

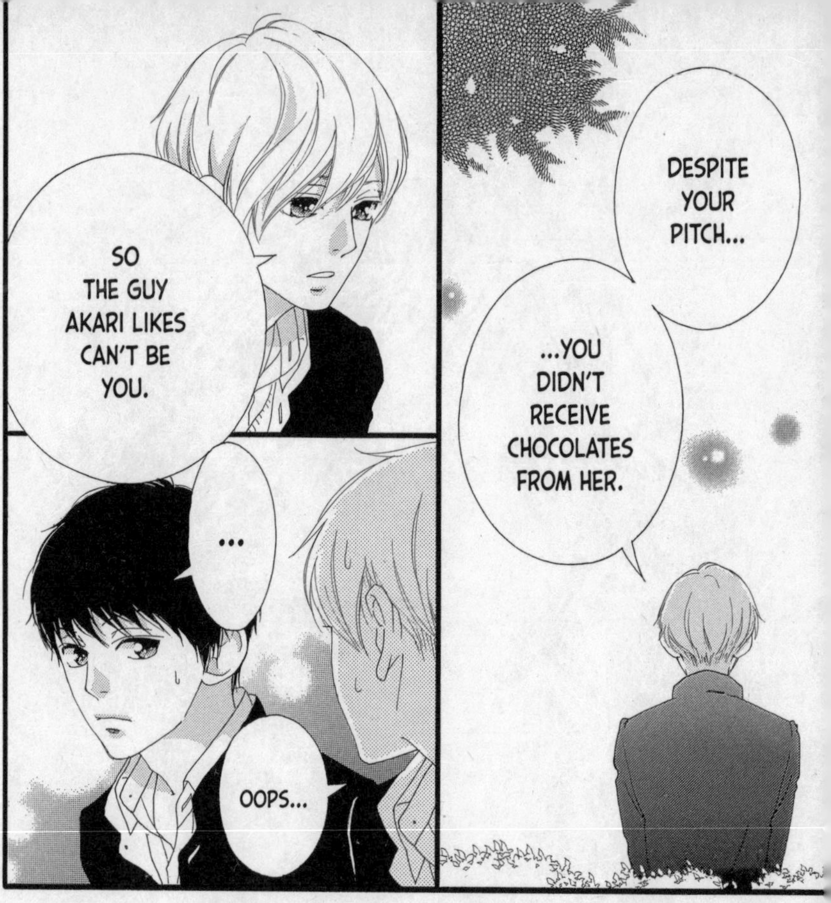
DESPITE YOUR PITCH...
...YOU DIDN'T RECEIVE CHOCOLATES FROM HER.
SO THE GUY AKARI LIKES CAN'T BE YOU.
...
OOPS...
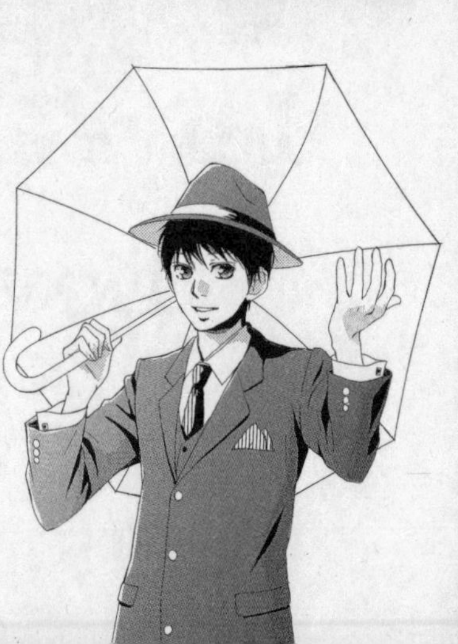

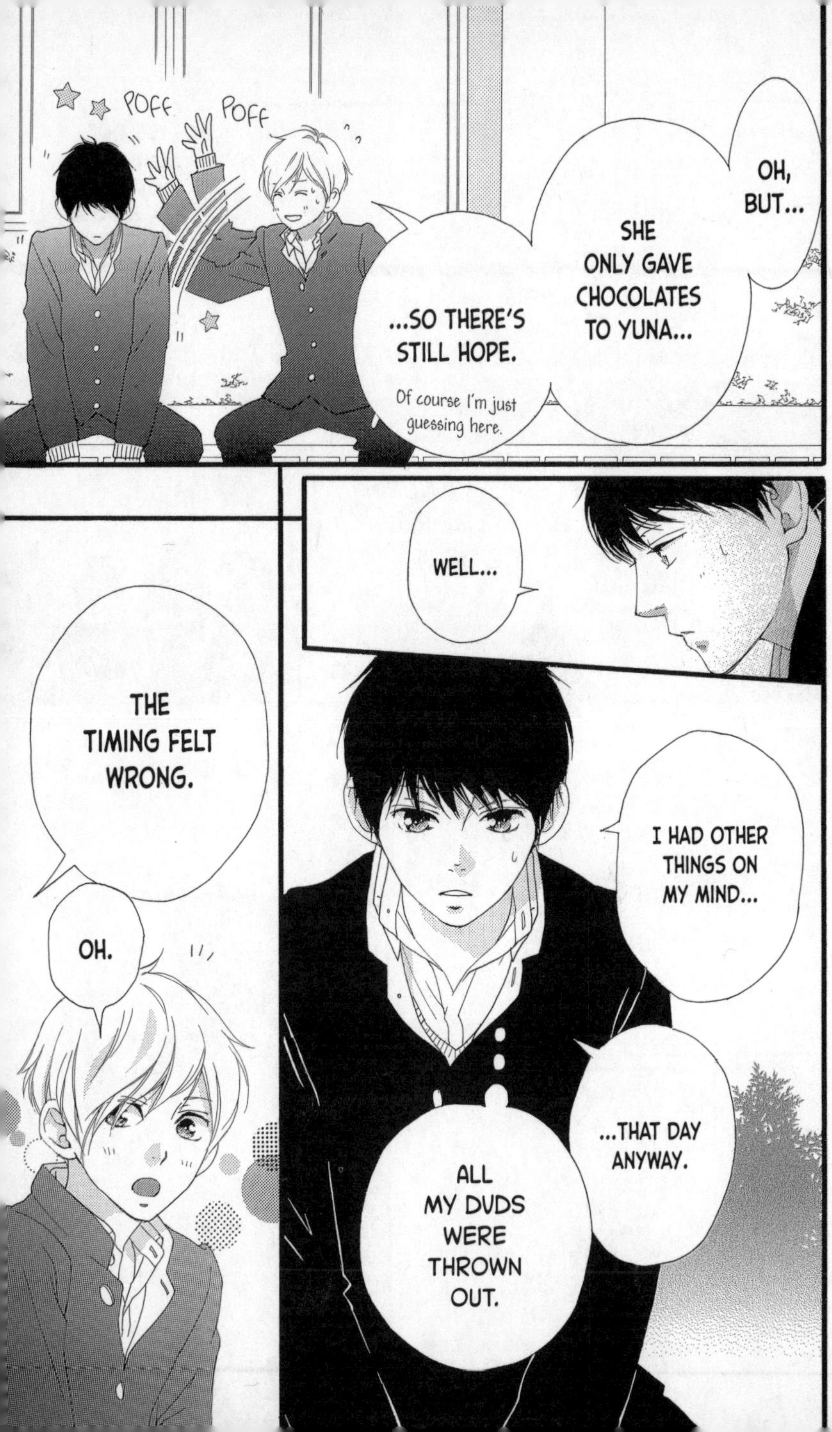
OH, BUT...
SHE ONLY GAVE CHOCOLATES TO YUNA...
...SO THERE'S STILL HOPE.
Of course I'm just guessing here.
POFF
POFF
WELL...
I HAD OTHER THINGS ON MY MIND...
...THAT DAY ANYWAY.
ALL MY DUDS WERE THROWN OUT.
THE TIMING FELT WRONG.
OH.

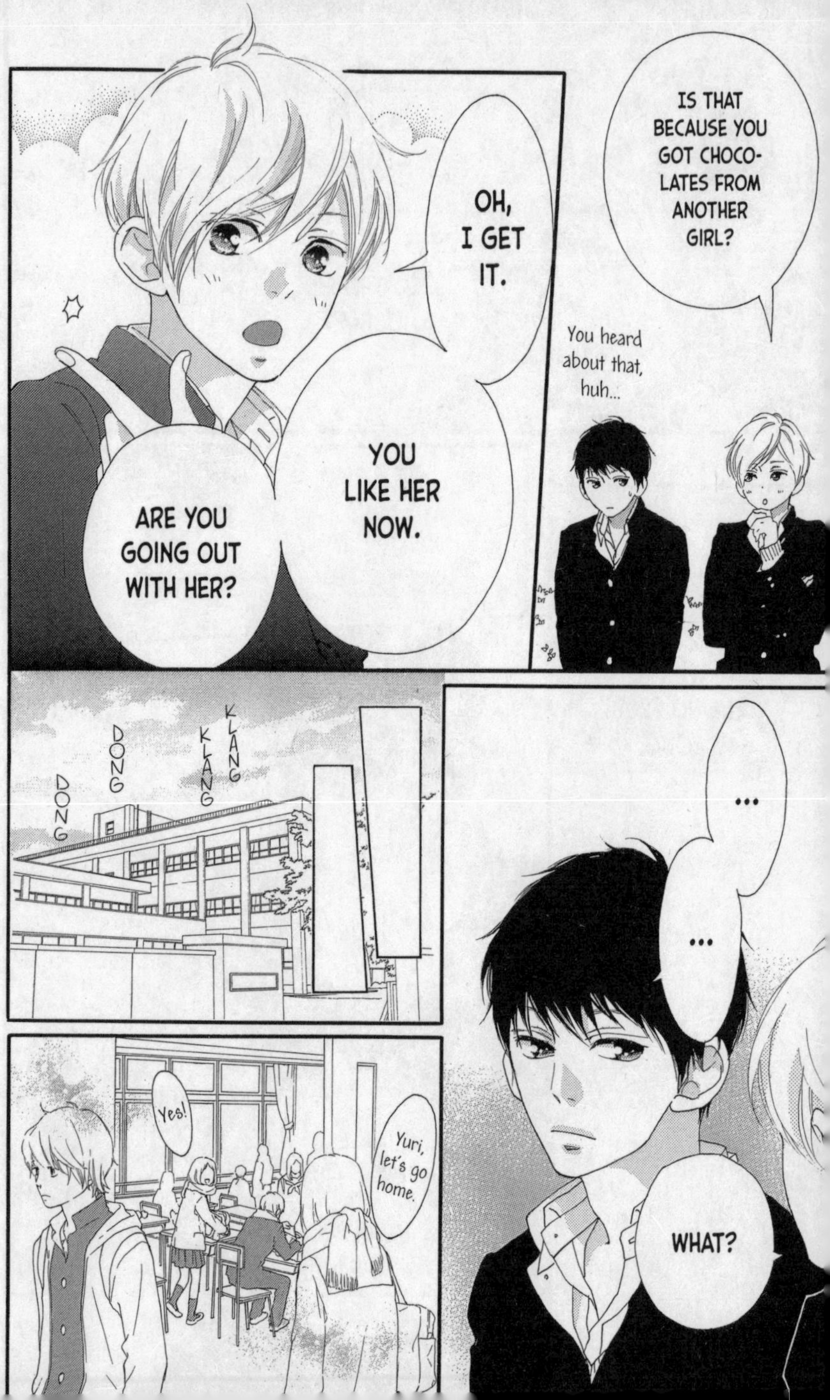
IS THAT BECAUSE YOU GOT CHOCO-LATES FROM ANOTHER GIRL?
You heard about that, huh...
OH, I GET IT.
YOU LIKE HER NOW.
ARE YOU GOING OUT WITH HER?
...
...
WHAT?
DONG
DONG
KLANG
KLANG
Yuri, let's go home.
Yes!

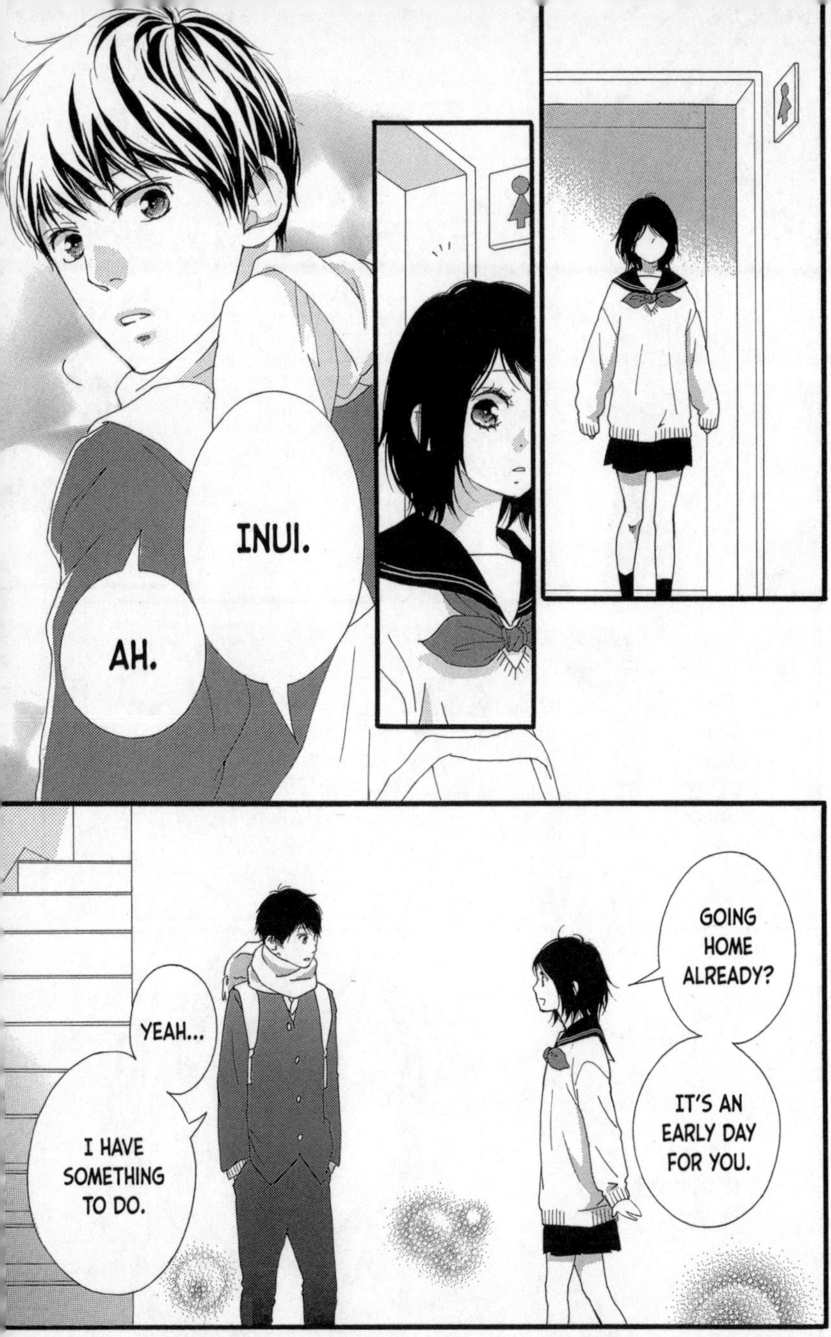
INUI.
AH.
GOING HOME ALREADY?
IT'S AN EARLY DAY FOR YOU.
YEAH...
I HAVE SOMETHING TO DO.

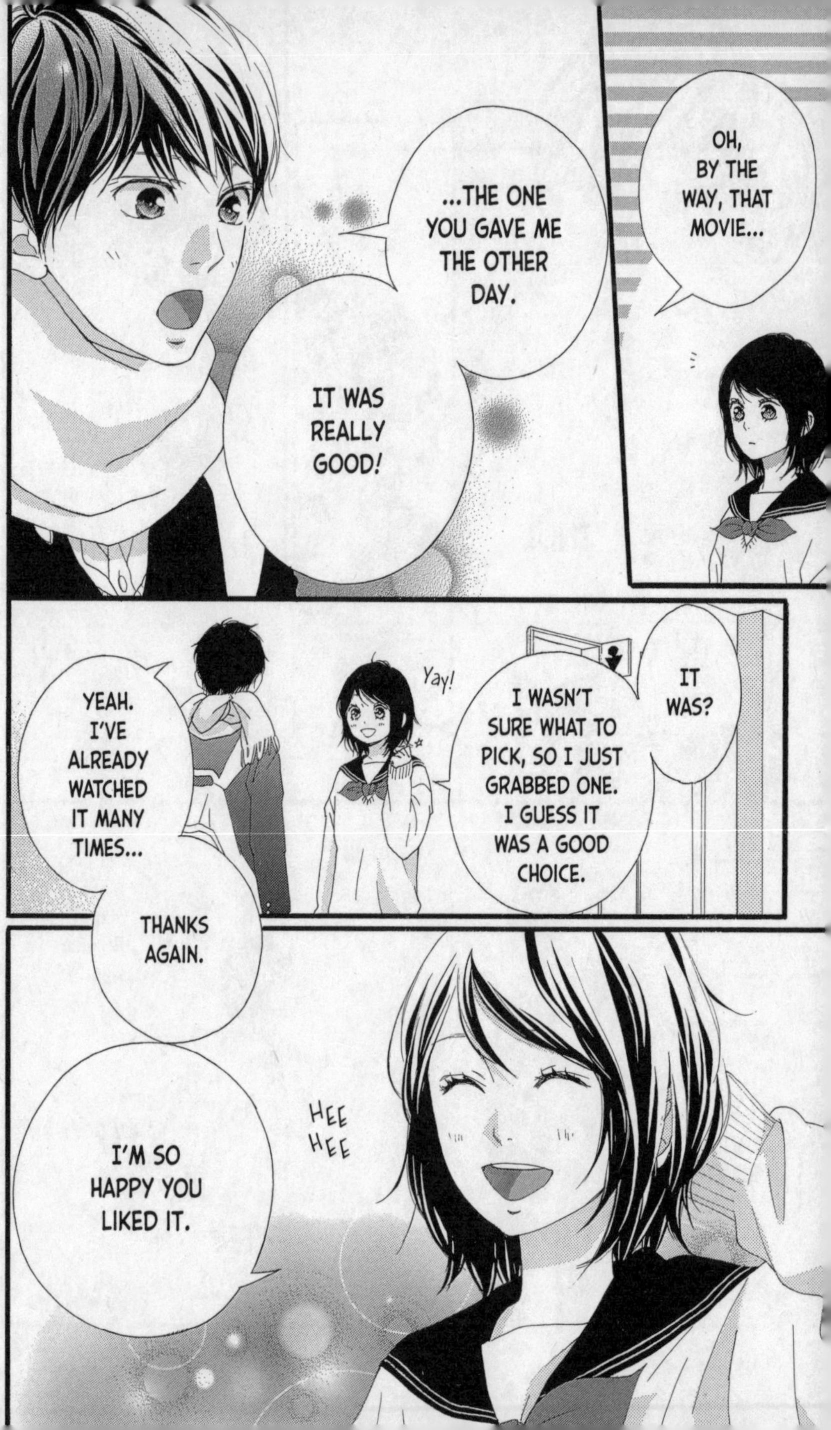
OH, BY THE WAY, THAT MOVIE...
...THE ONE YOU GAVE ME THE OTHER DAY.
IT WAS REALLY GOOD!
IT WAS?
I WASN'T SURE WHAT TO PICK, SO I JUST GRABBED ONE. I GUESS IT WAS A GOOD CHOICE.
Yay!
YEAH. I'VE ALREADY WATCHED IT MANY TIMES...
THANKS AGAIN.
HEE HEE
I'M SO HAPPY YOU LIKED IT.

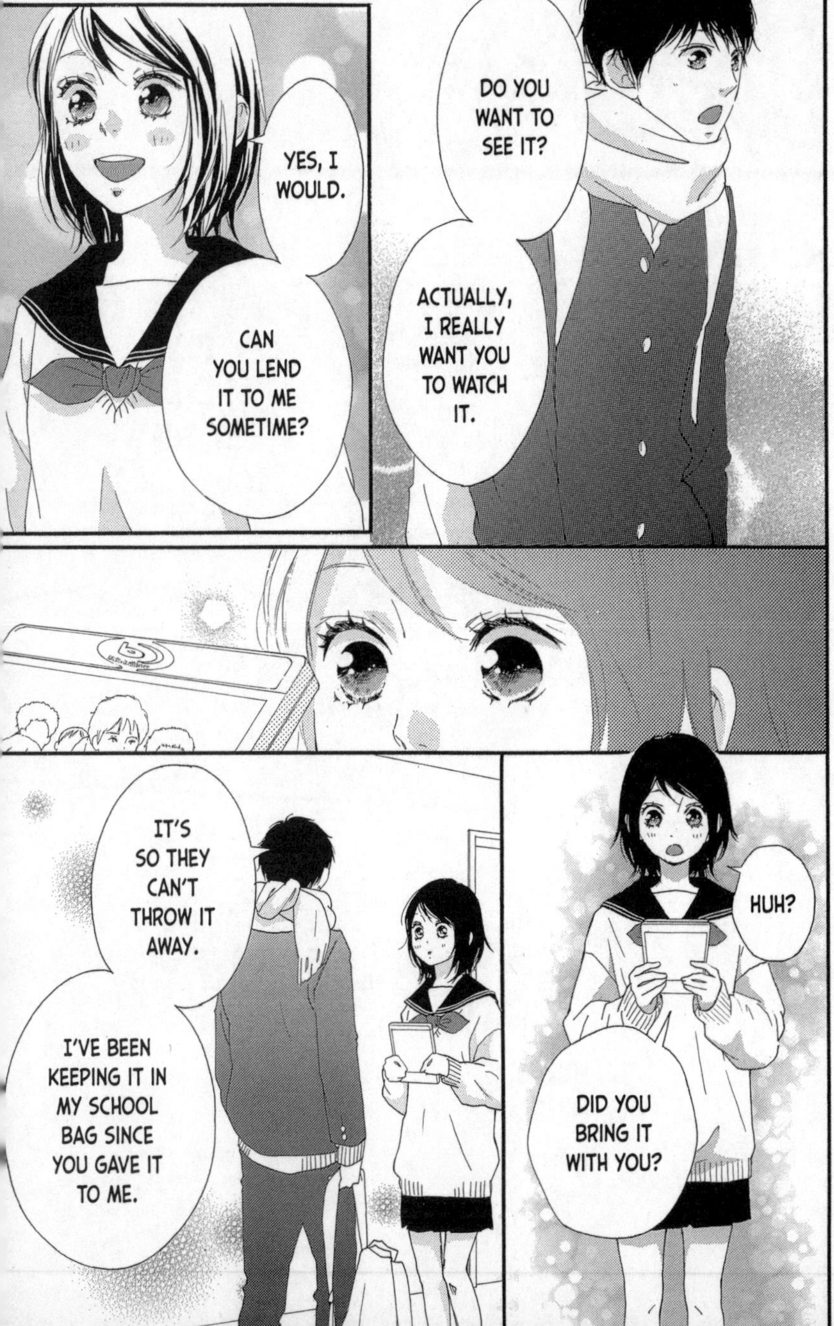
DO YOU WANT TO SEE IT?
ACTUALLY, I REALLY WANT YOU TO WATCH IT.
YES, I WOULD.
CAN YOU LEND IT TO ME SOMETIME?
HUH?
DID YOU BRING IT WITH YOU?
IT'S SO THEY CAN'T THROW IT AWAY.
I'VE BEEN KEEPING IT IN MY SCHOOL BAG SINCE YOU GAVE IT TO ME.

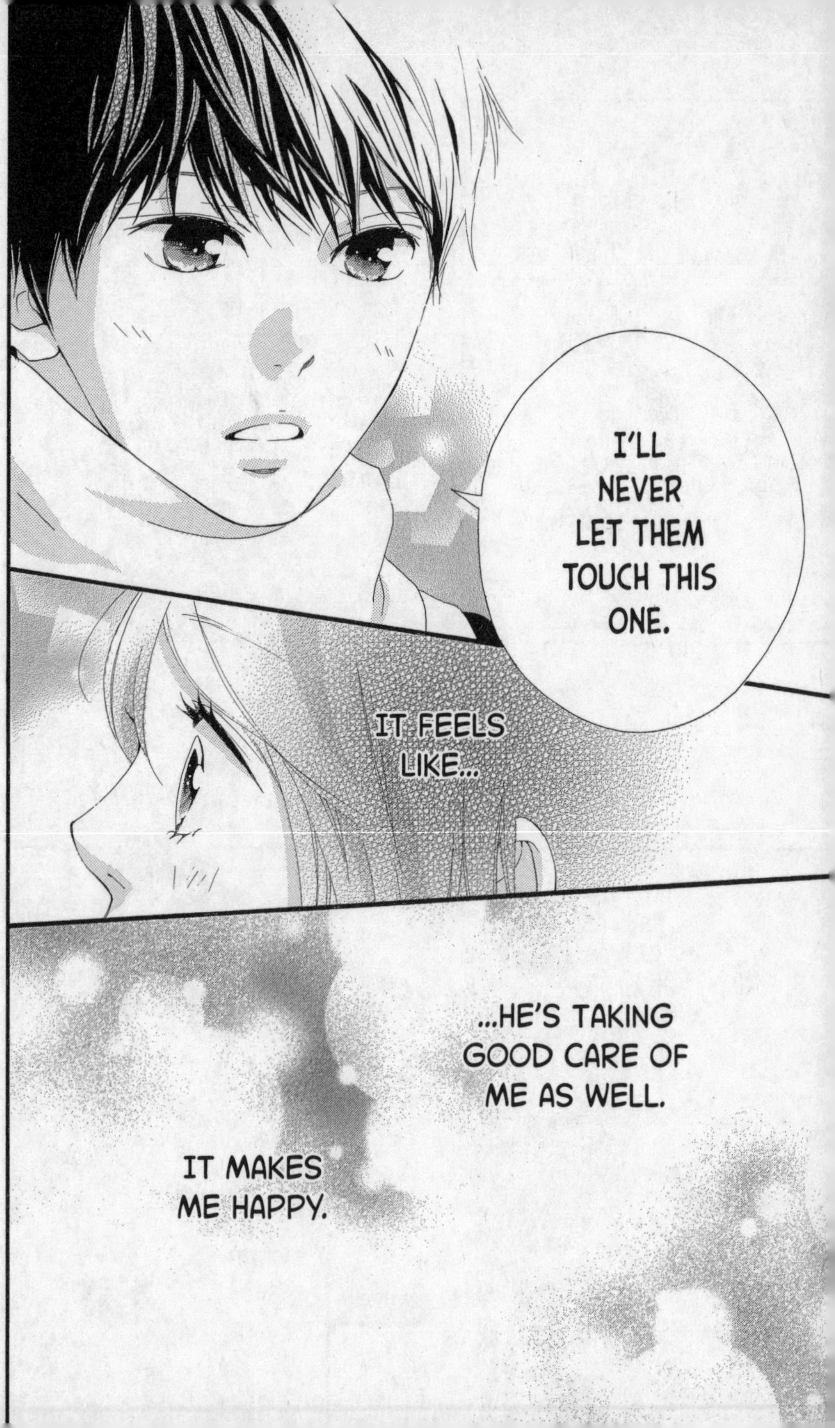
I'LL NEVER LET THEM TOUCH THIS ONE.
IT FEELS LIKE...
...HE'S TAKING GOOD CARE OF ME AS WELL.
IT MAKES ME HAPPY.

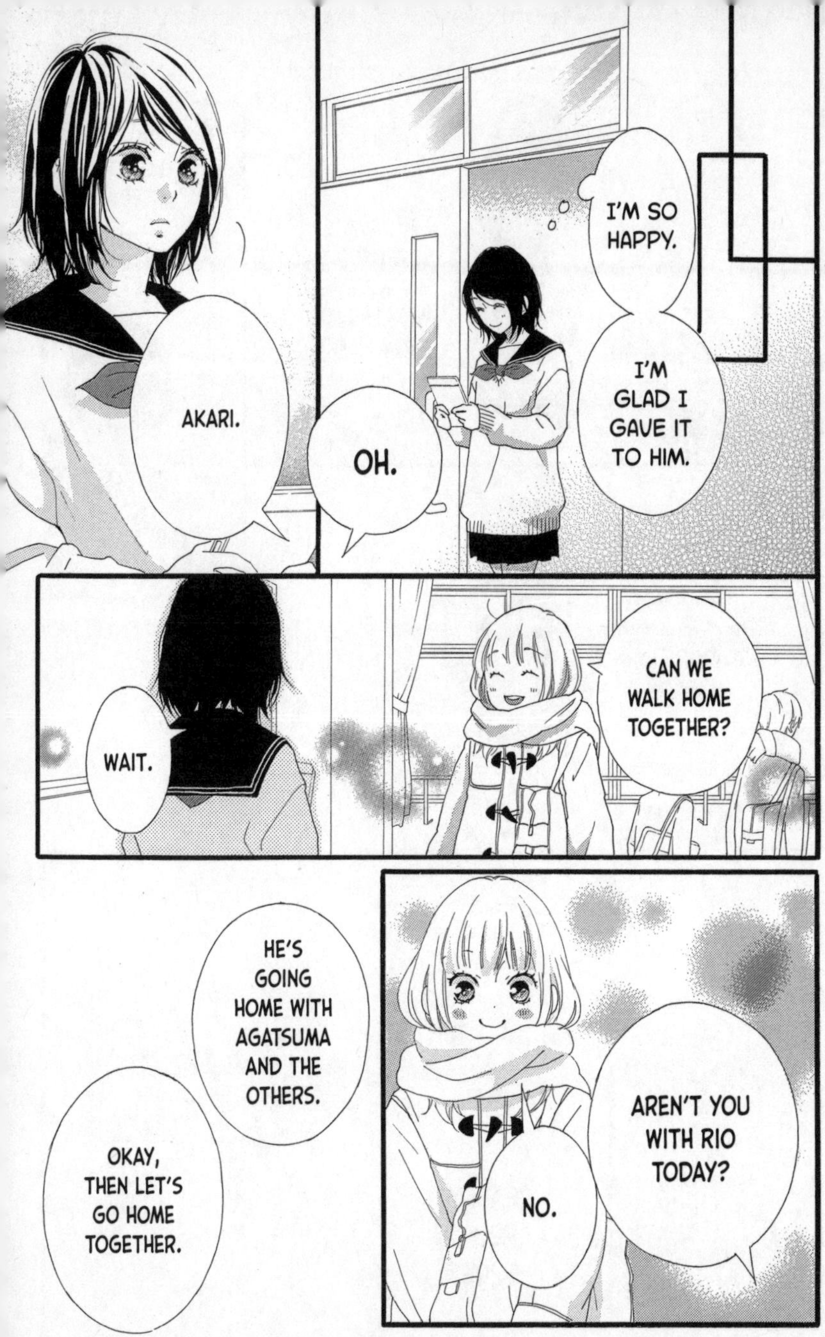
I'M SO HAPPY.
I'M GLAD I GAVE IT TO HIM.
OH.
AKARI.
CAN WE WALK HOME TOGETHER?
WAIT.
AREN'T YOU WITH RIO TODAY?
NO.
HE'S GOING HOME WITH AGATSUMA AND THE OTHERS.
OKAY, THEN LET'S GO HOME TOGETHER.

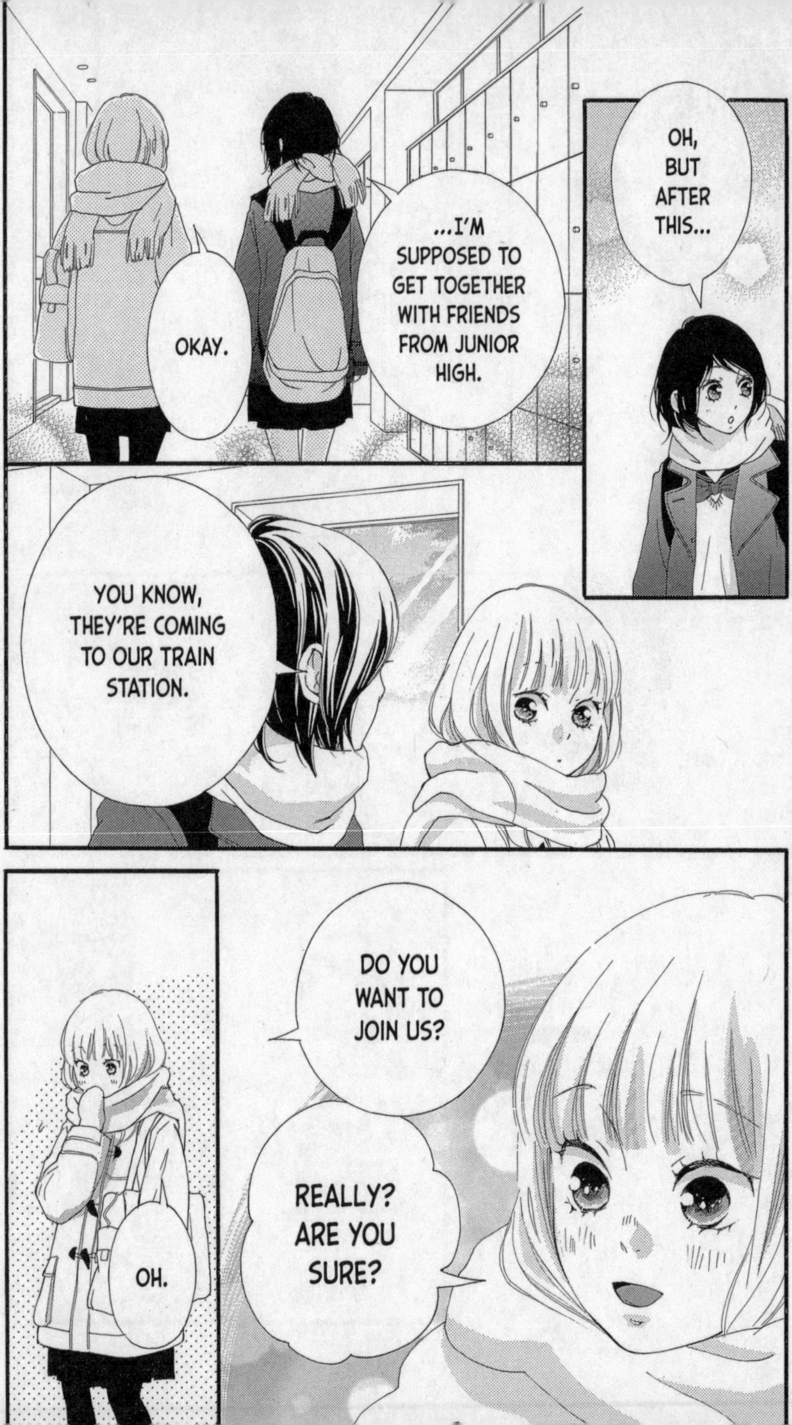
OH, BUT AFTER THIS...
...I'M SUPPOSED TO GET TOGETHER WITH FRIENDS FROM JUNIOR HIGH.
OKAY.
YOU KNOW, THEY'RE COMING TO OUR TRAIN STATION.
DO YOU WANT TO JOIN US?
REALLY? ARE YOU SURE?
OH.

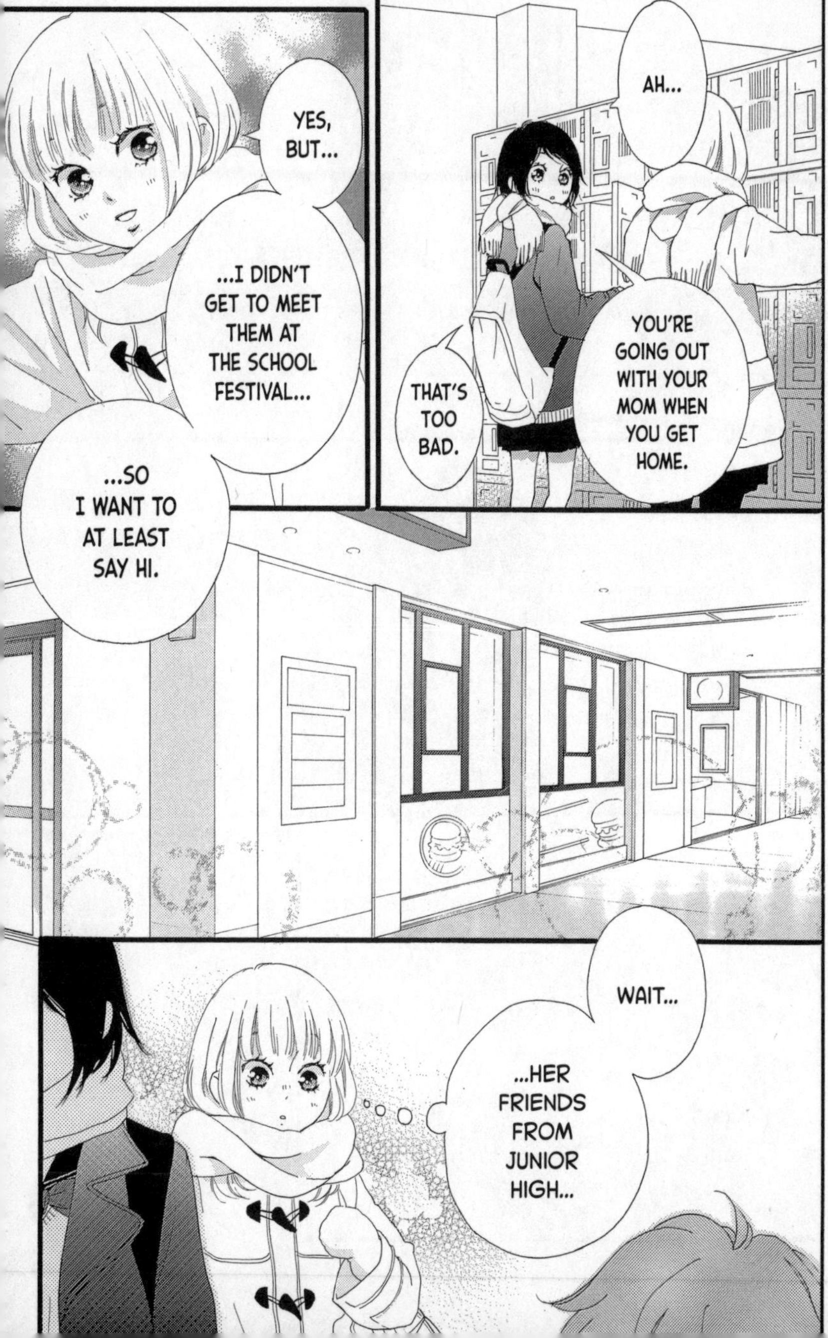
AH...
YOU'RE GOING OUT WITH YOUR MOM WHEN YOU GET HOME.
THAT'S TOO BAD.
YES, BUT...
...I DIDN'T GET TO MEET THEM AT THE SCHOOL FESTIVAL...
...SO I WANT TO AT LEAST SAY HI.
WAIT...
...HER FRIENDS FROM JUNIOR HIGH...

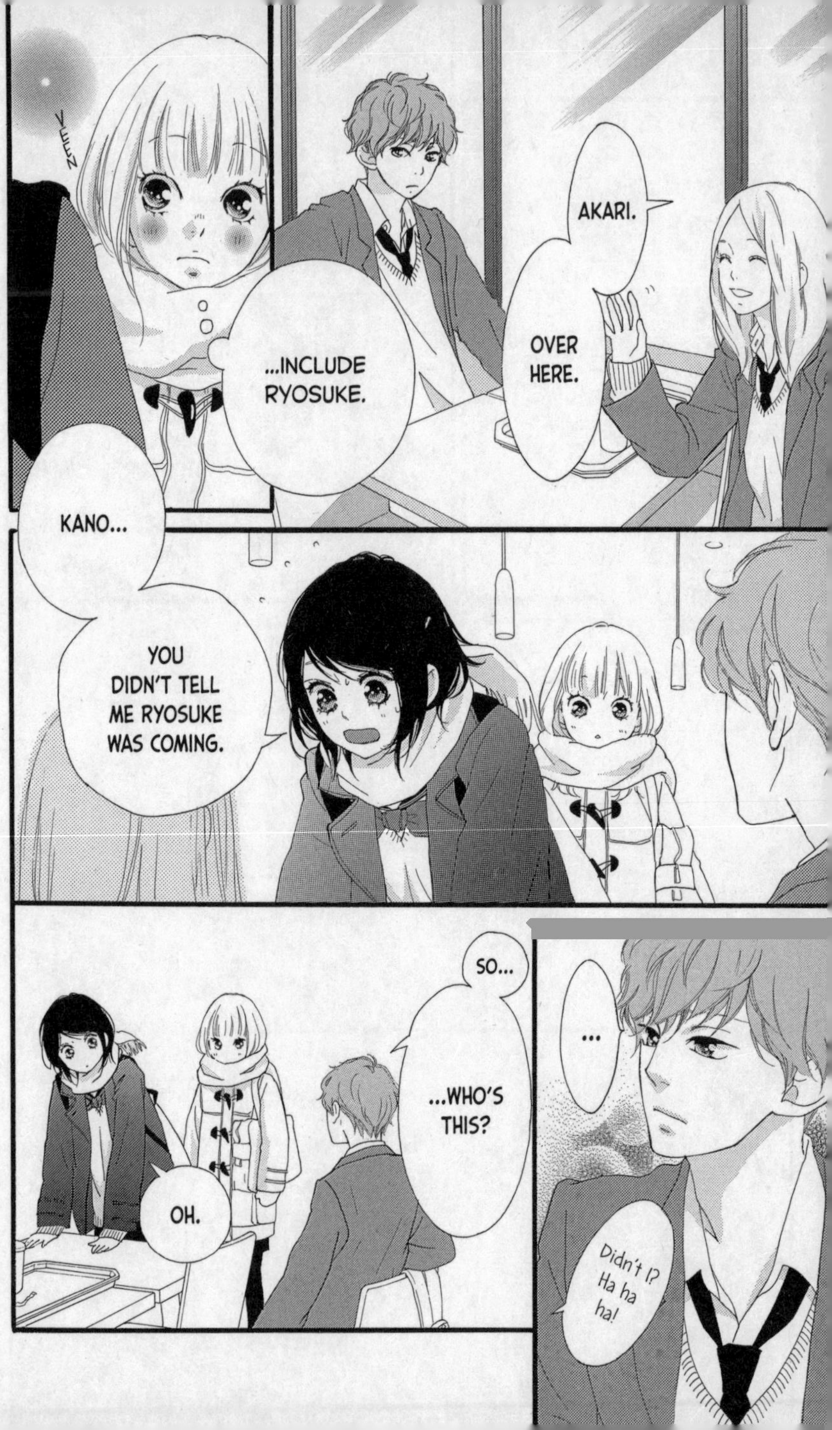
AKARI.
OVER HERE.
...INCLUDE RYOSUKE.
VEEN
KANO...
YOU DIDN'T TELL ME RYOSUKE WAS COMING.
...
Didn't I? Ha ha ha!
SO...
...WHO'S THIS?
OH.

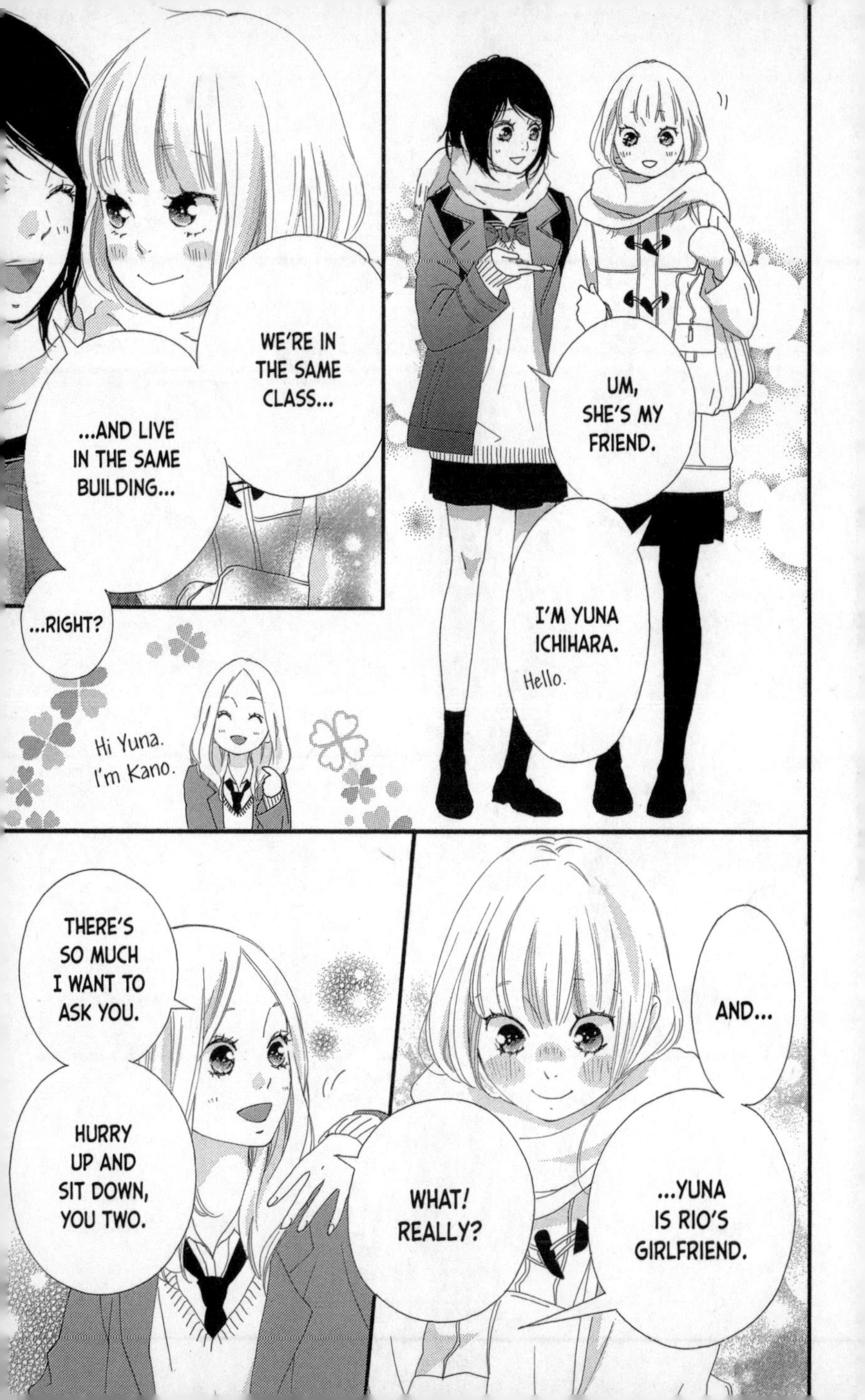
UM, SHE'S MY FRIEND.
I'M YUNA ICHIHARA.
Hello.
WE'RE IN THE SAME CLASS...
...AND LIVE IN THE SAME BUILDING...
...RIGHT?
Hi Yuna. I'm Kano.
AND...
...YUNA IS RIO'S GIRLFRIEND.
WHAT! REALLY?
THERE'S SO MUCH I WANT TO ASK YOU.
HURRY UP AND SIT DOWN, YOU TWO.

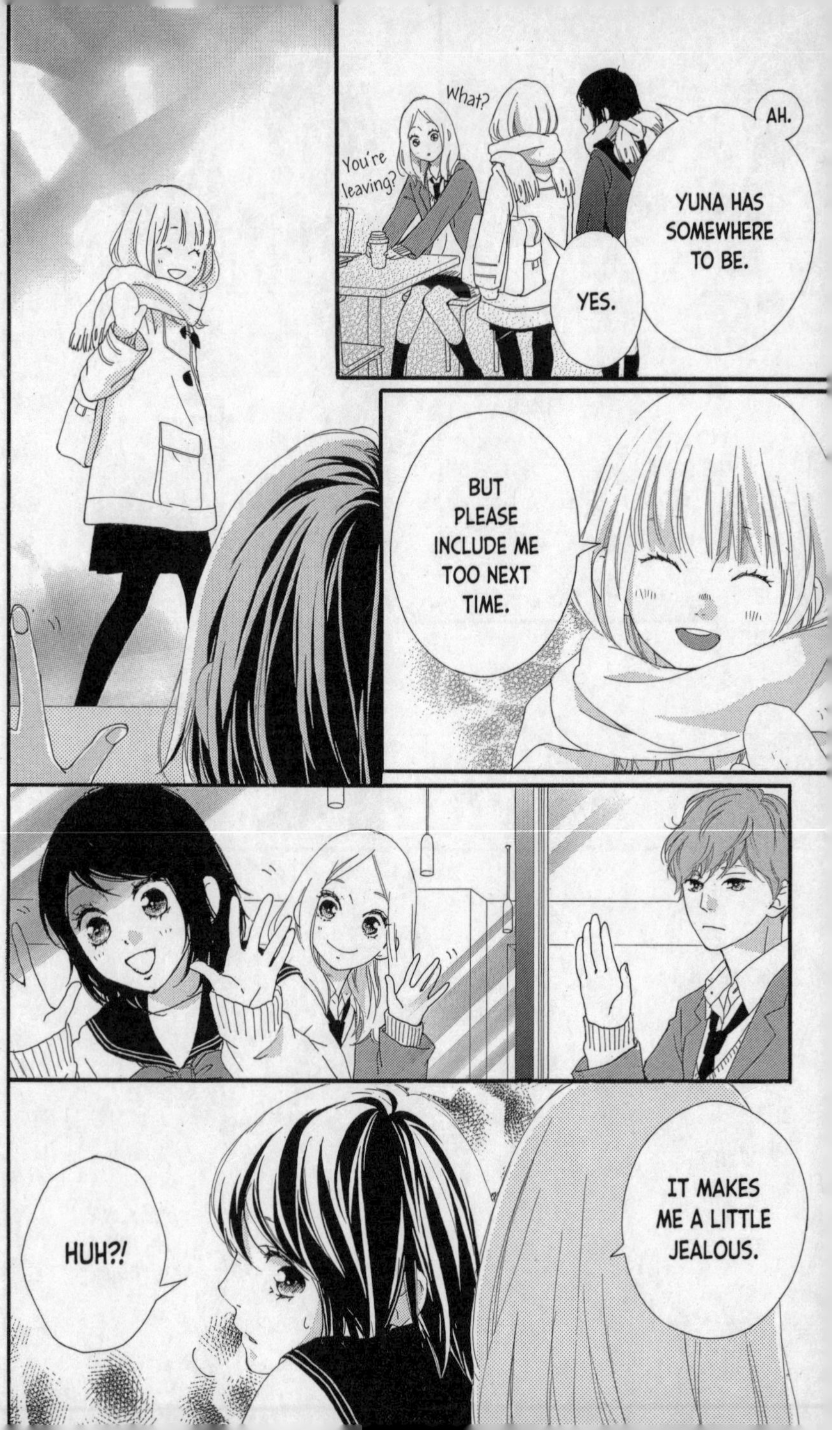
AH.
YUNA HAS SOMEWHERE TO BE.
YES.
What?
You're leaving?
BUT PLEASE INCLUDE ME TOO NEXT TIME.
IT MAKES ME A LITTLE JEALOUS.
HUH?!

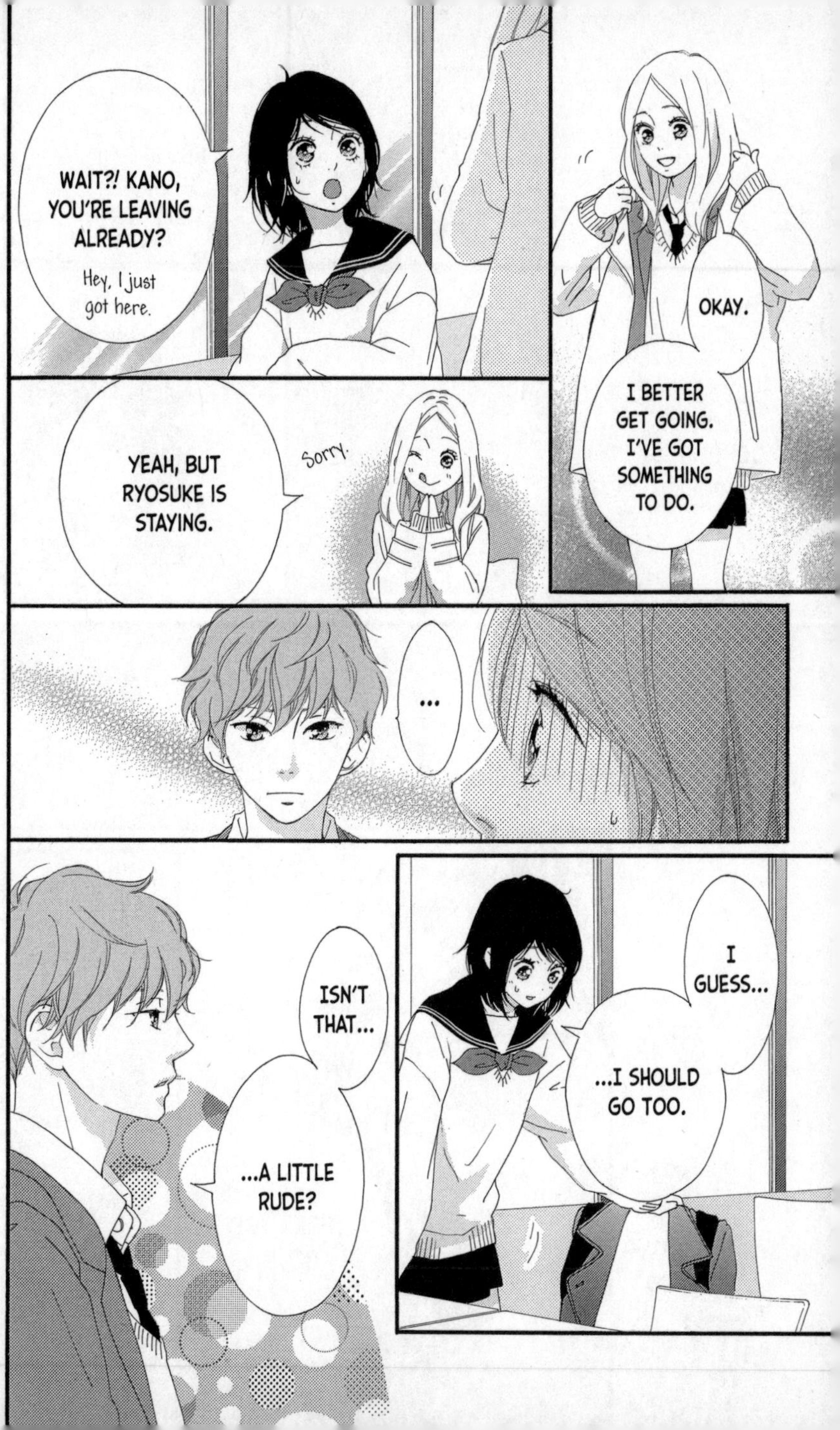
OKAY.
I BETTER GET GOING. I'VE GOT SOMETHING TO DO.
WAIT?! KANO, YOU'RE LEAVING ALREADY?
Hey, I just got here.
YEAH, BUT RYOSUKE IS STAYING.
Sorry.
...
I GUESS...
...I SHOULD GO TOO.
ISN'T THAT...
...A LITTLE RUDE?

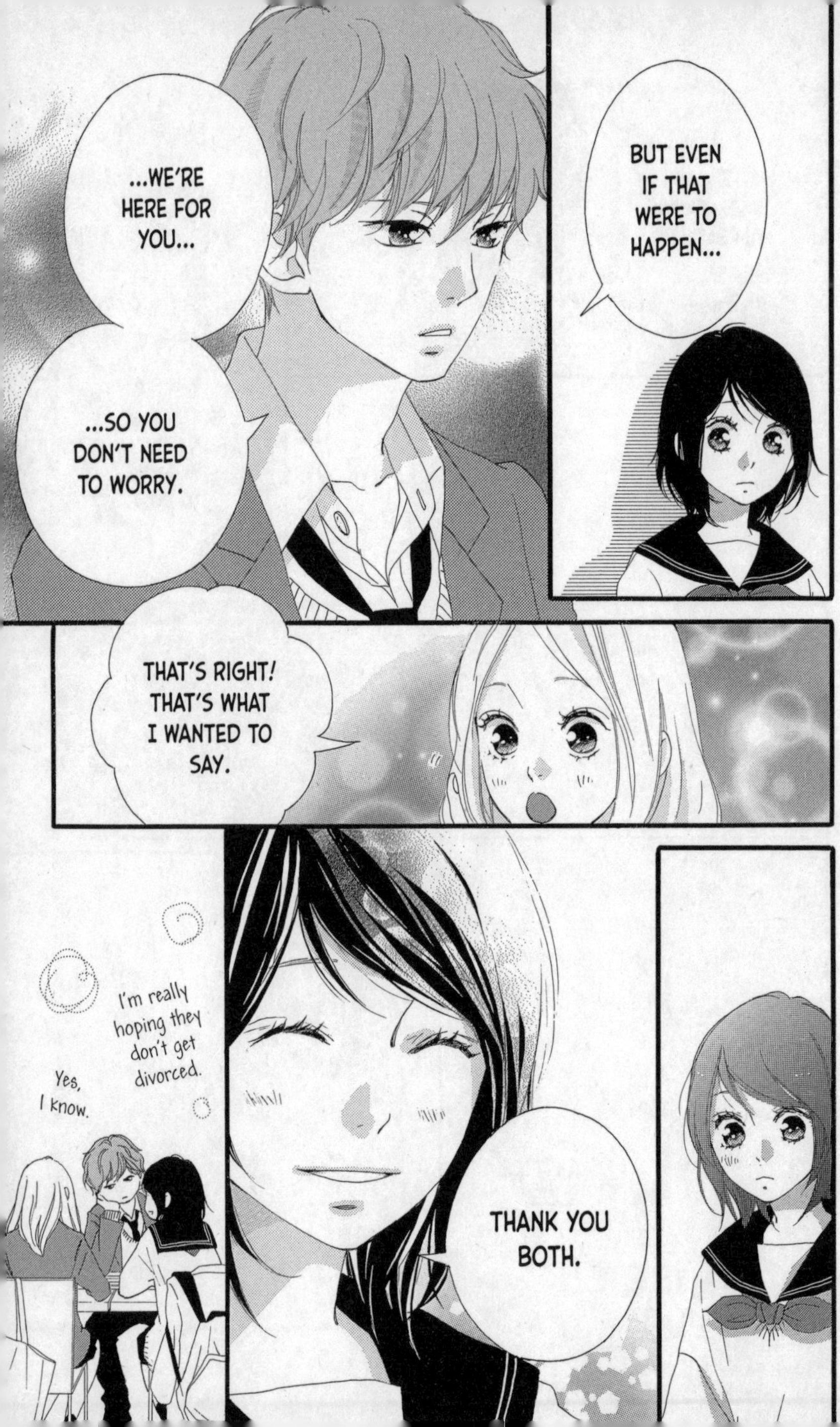
BUT EVEN IF THAT WERE TO HAPPEN...
...WE'RE HERE FOR YOU...
...SO YOU DON'T NEED TO WORRY.
THAT'S RIGHT! THAT'S WHAT I WANTED TO SAY.
THANK YOU BOTH.
I'm really hoping they don't get divorced.
Yes, I know.

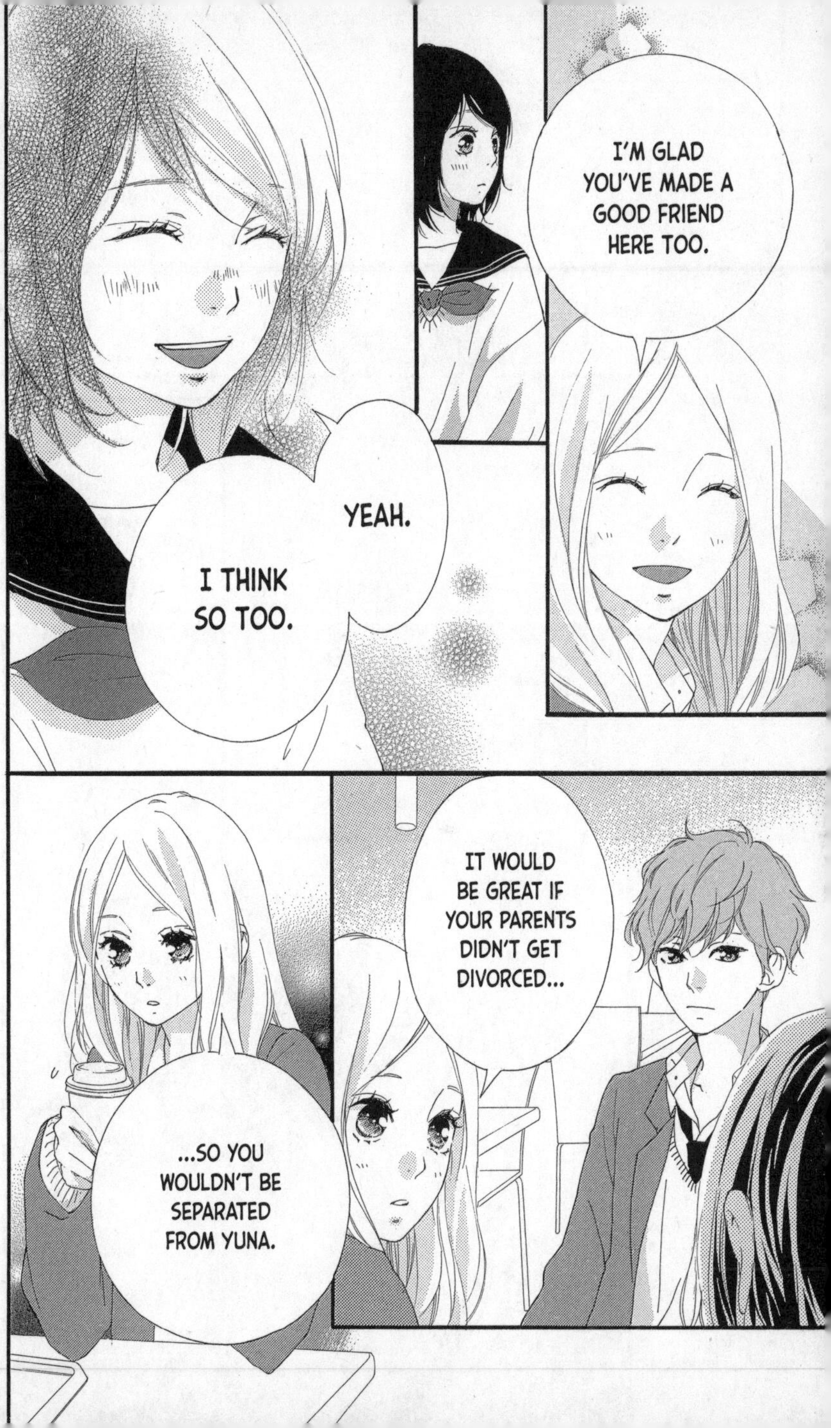
I'M GLAD YOU'VE MADE A GOOD FRIEND HERE TOO.
YEAH.
I THINK SO TOO.
IT WOULD BE GREAT IF YOUR PARENTS DIDN'T GET DIVORCED...
...SO YOU WOULDN'T BE SEPARATED FROM YUNA.

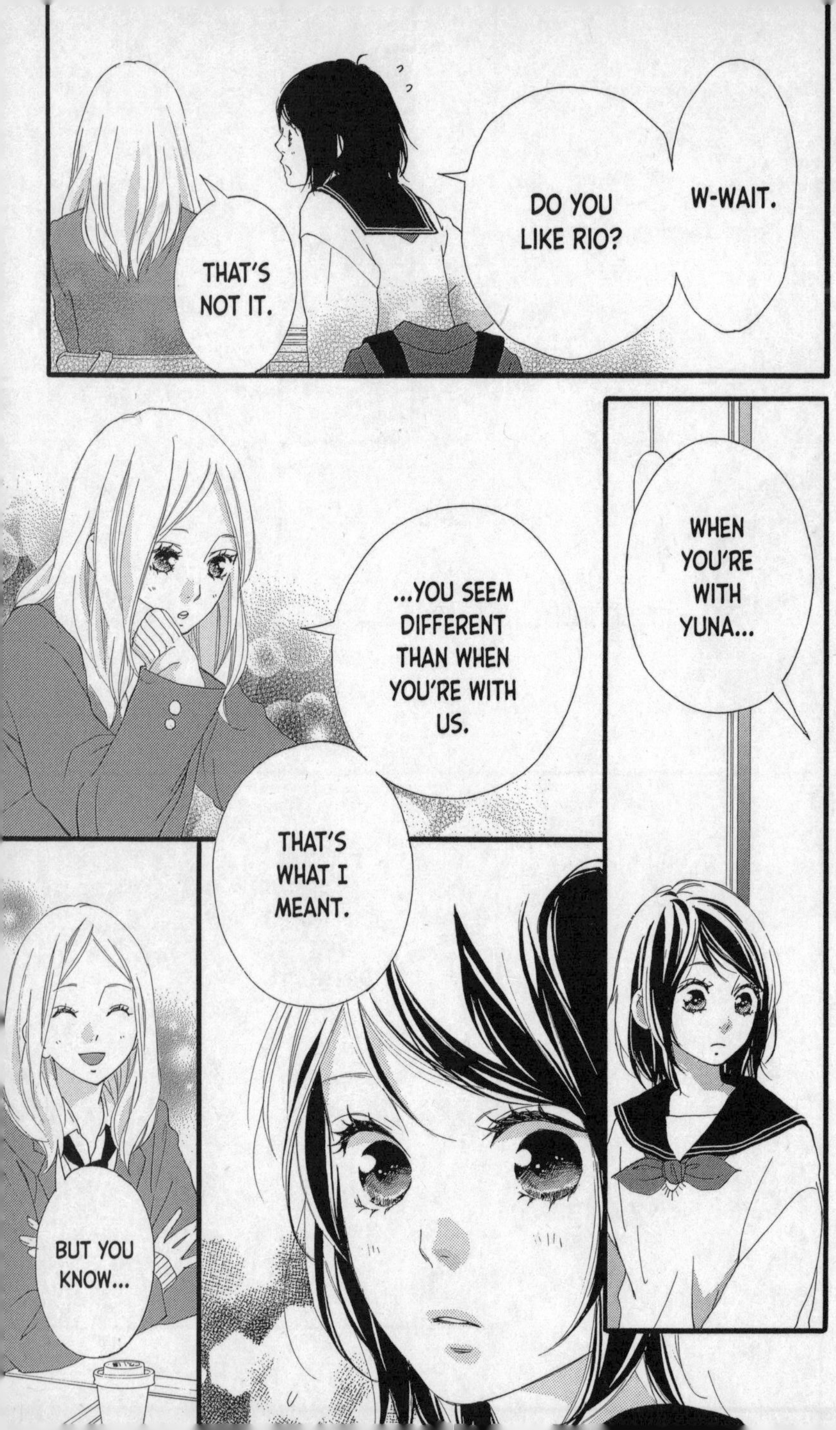
W-WAIT.
DO YOU LIKE RIO?
THAT'S NOT IT.
WHEN YOU'RE WITH YUNA...
...YOU SEEM DIFFERENT THAN WHEN YOU'RE WITH US.
THAT'S WHAT I MEANT.
BUT YOU KNOW...

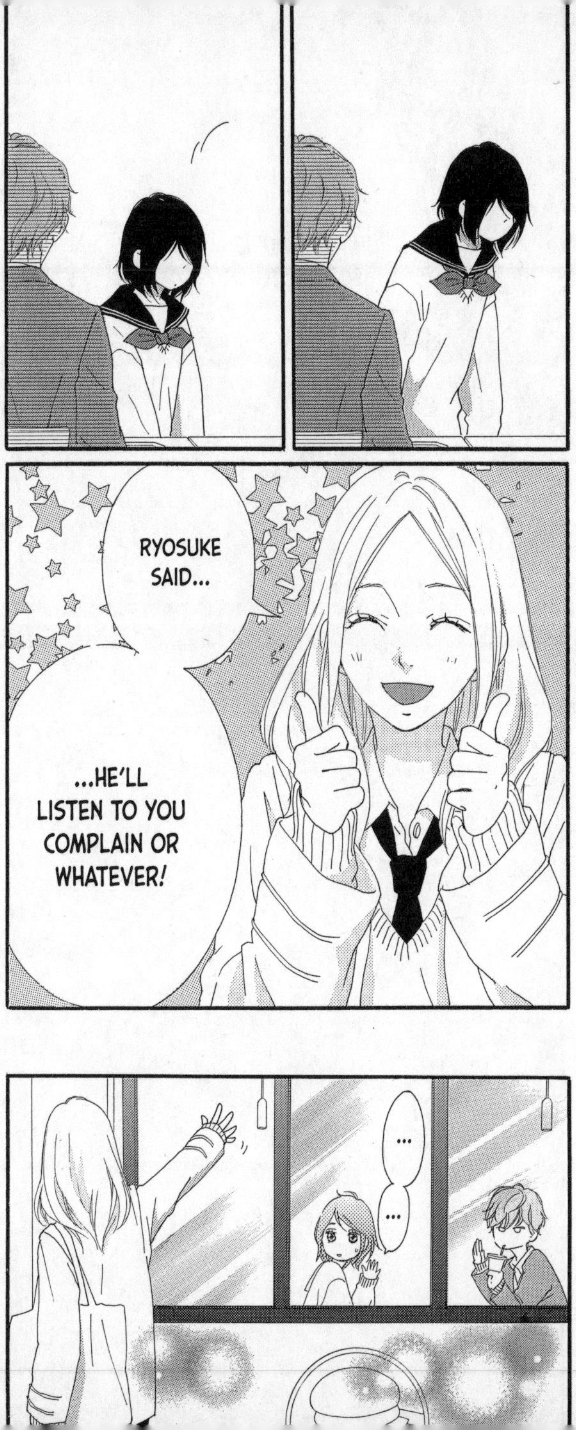
RYOSUKE SAID...
...HE'LL LISTEN TO YOU COMPLAIN OR WHATEVER!
...
...

I always appreciate reading letters from everyone. Sometimes people will write, "I don't know if you'll read this," but every letter I receive I read gratefully. I really look forward to not only your thoughts about my manga, but the things you share about your daily life. I often find myself giggling out loud. You guys give me lots of energy, so thank you so much. I want to keep writing the kind of manga that will make you think, "I want to write to her!" Thanks for your support.

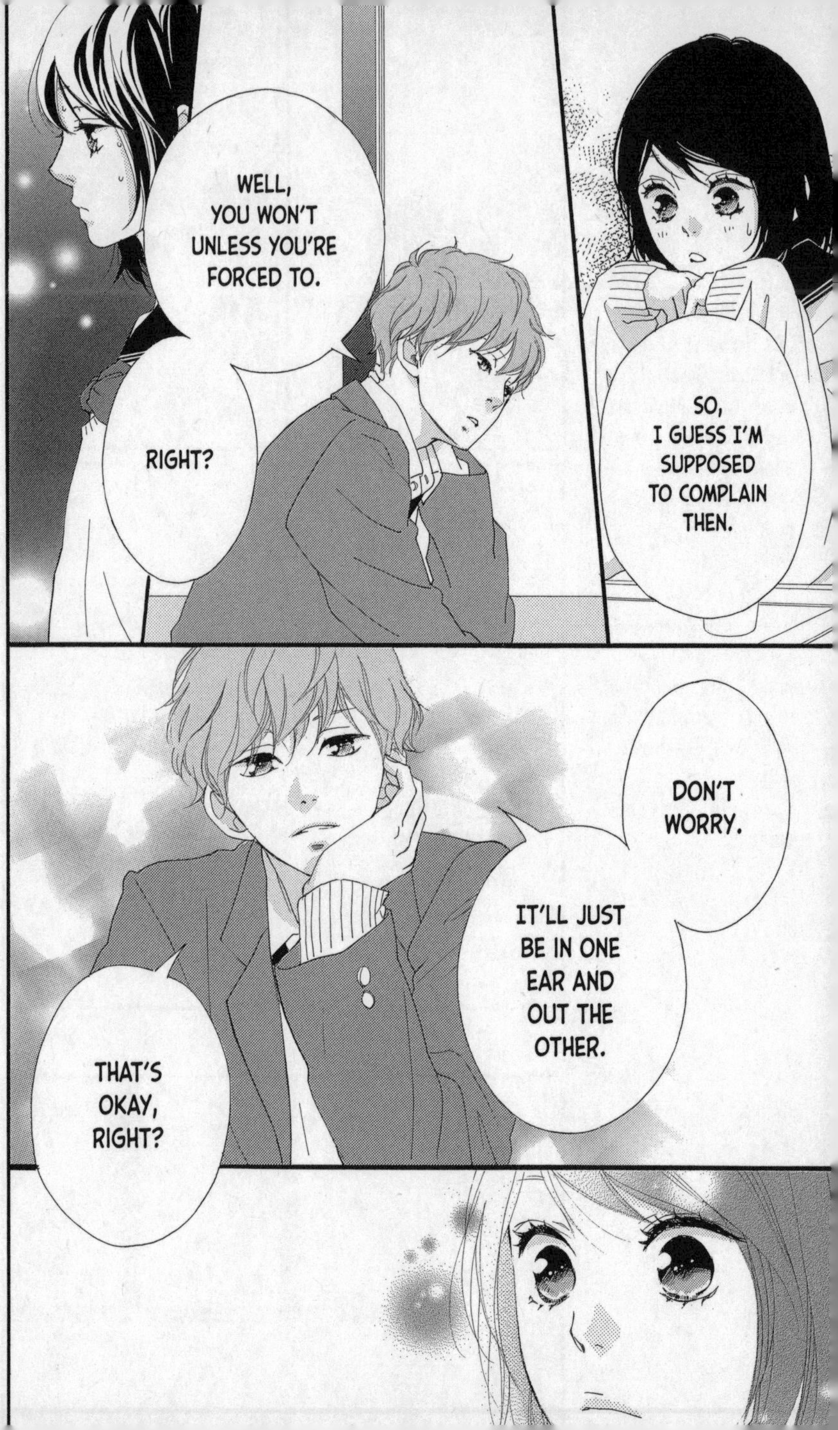
SO, I GUESS I'M SUPPOSED TO COMPLAIN THEN.
WELL, YOU WON'T UNLESS YOU'RE FORCED TO.
RIGHT?
DON'T WORRY.
IT'LL JUST BE IN ONE EAR AND OUT THE OTHER.
THAT'S OKAY, RIGHT?

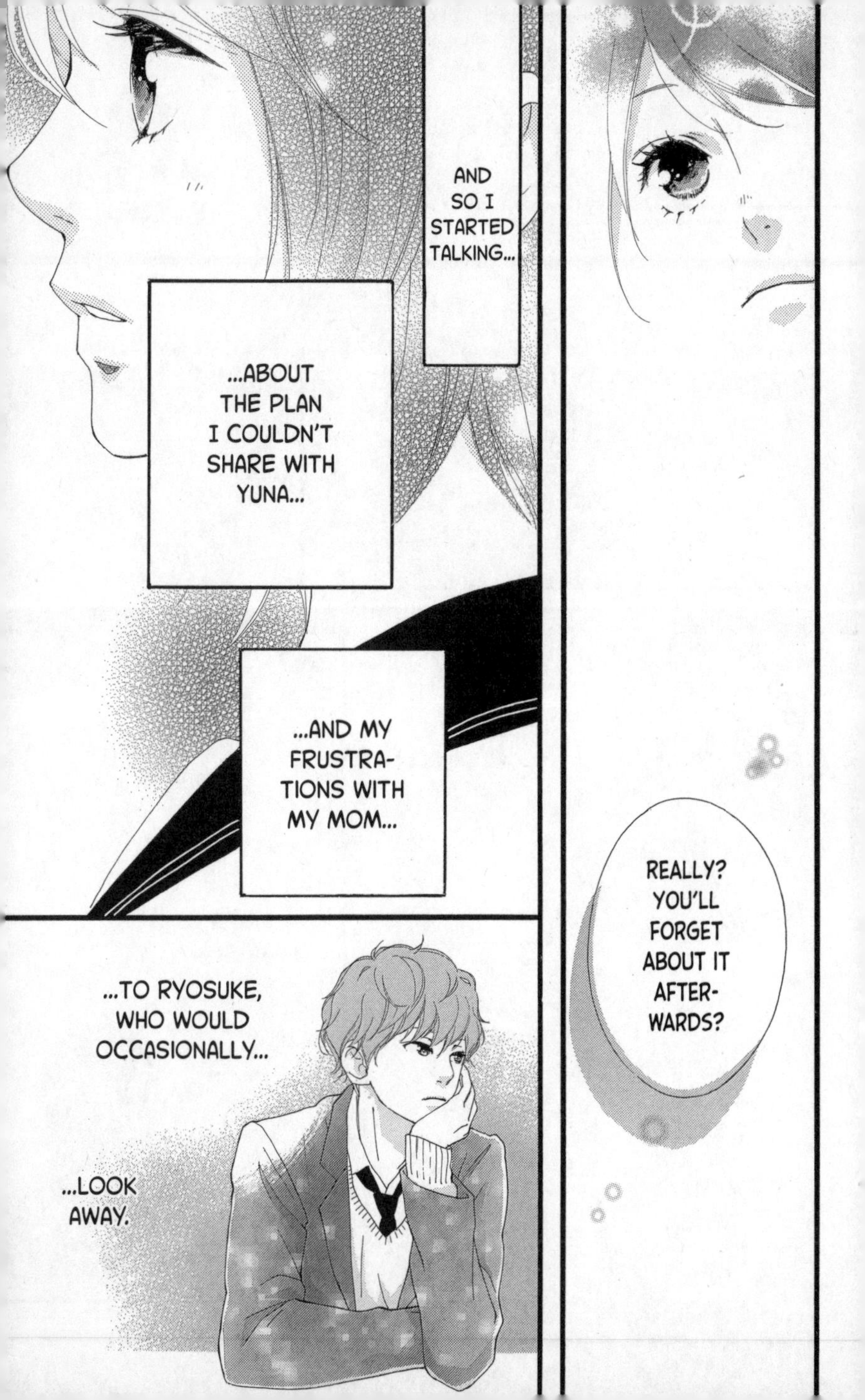
REALLY? YOU'LL FORGET ABOUT IT AFTER-WARDS?
AND SO I STARTED TALKING...
...ABOUT THE PLAN I COULDN'T SHARE WITH YUNA...
...AND MY FRUSTRA-TIONS WITH MY MOM...
...TO RYOSUKE, WHO WOULD OCCASIONALLY...
...LOOK AWAY.

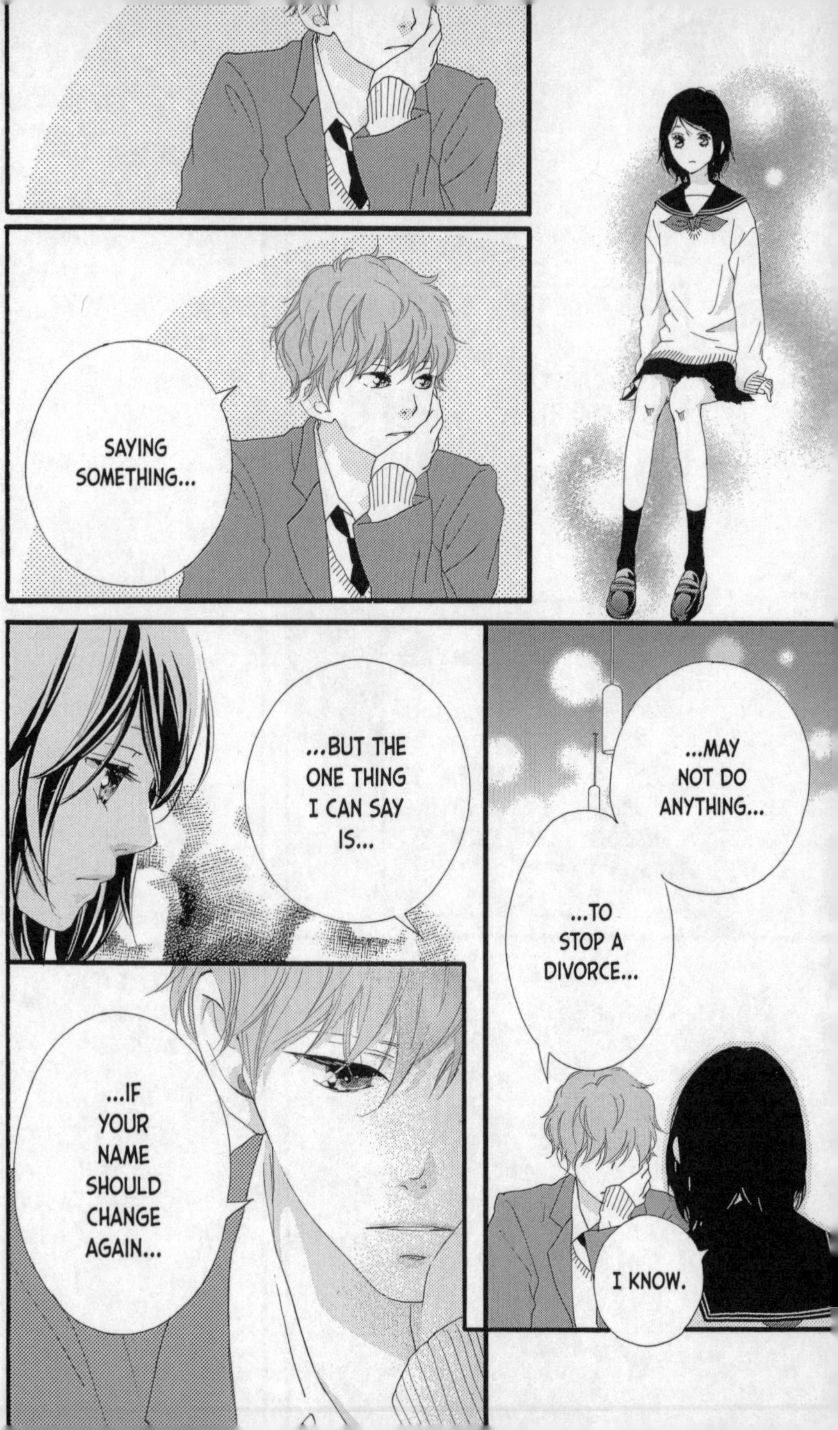
SAYING SOMETHING...
...MAY NOT DO ANYTHING...
...TO STOP A DIVORCE...
I KNOW.
...BUT THE ONE THING I CAN SAY IS...
...IF YOUR NAME SHOULD CHANGE AGAIN...

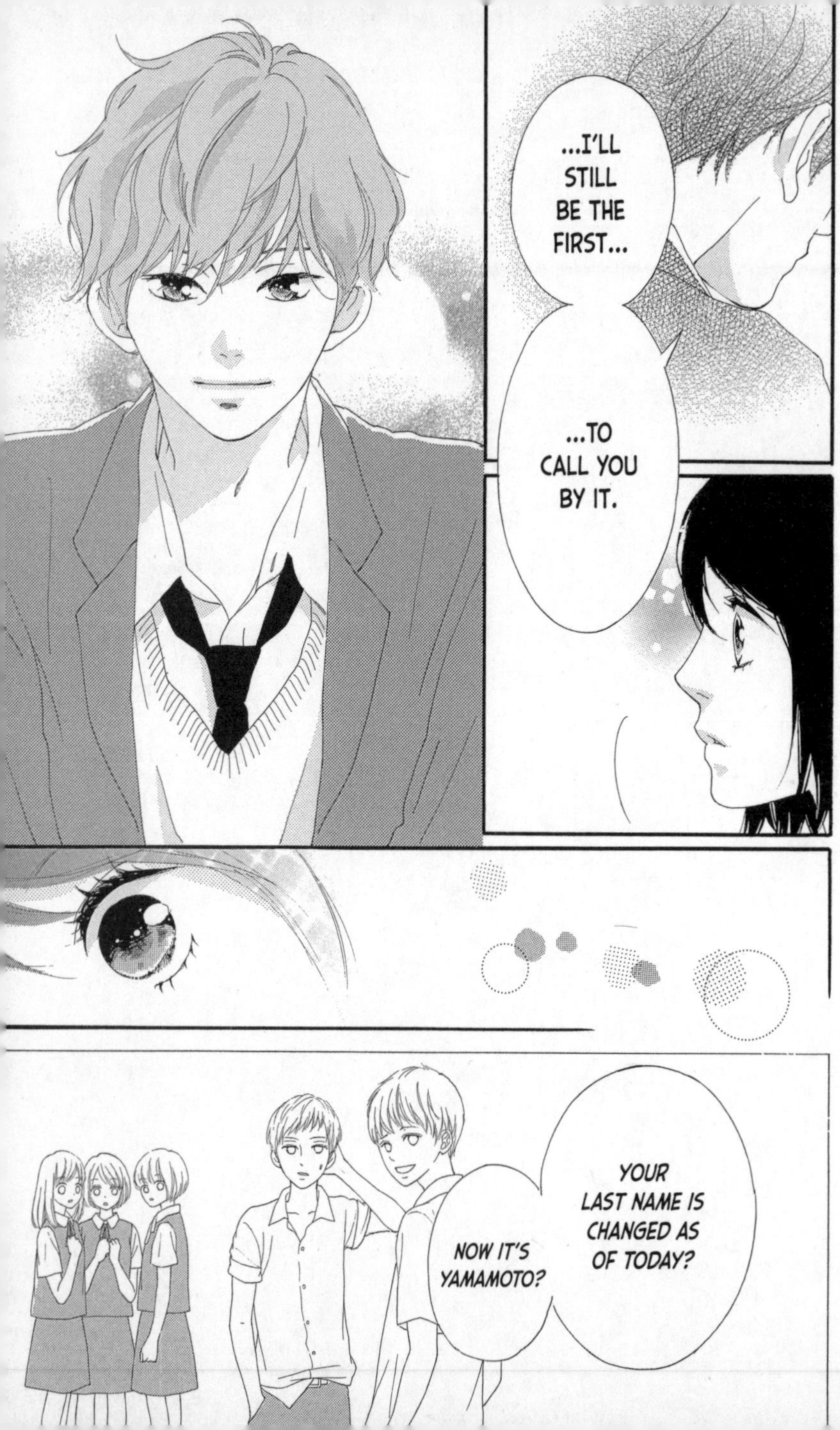
...I'LL STILL BE THE FIRST...
...TO CALL YOU BY IT.
YOUR LAST NAME IS CHANGED AS OF TODAY?
NOW IT'S YAMAMOTO?

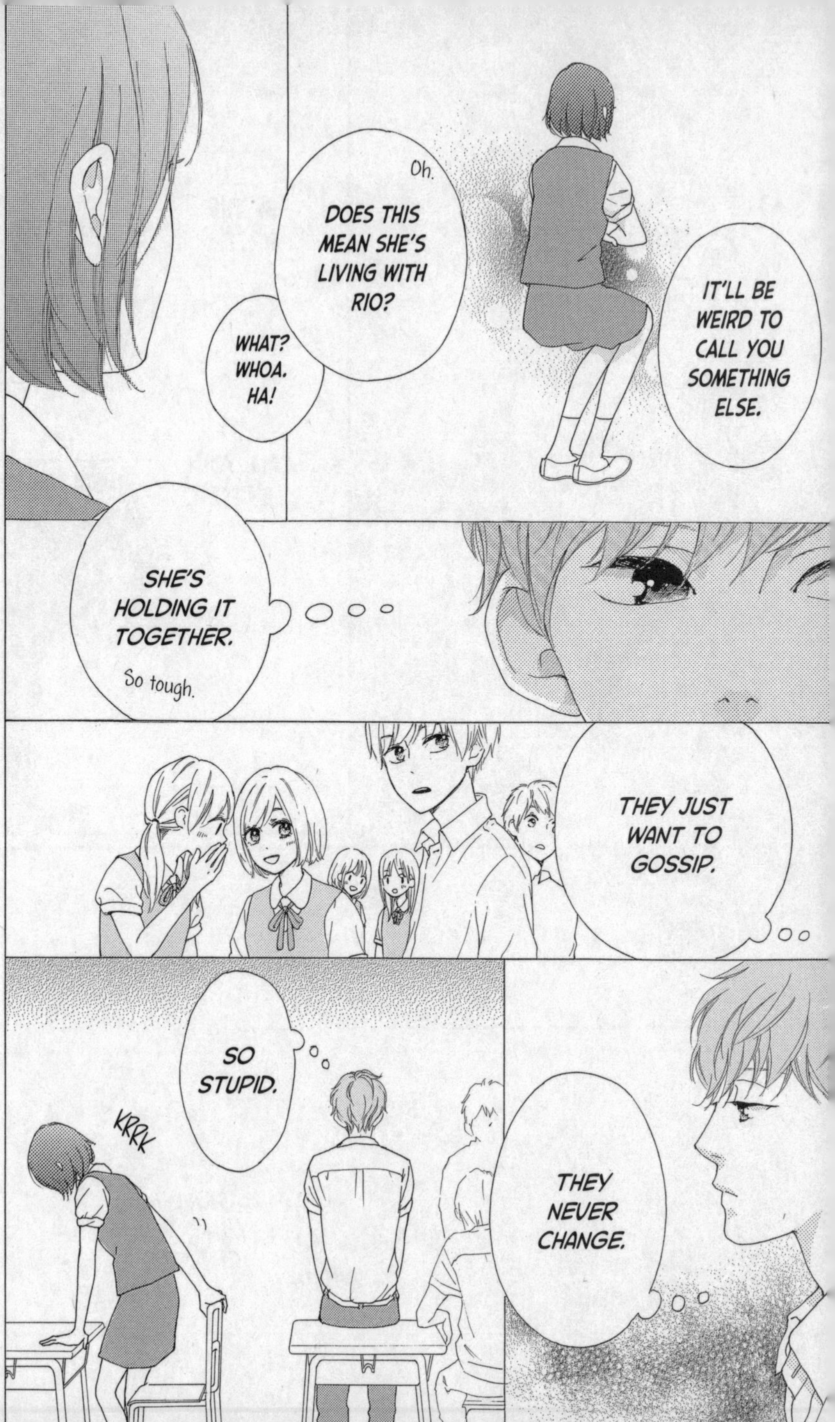
IT'LL BE WEIRD TO CALL YOU SOMETHING ELSE.
Oh.
DOES THIS MEAN SHE'S LIVING WITH RIO?
WHAT? WHOA. HA!
SHE'S HOLDING IT TOGETHER.
So tough.
THEY JUST WANT TO GOSSIP.
THEY NEVER CHANGE.
SO STUPID.
KRRK

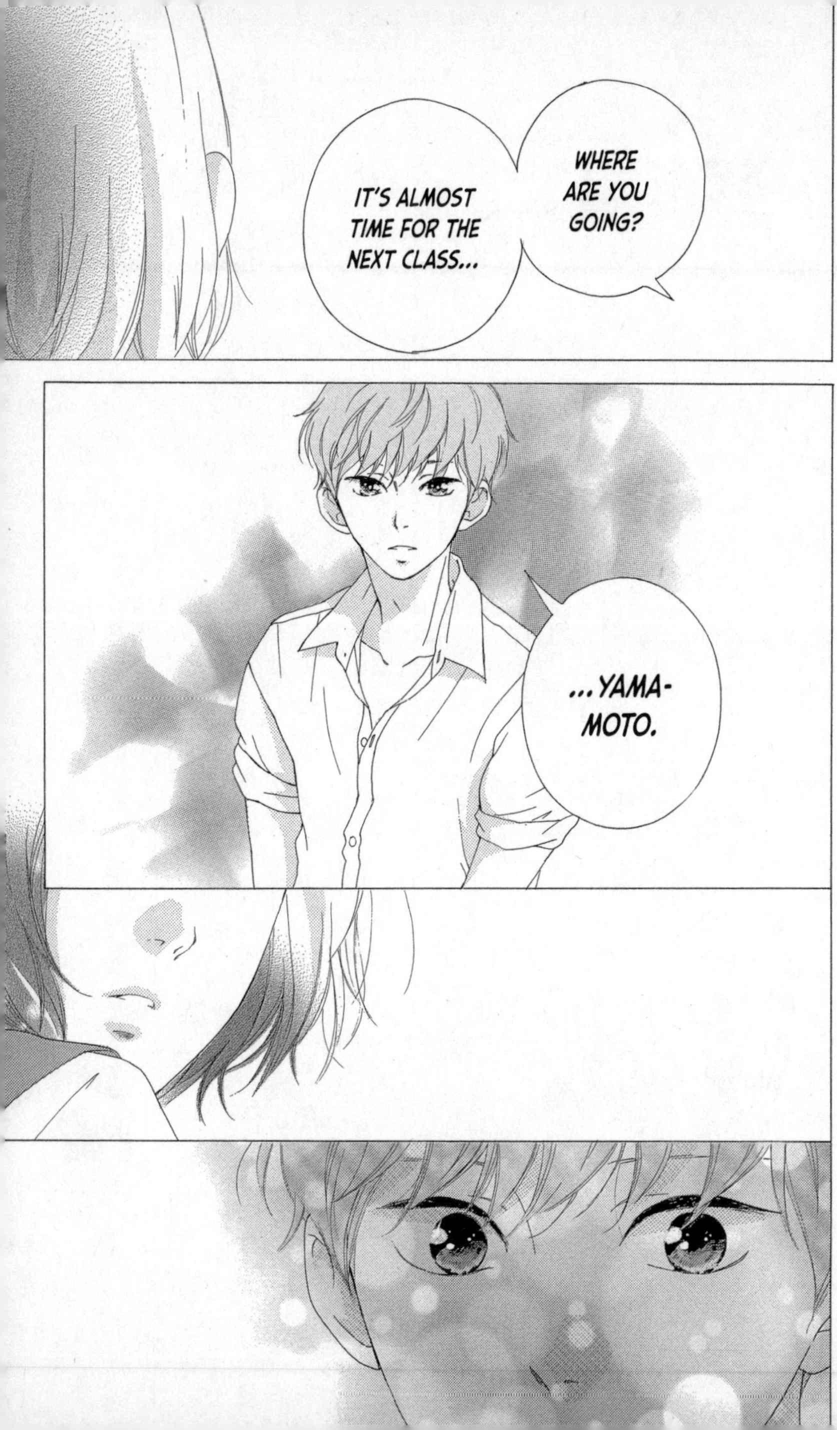
WHERE ARE YOU GOING?
IT'S ALMOST TIME FOR THE NEXT CLASS...
...YAMA-MOTO.

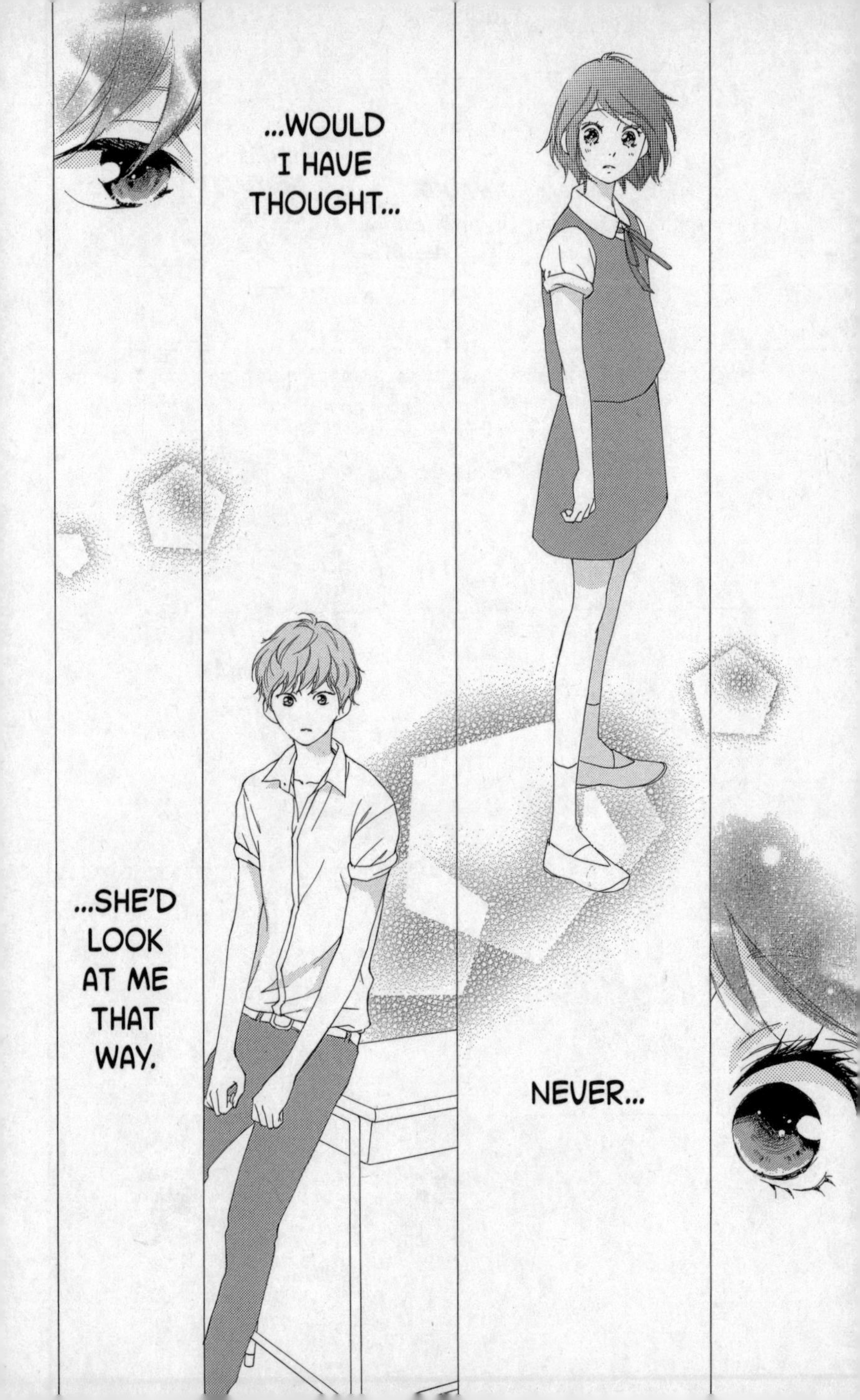
NEVER...
...WOULD I HAVE THOUGHT...
...SHE'D LOOK AT ME THAT WAY.

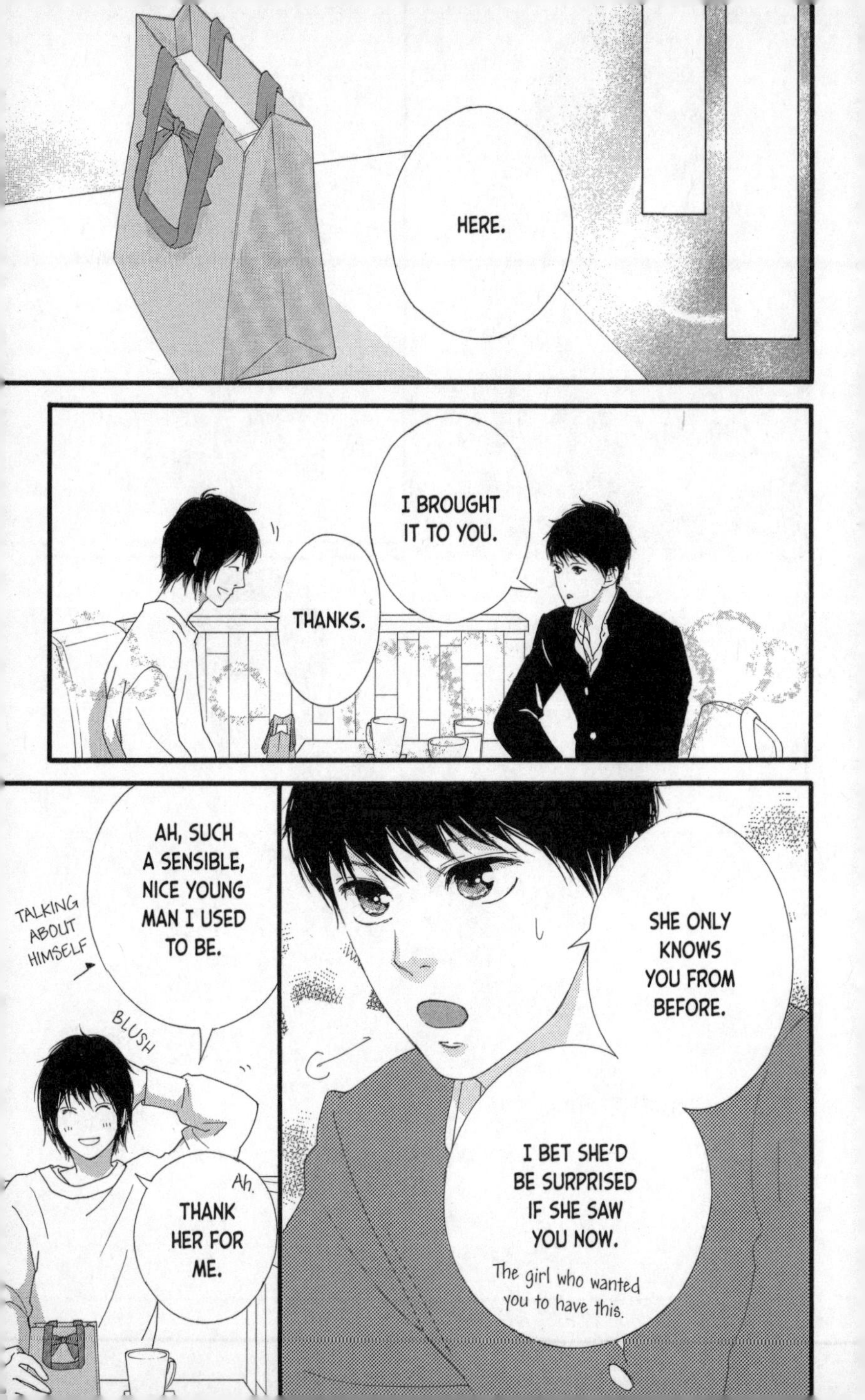
HERE.
I BROUGHT IT TO YOU.
THANKS.
SHE ONLY KNOWS YOU FROM BEFORE.
I BET SHE'D BE SURPRISED IF SHE SAW YOU NOW.
The girl who wanted you to have this.
AH, SUCH A SENSIBLE, NICE YOUNG MAN I USED TO BE.
TALKING ABOUT HIMSELF
BLUSH
Ah.
THANK HER FOR ME.

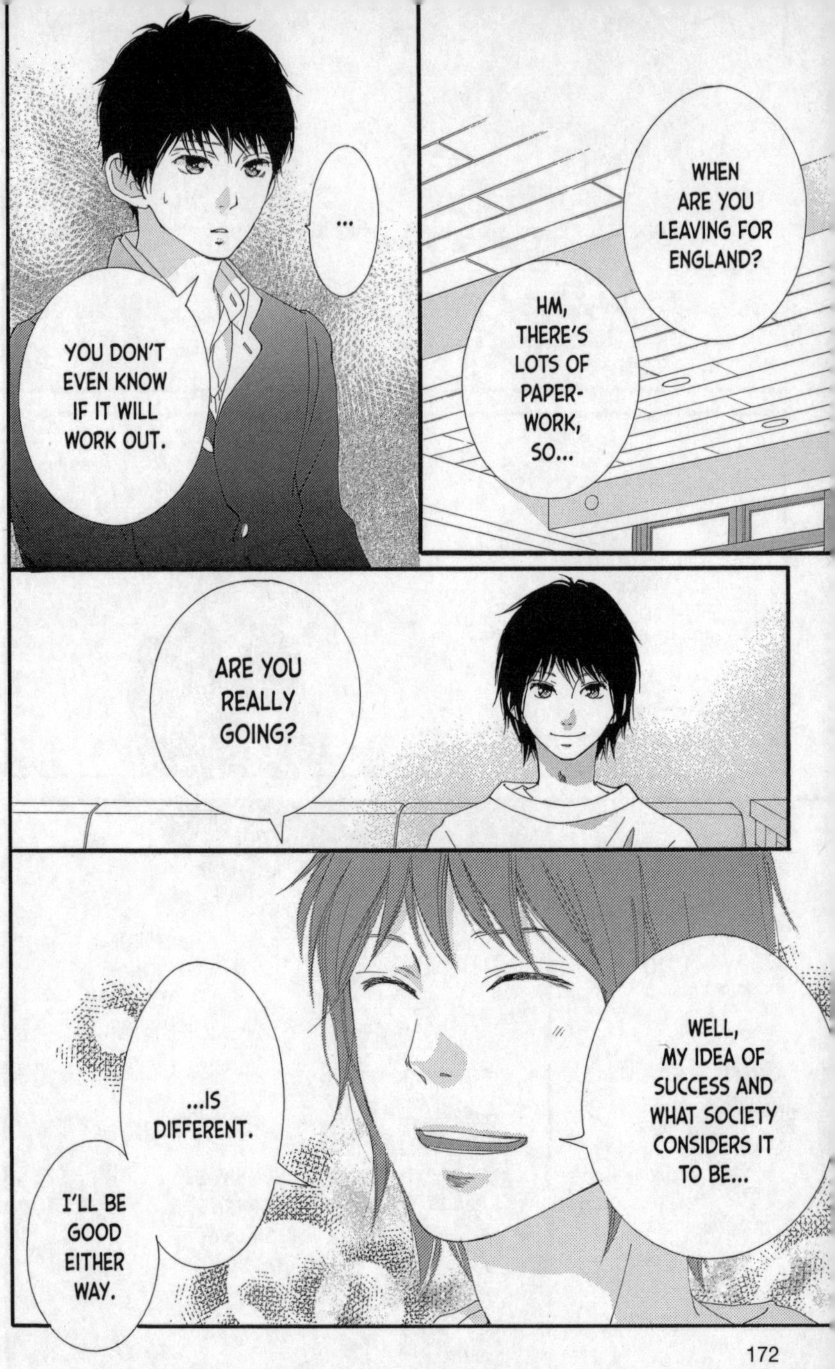
WHEN ARE YOU LEAVING FOR ENGLAND?
HM, THERE'S LOTS OF PAPER-WORK, SO...
...
YOU DON'T EVEN KNOW IF IT WILL WORK OUT.
ARE YOU REALLY GOING?
WELL, MY IDEA OF SUCCESS AND WHAT SOCIETY CONSIDERS IT TO BE...
...IS DIFFERENT.
I'LL BE GOOD EITHER WAY.

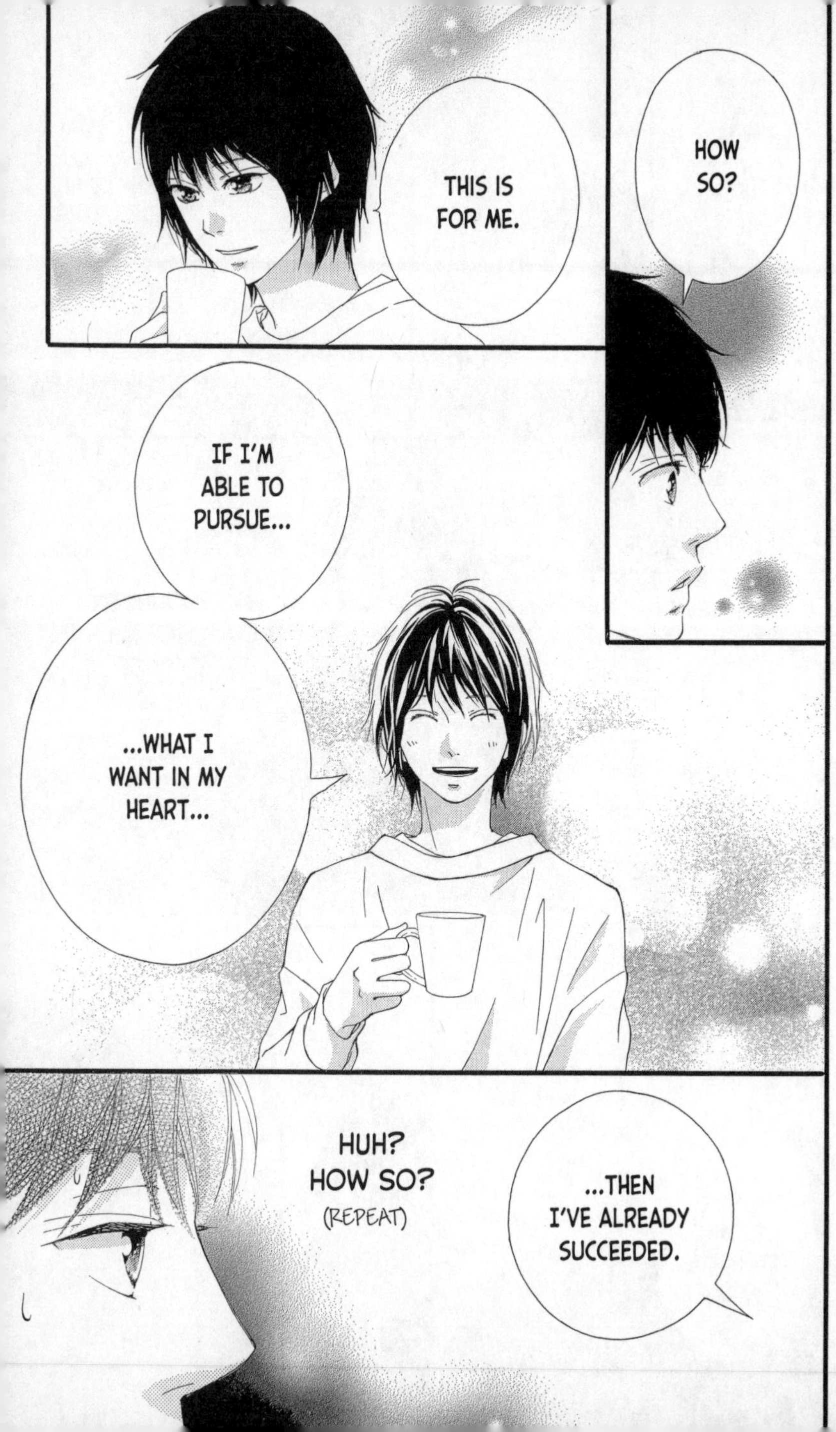
THIS IS FOR ME.
HOW SO?
IF I'M ABLE TO PURSUE...
...WHAT I WANT IN MY HEART...
...THEN I'VE ALREADY SUCCEEDED.
HUH? HOW SO?
(REPEAT)

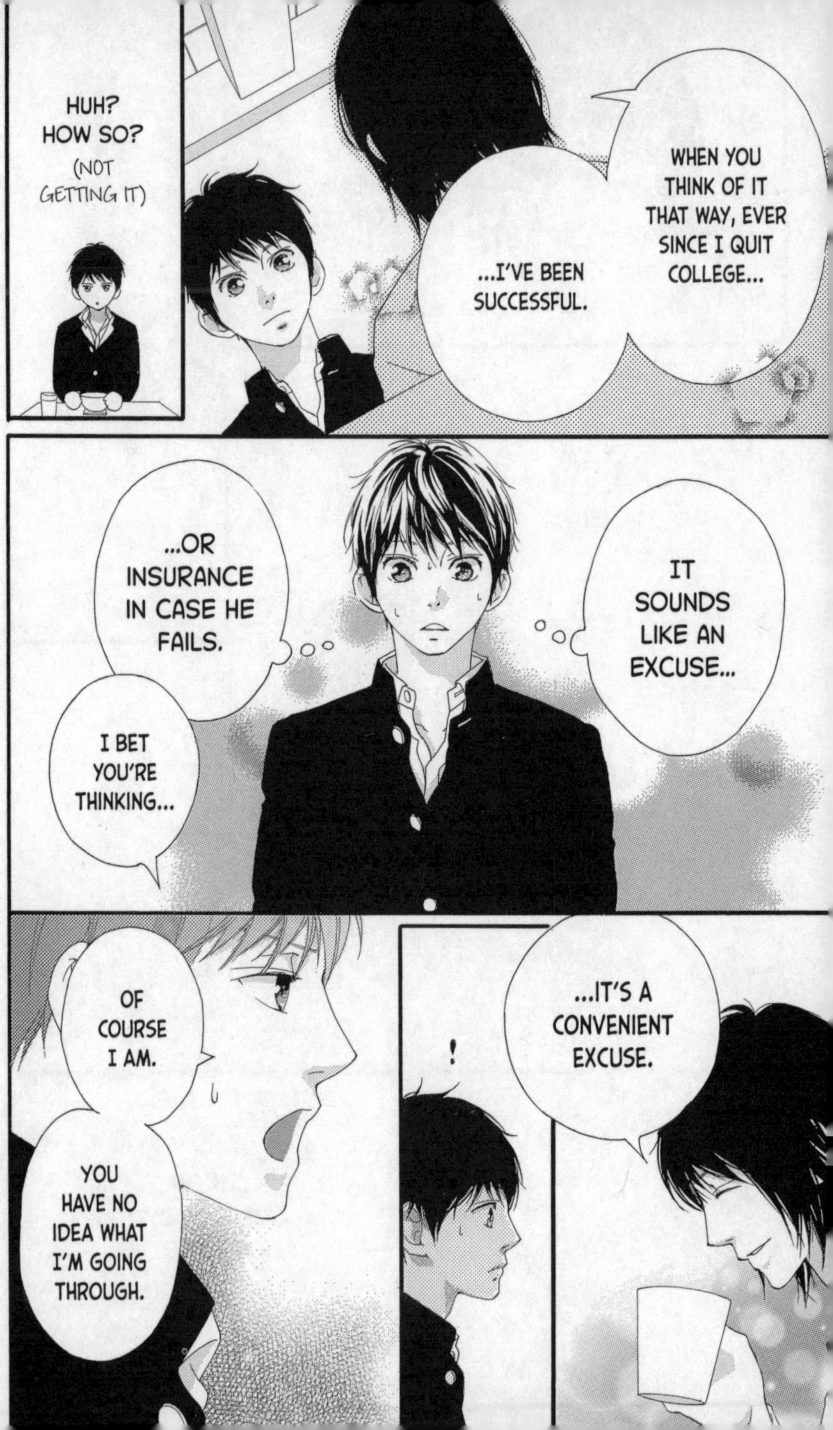
WHEN YOU THINK OF IT THAT WAY, EVER SINCE I QUIT COLLEGE...
...I'VE BEEN SUCCESSFUL.
HUH? HOW SO?
(NOT GETTING IT)
IT SOUNDS LIKE AN EXCUSE...
...OR INSURANCE IN CASE HE FAILS.
I BET YOU'RE THINKING...
...IT'S A CONVENIENT EXCUSE.
!
OF COURSE I AM.
YOU HAVE NO IDEA WHAT I'M GOING THROUGH.

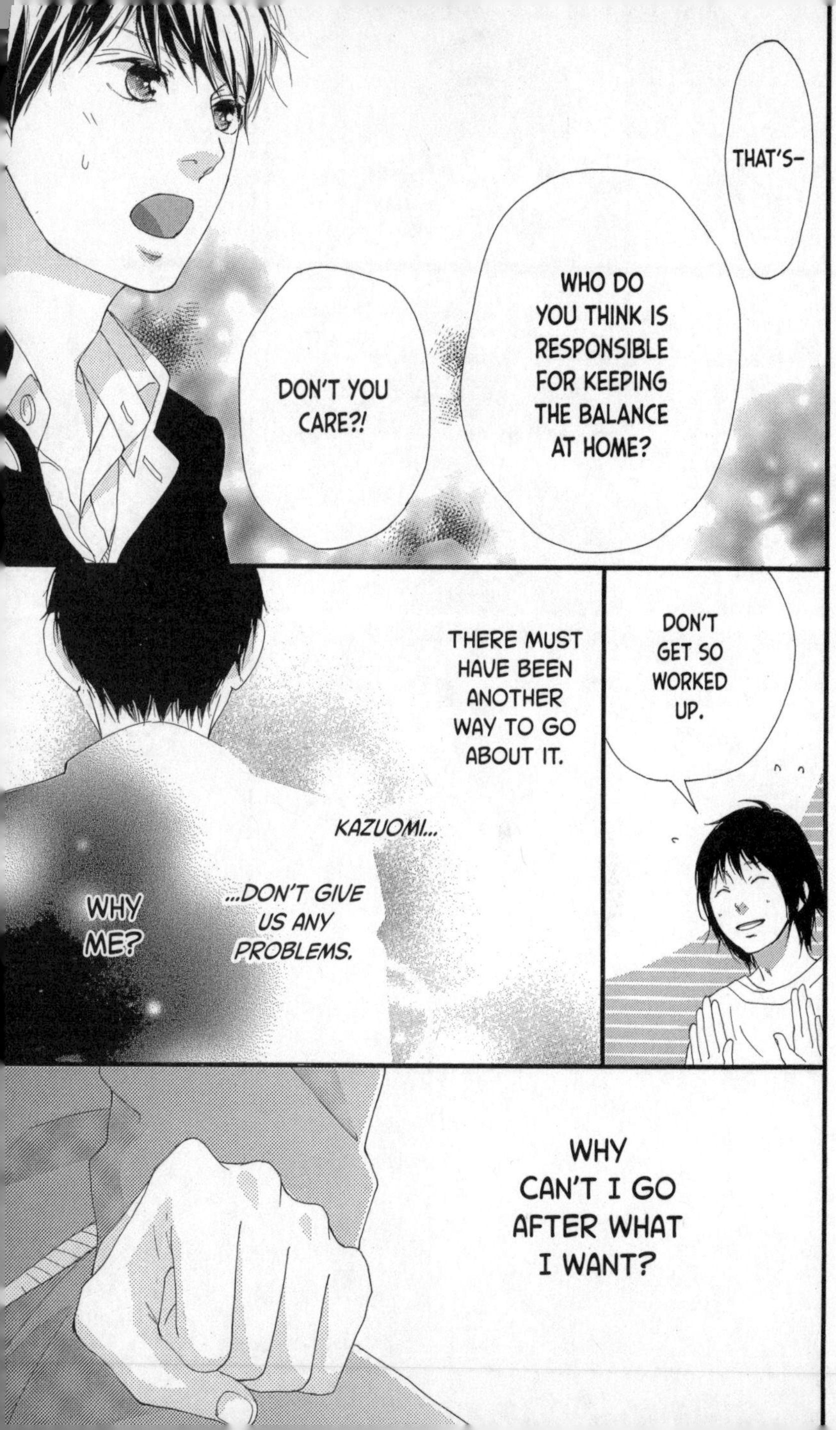
THAT'S-
WHO DO YOU THINK IS RESPONSIBLE FOR KEEPING THE BALANCE AT HOME?
DON'T YOU CARE?!
DON'T GET SO WORKED UP.
THERE MUST HAVE BEEN ANOTHER WAY TO GO ABOUT IT.
KAZUOMI...
...DON'T GIVE US ANY PROBLEMS.
WHY ME?
WHY CAN'T I GO AFTER WHAT I WANT?

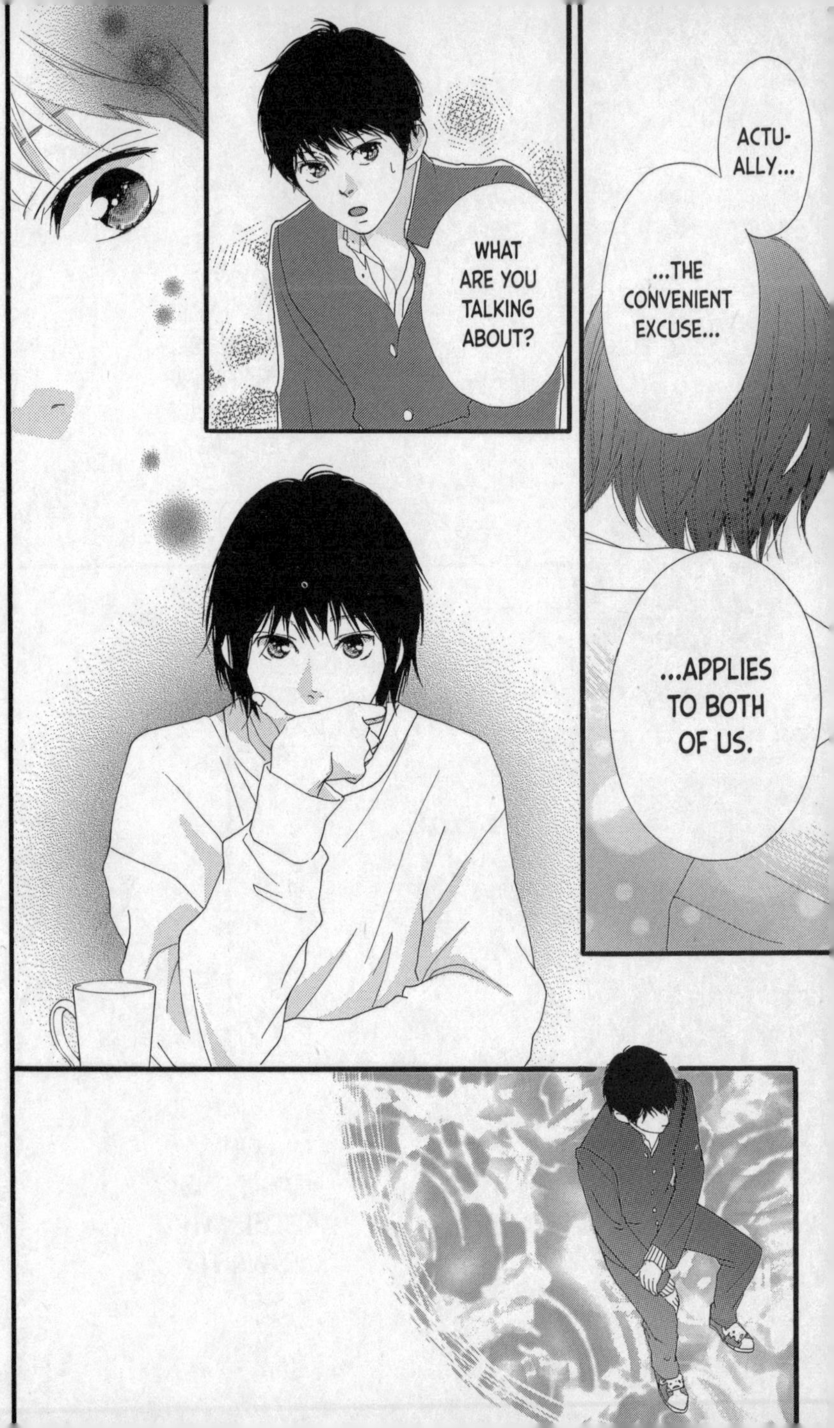
ACTU-ALLY...
...THE CONVENIENT EXCUSE...
...APPLIES TO BOTH OF US.
WHAT ARE YOU TALKING ABOUT?

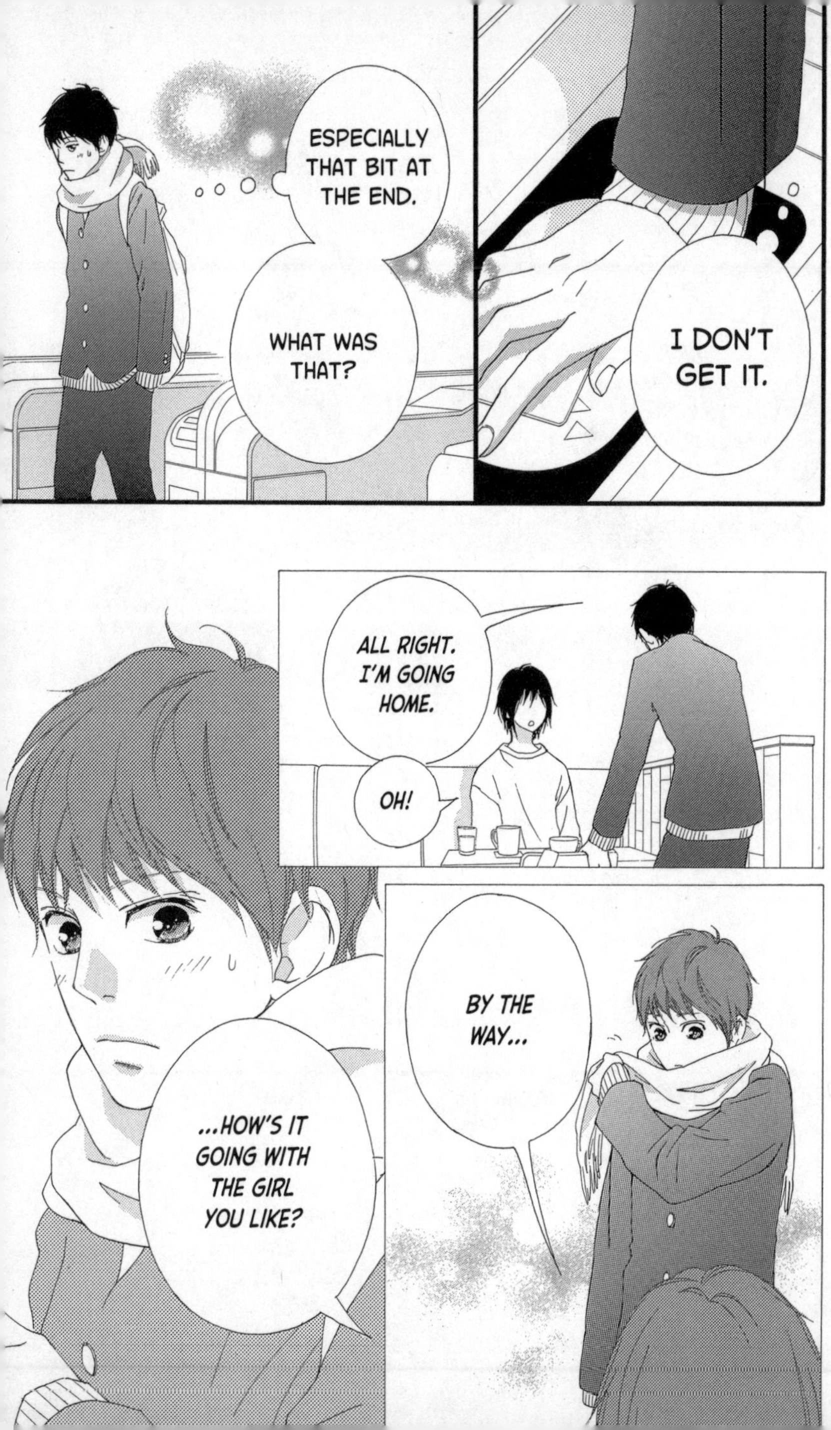
I DON'T GET IT.
ESPECIALLY THAT BIT AT THE END.
WHAT WAS THAT?
ALL RIGHT. I'M GOING HOME.
OH!
BY THE WAY...
...HOW'S IT GOING WITH THE GIRL YOU LIKE?

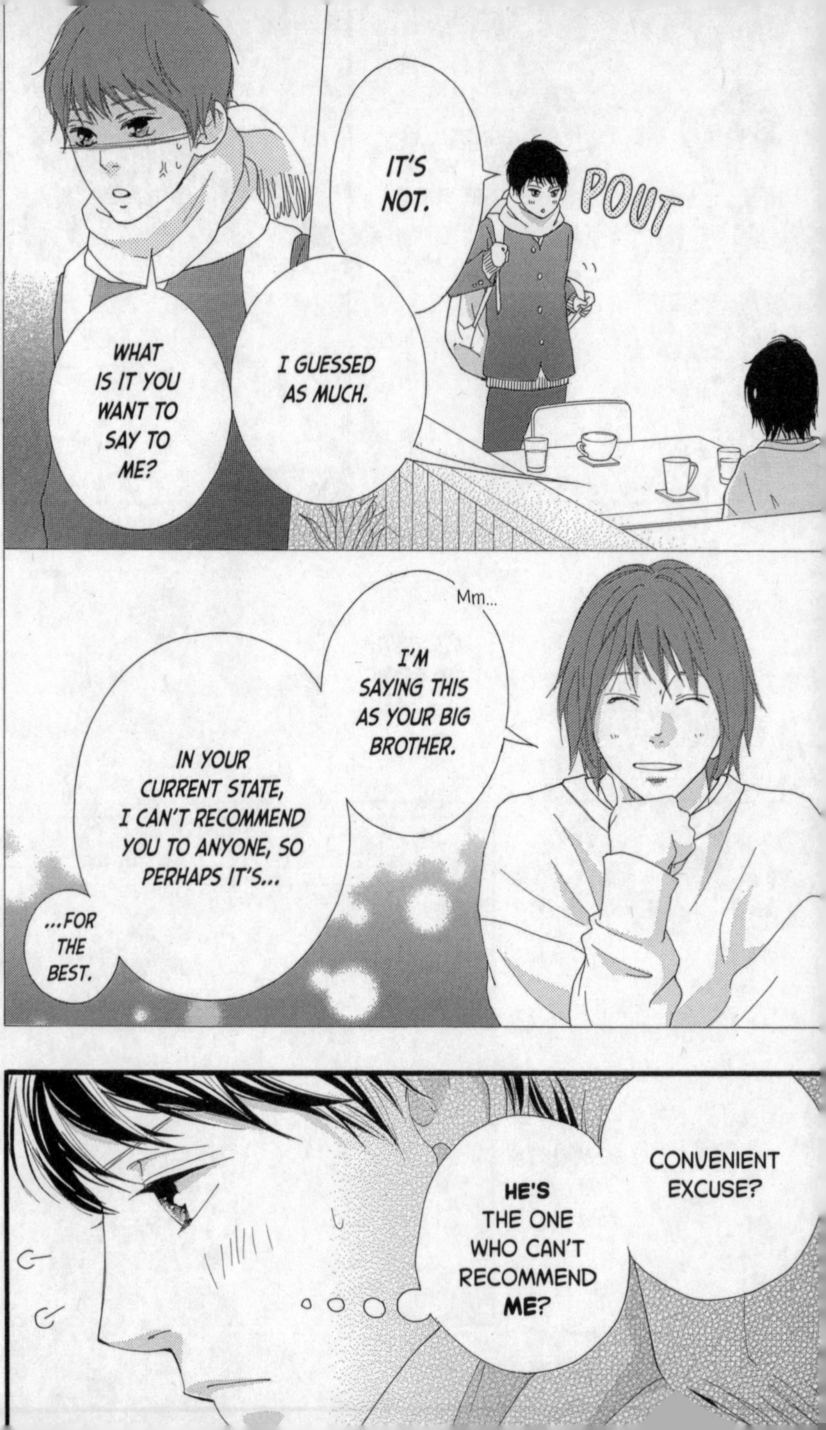
IT'S NOT.
POUT
I GUESSED AS MUCH.
WHAT IS IT YOU WANT TO SAY TO ME?
Mm...
I'M SAYING THIS AS YOUR BIG BROTHER.
IN YOUR CURRENT STATE, I CAN'T RECOMMEND YOU TO ANYONE, SO PERHAPS IT'S...
...FOR THE BEST.
CONVENIENT EXCUSE?
HE'S THE ONE WHO CAN'T RECOMMEND ME?

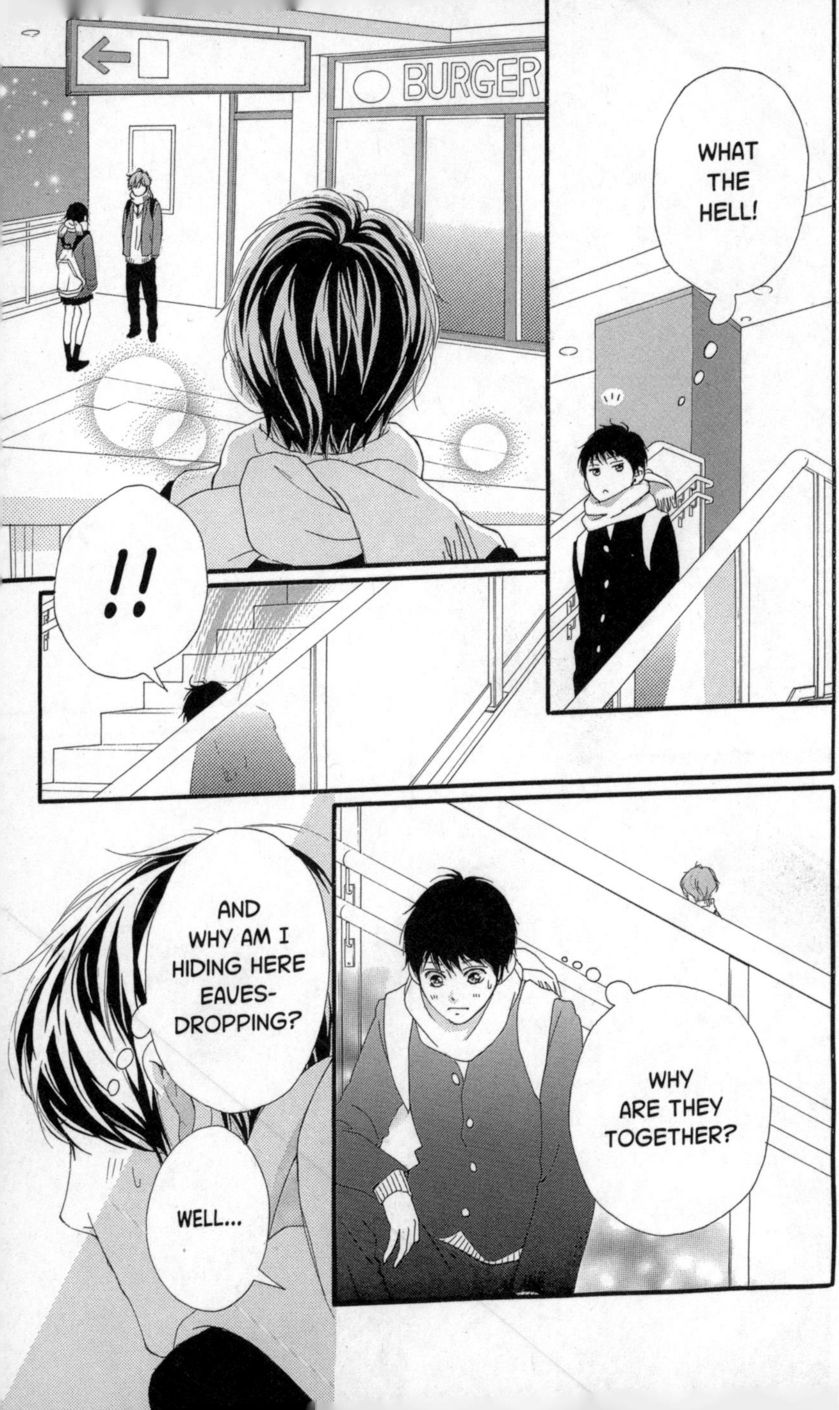
BURGER
WHAT THE HELL!
!!
WHY ARE THEY TOGETHER?
AND WHY AM I HIDING HERE EAVES-DROPPING?
WELL...

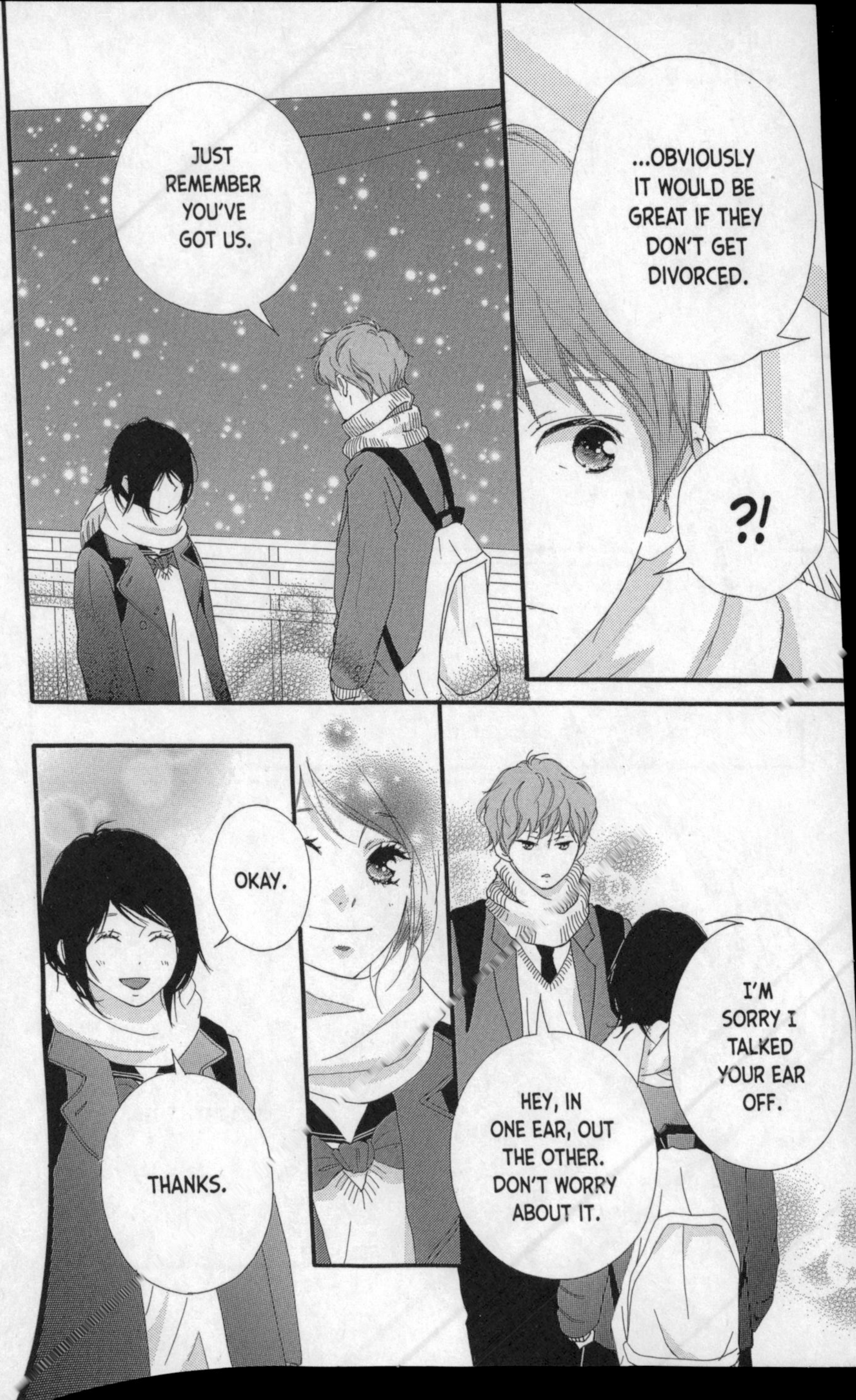
...OBVIOUSLY IT WOULD BE GREAT IF THEY DON'T GET DIVORCED.
?!
JUST REMEMBER YOU'VE GOT US.
I'M SORRY I TALKED YOUR EAR OFF.
HEY, IN ONE EAR, OUT THE OTHER. DON'T WORRY ABOUT IT.
OKAY.
THANKS.

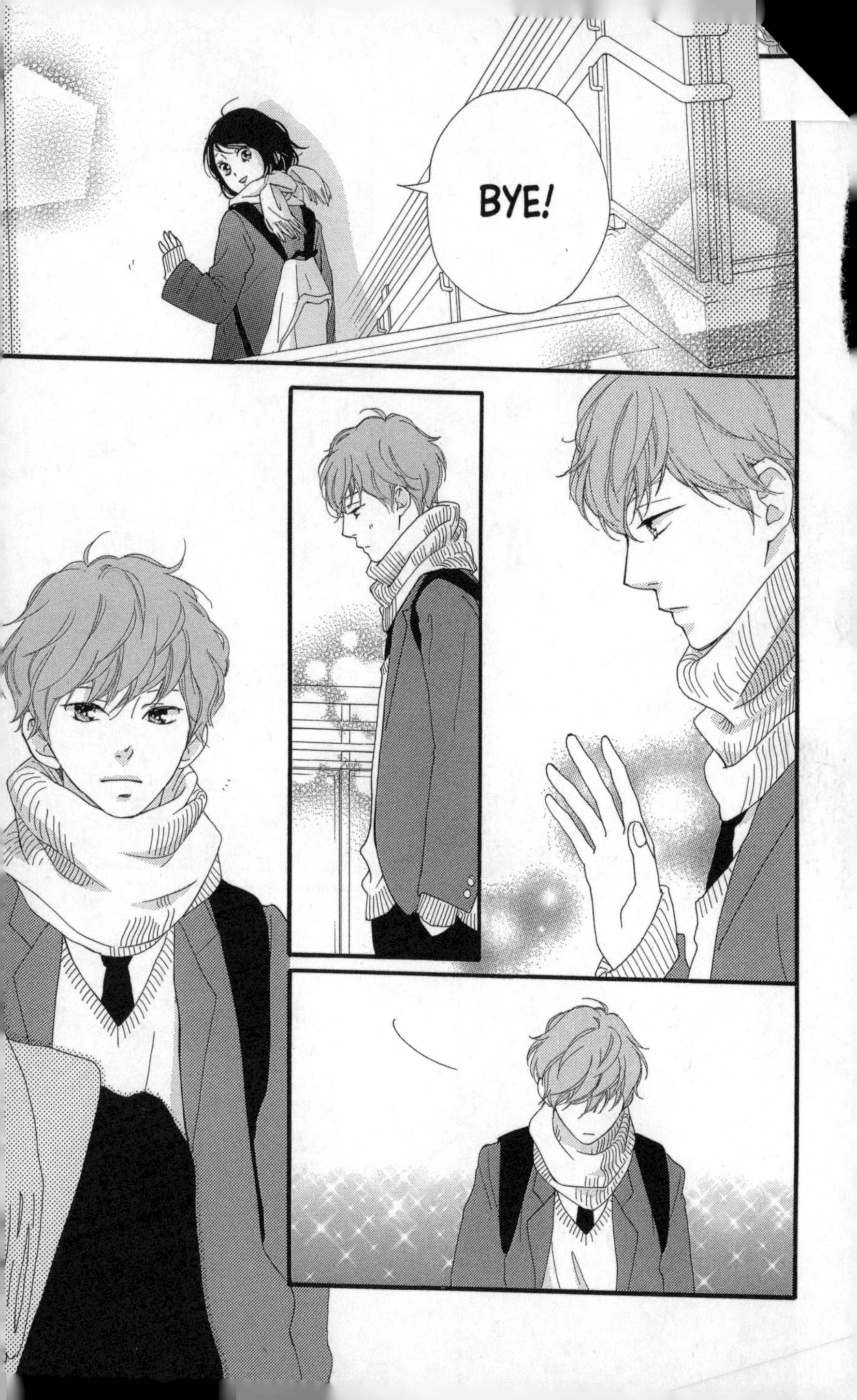
BYE!

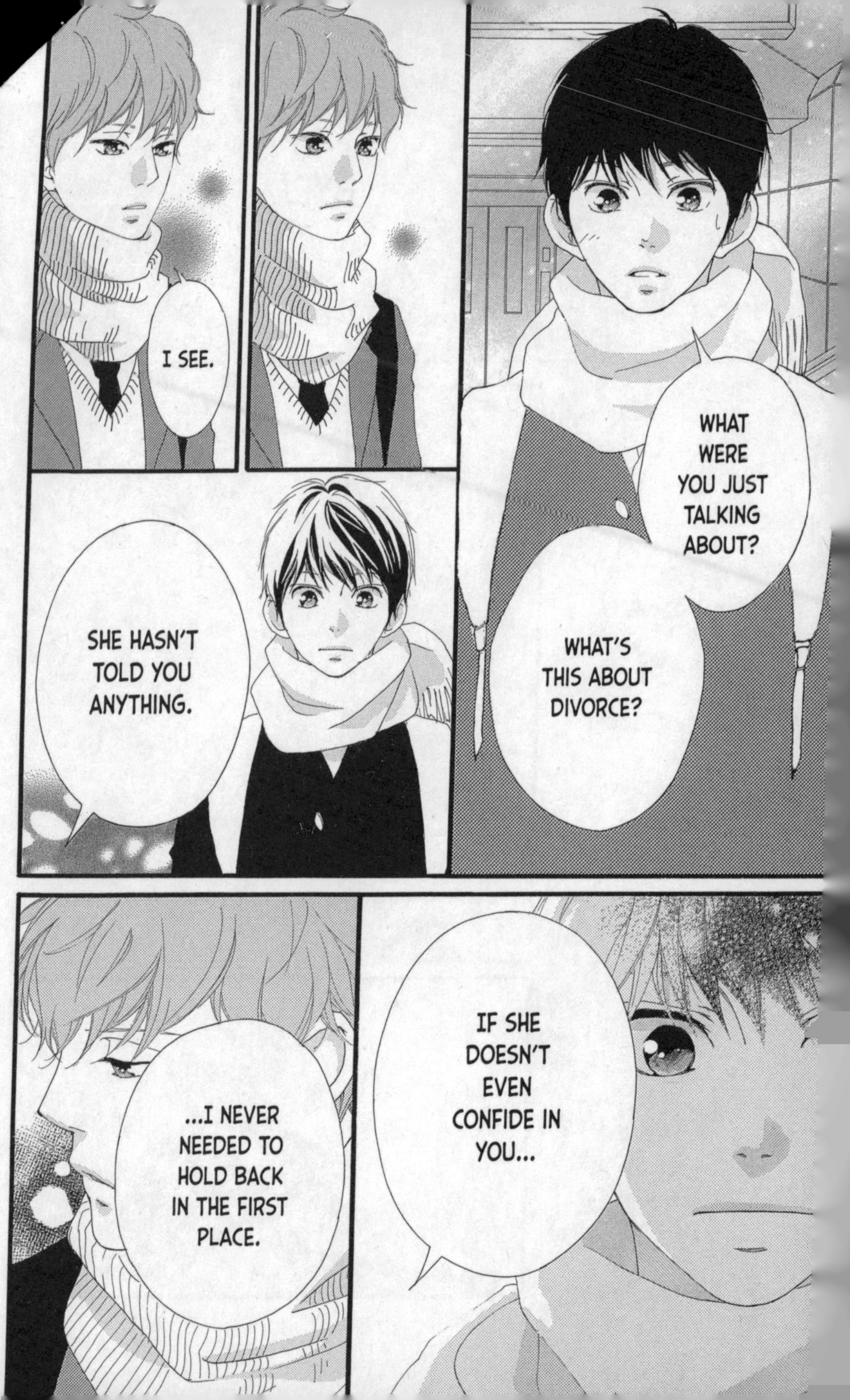
WHAT WERE YOU JUST TALKING ABOUT?
WHAT'S THIS ABOUT DIVORCE?
I SEE.
SHE HASN'T TOLD YOU ANYTHING.
IF SHE DOESN'T EVEN CONFIDE IN YOU...
...I NEVER NEEDED TO HOLD BACK IN THE FIRST PLACE.

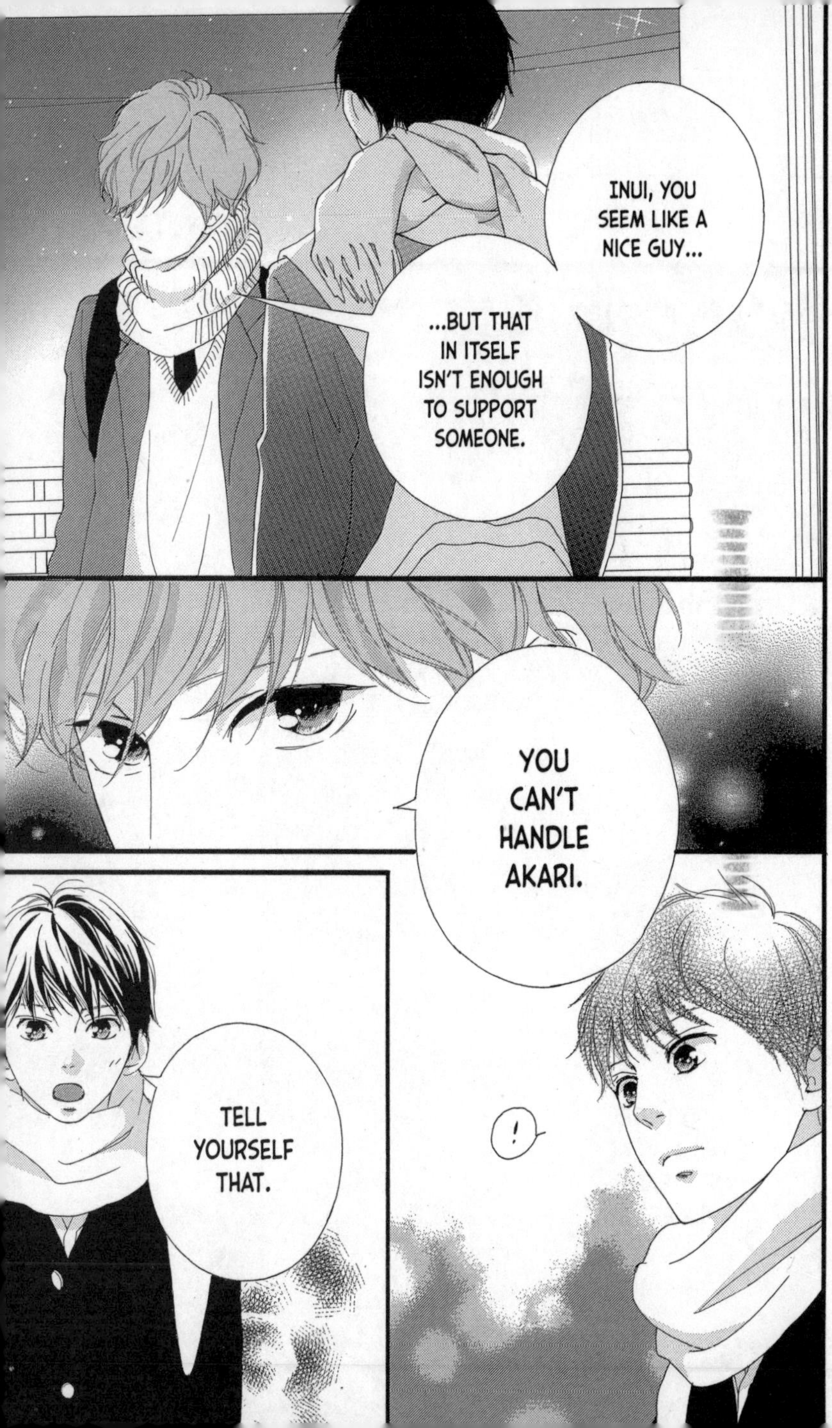
INUI, YOU SEEM LIKE A NICE GUY...
...BUT THAT IN ITSELF ISN'T ENOUGH TO SUPPORT SOMEONE.
YOU CAN'T HANDLE AKARI.
!
TELL YOURSELF THAT.

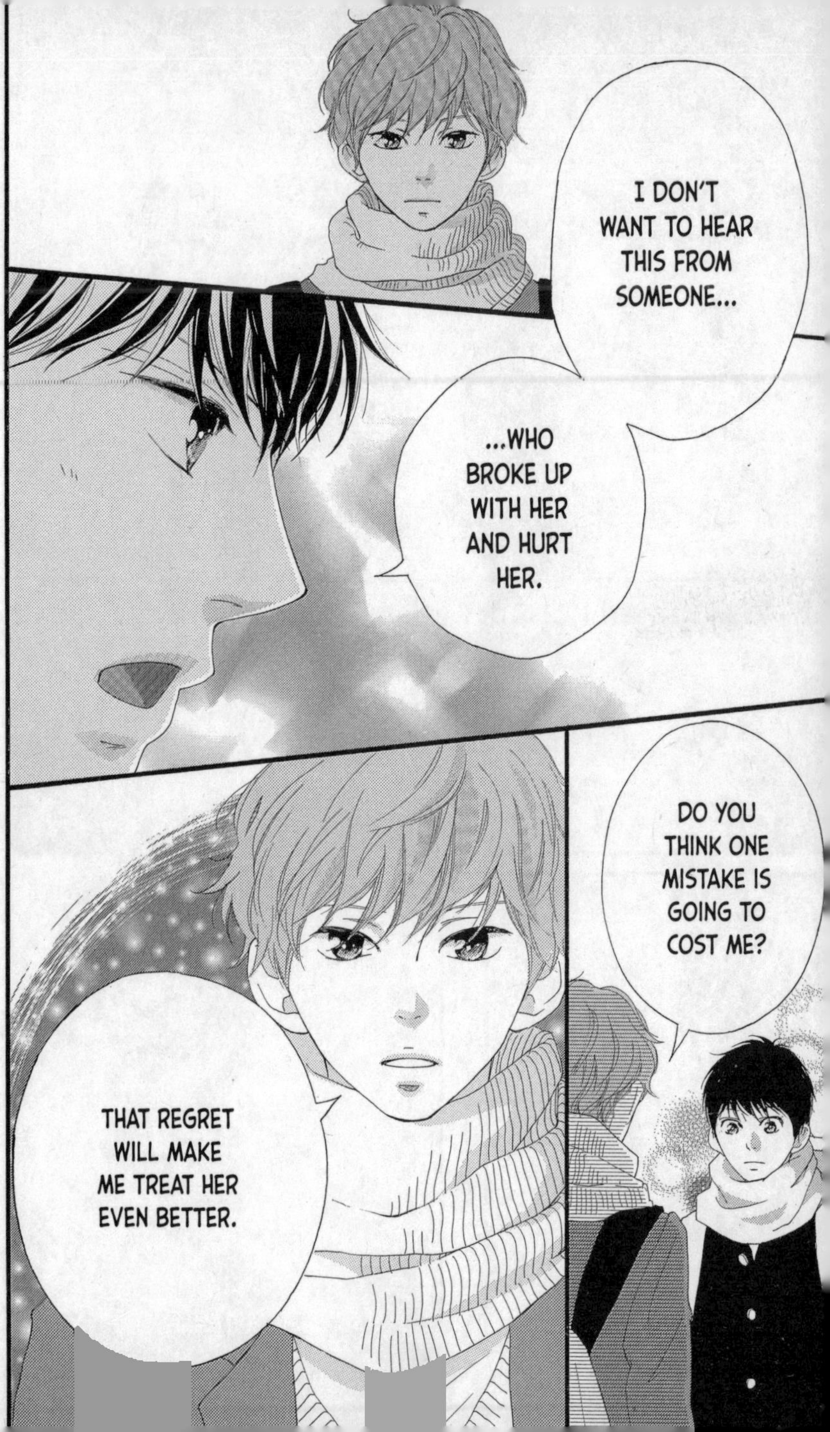
I DON'T WANT TO HEAR THIS FROM SOMEONE...
...WHO BROKE UP WITH HER AND HURT HER.
DO YOU THINK ONE MISTAKE IS GOING TO COST ME?
THAT REGRET WILL MAKE ME TREAT HER EVEN BETTER.

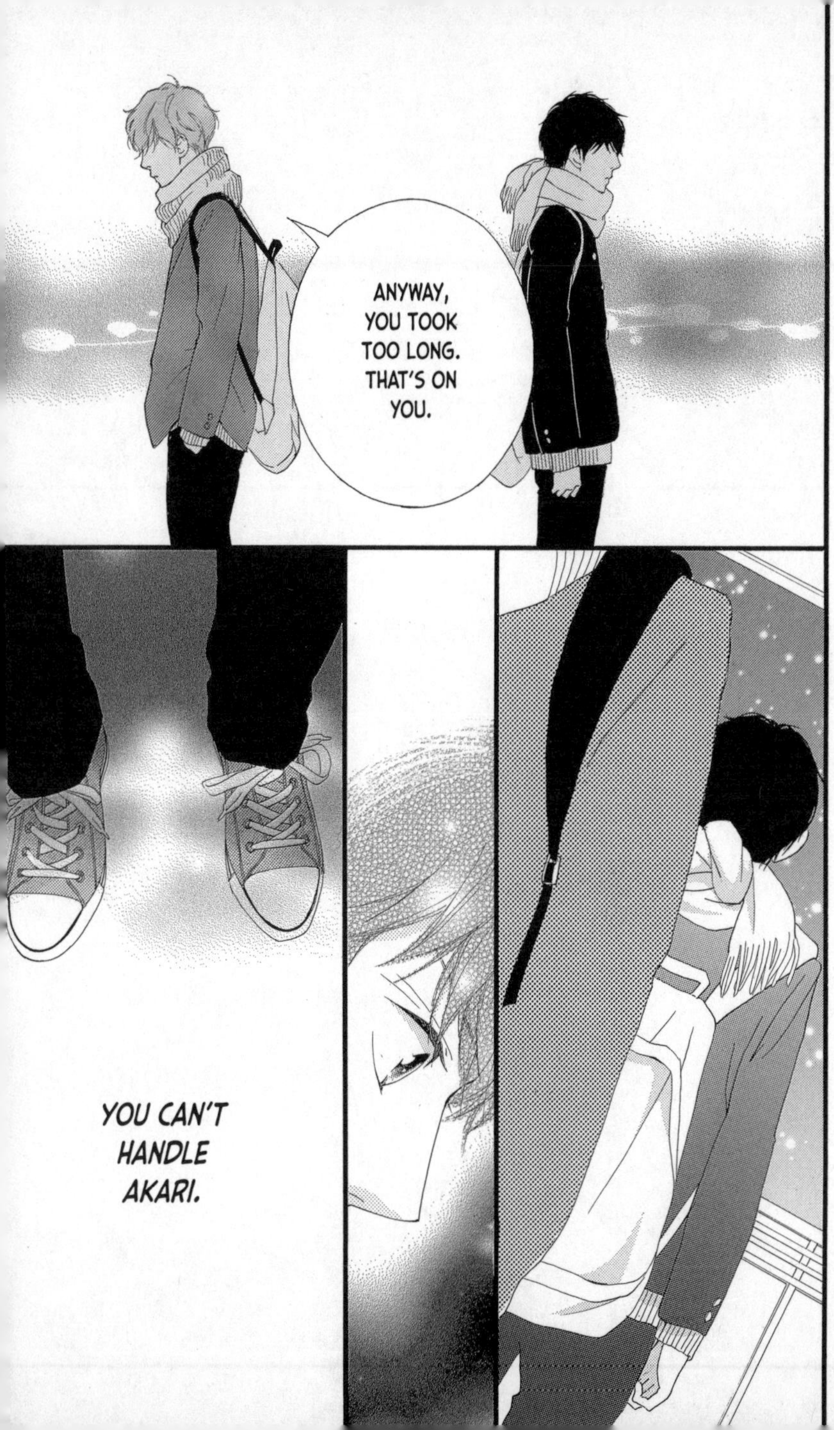
ANYWAY, YOU TOOK TOO LONG. THAT'S ON YOU.
YOU CAN'T HANDLE AKARI.

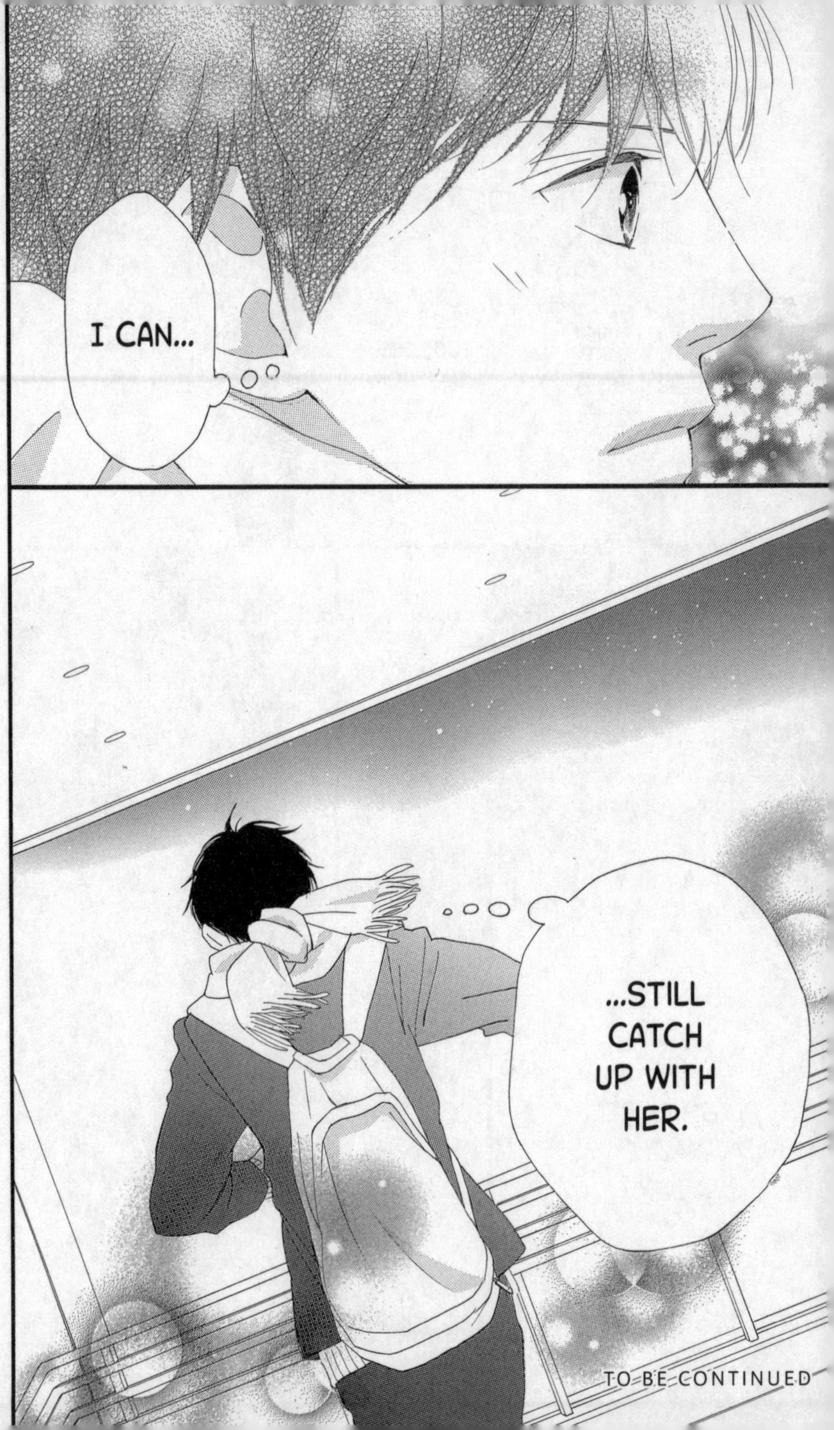
I CAN...
...STILL CATCH UP WITH HER.
TO BE CONTINUED

AFTERWORD

Thank you so much for reading this to the end.

Every time I write stories that take place around Valentine's Day, I'm reminded of when I was in junior high and gave chocolates to the first boy I liked. I was totally rejected. But it was so fun. I'm sure at the time I (probably) was really upset, but now it's just a happy memory. What a convenient memory. Since I have this ability to keep forgetting annoying and trying things, my days are pretty peaceful. I feel like that ability is increasing every year. But because of that, I often forget work deadlines. It's not that I dislike the work, I dislike the existence of deadlines. But if there were no such thing as deadlines, I would never start working. I'd just stare off into space, so it would be pretty terrible not to have them. I can't wholeheartedly hate deadlines.

See you in the next volume!

Io Sakisaka

A certain someone recommended a book to me. I thought it sounded interesting, and I bought it. But it's such a difficult read that it's taken me six months to read 30 pages. When I go to pick it up again, I'll have forgotten what happened before, so I'll have to start from the beginning again... This may go on forever.

Io Sakisaka

Born on June 8, Io Sakisaka made her debut as a manga creator with *Sakura, Chiru*. Her series *Strobe Edge* and *Ao Haru Ride* are published by VIZ Media's Shojo Beat imprint. *Ao Haru Ride* was adapted into an anime series in 2014, and *Love Me, Love Me Not* will be an animated feature film. In her spare time, Sakisaka likes to paint things and sleep.

Love Me, Love Me Not

Vol. 9
Shojo Beat Edition

STORY AND ART BY
Io Sakisaka

Adaptation/Nancy Thistlethwaite
Translation/JN Productions
Touch-Up Art & Lettering/Sara Linsley
Design/Yukiko Whitley
Editor/Nancy Thistlethwaite

OMOI, OMOWARE, FURI, FURARE © 2015 by Io Sakisaka
All rights reserved.
First published in Japan in 2015 by SHUEISHA Inc., Tokyo.
English translation rights arranged by SHUEISHA Inc.

The stories, characters and incidents mentioned in this
publication are entirely fictional.

Printed in the U.S.A.

Published by VIZ Media, LLC
P.O. Box 77010
San Francisco, CA 94107

10 9 8 7 6 5 4 3 2 1
First printing, July 2021

viz.com   shojobeat.com

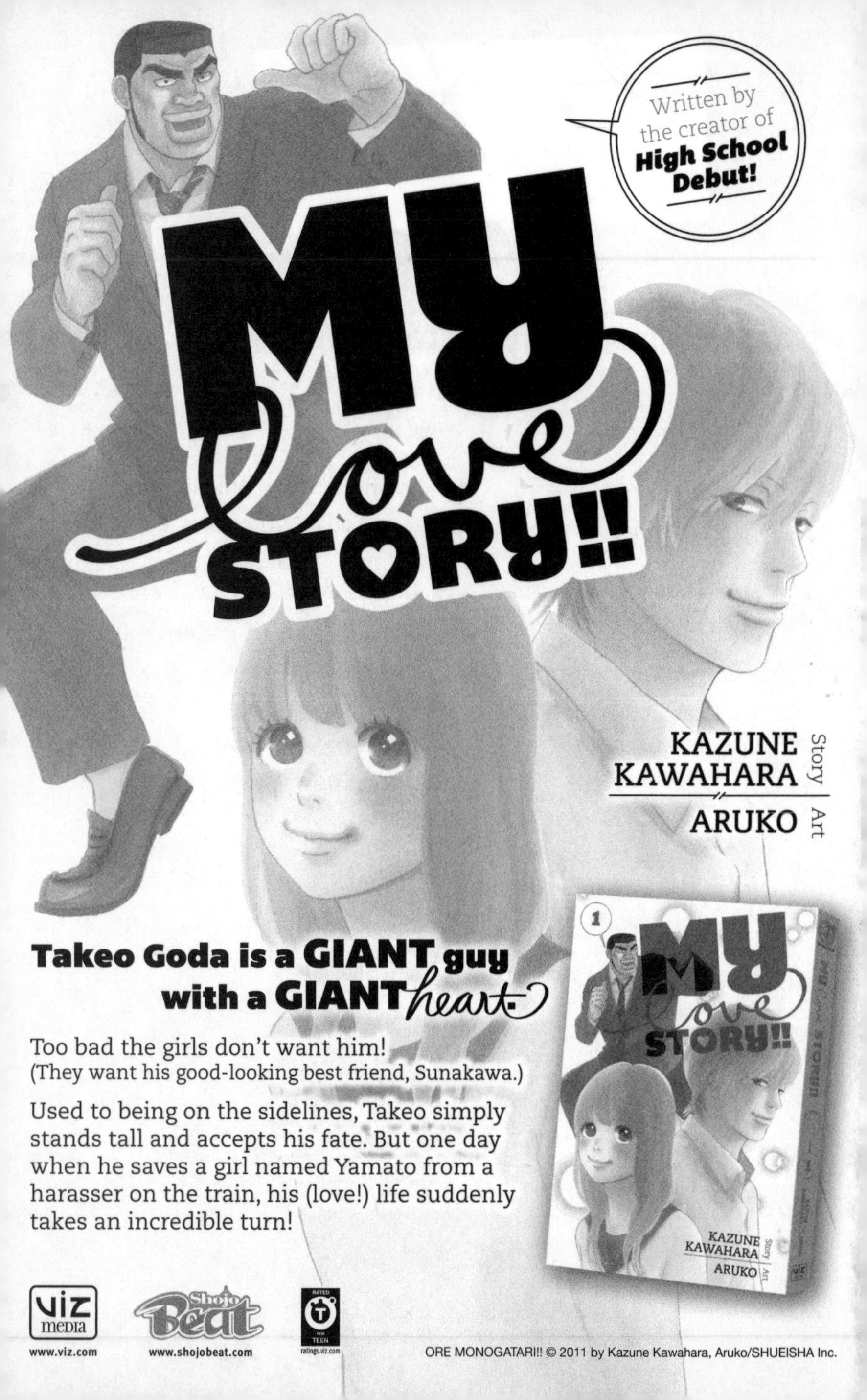
Written by the creator of High School Debut!
MY Love STORY!!
KAZUNE KAWAHARA Story
ARUKO Art
Takeo Goda is a GIANT guy with a GIANT heart
Too bad the girls don't want him!
(They want his good-looking best friend, Sunakawa.)
Used to being on the sidelines, Takeo simply stands tall and accepts his fate. But one day when he saves a girl named Yamato from a harasser on the train, his (love!) life suddenly takes an incredible turn!
1
MY Love STORY!!
KAZUNE KAWAHARA Story
ARUKO Art
VIZ media
www.viz.com
Shojo Beat
www.shojobeat.com
RATED T FOR TEEN
ratings.viz.com
ORE MONOGATARI!! © 2011 by Kazune Kawahara, Aruko/SHUEISHA Inc.

Stop!

You may be reading the wrong way.

In keeping with the original Japanese comic format, this book reads from right to left—so action, sound effects and word balloons are completely reversed to preserve the orientation of the original artwork. Check out the diagram shown here to get the hang of things, and then turn to the other side of the book to get started!

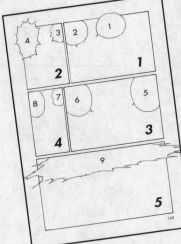